John Berendt

MIDNIGHT IN THE GARDEN OF GOOD AND EVIL

A Savannah Story

First published in Vintage 1995

10 9

Grateful acknowledgement is made to the following for permission to reprint previously published material: CPP/BELWIN, INC.: Ten lines from 'Sentimental Gentleman from Georgia' by Mitchell Parish and Frank Perkins. Copyright © 1932 (renewed 1960) by Mills Music c/o EMI Music Publishing. World print rights administered by CPP/Belwin, Inc., Miami, Florida. All rights reserved. Reprinted by permission. WARNER CHAPPELL MUSIC, INC.: Excerpt from 'Summer Wind' by Johnny Mercer, Henry Mayer, and Hans Bradke. Copyright © 1965 by Warner Bros. Inc. All rights reserved. Reprinted by permission.

First published in Great Britain by
Chatto & Windus Ltd, 1994

Vintage Books
Random House, 20 Vauxhall Bridge Road, London SW1V 2SA

Random House Australia (Pty) Limited
16 Dalmore Drive, Scoresby, Victoria 3179, Australia

Random House New Zealand Limited
18 Poland Road, Glenfield
Auckland 10, New Zealand

Random House South Africa (Pty) Limited
PO Box 2263, Rosebank 2121, South Africa

Random House UK Limited Reg. No. 954009

A CIP catalogue record for this book
is available from the British Library

Papers used by Random House UK Limited are natural, recyclable products made from wood grown in sustainable forests. The manufacturing processes conform to the environmental regulations of the country of origin

ISBN 0 09 952101 6

Printed and bound in Great Britain by
Cox & Wyman Ltd, Reading, Berkshire

Midnight in the Garden of Good and Evil

John Berendt writes a monthly column for *Esquire* and lives in New York.

For my parents

Preface to this edition

For the first edition of this book, I wrote an author's note to explain that, although I cast the book in the form of a novel, it is a work of nonfiction: all the characters are real and their stories are true. My note appeared at the *end* of the book, however, rather than at the beginning, with the result that quite a few readers got halfway through – and some even finished the book – before they discovered that what they'd been reading was journalism, not fiction.

With this revised author's note, the reader is put on notice at the outset. But even a forewarned reader may notice that, quite apart from the novelized style of the narrative, the story itself has a fictional quality. That is because the book is set in the magical city of Savannah, which I visited by chance some years ago and where I encountered an assortment of truly extraordinary people. Very few writers get this lucky. As the novelist-narrator in Philip Roth's novel *The Counterlife* wearily observes, 'People don't turn themselves over to writers as full-blown literary characters – generally they give you very little to go on and, after the impact of the initial impression, are barely any help at all. Most people (beginning with the novelist – himself, his family, just about everyone he knows) are absolutely unoriginal, and [the writer's] job is to make them appear otherwise.' It was my good fortune that the people I met and wrote about were highly original, full-blown literary characters who were absolutely compelling without any help from me.

The question that arises, then, is why there should be so many larger-than-life characters in Savannah. One reason is that Savannahians have a high tolerance for eccentric behavior. They dote on it, they encourage it. Savannah is a small, inward-looking, isolated town that thrives on gossip. Naturally, the main topic of gossip is the behavior of other people; therefore, the stranger the behavior, the better the gossip. Thus it follows that eccentric characters are appreciated in Savannah, if only because they give people something to talk about. The eccentrics know this, and it encourages them to outdo themselves. You don't find this happening in larger cities. A person who behaves oddly in, let us say, Indianapolis, will be viewed with suspicion and shunned. In Savannah, that same person will bask in the spotlight of gossip, knowing he is cherished for his loopy antics and for the entertainment he provides.

In my original author's note, I did acknowledge that I changed some names in order to protect the privacy of certain individuals, but there were relatively few of those. Most of the main characters appear under their own names – Jim Williams, Danny Hansford, The Lady Chablis, Joe Odom, Emma Kelly, Lee Adler, Sonny Seiler and the bulldog UGA. Several have been interviewed by the press and appeared on television, which is further proof that they are flesh and blood. One – The Lady Chablis – has even written her own book.

A few weeks after the release of the book in America in January 1994, Savannah began to notice an increase in the number of tourists in town. After eight months, the Georgia Department of Trade and Tourism announced that tourism to Savannah had grown by an astonishing 46 percent. A year later it had virtually doubled. Given this invasion of outsiders, it is fair to ask whether by revealing the quirky charms of Savannah I might have unintentionally brought about its ruin.

I am happy to report that no such thing has happened. According to a Bloomberg Business News wire story on the 'economic explosion' visited upon Savannah by *Midnight*, convention bookings in Savannah grew 40 percent in 1994 and another 30 percent in 1995; nineteen new businesses opened in formerly vacant storefronts on Savannah's main shopping thoroughfare, Broughton Street; and 1,500 new jobs have been created.

Savannah's head has not been turned by any of this. The city remains as gracious as ever to its visitors, but it continues to be steadfastly impervious to outside influence. There may be more tourists spending more money in Savannah than ever before, but eventually they do what tourists always do: they go home. And that suits Savannah just fine.

John Berendt
New York City
April, 1996

CONTENTS

PART ONE

PART TWO

PART ONE

Chapter 1

AN EVENING IN MERCER HOUSE

He was tall, about fifty, with darkly handsome, almost sinister features: a neatly trimmed mustache, hair turning silver at the temples, and eyes so black they were like the tinted windows of a sleek limousine—he could see out, but you couldn't see in. We were sitting in the living room of his Victorian house. It was a mansion, really, with fifteen-foot ceilings and large, well-proportioned rooms. A graceful spiral stairway rose from the center hall toward a domed skylight. There was a ballroom on the second floor. It was Mercer House, one of the last of Savannah's great houses still in private hands. Together with the walled garden and the carriage house in back, it occupied an entire city block. If Mercer House was not quite the biggest private house in Savannah, it was certainly the most grandly furnished. *Architectural Digest* had devoted six pages to it. A book on the interiors of the world's great houses featured it alongside Sagamore Hill, Biltmore, and Chartwell. Mercer House was the envy of house-proud Savannah. Jim Williams lived in it alone.

Williams was smoking a King Edward cigarillo. "What I

enjoy most," he said, "is living like an aristocrat without the burden of having to *be* one. Blue bloods are so inbred and weak. All those generations of importance and grandeur to live up to. No wonder they lack ambition. I don't envy them. It's only the trappings of aristocracy that I find worthwhile—the fine furniture, the paintings, the silver—the very things they have to sell when the money runs out. And it always does. Then all they're left with is their lovely manners."

He spoke in a drawl as soft as velvet. The walls of his house were hung with portraits of European and American aristocrats—by Gainsborough, Hudson, Reynolds, Whistler. The provenance of his possessions traced back to dukes and duchesses, kings, queens, czars, emperors, and dictators. "Anyhow," he said, "royalty is better."

Williams tapped a cigar ash into a silver ashtray. A dark gray tiger cat climbed up and settled in his lap. He stroked it gently. "I know I'm apt to give the wrong impression, living the way I do. But I'm not trying to fool anyone. Years ago I was showing a group of visitors through the house and I noticed one man giving his wife the high sign. I saw him mouth the words 'old money!' The man was David Howard, the world's leading expert on armorial Chinese porcelain. I took him aside afterward and said, 'Mr. Howard, I was born in Gordon, Georgia. That's a little town near Macon. The biggest thing in Gordon is a chalk mine. My father was a barber, and my mother worked as a secretary for the mine. My money—what there is of it—is about eleven years old.' Well, the man was completely taken aback. 'Do you know what made me think you were from an old family,' he said, 'apart from the portraits and the antiques? Those chairs over there. The needlework on the covers is unraveling. New money would mend it right away. Old money would leave it just as it is.' 'I know that,' I told him. 'Some of my best customers are old money.' "

—

I had heard Jim Williams's name mentioned often during the six months I had lived in Savannah. The house was one reason, but there were others. He was a successful dealer in antiques and a restorer of old houses. He had been president of the Telfair Academy, the local art museum. His by-line had appeared in *Antiques* magazine, and the magazine's editor, Wendell Garrett, spoke of him as a genius: "He has an extraordinary eye for finding stuff. He trusts his own judgment, and he's willing to take chances. He'll hop on a plane and go anywhere to an auction—to New York, to London, to Geneva. But at heart he's a southern chauvinist, very much a son of the region. I don't think he cares much for Yankees."

Williams had played an active role in the restoration of Savannah's historic district, starting in the mid-1950s. Georgia Fawcett, a longtime preservationist, recalled how difficult it had been to get people involved in saving downtown Savannah in those early days. "The old part of town had become a slum," she said. "The banks had red-lined the whole area. The great old houses were falling into ruin or being demolished to make way for gas stations and parking lots, and you couldn't borrow any money from the banks to go in and save them. Prostitutes strolled along the streets. Couples with children were afraid to live downtown, because it was considered dangerous." Mrs. Fawcett had been a member of a small group of genteel preservationists who had tried since the 1930s to stave off the gas stations and save the houses. "One thing we did do," she said. "We got the bachelors interested."

Jim Williams was one of the bachelors. He bought a row of one-story brick tenements on East Congress Street, restored the whole row, and sold it. Soon he was buying, restoring, and selling dozens of houses all over downtown Savannah. Stories in the newspapers drew attention to his restorations, and his antiques business grew. He started going to Europe once a year on buying trips. He was discovered by society hostesses. The improvement in Williams's fortunes paralleled the renaissance of Savannah's historic district. By the early 1970s, couples with children came back downtown, and the prostitutes moved over to Montgomery Street.

Feeling flush, Williams bought Cabbage Island, one of the sea islands that form an archipelago along the Georgia coast. Cabbage Island was a folly. It covered eighteen hundred acres, all but five of which lay under water at high tide. He paid $5,000 for it in 1966. Old salts at the marina told him he had been duped: Cabbage Island had been on the market for half that sum the year before. Five thousand dollars was a lot of money for a soggy piece of real estate you couldn't even build a house on. But a few months later phosphates were discovered under several coastal islands, including Cabbage Island. Williams sold out to Kerr-McGee of Oklahoma for $660,000. Several property owners on neighboring islands laughed at him for jumping at the bait too quickly. They held out for a higher price. Weeks later, the state of Georgia outlawed drilling along the coast. The phosphate deal was dead, and as it turned out, Williams was the only one who had sold in time. His after-tax profit was a half million dollars.

Now he bought far grander houses. One of them was Armstrong House, a monumental Italian Renaissance palazzo directly across Bull Street from the staid Oglethorpe Club. Armstrong House dwarfed the Oglethorpe Club, and, according to local lore, that was very much its purpose. George Armstrong, a shipping magnate, was said to have built the house in 1919 in response to being blackballed by the club. Although that story was not, in fact, true, Armstrong House was a lion of a house. It gloated and glowered and loomed. It even had a curving colonnade that reached out like a giant paw as if to swat the Oglethorpe Club off its high horse across the street.

The outrageous magnificence of Armstrong House appealed to Williams and to his growing appetite for grandeur. He was not a member of the Oglethorpe Club. Bachelors from middle Georgia who sold antiques were not likely to be asked to join—not that it bothered him. He installed his antiques shop in Armstrong House for a year and then sold the house to the law firm of Bouhan, Williams and Levy and went on about the business of living like, if not being, an aristocrat. He made more frequent buying trips to Europe—in style now, on the *QE2*—and sent back whole container loads of important paintings and fine English furniture. He bought his first pieces of Fabergé. Williams was gaining stature in Savannah, to the irritation of certain blue bloods. "How does it feel to be *nouveau riche*?" he was asked on one occasion. "It's the *riche* that counts," Williams answered. Having said that, he bought Mercer House.

Mercer House had been empty for more than ten years. It stood at the west end of Monterey Square, the most elegant of Savannah's many tree-shaded squares. It was an Italianate mansion of red brick with tall, arched windows set off by ornate ironwork balconies. It sat back from the street, aloof behind its apron of lawn and its cast-iron fence, not so much looking out on the square as presiding over it. The most recent occupants of the house, the Shriners, had used it as the Alee Temple. They had hung a neon-lit scimitar over the front door and driven around inside on motorcycles. Williams set about restoring the house to something greater than its original elegance. When work was completed in 1970, he gave a black-tie Christmas party and invited the cream of Savannah society. On the night of his party, every window of Mercer House was ablaze with candlelight; every room had sparkling chandeliers. Clusters of onlookers stood outside watching the smart arrivals and staring in amazement at the beautiful house that had been dark for so long. A pianist played cocktail music on the grand piano downstairs; an organist played classical pieces in the ballroom above. Butlers in white jackets circulated with silver trays. Ladies in long gowns moved up and down the spiral stairs in rivers of satin and silk chiffon. Old Savannah was dazzled.

The party soon became a permanent fixture on Savannah's social calendar. Williams always scheduled it to occur at the climax of the winter season—the night before the Cotillion's debutante ball. That Friday night became known as the night of Jim Williams's Christmas party. It was the Party of the Year, and this was no small accomplishment for Williams. "You have to understand," a sixth-generation Savannahian declared, "Savannah takes its parties very seriously. This is a town where gentlemen own their own white tie and tails. We don't rent them. So it's quite a tribute to Jim that he has been able to make so prominent a place for himself on the social scene, in spite of not being a native Savannahian and being a bachelor."

The food at Williams's parties was always provided by Savannah's most sought-after cateress, Lucille Wright. Mrs. Wright was a light-skinned black woman whose services were so well regarded that Savannah's leading hostesses had been known to change the date of a party if she was not available. Mrs. Wright's touch was easy to spot. Guests would nibble on a cheese straw or eat a marinated shrimp or take a bite of a tomato finger sandwich and smile knowingly. "Lucille . . . !" they would say, and nothing more needed to be said. (Lucille Wright's tomato sandwiches were never soggy. She patted the tomato slices with paper towels first. That was just one of her many secrets.) Her clients held her in high esteem. "She's a real lady," they often said, and you could tell from the way they said it that they considered that high praise for a black woman. Mrs. Wright admired her patrons in return, although she did confide that Savannah's hostesses, even the rich ones, tended to come to her and say, "Now, Lucille, I want a nice party, but I don't want to spend too much money." Jim Williams was not like that. "He likes things done in the grand style," Mrs. Wright said, "and he's very liberal with his money. Very. Very. He always tells me, 'Lucille, I'm having two hundred people and I want low-country food and plenty of it. I don't want to run out. Get what you need. I don't care what it costs.' "

Jim Williams's Christmas party was, in the words of the *Georgia Gazette,* the party that Savannah socialites "lived for." Or lived without, for Williams enjoyed changing his guest list from year to year. He wrote names on file cards and arranged them in two stacks: an In stack and an Out stack. He shunted the cards from one stack to the other and made no secret of it. If a person had displeased him in any way during the year, that person would do penance come

Christmas. "My Out stack," he once told the *Gazette*, "is an inch thick."

—

An early-evening mist had turned the view of Monterey Square into a soft-focus stage set with pink azaleas billowing beneath a tattered valance of live oaks and Spanish moss. The pale marble pedestal of the Pulaski monument glowed hazily in the background. A copy of the book *At Home in Savannah—Great Interiors* lay on Williams's coffee table. I had seen the same book on several other coffee tables in Savannah, but here the effect was surreal: The cover photograph was of this very room.

For the better part of an hour, Williams had taken me on a tour of Mercer House and his antiques shop, which was quartered in the carriage house. In the ballroom, he played the pipe organ, first a piece by Bach, then "I Got Rhythm." Finally, to demonstrate the organ's deafening power, he played a passage from César Franck's "Pièce Héroïque." "When my neighbors let their dogs howl all night," said Williams, "this is what they get in return." In the dining room, he showed me his royal treasures: Queen Alexandra's silverware, the Duchess of Richmond's porcelain, and a silver service for sixty that had belonged to a Russian grand duke. The coat of arms from the door of Napoleon's coronation carriage hung on the wall in the study. Here and there around the house lay Fabergé objects—cigarette cases, ornaments, jewel boxes—the trappings of aristocracy, nobility, royalty. As we moved from room to room, tiny red lights flickered in electronic recognition of our presence.

Williams was wearing gray slacks and a blue cotton shirt turned up at the sleeves. His heavy black shoes and thick rubber soles were oddly out of place in the elegance of Mercer House, but practical; Williams spent several hours a day on his feet restoring antique furniture in his basement workshop. His hands were raw and callused, but they had been scrubbed clean of stains and grease.

"If there's a single trait common to all Savannahians," he

was saying, "it's their love of money and their unwillingness to spend it."

"Then who buys those high-priced antiques I just saw in your shop?" I asked.

"That's exactly my point," he said. "People from out of town. Atlanta, New Orleans, New York. That's where I do most of my business. When I find an especially fine piece of furniture I send a photograph of it to a New York dealer. I don't waste time trying to sell it here in Savannah. It's not that people in Savannah aren't rich enough. It's just that they're very cheap. I'll give you an example.

"There's a woman here, a *grande dame* at the very apex of society and one of the richest people in the Southeast, let alone Savannah. She owns a copper mine. She built a big house in an exclusive part of town, a replica of a famous Louisiana plantation house with huge white columns and curved stairs. You can see it from the water. Everybody goes, 'Oooo, look!' when they pass by it. I adore her. She's been like a mother to me. But she's the cheapest woman who ever lived! Some years ago she ordered a pair of iron gates for her house. They were designed and built especially for her. But when they were delivered she pitched a fit, said they were horrible, said they were filth. 'Take them away,' she said, 'I never want to see them again!' Then she tore up the bill, which was for $1,400—a fair amount of money in those days.

"The foundry took the gates back, but they didn't know what to do with them. After all, there wasn't much demand for a pair of ornamental gates exactly that size. The only thing they could do was to sell the iron for its scrap value. So they cut the price from $1,400 to $190. Naturally, the following day the woman sent a man over to the foundry with $190, and today those gates are hanging on her gateposts where they were originally designed to go. That's pure Savannah. And that's what I mean by cheap. You mustn't be taken in by the moonlight and magnolias. There's more to Savannah than that. Things can get very murky." Williams stroked his cat and tapped another ash into the ashtray.

"We had a judge back in the nineteen-thirties, a member of one of the city's leading families. He lived one square over from here in a big house with tall white columns. His older son was going around town with a gangster's girlfriend. The gangster warned him to stop, but the judge's son kept right at it. One night the doorbell rang and when the judge opened the door, he found his son lying on the porch bleeding to death with his private parts tucked under his lapel. The doctors sewed his genitals back on, but the body rejected them and he died. The next day, the headline in the paper read FALL FROM PORCH PROVES FATAL. Most members of that family still deny the murder ever happened, but the victim's sister tells me it's true.

"It doesn't end there. The same judge had another son. This one lived in a house on Whitaker Street. He and his wife used to fight. I mean really go at it, throw each other across rooms and that sort of thing. During one of those fights, their three-year-old daughter came downstairs unnoticed, just when the husband was getting ready to fling his wife into a marble-topped table. When the woman hit the table, it overturned and crushed the little girl. They didn't find out about it until an hour later when they were picking up the debris from the fight. As far as the family is concerned, that incident never happened either."

Williams picked up the decanter of Madeira and refilled our glasses. "Drinking Madeira is a great Savannah ritual, you know," he said. "It's a celebration of failure, actually. The British sent whole shiploads of grapevines over from Madeira in the eighteenth century in hopes of turning Georgia into a wine-producing colony. Savannah's on the same latitude as Madeira. Well, the vines died, but Savannah never lost its taste for Madeira. Or any other kind of liquor for that matter. Prohibition didn't even slow things down here. Everybody had a way of getting liquor, even little old ladies. Especially the old ladies. A bunch of them bought a Cuban rumrunner and ran it back and forth between here and Cuba."

Williams sipped his Madeira. "One of those ladies died

just a few months ago. Old Mrs. Morton. She was a marvel. She did exactly as she pleased all her life, God bless her. Her son came home for Christmas vacation one year and brought his college roommate with him. Mama and the college roommate fell in love; the roommate moved into the master bedroom with her; Daddy moved into the guest bedroom, and the son went back to college and never came home again. From then on, Mr. and Mrs. Morton and the roommate lived in that house under those circumstances until the old man died. They kept up appearances and pretended nothing at all outrageous had happened. Mama's young lover served as her chauffeur. Whenever he dropped her off and picked her up at her bridge parties, the other ladies would peer out at them through the venetian blinds. But they never let on that they were interested, because nobody, *nobody* ever mentioned his name in her presence."

Williams fell silent for a moment, no doubt reflecting upon the recently departed Mrs. Morton. Through the open window, Monterey Square was quiet except for the rasp of a cricket and the passing, now and then, of a car unhurriedly negotiating the turns around the square.

"What do you suppose would happen," I asked, "if the tour guides told that sort of story to their busloads of tourists?"

"Not possible," said Williams. "They keep it very prim and proper."

I told Williams that as I was coming up the walk earlier I had heard the guide on one of the tour buses talking about this house.

"Bless their boring little hearts," said Williams. "What did the guide say?"

"She said that the house was the birthplace of the famous songwriter Johnny Mercer, the man who wrote 'Moon River,' 'I Wanna Be Around,' 'Too Marvelous for Words,' and other standards."

"Wrong, but not completely off base," said Williams. "What else?"

"That last year Jacqueline Onassis offered to buy the house and everything in it for two million dollars."

"The guide gets C minus for accuracy," said Williams. "And now, I'll tell you what really happened:

"Construction of the house was begun in 1860 by the Confederate general Hugh Mercer, Johnny Mercer's great-grandfather. It was unfinished when the Civil War broke out, and after the war, General Mercer was imprisoned and tried for the murder of two army deserters. He was eventually acquitted, largely on the testimony of his son, and released from jail a broken and very angry man. He sold the house, and the new owners completed it. So none of the Mercers ever lived here, including Johnny. Late in his life, though, Johnny used to drop in when he was in town. In fact, he taped a Mike Douglas show in the front yard. He once offered to buy the house, but I told him, 'Johnny, you don't need it, you'll end up playing houseboy to it just as I have.' And that's as close as he came to ever living here."

Williams leaned back and sent a thin stream of cigar smoke ceilingward. "I'll come to Jacqueline Onassis in a moment," he said, "but first I want to let you in on another piece of history that the tour guides never mention. It's an incident I call 'Flag Day.' It happened a couple of years ago."

He stood up and went over to the window. "Monterey Square is lovely," he said. "In my opinion, it's the most beautiful of all the squares in Savannah. The architecture, the trees, the monument, the way it all fits together. Moviemakers love it. Something like twenty feature films have been shot in Savannah in the past six years, and Monterey Square is one of their favorite shooting locations.

"Every time filming begins the town goes wild. Everybody wants to be an extra and meet the stars and watch from the sidelines. The mayor and the city councilmen think it's wonderful because the film companies will spend money here, and Savannah will become famous, and that will help tourism.

"But it really isn't so wonderful at all. The moviemakers pay local extras the minimum wage, and Savannah doesn't get publicity after all, because the audiences usually haven't the vaguest idea where the movies have been shot. In fact, the costs to Savannah turn out to be greater than the return, if you add up the overtime pay for sanitation men and police and the disruption of traffic. And the film crews are invariably rude. They leave piles of litter. They destroy shrubbery. They trample the grass. One crew even cut down a palm tree across the square, because it didn't happen to suit them.

"Well, the rudest bunch of all came to town a couple of years ago to film a CBS made-for-TV movie about the assassination of Abraham Lincoln. They selected Monterey Square for an important outdoor scene, but naturally we were not consulted. The night before filming was to begin, the police went around and abruptly ordered all of us to move our cars out of the square and not to enter or exit our houses between ten in the morning and five that afternoon. The film crew then dumped eight truckloads of dirt onto the street and spread it around to make it look like the unpaved streets of 1865. The next morning we awoke to find the square full of horses and wagons and ladies in hoopskirts and a thick coating of dust all over everything. It was intolerable. The cameras were in the middle of the square aimed directly at this house.

"Several of my neighbors asked me, as a founder and past president of the Downtown Neighborhood Association, to do something about it. I went out and asked the producer to make a thousand-dollar contribution to the Humane Society to show his good intentions. He said he would think it over and get back to me by noon.

"Noon came and went. The producer never responded. Instead, the cameras began to roll. I decided to ruin his shot, and this is how I did it."

Williams opened a cabinet to the left of the window and took out a bolt of red cloth. He held it up over his head and unfurled it with a snap of his wrist. It was an eight-foot Nazi banner.

"I draped this over the balcony outside the window," he said. He held the banner up so I could get a good look at the big black swastika against a circle of white on a field of bright red.

"I bet that stopped the shooting," I said.

"Yes, but only temporarily," he said. "The cameraman switched to the other side of the house, so I moved the flag to the window in the study. They eventually got the shot they wanted, but at least I made my point."

Williams rolled up the banner and put it back in the cabinet. "The furor it caused was something I hadn't expected. The *Savannah Morning News* splashed the story across its front page, complete with photographs. They wrote vituperative editorials and published angry letters. The wire services picked it up too, and so did the television network evening news.

"I found myself having to explain that, no, I was not a Nazi and that I had used the flag to create a time warp in order to stop some very inconsiderate filmmakers, who were not Jewish as far as I knew. But I did make one terrible oversight. I had forgotten that the Temple Mickve Israel synagogue is located directly across the square. The rabbi wrote me a letter asking how I happened to have a Nazi flag handy. I wrote back saying my uncle Jesse had brought it back as a trophy from the Second World War. I also told him I collected relics of all sorts of fallen empires and that the flag and a few other World War Two items were simply part of that group."

"Then I wasn't mistaken," I said. "That was a Nazi dagger I saw on a table in the rear parlor."

"I have several," said Williams, "plus a few sidearms and a hood ornament from a Nazi staff car. That's about the extent of it, though. Artifacts of Hitler's regime are not popular, but they do have historic value. Most people understand that point and know there was nothing political about my protest. The firestorm abated after a couple of weeks, but every so often I encounter a smoldering ember in the form of glaring eyes or people crossing the street to avoid me."

"But I gather you haven't been ostracized."

"Not at all. Six months after Flag Day, Jacqueline Onassis came to call."

Williams crossed the room and lifted the lid of a slant-top desk. "Twice a year," he said, "Christie's auction house has

Fabergé sales in Geneva. Last year, the star item in the sale was an exquisite little jade box. It had been widely advertised, and there was a lot of excitement about it. The man in charge of those sales was Geza von Habsburg; he'd be archduke of the Austro-Hungarian Empire today if it still existed. Geza's a friend of mine. I've attended those sales for years. Naturally, I flew over for this one, and I said, 'Geza, I'm here to buy that little box.' Geza laughed and said, 'Jim, quite a number of people are here to buy that little box.' I had visions of having to bid against Malcolm Forbes and his ilk, but I thought at least I'd have fun driving up the price. So I said, 'Well, Geza, let's put it this way: If somebody outbids me and buys that box they're gonna, by God, know they bought a box!' The bidding started at the highest estimate. I finally bought the box for seventy thousand dollars. Then I flew back over the Atlantic on the Concorde and had a champagne cocktail with the little box sitting on my linen-covered tray.

"The very next morning, I was down in my basement workshop restoring furniture, jet-lagged and unshaven, when the doorbell rang. I sent one of my assistants, Barry Thomas, up to answer it. He came running back downstairs all out of breath and said a tour guide was at the door and wanted to know if I would show Jacqueline Onassis through the house. I thought, 'This is a bunch of bull,' but I came up anyway and there was the tour guide, and indeed she had Mrs. Onassis waiting in the car.

"I asked her to drive around the block a few times and give me a chance to shave and get the house pulled together. While she did that, I got myself ready and told the boys to do what we call a tour-of-homes lighting. It's a set routine that takes a full ten minutes of turning on lamps, opening shutters, emptying ashtrays and clearing away newspapers. Just as we were finishing, the doorbell rang again, and there was Mrs. Onassis and her friend Maurice Tempelsman. 'I'm awfully sorry I sent you away before,' I said, 'but I just got back last night from the Fabergé sale in Geneva.' With that, Mr. Tempelsman said, 'Who bought the box?' I said, 'Won't you come in and see?' Without another word, he took Mrs. Onassis by the arm and said, 'There it is. I told you we should have bought it.' "

Williams handed me the box. It was a rich deep green, about four inches square. The top was covered with a brilliant latticework of diamonds punctuated with cabochon rubies. In the center, a white oval enamel medallion bore the cipher of Nicholas II in diamonds and gold.

"They were in the house an hour or so," said Williams. "They looked at everything. We went upstairs, and I played the pipe organ, and then we all played roulette. They were completely charming. Tempelsman had what I call a topside dye job. You take a man and dip him bottom side up in hair dye and stop right at the ears. He was an interesting man, very knowledgeable about antiques. In fact, they both were. They'd been traveling down the coast on his yacht, but Mrs. Onassis was very down-to-earth. She was wearing a white linen suit and didn't even bother brushing the dust off her chair when we sat down in the garden. She invited me to come visit her in her 'hovel' the next time I came to New York. When they left, she asked how to get to the nearest Burger King."

"What about offering to buy the house for two million dollars?" I asked.

"She did nothing as crass as that, but she apparently told Tempelsman in front of the tour guide—who reported it to the newspapers, of course—that she wished she owned the house and everything in it. 'But not Jim Williams,' she said, 'I couldn't afford him.' "

I ran my hands over the Fabergé box. The lid swung smoothly on its hinges. The gold clasp fastened with a muted click. As I gazed at this dazzling object, I was only half-aware of a key turning in the front door of Mercer House and of footsteps approaching in the entrance hall. Suddenly, a sharp voice cut the air.

"Goddammit! Goddamn *bitch*!"

A blond boy stood in the doorway. He appeared to be about nineteen or twenty. He was wearing blue jeans and a sleeveless black T-shirt with the words FUCK YOU printed in white across the front. He was trembling with barely controlled fury. His sapphire-blue eyes were blazing.

"What seems to be the problem, Danny?" Williams asked calmly, without rising from his chair.

"Bonnie! Goddamn bitch. She stood me up! She's runnin' around at all the southside bars. Dammit! I ain't takin' her shit no more!"

The boy grabbed a vodka bottle from the table and filled a crystal glass to the brim. He gulped it down. His arms were tattooed—a Confederate flag on one arm, a marijuana plant on the other.

"Get hold of yourself now, Danny," Williams said, speaking deliberately. "Just tell me what happened."

"Maybe I was a few minutes late! I got throwed off in my timing. So what! Shit! Her girlfriend said she left 'cause I wasn't there when I said I'd be." He glared at Williams. "Gimme twenty dollars! I need the money. I'm pissed off!"

"What do you need it for?"

"None of your goddamn business! I need to get fucked up tonight, if you really wanna know. That's what!"

"I think you've already accomplished that, Sport."

"I ain't anywhere near fucked up enough yet!"

"Now, Danny, don't go doing that and driving your car. You'll get arrested for sure if you do. You've already got charges against you from the last time you got, quote, fucked up. They're really gonna nail you this time."

"I don't give a goddamn about you or Bonnie or the goddamn police!"

With that, the boy turned and abruptly left the room. The front door slammed. Outside, a car door opened and closed. A sharp, prolonged squeal of tires pierced the evening stillness. There was another squeal as the car rounded the corner of Monterey Square, then another as it turned again and sped down Bull Street. Then all was quiet.

"I'm sorry," said Williams. He got up and poured himself a drink, not Madeira this time but straight vodka. Then silently, almost imperceptibly, he released a sigh and allowed his shoulders to relax.

I looked down and saw that I was still holding the Fabergé box. I was clutching it so tightly I was afraid for a moment I might have dislodged a jewel or two from the top. It seemed intact. I handed it back to Williams.

"That was Danny Hansford," he said. "He works for me part-time refinishing furniture in my workshop."

Williams studied the end of his cigar. He was calm, controlled.

"This is not the first time something like this has happened," he said. "I have an idea how it will end up. Later tonight, about three-thirty, the telephone will ring. It'll be Danny. He'll be charming and sweet-natured. He'll say, 'Hey, Jim! This is Danny. I'm real sorry to wake you up. *Boy*, did I fuck up tonight! Ma-a-a-an, did I make some big mistakes!' And I'll say, 'Well, Danny, what happened this time?' And he'll say, 'I'm callin' from the jailhouse. Yeah, they put me in here again. But I ain't done nothin' wrong. I was goin' down Abercorn Street, see if I could find Bonnie, and I burned a little rubber and turned left real quick, and there was this goddamn police car! Blue lights, sirens. Man, I'm in trouble. Hey, Jim? Think you could come down and get me out?' And I'll say, 'Danny, it's late, I'm tired of this. Why don't you just cool it and relax yourself tonight. In jail.'

"Now, Danny won't like this one bit, but he won't lose his cool. Not now. He'll keep it calm. He'll say, 'I know what you mean, and you're right. I oughta stay in here the rest of my goddamn life. It's been a messed-up life anyhow.' He'll be working on my sympathy now. 'It's okay, Jim,' he'll say. 'Just leave me here. Don't worry about it. Hell, I don't even care. I hope I didn't get you upset. Hope you can get back to sleep all right. See you later.'

"Inside, Danny will be seething because I won't come right down there. He won't show it, though, because he knows I'm the only one who'll help him. He knows I'll call the bondsman and tell them to go get him out, and they will. But I won't do that until morning, after the drugs have worn off."

Williams gave no outward sign that he was at all embarrassed by the human tornado that had just passed through his house.

"Danny has two distinct personalities," he said. "He can switch from one to the other like turning the pages of a book." Williams was speaking about Danny with calm detachment, just as he had spoken earlier about the Waterford crystal chandelier in the dining room, the portrait by Jeremiah Theus in the parlor, and the judge's son and the gangster's moll. But he did not address the most curious question of all: Danny's presence in Mercer House and the fact that he apparently had the run of it. The incongruity was startling. Perhaps it registered on my face, because Williams offered something of an explanation.

"I have hypoglycemia," he said, "and lately I've been blacking out. Danny stays here sometimes to baby-sit me when I'm not feeling well."

It may have been the Madeira, or the atmosphere of frankness that Williams had inspired with his stories—at any rate, I felt free to observe that blacking out alone might be preferable to having this person running loose in the house. Williams laughed. "Actually, I think Danny may be improving a little."

"Improving? Over what?"

"Two weeks ago, we had a similar scene, but it ended a bit more dramatically. Danny was agitated that time because his best friend had made a disparaging remark about his car, and his girlfriend had refused to marry him. Danny came back to the house and carried on about it, and before I knew what was happening, he had stomped a small table, thrown a bronze lamp against the wall, and slammed a cut-glass water pitcher on the floor with so much force it made a permanent imprint on the heart-pine floorboards. But he wasn't through yet. He took one of my German Lugers and fired a bullet into the floor upstairs. Then he ran out the front door and fired another shot into Monterey Square, trying to knock out a streetlight.

"Naturally, I called the police. But when Danny heard the sirens, he tossed the gun into the bushes, ran indoors, flew up the stairs, and jumped into bed with all his clothes on. The cops were no more than a minute behind him, but by the time they got upstairs, Danny was pretending to be fast asleep. When they 'woke' him, he put on an act of confusion and denied he'd broken anything or shot any guns. But the police noticed tiny drops of blood on his arms from the little splinters of glass that had shot up when he smashed the pitcher on the floor. So they took him off to jail. I figured the longer I left him there the madder he'd get, so the next morning I dropped the charges and got him out."

I did not ask the obvious question: Why do you have anything to do with him? Instead, I asked a question of more immediate concern: "You said Danny had fired 'one of' your German Lugers. How many do you have?"

"Several," said Williams. "I need them for security. I'm here by myself a lot, and I've had a couple of robberies. The second robbery was pulled off by a man who was armed with a submachine gun, and I was asleep upstairs at the time. That's when I installed the alarm system. It works fine when I'm out of the house or upstairs, but I can't throw the switch when I'm walking around down here on the main floor, because it'll summon the police. So I keep pistols in strategic places. There's a Luger in the rear library, another in a desk drawer in my office, a third in the Irish linen press in the hall, and a Smith and Wesson in the living room. I've also got a shotgun and three or four rifles upstairs. The pistols are loaded."

"That's four loaded pistols," I said.

"There's a risk, I know. But I'm a gambler. I have been all my life. You have to be if you deal in antiques and restore houses and go into debt for all of it as I have. But when I gamble I know how to improve the odds. Come, I'll show you."

Williams led me over to a small backgammon table. He removed the backgammon board and replaced it with another plain board lined with green felt.

"I believe in mind control," he said. "I think you can influence events by mental concentration. I've invented a game called Psycho Dice. It's very simple. You take four dice and call out four numbers between one and six—for example, a four, a three, and two sixes. Then you throw the dice, and if any of your numbers come up, you leave those dice standing on the board. You continue to roll the remaining dice until all the dice are sitting on the board, showing your set of numbers. You're eliminated if you roll three times in succession without getting any of the numbers you need. The object is to get all four numbers in the fewest rolls."

Williams was sure he could improve the odds by sheer concentration. "Dice have six sides," he said, "so you have a one-in-six chance of getting your number when you throw them. If you do any better than that, you beat the law of averages. Concentration definitely helps. That's been proved. Back in the nineteen-thirties, Duke University did a study with a machine that could throw dice. First they had it throw dice when nobody was in the building, and the numbers came up strictly according to the law of averages. Then they put a man in the next room and had him concentrate on various numbers to see if that would beat the odds. It did. Then they put him in the same room, still concentrating, and the machine beat the odds again, by an even wider margin. When the man rolled the dice himself, using a cup, he did better still. When he finally rolled the dice with his bare hand, he did best of all."

From the few rounds we played, I could not say whether Psycho Dice really worked. Williams had no doubt that it did. He saw proof of it at every turn. When I needed a five and rolled a two, he proclaimed, "Aha! You know what's on the other side of a two, don't you? Five!"

I could not let this pass. "If we'd been betting, I would have lost anyway, wouldn't I?"

"Yes, but look how close you came. You see, the same concentration that makes Psycho Dice work can make most things in life work. I've never been sick a day in my life except for a common cold once in a while. I just can't be bothered. I don't have the time. Being sick is a luxury. I concentrate on being well. Danny didn't do more than let off steam tonight, because I cooled him down. I was concentrating on that."

I was tempted not to let that remark pass, either. But it was late. I rose to leave. "Isn't it possible that other people will turn their mental energy on you?" I asked.

"They try to all the time," Williams said with a wry smile. "I'm told a lot of people pray fervently night after night that I'll invite them to my Christmas parties."

"I can understand that," I said. "From what I've heard, it's the best party in Savannah."

"I'll invite you to the next one, and you can judge for yourself." Williams fixed me with an impenetrable look. "You know I have two Christmas parties, not just one. Both are black-tie. The first party is the famous one. It's the one that gets written up in the newspapers, the one the high and mighty of Savannah come to. The second party is the next night. It's the one the papers never write about. It's . . . for gentlemen only. Which party would you like to be invited to?"

"The one," I said, "least likely to involve gunfire."

Chapter 2

DESTINATION UNKNOWN

It would be stretching things to say that I had left New York and come to Savannah as a result of eating a paillard of veal served on a bed of wilted radicchio. But there is a connection.

I had lived in New York for twenty years, writing and editing for magazines. Thomas Carlyle once said that magazine work is below street-sweeping as a trade, but in mid-twentieth-century New York it was a reasonably respectable calling. I wrote for *Esquire* and had served as editor of *New York* magazine. At any rate, in the early 1980s it happened that New York City had embarked on a *nouvelle cuisine* eating binge. Every week, two or three elegant new restaurants would open to great fanfare. The décor would be sleek postmodern, the food superlative, and the prices steep. Dining out became the most popular leisure activity in town; it replaced going to discotheques, the theater, and concerts. Talk of food and restaurants dominated conversations. One evening, as a waiter at one of these places was reciting a lengthy monologue of specials, I scanned the prices of entrées on the menu—$19, $29, $39, $49—and it occurred to me that I had seen that very same column of figures earlier in the day. But where? It suddenly came to me. I had seen it in a newspaper ad for supersaver airfares from New York to cities all across America. As I recall, the veal-and-radicchio entrée cost as much as a flight from New York to Louisville or any of six equidistant cities. With everything included—drinks, dessert, coffee, and tip—the bill for each person that night came to what it would have cost to spend a three-day weekend in another town.

A week later I passed up the veal and radicchio and flew to New Orleans.

After that, every five or six weeks I took advantage of the newly deregulated airfares and flew out of New York in the company of a small group of friends interested in a change of scene. One of those weekend jaunts took us to Charleston, South Carolina. We drove around in a rented car with a map lying open on the front seat. At the bottom of the map, about a hundred miles down the coast, lay Savannah.

I had never been to Savannah, but I had a vivid image of it anyway. Several images, in fact. The most memorable, because it was formed in my childhood, was one associated with *Treasure Island,* which I had read at the age of ten. In *Treasure Island,* Savannah is the place where Captain John Flint, the murderous pirate with the blue face, has died of rum before the story begins. It is on his deathbed in Savannah that Flint bellows his last command—*"Fetch aft the rum, Darby!"*—and hands Billy Bones a map of Treasure Island. "He gave it me at Savannah," says Bones, "when he lay a-dying." The book had a drawing of Flint's map in it with an X marking the location of his buried treasure. I turned to the map again and again as I read, and every time I did I was reminded of Savannah, for there at the bottom was Billy Bones's scrawled notation, "Given by above JF to Mr W. Bones. Savannah this twenty July 1754."

I next came across Savannah in *Gone with the Wind,* which was set a century later. By 1860, Savannah was no longer the pirates' rendezvous I'd pictured. It had become, in

Margaret Mitchell's words, "that gently mannered city by the sea." Savannah was an offstage presence in *Gone with the Wind*, just as it had been in *Treasure Island*. It stood aloof on the Georgia coast—dignified, sedate, refined—looking down its nose at Atlanta, which was then a twenty-year-old frontier town three hundred miles inland. From Atlanta's point of view, specifically through the eyes of the young Scarlett O'Hara, Savannah and Charleston were "like aged grandmothers fanning themselves placidly in the sun."

My third impression of Savannah was somewhat quirkier. I got it from the yellowed pages of an old newspaper that had been used to line the inside of an antique wooden chest that I kept at the foot of my bed. It was from the *Savannah Morning News*, April 2, 1914. Whenever I lifted the lid of the chest, I was confronted by a brief story that read as follows:

> TANGO IS NO SIGN OF INSANITY, HOLDS JURY
>
> DECIDES THAT SADIE JEFFERSON IS NOT INSANE
>
> It is no indication of insanity to tango. This was settled yesterday by a lunacy commission which decided that Sadie Jefferson is sane. It was alleged the woman tangoed all the way to police headquarters recently when she was arrested.

That was the story in its entirety. Sadie Jefferson was not further identified, and nothing was said about why she had been arrested in the first place. I imagined she had drunk more than her share of the rum left over from Captain Flint. Whatever it was, Sadie Jefferson seemed to be cut from the same cloth as the heroine of the song "Hard-hearted Hannah, the Vamp of Savannah." Those two women lent an exotic dimension to the picture of Savannah that was forming in my mind.

Then Johnny Mercer died in the mid-1970s, and I read that he had been born and raised in Savannah. Mercer had written the lyrics and sometimes also the music for dozens of songs I'd known since childhood, gentle songs that had a mellow eloquence: "Jeepers Creepers," "Ac-Cent-Tchu-Ate the Positive," "Blues in the Night," "One for My Baby," "Goody Goody," "Fools Rush In," "That Old Black Magic," "Dream," "Laura," "Satin Doll," "In the Cool, Cool, Cool of the Evening," and "On the Atchison, Topeka and the Santa Fe."

According to his obituary, Mercer had never lost touch with his hometown. Savannah, he said, had been "a sweet, indolent background for a boy to grow up in." Even after he moved away, he kept a home on the outskirts of town so he could visit whenever he wanted. The back porch of his house looked out on a tidal creek that meandered through a broad expanse of marshland. In his honor, Savannah had renamed the creek after one of the four Academy Award–winning songs for which he'd written the lyrics, "Moon River."

These, then, were the images in my mental gazetteer of Savannah: rum-drinking pirates, strong-willed women, courtly manners, eccentric behavior, gentle words, and lovely music. That and the beauty of the name itself: Savannah.

On Sunday, my traveling companions went back to New York, but I stayed on in Charleston. I had decided to drive down to Savannah, spend the night, and fly back to New York from there.

—

There being no direct route to Savannah from Charleston, I followed a zigzagging course that took me through the tidal flatlands of the South Carolina low country. As I approached Savannah, the road narrowed to a two-lane blacktop shaded by tall trees. There was an occasional produce stand by the side of the road and a few cottages set into the foliage, but nothing resembling urban sprawl. The voice on the car radio informed me that I had entered a zone called the Coastal

Empire. "The weather outlook for the Coastal Empire," it said, "is for highs in the mid-eighties, with moderate seas and a light chop on inland waters."

Abruptly, the trees gave way to an open panorama of marsh grass the color of wheat. Straight ahead, a tall bridge rose steeply out of the plain. From the top of the bridge, I looked down on the Savannah River and, on the far side, a row of old brick buildings fronted by a narrow esplanade. Behind the buildings a mass of trees extended into the distance, punctuated by steeples, cornices, rooftops, and cupolas. As I descended from the bridge, I found myself plunging into a luxuriant green garden.

Walls of thick vegetation rose up on all sides and arched overhead in a lacy canopy that filtered the light to a soft shade. It had just rained; the air was hot and steamy. I felt enclosed in a semitropical terrarium, sealed off from a world that suddenly seemed a thousand miles away.

The streets were lined with townhouses of brick and stucco, handsome old buildings with high front stoops and shuttered windows. I entered a square that had flowering shrubs and a monument at the center. A few blocks farther on, there was another square. Up ahead, I could see a third on line with this one, and a fourth beyond that. To the left and right, there were two more squares. There were squares in every direction. I counted eight of them. Ten. Fourteen. Or was it twelve?

"There are exactly twenty-one squares," an elderly lady told me later in the afternoon. Her name was Mary Harty. Acquaintances in Charleston had put us in touch; she had been expecting me. She had white hair and arched eyebrows that gave her a look of permanent surprise. We stood in her kitchen while she mixed martinis in a silver shaker. When she was finished, she put the shaker into a wicker basket. She was going to take me on an excursion, she said. It was too nice a day, and I had too little time in Savannah for us to waste it indoors.

As far as Miss Harty was concerned, the squares were the jewels of Savannah. No other city in the world had anything like them. There were five on Bull Street, five on Barnard, four on Abercorn, and so on. James Oglethorpe, the founder of Georgia, had been responsible for them, she said. He had decided Savannah was going to be laid out with squares, based on the design of a Roman military encampment, even before he set sail from England—before he even knew exactly where on the map he was going to put Savannah. When he arrived in February 1733, he chose a site for the city on top of a forty-foot bluff on the southern bank of the Savannah River, eighteen miles inland from the Atlantic. He had already sketched out the plans. The streets were to be laid out in a grid pattern, crossing at right angles, and there would be squares at regular intervals. In effect, the city would become a giant parterre garden. Oglethorpe built the first four squares himself. "The thing I like best about the squares," Miss Harty said, "is that cars can't cut through the middle; they must go *around* them. So traffic is obliged to flow at a very leisurely pace. The squares are our little oases of tranquillity."

As she spoke, I recognized in her voice the coastal accent described in *Gone with the Wind*—"soft and slurring, liquid of vowels, kind to consonants."

"But actually," she said, "the whole of Savannah is an oasis. We are isolated. Gloriously isolated! We're a little enclave on the coast—off by ourselves, surrounded by nothing but marshes and piney woods. We're not easy to get to at all, as you may have noticed. If you fly here, you usually have to change planes at least once. And trains are not much better. Somebody wrote a novel in the nineteen-fifties that captured it rather well, I thought. *The View from Pompey's Head*. It's by Hamilton Basso. Have you read it? The story opens with a young man taking the train from New York to Pompey's Head and having to get off at the ungodly hour of five in the morning. Pompey's Head is supposed to be Savannah, and I have no quibble with that. We're a terribly inconvenient destination!"

Miss Harty's laughter was as light as wind chimes. "There used to be a train that ran between here and Atlanta. The

Nancy Hanks. It shut down altogether twenty years ago, and we don't miss it at all."

"Don't you feel cut off?" I asked.

"Cut off from what?" she replied. "No, on the whole I'd say we rather enjoy our separateness. Whether that's good or bad I haven't any idea. Manufacturers tell us they like to test-market their products in Savannah—toothpastes and detergents and the like—because Savannah is utterly impervious to outside influence. Not that people haven't *tried* to influence us! Good Lord, they try all the time. People come here from all over the country and fall in love with Savannah. Then they move here and pretty soon they're telling us how much more lively and prosperous Savannah could be if we only knew what we had and how to take advantage of it. I call these people 'Gucci carpetbaggers.' They can be rather insistent, you know. Even rude. We smile pleasantly and we nod, but we don't budge an inch. Cities all around us are booming urban centers: Charleston, Atlanta, Jacksonville—but not Savannah. The Prudential Insurance people wanted to locate their regional headquarters here in the nineteen-fifties. It would have created thousands of jobs and made Savannah an important center of a nice, profitable, nonpolluting industry. But we said no. Too big. They gave it to Jacksonville instead. In the nineteen-seventies, Gian Carlo Menotti considered making Savannah the permanent home for his Spoleto U.S.A. Festival. Again, we were not interested. So Charleston got it. It's not that we're trying to be difficult. We just happen to like things exactly the way they are!"

Miss Harty opened a cupboard and took out two silver goblets. She wrapped each of them in a linen napkin and placed them carefully in the wicker basket beside the martinis.

"We may be standoffish," she said, "but we're not hostile. We're famously hospitable, in fact, even by southern standards. Savannah's called the 'Hostess City of the South,' you know. That's because we've always been a party town. We love company. We always have. I suppose that comes from being a port city and having played host to people from faraway places for so long. Life in Savannah was always easier than it was out on the plantations. Savannah was a city of rich cotton traders, who lived in elegant houses within strolling distance of one another. Parties became a way of life, and it's made a difference. We're not at all like the rest of Georgia. We have a saying: If you go to Atlanta, the first question people ask you is, 'What's your business?' In Macon they ask, 'Where do you go to church?' In Augusta they ask your grandmother's maiden name. But in Savannah the first question people ask you is 'What would you like to drink?' "

She patted the basket of martinis. I could hear the echo of Captain Flint shouting for rum.

"Savannah's always been wet," she said, "even when the rest of Georgia was dry. During Prohibition, filling stations on Abercorn Street sold whiskey out of gas pumps! Oh, you could always get a drink in Savannah. That's never been any secret. I remember when I was a child, Billy Sunday brought his holy-revival crusade to town. He set himself up in Forsyth Park, and everybody went to hear him. There was great excitement! Mr. Sunday got up and declared at the top of his voice that Savannah was *the wickedest city in the world!* Well, of course, we all thought that was perfectly marvelous!"

Miss Harty handed me the basket and led the way through the hall and out the front door to my car. With the basket on the seat between us, she guided me as I drove through the streets.

"I'm going to take you to visit the dead," she said.

We had just turned onto Victory Drive, a long parkway completely covered by an arch of live oaks dripping with Spanish moss. In the center, a double colonnade of palms marched along the median strip as if lending architectural support to the canopy of oaks and moss.

I glanced at her, not sure I'd heard correctly. "The dead?"

"The dead are very much with us in Savannah," she said. "Everywhere you look there is a reminder of things that were, people who lived. We are keenly aware of our past. Those palms, for example. They were planted in honor of soldiers from Georgia who died in the First World War."

After driving three or four miles, we turned off Victory Drive onto a winding road that took us to the gates of Bonaventure Cemetery. A live-oak forest of a primeval dimension loomed before us. We parked the car just inside the gate and continued on foot, coming almost at once to a large white marble mausoleum.

"Now, if you should die during your stay in Savannah," Miss Harty said with a gentle smile, "this is where we'll put you. It's our Stranger's Tomb. It was built in honor of a man named William Gaston. He was one of Savannah's greatest hosts and party givers, and he died in the nineteenth century. This tomb is a memorial to his hospitality. It has an empty vault in it that's reserved for out-of-towners who die while visiting Savannah. It gives them a chance to rest awhile in one of the most beautiful cemeteries in the world, until their families can make arrangements to take them away."

I remarked that I hoped I would not tax Savannah's hospitality to that extent. We moved on past the tomb along an avenue bordered by magnificent oaks. On both sides, moss-covered statues stood in an overgrowth of shrubbery like the remnants of an abandoned temple.

"In Colonial times, this was a lovely plantation," Miss Harty said. "Its centerpiece was a mansion made of bricks brought over from England. There were terraced gardens extending all the way down to the river. The estate was built by Colonel John Mulryne. When Mulryne's daughter married Josiah Tattnall the bride's father commemorated the happy union of the two families by planting great avenues of trees forming the initials M and T intertwined. I'm told enough of the original trees survive that you can still trace the monogram, if you put your mind to it." Miss Harty paused as we approached a vine-covered mound by the side of the path.

"This is all that's left of the plantation house," she said. "It's a piece of the foundation. The house burned sometime in the late seventeen-hundreds. It was a spectacular fire, by all accounts. A formal dinner party had been in progress, with liveried servants standing behind every chair. In the middle of dinner, the butler came up to the host and whispered that the roof had caught fire and that nothing could be done to stop it. The host rose calmly, clinked his glass, and invited his guests to pick up their dinner plates and follow him into the garden. The servants carried the table and chairs after them, and the dinner continued by the light of the raging fire. The host made the best of it. He regaled his guests with amusing stories and jests while the flames consumed his house. Then, in turn, each guest rose and offered a toast to the host, the house, and the delicious repast. When the toasts were finished, the host threw his crystal glass against the trunk of an old oak tree, and each of the guests followed suit. Tradition has it that if you listen closely on quiet nights you can still hear the laughter and the shattering of crystal glasses. I like to think of this place as the scene of the Eternal Party. What better place, in Savannah, to rest in peace for all time—where the party goes on and on."

We resumed our walk and in a few moments came to a small family plot shaded by a large oak tree. Five graves and two small date palms lay inside a low curbstone. One of the graves, a full-length white marble slab, was littered with dried leaves and sand. Miss Harty brushed the debris away, and an inscription emerged: JOHN HERNDON MERCER (JOHNNY).

"Did you know him?" I asked.

"We all knew him," she said, "and loved him. We always thought we recognized something of Johnny in each of his songs. They had a buoyancy and a freshness, and that's the way he was. It was as if he'd never really left Savannah." She brushed away more of the leaves and uncovered an epitaph: AND THE ANGELS SING.

"For me," she said, "Johnny was literally the boy next door. I lived at 222 East Gwinnett Street; he lived at 226. Johnny's great-grandfather built a huge house on Monterey Square, but Johnny never lived in it. The man who lives there now has restored it superbly and made it into quite a showplace. Jim Williams. My society friends are wild about him. I'm not."

Miss Harty squared her shoulders and said no more about the Mercers or Jim Williams. We continued along the path toward the river, which was just now visible up ahead under the trees. "And now I have one more thing to show you," she said.

We walked to the crest of a low bluff overlooking a broad, slow-moving expanse of water, clearly the choicest spot in this most tranquil of settings. Miss Harty led me into a small enclosure that had a gravestone and a granite bench. She sat down on the bench and gestured for me to sit next to her.

"At last," she said, "we can have our martinis." She opened the wicker basket and poured the drinks into the silver goblets. "If you look at the gravestone," she said, "you'll see it's a bit unusual." It was a double gravestone bearing the names of Dr. William F. Aiken and his wife, Anna. "They were the parents of Conrad Aiken, the poet. Notice the dates."

Both Dr. and Mrs. Aiken had died on the same day: February 27, 1901.

"This is what happened," she said. "The Aikens were living on Oglethorpe Avenue in a big brick townhouse. Dr. Aiken had his offices on the ground floor, and the family lived on the two floors above. Conrad was eleven. One morning, Conrad awoke to the sounds of his parents quarreling in their bedroom down the hall. The quarreling subsided for a moment. Then Conrad heard his father counting, 'One! Two! Three!' There was a half-stifled scream and then a pistol shot. Then another count of three, another shot, and then a thud. Conrad ran barefoot across Oglethorpe Avenue to the police station where he announced, 'Papa has just shot Mama and then shot himself.' He led the officers to the house and up to his parents' bedroom on the top floor."

Miss Harty lifted her goblet in a silent toast to Dr. and Mrs. Aiken. Then she poured a few drops onto the ground.

"Believe it or not," she said, "one of the reasons he killed her was . . . parties. Aiken hinted at it in 'Strange Moonlight,' one of his short stories. In the story, the father complains to the mother that she's neglecting her family. He says, 'It's two parties *every* week, and sometimes three or four, that's excessive.' The story was autobiographical, of course. The Aikens were living well beyond their means at the time. Anna Aiken went out to parties practically every other night. She'd given six dinner parties in the month before her husband killed her.

"After the shooting, relatives up north took Conrad in and raised him. He went to Harvard and had a brilliant career. He won the Pulitzer Prize and was appointed to the poetry chair at the Library of Congress. When he retired, he came back to spend his last years in Savannah. He always knew he would. He'd written a novel called *Great Circle;* it was about ending up where one started. And that's the way it turned out for Aiken himself. He lived in Savannah his first eleven years and his last eleven years. In those last years, he lived *next door* to the house where he'd lived as a child, separated from his tragic childhood by a single brick wall.

"Of course, when he moved back to Savannah, the poetry society was all aflutter, as you can imagine. But Aiken kept pretty much to himself. He politely declined most invitations. He said he needed the time for his work. Quite often, though, he and his wife would come out here and sit for an hour or so. They'd bring a shaker of martinis and silver goblets and talk to his departed parents and pour libations to them."

Miss Harty raised her goblet and touched it to mine. A pair of mockingbirds conversed somewhere in the trees. A shrimp boat passed at slow speed.

"Aiken loved to come here and watch the ships go by," she said. "One afternoon, he saw one with the name *Cosmos Mariner* painted on the bow. That delighted him. The word 'cosmos' appears often in his poetry, you know. That evening he went home and looked for mention of the *Cosmos Mariner* in the shipping news. There it was, in tiny type on the list of ships in port. The name was followed by the comment 'Destination Unknown.' That pleased him even more."

"Where is Aiken buried?" I asked. There were no other gravestones in the enclosure.

"Oh, he's here," she said. "In fact, we are very much his personal guests at the moment. It was Aiken's wish that people should come to this beautiful place after he died and drink martinis and watch the ships just as he did. He left a gracious invitation to that effect. He had his gravestone built in the shape of a bench."

An involuntary reflex propelled me to my feet. Miss Harty laughed, and then she too stood up. Aiken's name was inscribed on the bench, along with the words COSMOS MARINER, DESTINATION UNKNOWN.

—

I was beguiled by Savannah. The next morning, as I checked out of the hotel, I asked the desk clerk how I might go about renting an apartment for a month or so—not right then, but soon perhaps.

"Dial 'bedroom,' " she said. "On the telephone. B-E-D-R-O-O-M. It's the number of a referral service for guest houses. They have listings."

I suspected that in Savannah I had stumbled on a rare vestige of the Old South. It seemed to me that Savannah was in some respects as remote as Pitcairn Island, that tiny rock in the middle of the Pacific where the descendants of the mutineers of the H.M.S. *Bounty* had lived in inbred isolation since the eighteenth century. For about the same length of time, seven generations of Savannahians had been marooned in their hushed and secluded bower of a city on the Georgia coast. "We're a very cousiny people," Mary Harty told me. "One must tread very lightly here: Everyone is kin to everyone else."

An idea was beginning to take shape in my mind, a variation of my city-hopping weekends. I would make Savannah my second home. I would spend perhaps a month at a time in Savannah, long enough to become more than a tourist if not quite a full-fledged resident. I would inquire, observe, and poke around wherever my curiosity led me or wherever I was invited. I would presume nothing. I would take notes.

Over a period of eight years I did just that, except that my stays in Savannah became longer and my return trips to New York shorter. At times, I came to think of myself as living in Savannah. I found myself involved in an adventure peopled by an unusual assortment of characters and enlivened by a series of strange events, up to and including murder. But first things first. I went to the telephone and dialed "bedroom."

Chapter 3

THE SENTIMENTAL GENTLEMAN

The voice that spoke to me from "bedroom" led me to my new home in Savannah—the second floor of a carriage house on East Charlton Lane. I had two small rooms that looked out on a garden and the rear of a townhouse. The garden had a fragrant magnolia and a small banana tree.

The apartment's furnishings included an old navigator's globe on a stand. On my first night in residence, I put my finger on Savannah and, turning the globe, followed the thirty-second parallel around the world. Marrakesh, Tel Aviv, and Nanking passed beneath my finger. Savannah stood on the westernmost point of the East Coast, due south of Cleveland. It was south of New York by nine degrees of latitude, which should have been enough to make a difference in the angle of the moon in the sky, I figured. The crescent would be turned clockwise slightly tonight, so that it would look more like the letter U than the letter C it had been the night before in New York. Or would it be the other way around? I looked out the window to see, but the moon had slipped behind a cloud.

It was at about that time, as I was attempting to fix my exact location in the universe, that I became aware of laughing voices and the sound of a honky-tonk piano coming over the garden wall. The song was "Sweet Georgia Brown," and it was sung by a smooth baritone voice. The next song was "How Come You Do Me Like You Do?" A party was in progress a few houses away, and I took this to be a good sign. The music made an agreeable background sound, if a little corny, and the piano player was very good. Tireless, too. The last song I remember that night before falling asleep was "Lazybones." It was written, appropriately enough, by Johnny Mercer.

A few hours later, shortly after dawn, the music started in again. "Piano-roll Blues" was the first tune of the morning, as I recall; then came "Darktown Strutters' Ball." The music continued in that vein, off and on, throughout the day and late into the evening. It did the same the following day and the day after that. The piano was a permanent part of the atmosphere, apparently, and so was the party—if a party was what it was.

I traced the music to 16 East Jones Street, a yellow stuccoed townhouse four houses away. In most respects, the house was like all the others on the block except for a steady stream of visitors who came and went at all hours of the day and night. There was no common denominator among them—they were young and old, alone and in groups, white and black—but I did notice that none of them rang the bell or knocked. They just pushed the door open and walked in. Unlocked doors were highly unusual, even in Savannah. I assumed that eventually all of this would explain itself, and in the meantime I set about becoming acquainted with my new surroundings.

The garden part of the city with its geometrical arrangement of squares encompassed the three-square-mile historic district, which was built before the Civil War. City fathers abandoned the squares later on when the city expanded southward. Immediately south of the historic district lay a wide swath of Victorian gingerbread houses. These gave way to Ardsley Park, an enclave of early twentieth-century houses with proud façades that featured columns, pediments, porticoes, and terraces. South of Ardsley Park, the scale of the houses diminished. There were bungalows built in the thirties and forties, then ranch houses of the fifties and sixties, and finally the southside, a flat semirural terrain that could have been anywhere in America except for occasional echoes of Dixie such as the Twelve Oaks Shopping Plaza and the Tara Cinemas.

At the Georgia Historical Society, an obliging librarian clarified a few matters for me. No, she said, there had never been any such woman as Hard-hearted Hannah. The librarian suspected that Hannah had simply been the product of a songwriter needing a rhyme. She added with a sigh that sometimes she wished Hannah had been the vamp of Montana instead. Savannah could lay claim to enough real history, she said, that it had no need of false honors. Did I know, for instance, that Eli Whitney had invented the cotton gin at Mulberry Plantation in Savannah? Or that Juliette Gordon Low had founded the Girl Scouts of America in a carriage house on Drayton Street?

The librarian recited a list of Savannah's historic highlights: America's first Sunday school had been founded in Savannah in 1736, America's first orphanage in 1740, America's first black Baptist congregation in 1788, America's first golf course in 1796. John Wesley, the founder of Methodism, had been the minister of Christ Church in Savannah in 1736, and during his tenure had written a book of hymns that became the first hymnal used in the Church of England. A Savannah merchant had bankrolled the first steamship ever to cross the Atlantic, the *Savannah,* which made its maiden ocean voyage from Savannah to Liverpool in 1819.

The cumulative weight of all these historic firsts suggested that this sleepy city of 150,000 had once been more important in the general scheme of things than it was now. Sponsoring the world's first oceangoing steamship in 1819, for instance, would have been the equivalent of launching the first space shuttle today. President James Monroe had made a special trip to Savannah in honor of the maiden voyage—a fair indication of its importance.

I browsed among the books, prints, and maps in the society's reading room, a spacious hall with a high ceiling and a double tier of bookshelves along the walls. The Civil War loomed large in this room, and Savannah's role in it was a story that seemed to say a great deal about the city:

At the outbreak of fighting, Savannah was the world's leading cotton port. General William Tecumseh Sherman selected it as the climax for his triumphant march to the sea, bringing seventy thousand troops against Savannah's ten thousand. Unlike their counterparts in Atlanta and Charleston, Savannah's civic leaders were practical businessmen, and their secessionist passions were tempered by a sobering awareness of the devastation that was about to befall them. When Sherman drew near, the mayor of Savannah led a delegation out to meet him. They offered to surrender the city without a shot if Sherman promised not to burn it. Sherman accepted the offer and sent President Lincoln a famous telegram: I BEG TO PRESENT TO YOU, AS A CHRISTMAS GIFT, THE CITY OF SAVANNAH WITH ONE HUNDRED AND FIFTY GUNS AND PLENTY OF AMMUNITION, ALSO ABOUT TWENTY-FIVE THOUSAND BALES OF COTTON. Sherman stayed a month and then marched to Columbia, South Carolina, and burned it to the ground.

Savannah emerged from the war impoverished, but it recovered within a few years and prospered once again. By then, however, the city's financial underpinnings had begun to erode. Rural labor was being drawn away to the industrialized North; years of growing nothing but cotton had leached the soil of nutrients, and the center of the Cotton Belt had moved westward. In the financial panic of 1892, the price of a pound of cotton dropped from a dollar to nine cents. By 1920, the boll weevil had wiped out what little cotton activity was left. From that time onward, Savannah slipped into decline. Many of its once-great houses fell into disrepair. Lady Astor, passing through in 1946, remarked that Savannah was like "a beautiful woman with a dirty face." Stung by the criticism, a group of concerned citizens began in the 1950s to restore Savannah's downtown. Their effort resulted in the preservation of Savannah's historic district.

Before leaving the reading room, I thought to look in the 1914 city directory for the name of Sadie Jefferson, the woman who had tangoed all the way to the police station. She was not listed. No Jeffersons were listed at all, in fact. The librarian looked at my old newspaper clipping and told me I had probably consulted the wrong part of the city directory.

"You can tell from the wording of the news item that Sadie Jefferson was black," she said, "because the courtesy title of 'Mrs.' or 'Miss' is omitted. That was the practice until integration. It was also the practice to list blacks in a separate section of the city directory. That's probably why you didn't find her." Indeed, Sadie Jefferson was listed in the "Colored" section of the 1914 city directory—the wife of James E. Jefferson, a barber. She died in the 1970s.

The story of blacks in Savannah was, of course, a very different one from that of whites. Slavery was forbidden in Georgia in 1735 (Oglethorpe called it "a horrid crime"), but in 1749 the colony's Trustees gave in to pressure from the settlers and legalized it. Despite a long history of oppression, the 1960s civil rights movement in Savannah was almost entirely nonviolent. Civil rights leaders staged sit-ins at lunch counters, swim-ins at the beach, kneel-ins in churches, and a fifteen-month boycott of segregated stores. Tensions rose, but peace prevailed, largely because of the tireless efforts of a forward-thinking mayor, Malcolm Maclean, and a nonviolent strategy adopted by black leaders, notably W. W. Law, the head of the local branch of the NAACP. In 1964, Martin Luther King declared Savannah "the most desegregated city in the South." In 1980, the population of Savannah was half white and half black.

—

There was ample evidence in the records of the historical society that in Savannah's palmier days it had been a cosmopolitan city and its citizens an unusually worldly sort. Mayor Richard Arnold, the man who had sweet-talked General Sherman in and out of town during the Civil War, was typical of the breed. He was a physician, a scholar, an epicure, a connoisseur of fine wines, and a gentleman who took his social obligations seriously. He wrote in one letter, "Yesterday, I entertained the Hon. Howell Cobb at a sociable dinner party. We sat down at 3 o'clock and got up at half past nine." Mayor Arnold's six-and-a-half-hour dinner lent weight to what I had been told about Savannah's fondness for parties, and it put me in mind of the genteel merriment going on nonstop in the townhouse down the street from me at 16 East Jones Street.

My casual surveillance of the house paid off one day at noontime. A car drew up to the curb and screeched to a jolting stop. At the wheel was a neatly dressed elderly lady with white hair as neat as pie crust. She had made no attempt to parallel park but had instead pulled into the space front end first as if tethering a horse to a hitching post. She got out and marched to the front door, took a ball-peen hammer out of her purse and methodically smashed all the little panes of glass around the door. Then she put the hammer back in her purse and walked back to her car. The incident did not seem to make any difference to the people in the house. The piano went right on playing, and the voices kept on laughing. The panes of glass were replaced, but not until several days later.

As I expected, it all became perfectly clear soon enough. One night after dinner, I heard the click of spike heels coming up the steps followed by a gentle knock on the door. I opened it to behold a beautiful woman standing in the moonlight. Her head was tucked into a platinum cloud of cotton-candy hair. She wore a low-cut pink dress, which she filled voluptuously, and she was giggling.

"Wouldn't you know," she said, "they've gone and turned off Joe's electricity again."

"They have?" I answered. "Who is Joe?"

She was momentarily confused. "You don't know Joe? I thought everybody knew Joe. He's your neighbor. I mean, he's almost your neighbor. Joe Odom." She waved in a westerly direction. "He lives a couple of houses down that way."

"Not the house with the piano?"

This comment sent the woman into gales of pretty laughter. "Uh-huh. You got it."

"And is Joe Odom the one who plays the piano?"

"He sure is," she said, "and I'm Mandy. Mandy Nichols. I don't mean to disturb you or anything, but I saw your light on. Anyway, we've run out of ice, and I was sort of hoping you could spare some."

I invited her in. As she brushed by me I breathed the essence of gardenia. I recognized her now as one of the many people I had seen going into the house down the street. There was no way I could possibly have forgotten her. She was a statuesque beauty with not a single angular contour on her soft and lovely body. Her blue eyes were set off by a bright framework of lavishly applied cosmetics. I took four ice trays out of the freezer and emptied them into an ice bucket. I told her I had been wondering who lived in that house.

"Officially, it's just Joe," she said, "but sometimes it's hard to tell, with so many people spending the night, or the week, or a few months. I live in Waycross, and I drive in to Savannah six days a week to sing at the clubs here in town. If I'm too tired to drive home at night, I just stay at Joe's."

Mandy said she had gone to the University of Tennessee on a half-scholarship for twirling. She also said she had been crowned Miss BBW in Las Vegas a year before.

"Miss BBW?"

"That stands for Miss Big Beautiful Woman," she said. "It's a beauty contest for large women. They put out a magazine and a line of clothing—the whole nine yards. I didn't really plan on entering the pageant, though. My friends sent in the application."

I gave her the ice bucket.

"Hey," she said, "why don't you come on over and join us for a drink."

I had been about to suggest that very thing myself, so I accepted without hesitation and followed her down the stairs and into the lane. Mandy walked gingerly; the pebbles clicked and skittered under her spike heels.

"It's a long drive from Waycross to Savannah, isn't it?" I asked.

"About an hour and a half," she said, "each way."

"Doesn't that get a little boring, day after day?"

"Not really. It gives me a chance to do my nails."

"Your nails?"

"Of course," she giggled. "Why not?"

"I don't know. It just sounds a little complicated," I said. "Doing your nails and driving at the same time."

"It's real easy once you get the hang of it," she said. "I drive with my knees."

"Your knees!"

"Uh-huh. Actually, I save my nails for last. I do my makeup first and then my hair."

I looked at the brilliant palette of colors on Mandy's smiling face. This was no simple application of lipstick and mascara. It was a complex composition that involved the blending of many hues and tints. There were pinks and blues and umber, topped by the platinum-blond nimbus of her hair.

"I back-comb my hair," she said.

"You must attract a lot of attention on the road," I said, "doing all that."

"Yeah, sometimes," she said. "Yesterday, I pulled into a gas station, and this truck driver followed right behind me and pulled up alongside. He said, 'Ma'am, I have been driving behind you for the last forty-five minutes, and I've been watching. First you did your makeup. Then you did your hair. Then you did your nails. I just wanted to get up close and see what you looked like.' He gave me a big wink and told me I was right pretty. But then he said, 'Let me ask you something. I noticed every couple of minutes you've been reaching over and foolin' with something on the seat next to you. Whatcha got over there?' 'That's my TV,' I told him. 'I can't miss my soaps!' "

We walked from the lane into Joe Odom's garden. Candlelight flickered in the windows of the darkened house. Two men crouched by the garden wall. One held a flashlight while the other knelt in front of the electric meter. The kneeling man wore big rubber gloves with which he gripped a large pair of pliers. He appeared to be splicing two cables together.

"Careful, Joe," the man with the flashlight said.

A shower of sparks jumped from the cable, and the lights in the house next door dimmed for a moment. As they came back up to full strength, the lights in Joe's house blinked on. Cheers came from inside. Joe stood up.

"Well, I guess I didn't get electrocuted this time," he said. "Maybe next time." He bowed silently to the neighboring house.

Joe Odom had a mustache and graying blond hair. He wore a light blue shirt open at the neck, chinos, and brown-and-white saddle shoes. He was about thirty-five and looked remarkably calm, I thought, for someone who had just pulled off a life-threatening, high-voltage act of larceny.

"I've got ice," said Mandy.

"And an ice man too, I see." Joe flashed a bright smile. "I don't usually putter around in the garden this late at night," he said, "but, well . . . we had a few problems out here that needed tending to."

He took off the rubber gloves. "I reckon I'm getting pretty good at this. I can turn water and gas back on too. Remember that. Someday you may need my services. I'm only fair at telephones, though. I can reconnect a phone that's been cut off, but I can't make it do anything but receive incoming calls. No outgoing."

Somewhere under the steps an air-conditioning condenser clicked on.

"Lovely sound, isn't it!" said Joe. "Why don't we all go inside and drink a toast to it—and to the lights, and the dishwasher, and the microwave, and the refrigerator, and the Savannah Electric and Power Company. And to . . ." He raised an imaginary glass in the direction of the house next door. "Whoever."

Joe Odom's townhouse was furnished in a manner I would not have expected for the home of a utilities deadbeat. On the parlor floor I saw a fine English sideboard, several good eighteenth-century oil portraits, a pair of antique silver sconces, a Steinway grand piano, and two or three impressive oriental carpets. There were people in every room, it seemed—not quite a party, more an open house.

"I'm a tax lawyer," said Joe, "and a real estate broker and a piano player. I used to be a partner in a law firm, but a couple of years ago I quit and moved my office into this house so I could mix business and pleasure in whatever proportion I wanted. That's when my third wife left me."

Joe nodded toward a young man asleep on a couch in the living room. "That's Clint. If you ever need a ride to Atlanta, Clint will be happy to take you. He drives trailer trucks back and forth, and he likes to have company in the cab. I should warn you, though, he makes the trip in just under three hours. Nobody who's ever been on one of those wild rides has ever gone back for a second one."

A girl with a red ponytail was talking on the telephone in the kitchen. Joe told me she was a disk jockey for one of Savannah's Top 40 radio stations. He added that a man she was dating had just been arrested for dealing cocaine and for making terroristic threats against the police. In the dining room, a blond man dressed in a white shirt and white slacks was cutting a woman's hair. "That's Jerry Spence," said Joe. "He cuts all our hair, and right now he's doing Ann, my first and second wife. Ann and I were childhood sweethearts. We got married the first time while I was in law school and the second time on the anniversary of our first divorce. And, of course, you've met Mandy here. She's my fourth wife-in-waiting."

"What's she waiting for?" I asked.

"For her divorce to come through," said Joe. "There's no telling when that will happen, because her attorney's a lazy cuss who hasn't gotten around to filing the papers yet. I guess we can't complain about it, though, because I'm her attorney."

The social center of the house was the kitchen, which

overlooked the garden. It had a piano in it, and it was from this room that the music and laughter spilled out over the garden walls up and down the street.

"I notice you leave your front door unlocked," I said.

"That's right. It got to be too much trouble going down to answer it all the time. That was one of my third wife's grievances." Odom laughed.

"Well, the front door happens to be one of my grievances too," said Mandy. "Especially since the burglary last week. Joe says it wasn't a burglary, but I say it was. It was four o'clock in the morning, and we were both in bed. I woke up and heard noises downstairs, and I shook Joe. 'Joe, we got burglars,' I said. But he didn't care. 'Oh, it could be anybody,' he said. But I was sure it was burglars. They were opening cupboards and drawers and I don't know what-all. So I shook him again and I said, 'Joe, go down and see.' Well, Mr. Cool just lifted his head a few inches off the pillow and hollered, 'Angus? That you, Angus?' There was total silence, of course. So Joe says to me, 'Well, if we got a burglar, his name ain't Angus.' Then he went back to sleep. But it *was* a burglar, and we were lucky we weren't murdered."

Joe started to play the piano in the middle of Mandy's story. "In the morning," he said, "three bottles of liquor and a half dozen glasses were missing. That doesn't sound like a burglary to me. It sounds like a party. And the only thing that annoys me about it is we weren't invited."

Joe's smile indicated that the matter was closed, at least as far as he was concerned. "Anyway, as I was saying, I originally left the door unlocked as a matter of convenience. But pretty soon I realized that whenever the doorbell *did* ring, it was someone I didn't know. So the bell became a signal that a stranger was at the door. I've learned never to answer it myself when that happens, because it's likely to be a deputy sheriff wanting to serve me with some kind of paper, and of course I don't need to be home for that."

"Or for little old ladies with hammers in their hands," I said.

"Hammers? I don't believe I know any old ladies who carry hammers."

"The one who punched out your windows certainly had a hammer."

"A little old lady did that?" Joe looked surprised. "I was wondering how that happened. We thought somebody slammed the door too hard. You mean you saw her do it?"

"I did."

"Well, we've got our share of little old ladies here in Savannah," said Joe, "and it looks like one of them's unhappy with me." He did not seem the least bit concerned. "Well, now you know something about us," he said. "Tell us about yourself."

I said I was a writer from New York.

"Ah, then you must be the new Yankee I've been hearing about. Nothing escapes our notice, you know. Savannah's a real small town. It's so small everybody knows everybody else's business, which can be a pain, but it also means we know who all the undercover cops are, which can be a plus. Now, as for you, I should tell you that you've already aroused a fair amount of curiosity. People think you're writing an exposé about Savannah, so they're a little wary of you. You don't need to fret about that, though. Secretly they all hope you'll put them in your book." Joe laughed and winked.

"Savannah's a peculiar place, but if you just listen to your Cousin Joe you'll get along fine. You need to know about a few basic rules though.

"Rule number one: *Always stick around for one more drink*. That's when things happen. That's when you find out everything you want to know."

"I think I can live with that one," I said.

"Rule number two: *Never go south of Gaston Street.* A true Savannahian is a NOG. NOG means 'north of Gaston.' We stay in the old part of town. We don't do the Mall. We don't do the southside unless we're invited to a party for rich people out at The Landings. Everything south of Gaston Street is North Jacksonville to us, and ordinarily we leave it alone.

"Rule number three: *Observe the high holidays—Saint Patrick's Day and the day of the Georgia-Florida football game.* Savannah has the third-biggest Saint Patrick's Day parade in America. People come from all over the South to see it. Businesses close for the day, except for restaurants and bars, and the drinking starts at about six A.M. Liquor is a major feature of the Georgia-Florida game, too, but the similarity ends there. The game is nothing less than a war between the gentlemen of Georgia and the Florida barbarians. We get all keyed up for it a week ahead of time, and then afterwards it takes a week to ten days to deal with the emotional strain of having won or lost. Georgia men grow up understanding the seriousness of that one game."

"Georgia women grow up understanding it too," said Mandy. "Ask any girl in south Georgia. She'll tell you flat out: You don't start wearing panty hose until *after* the Georgia-Florida game." I felt myself becoming a fast friend of Joe and Mandy.

"So, look here," Joe said. "Now that you've come under our protective custody, we'll be unhappy with you if you need anything and don't ask for it, or if you get into trouble and don't holler."

Mandy climbed into Joe's lap and nuzzled his ear.

"Just make sure you put us in your book," he said. "You understand, of course, that we'll want to play ourselves in the movie version. Won't we, Mandy?"

"Mm-hmmm," she said.

Joe played a few bars of "Hooray for Hollywood" (another Johnny Mercer tune).

"In that book of yours," he said, "you can use my real name if you want to. Or you can just call me the 'Sentimental Gentleman from Georgia,' because that's pretty much who I am.

I'm just a sentimental gentleman from Georgia, Georgia,
Gentle to the ladies all the time.
And when it comes to lovin' I'm a real professor,
Yes sir!
Just a Mason-Dixon valentine.

Oh, see those Georgia peaches
Hangin' around me now.
'Cause what this baby teaches nobody else knows how.
This sentimental gentleman from Georgia, Georgia,
Gentle to the ladies all the time.

Joe sang with such winsome charm, I had to remind myself that he was the same person who had tapped into the electricity of the house next door and who was, by his own admission, dodging process servers for financial transgressions of God-knew-what proportion. His ingratiating manner made everything he did seem like good-natured fun. Later, as he saw me to the door, he joked and bantered with such easy grace that I did not fully realize until I got home that in the course of saying good-bye he had borrowed twenty dollars from me.

Chapter 4

SETTLING IN

Having made what I took to be a promising, if unorthodox, start on a social life, I set about arranging my apartment so I could live and work in it comfortably. For essential things like bookshelves, file cabinets, and reading lamps, I visited a junk shop on the edge of town. It was a cluttered, barnlike warehouse that extended back into a series of rooms filled with Formica dinette sets, sofas, office furniture, and all manner of machinery from washer-dryers to apple corers. The owner sat like a Buddha behind a desk, barking hellos to customers and instructions to his salesman.

The salesman was an expressionless man in his mid-thirties. He had mousy brown hair parted at the center, and his arms hung loosely at his sides. His clothes were clean but faded, like the suits and shirts on a rack in one corner of the store. I was immediately impressed by the man's instant recall of the store's vast inventory. "We have seven of that type item," he would say. "One's like new, four work pretty good, one's broke but could be fixed, and the other's on lay-away." In addition to having a mental catalog of the place, the salesman was a virtuoso on the strengths and weaknesses of practically any brand of appliance, particularly brands no longer in existence. "Kelvinator made a good one in the early fifties," he'd say. "It had five speeds. It was real easy to clean, and you could get replacement parts right quick."

Impressed as I was by all of that, I was struck even more by something else—a carefully applied arc of purple eye shadow that blazed like a lurid sunset on his left eyelid.

At first I found it difficult to listen to what he was saying, distracted as I was by the eye shadow. I wondered what nocturnal transformation was built around this painted eye. I envisioned a tiara and a strapless gown, a fluttering ostrich fan at the end of a long white glove. Or was this something quite different? Was it, perhaps, the war paint of punk? Did this mild-mannered man spend his secret hours in jackboots, ripped T-shirts, and spiked hair?

Eventually, my attention wandered back to what the man was saying, and I bought what it was he was showing me. The next week, I dropped in at the shop again, and this time I tried very hard not to stare at the purple eye shadow on the man's left eye.

From time to time, while he was waiting on me, the boss would shout questions from his desk about whether such-and-such an item was in stock. The salesman would cock an ear and call out the answer over his shoulder without looking directly at his boss. After one such exchange, the salesman said in a low voice, "What the boss don't know won't hurt him."

"What do you mean?" I said.

"He didn't like this," the salesman said, pointing to his left eye. "I don't do drag or anything sick like that. I just do my eyes. I used to do my other eye the same way too. The boss told me to stop, and I was all set to walk out the door and never come back. But then I figured, 'Wait a minute. He never gets out of that chair, see, and my desk is over by his left side. If I only do the eye away from him, maybe he'll never notice.' That was two years ago and he ain't said nothin' about it since."

On my next visit to the shop, the salesman was out to lunch but due back soon. The boss and I chatted. "Jack's a good man," he said, speaking of his salesman. "Best I've ever seen. He's a strange one, though. He's a loner. This shop and everything in it is his whole life. I call him 'Jack the One-eyed Jill'—not to his face, of course. He used to put that eye makeup on both eyes, you know. God, it looked awful. I told him, *'I can't have this in my shop! No more or you're out!'* So what did he do? Came in the next day not wearin' any eye makeup at all as far as I could tell. But he was walkin' sideways around the store like a damned crab, twistin' this way and that. Then he went past a mirrored wardrobe, and I saw it plain as day: He'd put the makeup on the other eye.

"I was ready to kick his butt clear out the door, then and there. But he's good at what he does, and it doesn't seem to bother the customers. So I kept my mouth shut. And from that day to this, he's kept that eye turned away from me. He must take me for blind or some kind of idiot, but that's okay with me. He pretends he's not wearing makeup, and I pretend I don't know he's ignored my wishes. Meanwhile, he keeps walkin' sideways, twistin' around, speakin' outta the corner of his mouth, and hopin' I won't notice. And I make out like I don't. I don't know who's crazier, Jack the One-eyed Jill or me. But we get along just fine."

—

Before long, I found myself settling into a pattern of daily routines: an early-morning jog around Forsyth Park, breakfast at Clary's drugstore, a late-afternoon walk along Bull Street. I discovered that my activities coincided with the daily rituals of certain other people. No matter how widely our paths may have diverged for the rest of the day, we overlapped again and again at our appointed hour and place. The black man who jogged around Forsyth Park at the same hour I did was one such person.

He was lean, very dark, and a little over six feet tall. When I fell in behind him the first time, I noticed he was carrying a short blue leather strap. Most of it was wound around his hand; eight or ten inches of it protruded. He snapped the free end against his thigh every other step, producing a rhythmic *whap* that forced me to run in step or very much out of step. I ran in step; it was easier. As he turned the corner at the south end of the park that first day, he looked back in my direction but not quite at me, a little behind me. I looked over my shoulder. About fifty yards back, there was a blond woman jogging with a little terrier romping beside her.

The next time I started my run, the blond woman and her dog were running ahead of me. The dog would dart into the park and then double back to join her. As I drew near, she turned her head to look across the park toward Drayton Street on the other side. The black man was jogging along Drayton, having already made both turns at the far end. He looked back at her.

After this, I never saw one of them without also seeing the other. He always carried the little blue leather strap. She always had her dog with her. Sometimes he was in the lead; sometimes she was. They were always separated by at least a hundred yards.

One day I saw the man at the M&M supermarket pushing a shopping cart. Another time I caught sight of him getting into a late-model green Lincoln on Wright Square. But no blue strap and no blond woman. A few days later, I saw the blond woman coming out of a bank. She was unaccompanied except for her terrier, who trotted along beside her. He was straining at the end of a blue leather leash.

"We don't do black-on-white in Savannah," Joe Odom told me when I mentioned having seen this couple. "Especially black male on white female. A lot may have changed here in the last twenty years, but not that. Badness is the only woman I know of who had a black lover and got away with it. Badness was the wife of an influential Savannah businessman, and she had lovers during most of their marriage. That was all perfectly acceptable. Savannah will put up with public infidelity no matter how flagrant it is. Savannah loves it. Can't get enough of it. But even Badness knew enough to leave Savannah and go to Atlanta when she felt the urge to have an affair with a black man."

I understood all that, but I still wondered about certain small details concerning my jogging companions. Why, for instance, did he carry the leash? And when and where did they get close enough for her to give it to him? The whole point, I finally realized, was that I would never know.

—

If I happened to be walking along Bull Street in the late afternoon, I would invariably see a very old and very dignified black man. He always wore a suit and tie, a starched white shirt, and a fedora. His ties were muted paisleys and regimental stripes, and his suits were fine and well tailored, though apparently made for a slightly larger person.

Every day at the same time, the old man walked through the cast-iron gates of the grandiose Armstrong House at the north end of Forsyth Park. He turned left and proceeded up Bull Street all the way to City Hall and back. He was very much a gentleman. He tipped his hat and bowed in greeting. But I noticed that he and the people he spoke with—usually well-dressed businessmen—played a very odd game. The men would ask him, "Still walking the dog?" It was perfectly clear that the old man was not walking a dog, but he would respond by saying, "Oh, yes. Still walking the dog." Then he would look over his shoulder and say to the air behind him, "Come on, Patrick!" And off he would go.

One day, as I came through Madison Square, I saw him standing by the monument facing a semicircle of tourists. He was singing. I could not make out the words, but I could hear his reedy tenor voice. The tourists applauded when he was done, and one of the lady tour guides slipped something into his hand. He bowed and left them. We approached the crosswalk at the same time.

"That was very nice," I said.

"Why, thank you kindly," he replied in his courtly way. "My name is William Simon Glover."

I introduced myself and told Mr. Glover that it seemed we often took the same walk at the same hour. I said nothing about the dog, figuring that the subject would come up on its own.

"Oh, yes," he said. "I'm eighty-six years old, and I'm downtown at seven o'clock every morning. I'm retired, but I don't stay still. I work as a porter for the law firm of Bouhan, Williams and Levy." Mr. Glover's voice had a bounce to it. He pronounced the name of the law firm as if an exclamation mark followed each of the partners' names.

"I'm a porter, but everybody knows me as a singer," he said as we started to cross the street. "I learned to sing in church when I was twelve. I pumped the organ for a quarter while one lady played and another lady sang. I didn't know nothing about no German, French, or Italian, but by me hearing the lady sing so much, I learned to say the words whether I knew what they was or not. One Sunday morning, the lady didn't sing, so I sang instead. And I sang in Italian. I sang 'Hallelujah.' "

"How did it go?" I asked him.

Mr. Glover stopped and faced me. He opened his mouth wide and drew a deep breath. From the back of his throat came a high, croaking sound, "Aaaaa lay *loooo*-yah! A-*layyyy*-loo yah!" He had abandoned his tenor and was singing in a wavering falsetto. Forever in his mind, apparently, "Hallelujah" would be a soprano piece as sung by the lady in church so many years before. "Allay-*loo*-yah, a-lay-loo yah, a-lay-loo yah, a-*lay*-loo yah, a-lay-loo-yah, a-lay-loo-yah!" Mr. Glover stopped for a breath. "—And then the lady always finished by saying, '*AAAAAAAhhh* lay *looooooo* yah!' "

"So that was your debut," I said.

"That's right! That's how I started. That lady learned me to sing in German, French, and Italian! Oh, yes! And I've been musical director of the First African Baptist Church since 1916. I directed a chorus of five hundred voices for Franklin D. Roosevelt when he visited Savannah on November 18, 1933. I remember the date, because that was the very day my daughter was born. I named her Eleanor Roosevelt Glover. I can remember the song we sang too: 'Come By Here.' The doctor sent word up to me, 'Tell Glover he can sing "Come By Here" for the president all he damn pleases, but I just come by his house and left a baby girl and I want him to come by my office and pay me fifteen dollars.' "

When we parted at the corner of Oglethorpe Avenue, I realized I was still in the dark about the imaginary dog, Patrick. A week or so later, when I next fell in step with Mr. Glover, I made a mental note to bring the subject around to it. But Mr. Glover had other things to talk about first.

"You know about psychology," he said. "You learn that in school. You learn *people*-ology on the Pullman. I was a porter for the Pullman during the war. You had to keep the passengers well satisfied for 'em to tip you fifty cents or a dollar. You say, 'Wait a minute, sir. You going up to the club car? Your tie is crooked.' Now, his tie is really straight as an arrow, but you pull it crooked and then you pull it straight again, and he likes it. That's people-ology!

"Keep a whisk broom in your pocket, and brush him off! He don't need no brushing off, but he don't know it! Brush him off anyhow, and straighten his collar. Pull it crooked and straighten it again. Miss Mamie don't need a box for her hat, but you be sure and put her hat in a box! If you sit and don't do nothin', you won't get nothin'!

"Another thing I learned: Don't ever ask a man, 'How is Mrs. Brown?' You ask him, 'How is Miss Julia? *Tell her I ask about her.*' I never did ask Mr. Bouhan about Mrs. Bouhan. I ask him, 'How is Miss Helen? *Tell Miss Helen I ask about her.*' He liked it and she liked it. Mr. Bouhan gave me his old clothes and shoes. Miss Helen gave me records from her collection, all kinds of records. I got records I don't even know I got. I even got records of that great opera singer . . . Henry Coca-ruso!

"I keep busy," Mr. Glover said. "I don't sit down and hold my hand. I got five hundred dollars of life insurance, and it's all paid up. I paid twenty-five cents a week for seventy years! And last week the Metropolitan Life Insurance Company sent me a check for one thousand dollars!"

Mr. Glover's eyes were sparkling. "No, sir, I don't sit down and hold my hand."

"Glover!" came a booming voice from behind us. A tall white-haired man in a gray suit approached. "Still walking the dog?"

"Why, yes, sir, yes I am." Mr. Glover did his little bow and tipped his hat and gestured to the invisible dog behind him. "I'm still walking Patrick."

"Glad to hear it, Glover. Keep it up! Take care now." With that, the man walked away.

"How long have you been walking Patrick?" I asked.

Mr. Glover straightened up. "Oh, for a long time. Patrick was Mr. Bouhan's dog. Mr. Bouhan used to give him Chivas Regal scotch liquor to drink. I walked the dog, and I was the dog's bartender too. Mr. Bouhan said that after he died I was to be paid ten dollars a week to take care of Patrick. He put that in his will. I had to walk him and buy his scotch liquor. When Patrick died, I went to see Judge Lawrence. The judge was Mr. Bouhan's executor. I said, 'Judge, you can stop paying me the ten dollars now, because Patrick is dead.' And Judge Lawrence said, 'What do you mean Patrick is dead? How could he be? I see him right there! Right there on the carpet.' I looked behind me, and I didn't see no dog. But then I thought a minute and I said, 'Oh! I think I see him too, Judge!' And the judge said, 'Good. So you just keep walking him and we'll keep paying you.' The dog is dead twenty years now, but I still walk him. I walk up and down Bull Street and look over my shoulder and say, 'Come on, Patrick!' "

—

As for the mysterious old lady who punched out Joe Odom's windows with a hammer, I never saw her again. I did learn, however, that there were quite a few people in Savannah who might have felt justified in smashing Joe's windows as a result of having done business with him. The ranks of such people included any number of old ladies.

At least half a dozen people, for instance, had come to grief in Joe's most recent real estate development deal—the conversion of an office building into a luxurious apartment house: the Lafayette. Shortly before completing the renovation, Joe hosted a gala dinner-dance in the building as a preview party for prospective buyers. Sixteen of the guests signed up for apartments then and there, and six plunked down cash. The new owners were just about to move into the building when events took an unexpected turn: A mortgage company swooped down and repossessed their apartments. How could this happen? The people had paid for their apartments in full! The answer was not long in coming. Joe had defaulted on his construction loan and had never bothered to transfer the deeds to the new owners. At the moment of foreclosure, the apartments were still in his name, so they were seized as collateral. The rightful owners were forced to go to court to retrieve their apartments.

Joe never lost his good humor throughout the affair. Like an unflappable master of ceremonies, he cheerfully reassured his clients that things would sort themselves out. Whether they believed him or not, most chose to forgive him. One woman communed with the Lord, who told her not to sue. Another simply refused to believe that so lovely a young man could have done anything improper. "I suppose I should hate him," said an osteopath, who had lost money in another of Joe's financial schemes, "but he's too damned likable."

There were rumors that Joe had squandered the money from the construction loan for the Lafayette, that he had chartered a private plane and taken a dozen friends to New Orleans to select a chandelier for the lobby and, incidentally, attend the Sugar Bowl game. After the foreclosure, however, it was clear that Joe had in no way enriched himself in the fiasco. In fact, he had lost his car, his boat, his butler, his wife, and title to his house.

In the aftermath of the Lafayette affair, Joe had found it necessary to supplement his income by playing piano at private parties and by opening his house to busloads of tourists several days a week, at three dollars a head, as part of a tour package that included lunch in a historic townhouse. The tour companies would send caterers to Joe's house at 11:45

A.M. with platters and tureens of food; the tour buses would pull up at noon; the tourists would walk through the house, eat a buffet lunch, and listen to Joe play a few songs on the piano. Then at 12:45, the tourists would get back on the bus, and the caterers would pack up and leave.

Laughter and music continued to ring through 16 East Jones Street day and night as it had before, but Joe was merely a rent-paying tenant now. Neither the house nor anything in it belonged to him anymore. Not the portraits, not the carpets, not the silver. Not even the little panes of glass upon which the mysterious old lady, whoever she was, had taken out her fury.

Chapter 5

THE INVENTOR

The voice came over my shoulder like a murmuring breeze. "Oh, don't do that," it said. "Whatever you do, don't do that." I was standing at the sales counter in Clary's drugstore after breakfast one morning, and when I turned around, I was confronted by a scarecrow of a man. He had a long neck and a protruding Adam's apple. Lank brown hair hung over his forehead. The man's face reddened, as if he'd been caught thinking out loud. It struck me that if either of us should have been embarrassed, I was the one. I had just asked the salesgirl what I should do about the crystallized ring of black scum that would not come off my toilet bowl. The girl had told me to use steel wool.

The man smiled self-consciously. "Steel wool leaves big scratches in the porcelain," he said. "Those are calcium deposits you've got. It's from the water. You need to scrub them off with a red brick. A brick's harder than the calcium deposits, but it's not as hard as the porcelain and it won't scratch it."

I had seen this man several times before, right here in

Clary's drugstore. He was one of the regulars who came in for breakfast every morning. Although we had never spoken before, I knew who he was. That was one of the main things about Clary's drugstore. It was a clearinghouse of information, a bourse of gossip.

Despite the permanent smell of burned bacon grease and the likelihood that Ruth or Lillie would get the orders confused, Clary's had a loyal breakfast and lunch clientele. People sauntered in, sidled in, or stumbled in, and their condition was duly noted over the tops of newspapers. Customers greeted one another from table to table, or from table to soda fountain, and every word was overheard and passed along later. Patrons at any given moment might include a housewife, a real estate broker, a lawyer, an art student, and perhaps a pair of carpenters doing work in a townhouse down the street. One of the carpenters might be heard to say, "All we got to do today is seal up that doorway between her bedroom and his," and the news that a marital Ice Age had descended on the townhouse in question would be common coin by the end of the day. Overheard remarks were as much a commodity at Clary's drugstore as Goody's Powder or Chigarid.

The man who told me to scrub my toilet bowl with a brick performed a peculiar daily ritual at Clary's. He always ordered the same breakfast: eggs, bacon, a Bayer aspirin, and a glass of spirits of ammonia and Coca-Cola. But he didn't always consume it. Sometimes he just looked at it. He'd put both hands flat on the table as if to steady his gaze, and he'd stare at his plate. Then he would either begin to eat or get up without a word and walk out the door. The next day, Ruth would serve him the same breakfast and go back to her perch at the end of the soda fountain to take a drag on her cigarette and see what he would do. I, too, began to watch.

Whenever he left without touching his food, Ruth would say to no one in particular, "Luther's not eating." She'd clear his plate away and put his bill beside the cash register. From the remarks that followed these exits, I learned that the man's name was Luther Driggers and that some years back he had achieved a certain prominence in Savannah. He had made a discovery—involving a certain pesticide and its ability to pass through plastic—that had led to the invention of the flea collar and the no-pest strip.

In this respect, it could be said that Luther Driggers was the modern equivalent of Savannah's other famous inventor, Eli Whitney. As it happened, neither man had made a dime from his invention. Eli Whitney had carefully kept the cotton gin under wraps while he applied for a patent, but he made a tactical error when he allowed women to have a look at it, assuming that they would not understand what they were looking at. A male entrepreneur put on a dress one day and slipped in with a group of women visitors, then went home and made his own cotton gin. Luther Driggers's case was complicated by his having been a government employee at the time he had made his discovery. Government employees had no monetary claim to their work. The only way Driggers could have profited was by secretly selling the pertinent information to a private manufacturer. While he wrestled with the moral pros and cons of doing just that, one of his colleagues beat him to it.

Luther Driggers had a mournful expression, but his failure to make any money from the flea collar was not the only reason for it. His life seemed to be marked by a succession of unfortunate misadventures. His early marriage to his high school sweetheart had lasted little more than a year. Her father was the owner of a supermarket, and the girl's dowry consisted of a house and unlimited free groceries. When the marriage came to an end, the house and the groceries went with it. Luther moved into an old mortuary at the corner of Jones and Bull, where the first thing he did was to convert the tiled embalming room into a shower. Later, he sold some inherited property and bought an old townhouse. He leased the house to tenants and converted the carriage house behind it into living quarters for himself. In the process of renovation, he devoted considerable attention to one small design detail of the stairway—the so-called false step. The riser of the false step was one inch higher than the other steps so that it would trip up anybody unfamiliar with it and serve as a primitive burglar alarm. This was a device used in many old houses, but it proved to be a hazard for Driggers, since he generally arrived home in no shape to deal with normal stairs, let alone trick ones. Furthermore, once the stairs were built, he realized he'd overlooked a more important consideration: namely, where to put the stairway in the first place. He'd put it against the one wall that could have had windows and a view of the garden. As a result, the living room looked out onto a back alley and a big brown dumpster.

It was while nursing a bruised shin suffered from a fall over the false step that Luther went one afternoon to the Wright Square post office to check the weight of a pound of marijuana he was about to buy. He wanted to make sure he was not being cheated. To his amazement, he was stopped at the door, his package was seized, and he was arrested. As the *Savannah Evening Press* explained in its coverage of the event, the post office had received a bomb threat only minutes before. The story said Luther's parcel contained "slightly less than a pound of marijuana." Luther would have been short-changed, just as he'd feared.

Luther's misfortunes pained his friends, particularly the headstrong Serena Dawes. Luther and Serena were an unlikely pair. Serena was much older than Luther, and she spent most of her waking hours lounging in her four-poster bed, propped up against an embankment of tiny pillows. From her silken dais, Serena would cajole Luther to fix her a drink, look for her stockings, answer the door, get some ice, hand her a comb, fluff up her pillows, massage her ankles. Alternately, and without a hint of irony, she would exhort him to stand up for his rights. "A lady," she would say in her most languid, multisyllabic drawl, "expects a gentleman to take what belongs to him!" Whenever Serena took this line, she was usually thinking about the proceeds from the flea collar and the no-pest strip. Serena had calculated what baubles those proceeds could have bought.

Serena Vaughn Dawes had been a celebrated beauty in her

day. She was so alluring that Cecil Beaton had called her "one of the most perfect natural beauties I've ever photographed." The daughter of a socially prominent lawyer from Atlanta, Serena had met the young Simon T. Dawes of Pittsburgh, grandson of a steel tycoon, while on a vacation in Newport before the Second World War. Simon Dawes was smitten by Serena. Gossip columnists across the country breathlessly chronicled their whirlwind romance. But when the New York *Daily News* reported that the couple had become engaged, Dawes's mother—the formidable Theodora Cabot Dawes—telegraphed a haughty one-word comment that was blown up into headlines: SON ENGAGED? "ABSURD!" SAYS MRS. DAWES. Mrs. Dawes's opposition to the engagement was rendered moot by the subsequent elopement of Simon and Serena. After their honeymoon at the old DeSoto Hotel in Savannah, the newlyweds went back to live in Pittsburgh.

As Mrs. Simon T. Dawes, Serena became an icon of upper-crust glamour in the 1930s and 1940s. Her photograph adorned full-page cigarette ads in *Life* magazine. The copy always carried a message to the effect that Mrs. Simon T. Dawes of Pittsburgh was a lady of refined taste, that she traveled first class and resided in presidential suites wherever she went. In the ads, Serena would be sitting in quiet splendor, her head tilted back and a wisp of smoke rising from the cigarette held in her fair hand.

Beneath the serenity, however, there was fire, and Serena's mother-in-law knew it. The elder Mrs. Dawes did her best to bend Serena to her will. She admonished Serena to donate the fees from her endorsements to charity, and Serena did. But when Serena discovered that her mother-in-law secretly pocketed her own fees from such endorsements, she slapped the woman's face and called her "a heathen bitch." The two women loathed each other.

When Simon Dawes accidentally shot himself in the head and died, his mother took her revenge on Serena. The family affairs had been arranged so that the bulk of Simon's estate would circumvent Serena and go to their children. But Serena would not be outdone; she announced her intention to sell her mansion in Pittsburgh to a black family. A group of rich neighbors begged her to let them buy it first. She sold it to them for a king's ransom and moved to Savannah.

It was in Savannah that Serena plunged headlong into middle age. She gained weight, indulged herself endlessly, and became the soul of pampered self-absorption. She spent most of her day in bed, holding court, drinking martinis and pink ladies, and playing with her white toy poodle, Lulu.

As much as Serena detested her former in-laws, she reveled in her connection to them. She never tired of telling people that the bed she lay in had once belonged to Algernon Dawes, the steel millionaire. Photographs of Daweses and Cabots stood sentry on the night table. A full-length portrait of her hated mother-in-law hung in the dining room, just as her own Cecil Beaton photographs adorned the walls of her bedroom. Serena thrived in this museum of her former self. She had a wardrobe that consisted mostly of shortie nightgowns and peignoirs. They revealed her still-shapely legs and discreetly swathed her upper half in clouds of feathers and silk chiffon. She dyed her hair flaming red and painted her fingernails and toenails dark green. She bullied and wheedled; she railed and purred. She drawled and cussed and carried on. For emphasis, she threw objects across the room—pillows, drinks, even Lulu the poodle. Every now and then she would sweep the Daweses and Cabots off the night table with an oath and send them crashing to the floor.

Serena did not choose to mingle in Savannah's society, nor was she invited to do so. But Savannah's elite never tired of talking about her. "She has no couples as callers," said a woman who lived a few houses down Gordon Street, "only young men. You never see ladies going into her house at all. She is not, as far as I know, a member of any garden club. She's not neighborly." But after a fashion, Serena loved Luther and Luther loved Serena.

The unassuming, shy, and hapless Luther Driggers had a darker side. He was possessed by inner demons who showed themselves in disturbing ways. Chronic insomnia was one of them. Luther had once gone nine days without falling asleep. Sleep, when it came, was rarely peaceful. Luther usually slept with his teeth and his fists tightly clenched. By morning he would awake with sore jaws and little crescent-shaped cuts in his palms. People worried about Luther's demons. But they were not so much concerned with the uneaten breakfasts or the lost sleep or the bleeding palms. They were fearful about something much more serious.

It was rumored that Luther had in his possession a bottle of poison five hundred times more deadly than arsenic, a poison so lethal that if he ever dumped it into the city's water supply it would kill every man, woman, and child in Savannah. Years back, a delegation of nervous citizens had informed the police, and the police had searched Luther's house without finding anything. That satisfied no one, of course, and the rumors persisted.

Luther certainly knew all about poisons and how to use them. He was a technician at the government insectary on the outskirts of Savannah. His job required that he sift through jugs of barn sweepings, sort out the weevils and beetles, and raise them in colonies so that he could test various insecticides on them. The difficult part of the job was the requirement that Luther inject insecticide into the chest cavities of the individual insects. This operation demanded the dexterity of a watchmaker. It was hard enough to do sober; with a hangover and tremors it was nearly impossible. "God, it's tedious work," Luther said.

Sometimes, to relieve the boredom, Luther anesthetized ordinary house flies and glued lengths of thread to their backs. When the flies awoke, they flew around trailing the threads behind them. "It makes them easier to catch," he said.

On occasion, Luther walked through downtown Savannah holding a dozen or more threads in his hand, each a different color. Some people walked dogs; Luther walked flies. Now and then, when he visited friends, he took a few of the flies with him and let them loose in the living room.

At other times, Luther pasted the wings of a wasp on top

of a fly's own wings to improve its aerodynamics. Or he made one wing slightly shorter than the other so it would fly in circles the rest of its life.

It was just this side of Luther, his quirky tinkering, that left people with a lingering uneasiness about whether he might one day pour his bottle of poison into Savannah's water supply. They worried about this most of all when his well-known demons got the better of him. And whenever Luther walked out of Clary's without eating breakfast—which he had been doing of late—it was a sign that his demons were stirring.

This concern was uppermost in my mind, in fact, when Luther was explaining why I should scrub my toilet bowl with a brick. He was telling me about, of all things, Savannah's water supply. Savannah's water came from a limestone aquifer, he said. It was rich in calcium bicarbonate, which loses a molecule and turns into crystals of calcium carbonate when it dries. "Hey, listen," I wanted to say, "what's this I hear about you and a deadly poison?" But I didn't. I just thanked him for the advice.

The next morning when he sat down at the table next to me, I leaned over and gave him the news. "The brick worked," I said. "Thanks."

"Good," he said. "You could have used a pumice stone instead. That would have done just as well as a brick."

Ruth put Luther's breakfast in front of him, and as usual he began to stare at it. I noticed a bright green thread tied to the buttonhole of his lapel. It hung loosely down the front of his jacket. As Luther stared at his eggs, the green thread became taut; then it swung counterclockwise and came to rest along his left shoulder. It stayed there for a moment, then lifted into the air as if caught in an updraft. It hung aloft, still anchored to his lapel, then floated down and lay across his chest. Luther was oblivious to the movements of the thread and to the antics of the fly at the end of it.

He saw that I was watching him. "I dunno," he said with a sigh. "Sometimes I just can't face going through with breakfast."

"I've noticed," I said.

Luther blushed at the thought that his eating habits had been observed, and he started to eat. "I have a deficiency of stomach acid," he said. "It's not serious. It's called hypochlorhydria. I'm told Rasputin had the same condition, but I wouldn't know about that. All I know is that at times of stress, my gastric juices just quit on me and I can't digest food. But it passes."

"About these gastric juices," I said. "Have you been under a lot of tension lately?"

"Well, sort of," Luther said. "I'm working on something new. It's something that could make a lot of money, if it works. The problem is, I haven't got it to work yet." Luther paused for a moment, considering whether to let me into his confidence.

"Do you know what black lights are?" he asked. "Those purple fluorescent lights that make things glow in the dark? Well, you know, a lot of bars have fish tanks illuminated with black lights. The Purple Tree down on Johnson Square does. I got to thinking what a shame it was that goldfish didn't glow in the dark. So I'm trying to find a way to make them glow. If they did glow, they'd look as if they were floating in air like giant fireflies—just the kind of weird vision a guy getting drunk in a bar could spend hours looking at. I know *I* would. Every bar in America would have to have them. That's why I want to find a way to make them glow."

"Do you think you can?"

"I'm experimenting with fluorescent dye," he said. "The first thing I did was dip the goldfish directly into the dye, and it killed them. Then I took a slower approach and poured a teaspoon of dye into the fish tank and waited. After a week, a faint glow appeared on the gills and the tips of the fins, but it wasn't enough to make much of an impact in a bar. Little by little, I poured more dye into the water, but the fish didn't glow any brighter and the glow didn't spread to any other parts of the fish. All that happened was the pH factor of the water increased, and in a couple of days the fish were dead. That's where I'm at right now."

The fly had alighted on Luther's eyebrow. The green thread dangled down his cheek as if it were attached to a monocle.

Driggers's Golden Glowfish. Sure, why not? Fortunes had been built on less. "I like it," I said. "I hope you can make it happen."

"I'll let you know," said Luther.

Our conversations over the next few days were brief. Several times Luther just waved and gave me the thumbs-up sign. On one occasion, I thought I saw a small horsefly hovering over him. I could not tell whether it was attached by a thread, but it followed him up to the cash register, and when he left the premises he appeared to hold the door open for it.

One morning, when I came into Clary's, he waved me over. "I'm trying a new approach," he said. "I'm mixing the fluorescent dye with fish food, and I'm beginning to see results. The gills and the fin tips are glowing pretty good, and there's even some fluorescence in the eyes and around the mouth."

Luther told me he planned to go to the Purple Tree later that evening for the first public tryout. I was welcome to join him if I liked. I could meet him at the home of Serena Dawes at ten o'clock, and the three of us would proceed to the Purple Tree together.

—

At ten o'clock sharp, Serena Dawes's maid, Maggie, came to the door of her townhouse. She showed me into a front parlor, which was furnished in the grand manner—French Empire furniture, heavy swag curtains, and plenty of gold leaf. Then she disappeared to the rear of the house to attend her mistress. Judging from the sounds coming from that direction, Serena's appearance would be some time off. I could hear the high-pitched strains of a one-way conversation: "Put it back! Put it *back*!" she screeched. "It doesn't match, goddammit! Now hand me that other one. No, dammit, *that* one! I can't wear these shoes. Maggie, you're hurting me! Well, be more careful next time, and listen to what I say. Did you call the police like I told you to? Did they catch those nasty little redneck bastards? Did they? They oughta shoot 'em! Kill 'em! They nearly blew the goddamn house down. Luther, darling, hold the mirror higher so I can see. That's better. Lulu, come to Mama. Come to Mama, Lulu! Oooo! Mama's little love, Mama's little kissy-woo! Maggie, do something to my drink. Well, can't you see the ice is melted!"

At eleven o'clock, I looked up to see a pair of pale and shapely legs supporting a tumult of pink marabou surmounted by a picture hat. Serena's fingernails were a greenish black. Her face was thrown into shadow by the wide-brimmed hat, but it still showed evidence of the vision it had once been. She smiled, and an even row of perfectly white teeth gleamed between two brilliant red lips.

"I am so des-per-ate-ly sorry to have kept you waiting," she purred in a soft, coquettish drawl. "I do hope you will find it in your heart to forgive me, but I regret to say I have simply had no sleep. The dreadful little children from across the square threw a bomb under my bedroom window in the dead of night. My nerves are still unsettled. My life is in constant danger."

"Why, Miz Dawes," said Maggie, "it wutt'n them chirrin at all. It was on'y Jim Williams shootin' off a cap pistol. You know how he likes to get your goat. An' it wutt'n no death a night neither. It was noontime."

"Decent people were still resting!" said Serena. "And it was *not* a toy pistol! You don't understand these things, Maggie. It was a fuckin' bomb! It nearly tore the goddamn side off the house. I am quite sure my bedroom is structurally unsound as a result. And as for Jim Williams—that no-good, low-rent middle Georgia redneck—I will fix his wagon. You wait and see."

Luther appeared, carrying a Chinese food take-out carton. "Well, I've got the goldfish ready. Let's go."

Serena insisted on making the circuit of local nightspots rather than going directly to the Purple Tree. The effort of getting dressed warranted nothing less than a Grand Tour, she felt. We went first to the bar of the 1790 restaurant, then to the Pink House, then to the DeSoto Hilton. At each stop, Serena's friends gathered around. She paid attention only to the men among them, flattering and bullying them by turns and fanning herself with her cocktail napkin. "Oh, darlin', you look so handsome. Dear me, I left my cigarettes in the car. Now, be a love and go get them for me—here, take my keys. Goddamn, it's hot as a bitch in here. I swear I'll pass out unless somebody turns up the air. Oh, goodness, look at that, my drink's all gone! I simply must have another! Why, thaaaank yewwww. My nerves are still shattered from that bomb attack last night. Haven't you heard? A disappointed lover blew a hole in my bedroom wall. I'm still too upset to talk about it."

As the evening wore on, Luther became concerned that the fluorescence might wear off his goldfish and that they might begin to fade. "We need to get to the Purple Tree before it's too late," he said.

"We'll get there, darling," Serena trilled. "After we peek in at the Pirates' Cove." Luther opened the carton and sprinkled a little more fish food into it. After the Pirates' Cove, Serena insisted on a stop at Pinkie Master's. Luther added more fish food. At Pinkie Master's, several people peered into the carton.

"Goldfish," they said. "So what?"

"Come with us to the Purple Tree," said Luther. "You'll see." He put another dose of fish food into the carton. When we finally reached the Purple Tree, it was two-thirty, and our party of three had grown into a small crowd with Serena at the center of it. Luther was content to look after his goldfish and become quietly drunk. In the black-lit darkness of the Purple Tree, Serena's face was all but invisible under her hat, except for her teeth, which were all aglow. "If it wasn't a jealous lover," she said, "then it could have been the Mafia. They use explosives too, don't they? They'd give anything to get their hands on the magnificent jewels my late husband left me. He was one of the richest men in the world as you all know. After the attack last night I consider myself lucky to be alive."

Luther, none too steady on his feet by this time, stepped behind the bar. "Well, here goes," he said, and without further ceremony he poured the goldfish into the tank. They plunged into the water in a burst of bright green bubbles. Luther held his breath as the bubbles rose and the water cleared. There, swimming around the tank—brighter than the gills or the mouths or the eyes or the fins—were the glowing intestines of his six goldfish. Looping, coiled, knotty cores of light at the center of each of his fish. Luther could not believe it. Months of work had come to this. Glowing goldfish guts. He had overfed the fish.

A silence came over the patrons at the bar.

"Darling," said Serena, "what the hell is that?"

Others were quick to add their two cents.

"That's repulsive."

"It looks like X-ray fish."

"Yuck!"

Luther would not be consoled. "I don't care," he said. "It doesn't matter. I just don't care." He kept repeating "I don't care," over and over. In response to any question—*Do you want another drink? What should we do with the goldfish? Are they radioactive?*—he gave the same answer. "I don't care."

Luther was in no condition to drive. So, after we left Serena calling out "Nighty-night!" on her doorstep, I got behind the wheel of his car, drove him home, and deposited him in the living room of his carriage house—the living room that looked out on the dumpster instead of the garden. The night air seemed to revive him a little.

"I don't know why I ever fooled around with goldfish," he said. "I should have stuck to what I know best. Insects. It doesn't pay to try to change. I've often thought of changing my life completely, but it never works. I moved to Florida once, but I came back. I've got too much Savannah in me, I guess. My family's been here seven generations, and after that long a time I suppose it gets into your genes. It's like the control insects at the laboratory. Did I ever tell you about them? Well, we keep a lot of insect colonies in big glass jars out there. Some of them have been breeding for twenty-five years. That's a thousand generations. All they know about life is what goes on inside their jar. They haven't been exposed to pesticides or pollution, so they haven't developed immunities or evolved in any way. They stay the same, generation after generation. If we released them into the outside world, they'd die. I think something like that happens after seven generations in Savannah. Savannah gets to be the only place you can live. We're like bugs in a jar."

Luther excused himself and asked me to wait in the living room. He walked upstairs unsteadily but with exaggerated care, negotiating the false step without mishap. I could hear him cross the floor overhead. A dresser drawer opened and closed. When he returned, he was carrying a brown bottle with a black screw cap. The bottle was filled with a white powder.

"This is one way out," he said. "Sodium fluoroacetate. It's a poison. Five hundred times more lethal than arsenic." Luther held the bottle up to the light. It had a handwritten label that read: "Monsanto 3039."

"This is the same stuff the Finns dumped down their wells when the Russians invaded in 1939. The water in those wells is still undrinkable. I could kill damn near everybody in Savannah with this bottle. Tens of thousands of people anyway." A smile played across Luther's lips as he gazed at the bottle. "I was in charge of burying a lot of this stuff out on Oatland Island where we closed down a laboratory years ago. I kept some of it for myself, though. More than enough."

"Ever thought of using it?" I asked.

"Sure. I've always said I'd use it if niggers moved into the house next door. Then niggers did move in next door and made a liar out of me."

"Isn't it illegal to have it?"

"Highly."

"Then why do you keep it?"

"I just like the idea of it." Luther spoke in a taunting way, like a boy with an extra-powerful slingshot. "Every so often I hold it in my hand and think . . . poof!"

Luther handed me the bottle. As I looked at it, I held my breath for fear that the slightest leaking fumes would be lethal. I wondered what went through Luther's mind when he held this bottle and thought "poof!" Then I thought I knew. He probably saw the people of Savannah dropping dead one by one: businessmen sitting on benches in Johnson Square, young revelers carousing on River Street, slow-moving black women holding umbrellas aloft against the hot summer sun, butlers carrying silver trays in the Oglethorpe Club, whores in hotpants on Montgomery Street, tourists lined up in front of Mrs. Wilkes's boarding house.

He took the bottle back. "It's an odorless, tasteless poison," he said. "It kills without leaving a trace—just a slight residue of fluoride but no more than you could attribute to the use of fluoride toothpaste. The victim dies of a heart attack. It's the perfect murder weapon."

Luther went to the front door and opened it. I took this as a sign that the evening was over. But as I stood up, he grabbed hold of the door and pulled it sharply upward. The door lifted completely off its hinges. Luther laid it down flat on the living-room floor. "This is more than just an ordinary door," he said. "It's what's called a 'cooling board.' Cooling boards are for laying out corpses and preparing them for burial. It's a typical feature of old houses. The front door doubles as a cooling board. My family's houses have always had them, so I had one made for myself. When I go, they'll carry me out on this."

Luther sat cross-legged on top of the cooling-board door on the living-room floor with the bottle of poison in his hand. Yes, I thought, and when you go, how many others will you take with you? Luther closed his eyes. A smile spread across his face.

"You know," I said, "some people in Savannah, or at least some people in Clary's, are afraid you might dump that poison into the water supply someday."

"I know," he said.

"What if I were to grab that bottle out of your hands and run away with it?"

"I'd go back to Oatland Island and dig up some more, probably," said Luther. Whatever his intentions, Luther clearly relished the speculation about his sinister power.

"When you were a kid," I said, "were you the type who pulled the wings off flies?"

"No," he said, "but I caught June bugs and tied balloons to them."

—

The next morning at Clary's drugstore, Ruth set Luther's breakfast in front of him—his eggs, his bacon, his Bayer aspirin, and his glass of ammonia and Coca-Cola. Then she went back to the end of the soda fountain and took a drag on her cigarette.

"Ruth?" Luther asked. "Do you think you can live without glowing goldfish?"

"I can if you can, Luther," she answered.

Luther ate a mouthful of eggs and then some bacon. He took a swallow of Coke and proceeded to finish his entire breakfast. He had a mournful but peaceful air. Luther ate, he slept, and the demons within him were still. His deadly bottle of poison would remain a harmless curiosity. At least for now.

Chapter 6

THE LADY OF SIX THOUSAND SONGS

The stream of people going in and out of Joe Odom's house seemed to pick up tempo in the weeks after I met him. That might have been because I had joined the flow myself and was now viewing the phenomenon from midstream, so to speak. I often dropped in after breakfast, by which time the aroma of fresh coffee would be gaining the upper hand over the smell of stale cigarettes from the night before. Joe would be clean-shaven and well rested on three or four hours' sleep, and among the assorted company (bartenders, socialites, truck drivers, accountants) there would generally be at least one person who had spent the night on the sofa. Currents of activity swirled about the house even at this early hour. People entered and exited rooms, crisscrossing one's field of vision like characters in *La Dolce Vita*.

One morning, Joe sat at the grand piano in the living room having coffee, playing the piano, and talking to me. A fat man and a girl with braided hair walked through, completely engrossed in their own conversation.

"She tore up her mother's car yesterday," the girl said.

"I thought it was the TV."

"No, the TV was last week. . . ."

They continued out into the hall, whereupon a bald man in a business suit poked his head in.

"The meeting's at two," he said to Joe. "I'll call you when it's over. Wish me luck." Then he disappeared. At that point, Mandy came in from the kitchen, wrapped in a white sheet and looking like a voluptuous goddess. She plucked a cigarette from the pack in Joe's shirt pocket, kissed him on the forehead, whispered, "Draw up the damn divorce papers!" and then skipped back into the kitchen, where Jerry resumed cutting her hair. In the dining room, a young man hooted with laughter as he read Lewis Grizzard's column aloud to a white-haired woman who was not finding it at all funny. Overhead, the sound of high-heeled shoes clicked across the floor.

"Well, it's nine-thirty A.M.," said Joe, "and I ain't bored yet."

Joe was talking not just to me, but to a person at the other end of the telephone, which was tucked under his chin. Joe often engaged in split conversations of this sort. Sometimes you knew who the other party was, sometimes you did not.

"I woke up this morning at seven," he was saying, "and there was this big lump next to me under the covers, which I thought was strange because I had gone to bed alone. Mandy was in Waycross for the night and not due back here for an hour or so. So I lay there just looking at the lump, trying to figure out who or what it was. It was very big, bigger than anybody I knew. . . . What? . . . I was sure it was a human being and not a pile of laundry, because it was breathing. Then I noticed something strange about the breathing pattern: It was coming from two different parts of the lump. Finally, it dawned on me that the lump was two people, which meant I was odd man out, so I yanked the covers back, and sure enough, it was a boy and a girl. I had never seen either one of them before. They were both completely naked."

Joe paused for a moment to listen to the person at the other end of the telephone. "Heh-heh, you know me better than that, Cora Bett," he said. Then, speaking to both of us again, he continued: "Anyhow, before I had a chance to say anything, the boy asked me, 'Who are you?' Now, I'm pretty sure that's the first time I've ever been asked that question in my own bed. So I said, 'I happen to be the social director here, and I don't believe we've met.' I wasn't sure what to do next, but just then the telephone rang, and I learned that I had a busload of tourists coming at noon—forty people—and that I'd have to make lunch for them because the caterer is sick. . . .Yup, lunch for forty! . . .They're all members of a polka-dancing social club from Cleveland. Heh-heh." Joe smiled as he listened to the voice on the other end.

"Anyhow," he went on, "my two newest naked friends got dressed. The boy had tattoos on his arms—a Confederate flag on one arm and a marijuana plant on the other. He put on a really swell T-shirt. It had 'Fuck You' printed on it. At this very moment, both he and the girl are in the kitchen helping make shrimp salad for forty polka dancers. Jerry's in there too, cutting Mandy's hair, and that's why I say I ain't bored yet."

Joe said good-bye and hung up the telephone, and as he did a large blue caftan floated into the room. The caftan was topped by the round, smiling face of a woman of about seventy. She had powder-white skin set off by bright red lipstick, rouge, and mascara. Her jet-black hair was wound into a huge bun that sat on top of her head like a turban. "I'm off to Statesboro to play for the Kiwanis Club," she said, waving a set of car keys, "and then I have a beauty pageant in Hinesville at six. I should be back in Savannah by nine. But in case I'm late, can you get to the bar early and cover for me?"

"Yes, ma'am," said Joe, and with that the woman floated away in a rustle of silk and a jangle of keys.

Joe nodded at the spot where she had been standing. "That," he said, "was one of Georgia's greatest ladies. Emma Kelly. Come with us tonight and you'll see her in action. Around these parts she's known as 'The Lady of Six Thousand Songs.' "

—

For the past forty years, Emma Kelly had spent the better part of her waking hours driving across the landscape of south Georgia to play piano wherever she was needed. She played at graduations, weddings, reunions, and church socials. All anyone had to do was ask, and she would be there—in Waynesboro, Swainsboro, Ellabell, Hazlehurst, Newington, Jesup, and Jimps. She had played at senior proms for every high school within a hundred miles of Savannah. On a given day, she might drive to Metter to play for a ladies' fashion show, then on to Sylvania for a retired teachers' convention, and then to Wrens for a birthday party. Toward evening she would usually drive to Savannah to play piano at one of several nightspots. But no matter where her engagements took her, she would always be back home in Statesboro—an hour west of Savannah—to play at the Rotary Club lunch on Monday, the Lions on Tuesday, the Kiwanis on Thursday, and the First Baptist Church on Sunday. Emma played old standards and show tunes, blues and waltzes. She was a familiar sight with her flowing caftans and happy coats and that towering turban of black hair held in place by two lacquered chopsticks.

Emma was descended from the earliest English settlers in Georgia and South Carolina. She had met George Kelly when she was four and married him when she was seventeen. He was a sign painter, and by the time he died Emma had borne ten children, "not counting five miscarriages," as she would always say.

Being a devout Baptist, Emma never drank. But once, after playing at the Fort Stewart officers' club, she was stopped on suspicion of drunk driving. The M.P. who shined his light through the window told her she had been weaving all over the road for the last three miles. That was true, but the fact of the matter was that Emma had been trying to undo her corset and slip out of it at the time. She squinted into the glare of the flashlight, clutching her unfastened clothes about her and wondering how on earth she was going to step out of the car in this condition and convince the young man she was sober. It was Emma's good fortune that she had played piano at the M.P.'s senior prom years before. He recognized her and knew she never touched a drop, and in a moment she was on her way.

In fact, most of the highway patrolmen knew Emma's car, and when it zoomed past them late at night doing eighty or ninety, they generally let it go. Emma had the greatest compassion for the occasional rookie cop who would unknowingly pull her over, siren blaring, blue lights flashing. She would roll down the window and say softly, "You must be new." She'd be thinking ahead to the browbeating the young man was about to receive from a groggy sheriff. It would go something along the lines of: "What in blazes you think you doin', boy, draggin' Emma Kelly off the road! Tell you what you gone do now! You gone escort this fine lady all the way to Statesboro! See she gets home safe! A million pardons, Miss Emma. It won't happen again."

In Savannah, Emma's fans followed her from nightspot to nightspot like a cheerful caravan—from Whispers to the Pink House to the Fountain to the Live Oak Bowling Alley to the Quality Inn out by the airport. She was good business. Bar receipts always picked up sharply for the duration of her stay and fell off when it was over. For years, Emma's children had pleaded with her to open her own piano bar and cut down on the driving. After she killed her ninth deer on the highway, they stopped pleading and just plain insisted. "It breaks my heart," said Emma, "because I love animals so much, not to mention the damage it's done to the car." About opening a piano bar, she promised she would think it over.

Joe Odom, who had known Emma all his life, often came to hear her wherever she happened to be performing. At some point after his arrival, Emma would play "Sentimental Journey," which was the signal for Joe to come up and take over at the piano so she could rest a few minutes. Joe would happily oblige.

The night Emma collided with her tenth deer, she drove to Whispers and played "Sentimental Journey" as soon as Joe set foot in the door. "Go out and see how bad the car is, Joe, will you?" she said. "I can't bear to look at it myself." Six months later, she and Joe opened a piano bar in an old cotton warehouse overlooking the river. They called it Emma's.

Emma's was a long, narrow room, cozy as a book-filled den. Its tiny dance floor was nestled in the curve of a baby grand piano. A picture window looked out on the river and an occasional containership gliding by. Dozens of framed photographs of family and friends lined the shelves along one wall, and an alcove by the entrance was decorated with memorabilia of Johnny Mercer. It was Mercer, in fact, who had nicknamed Emma "The Lady of Six Thousand Songs." That was how many songs she knew, according to Mercer's calculations. He and Emma had paged through a pile of songbooks, Mercer checking off the songs Emma could sing from start to finish. After three years of checking off songs, Mercer made an educated guess as to the store of lyrics in Emma's head. He put it at six thousand.

The first time I came to Emma's, I was just taking my seat when Emma looked in my direction and asked, "What's your favorite song?" My mind went totally blank, of course. As I looked at her helplessly, a huge freighter came into view over her left shoulder. "Ship!" I said. "My ship has sails that are made of silk!"

"Oh, that's a lovely song," said Emma. "Kurt Weill, 1941." She played it, and from that time on, Emma always played "My Ship" whenever I came into the bar. "Bartenders know customers by the drinks they order," she said. "I know them by the songs they ask me to play. Whenever regulars walk in the door, I like to play their favorites. It tickles them and makes them feel they're home."

Emma had many regulars. There were the four ladies from Estill, South Carolina, who drove in several nights a week with or without their husbands. There was the real estate agent John Thorsen, who walked his dog every night before going to bed and more than once kept walking until he got to Emma's, where, dressed in pajamas and bathrobe and accompanied by the dog, he was shown to his regular table. Just as he was sitting down, Emma would play "Moments Like This," which was his favorite song. There was Wanda Brooks, a self-appointed greeter-hostess who wore rakish hats and a rhinestone brooch that advertised her telephone number in glittering numerals an inch high. Wanda had been a majorette in junior high school; now she sold tanning beds to suntan parlors in South Carolina and coastal Georgia. She would call out "Hey!" to perfect strangers, show them to a table, engage them in animated conversation, dance with them, and then move on to chat with others. Wanda was forever foraging in her purse for a lighter, swaying and leaning into the person next to her as she babbled amiably. Inevitably, her ever-present cigarette would tumble from her lips or slip out of her fingers in a shower of glowing ashes, sending the people in her immediate vicinity leaping to their feet and flailing at their clothes. Wanda had platinum-blond hair, and her entrance into Emma's was always accompanied by the playing of "New York, New York," which was her favorite song.

Though Emma's was a popular nightspot, it fell short of expectations in one respect: It failed to keep Emma off the road. She went right on making appearances from one end of south Georgia to the other and driving on to Savannah afterward to play until early morning. Occasionally, she spent the night in Joe Odom's carriage house after closing, but most of the time she found an excuse to drive home to Statesboro. On Saturday nights, she would drive home no matter what, because her Sundays in Statesboro started very early and ran very late, as I discovered firsthand. Emma invited me to join her one Sunday at church and stay with her throughout the day. This is how it went.

Emma pulled into the parking lot of the First Baptist Church in Statesboro Sunday morning at twenty minutes past eight. She was wearing a purple silk dress, a blue cape, turquoise eye shadow, and a touch of rouge. "Let me see," she said, "we closed Emma's at three o'clock last night, and I got home about four. I would have pulled off the highway and taken a fifteen-minute nap under the Ash Branch overpass, like I usually do, but there was a big old truck there ahead of me and it took all the room. So I got to bed by four-thirty, and then at a quarter past seven, Aunt Annalise called to make sure I got up in time for church. She's ninety." Emma adjusted the two lacquered chopsticks that anchored her bun. "I can keep going with just a couple hours sleep, but sometimes you can tell. My eyes get puffy." We went inside the church.

The preacher delivered a sermon entitled "Temptation and Decay from Within." A deacon then read a report on the forthcoming revival week, the theme of which was to be "Wake Up, America: God Loves You!" The deacon thought too many people were still very much asleep in regard to this message. "There are one hundred and eighty million people in America who do not claim Christ," he said. "Two million in the state of Georgia. Thousands in Statesboro alone."

The preacher then addressed the gathering. "Have we got any guests among us today?" Emma whispered that I should stand up. All heads turned. "Welcome," the preacher said heartily. "So glad you could join us."

After the service, Emma and I walked to a smaller chapel where the older people were to attend their weekly senior assembly. We were slowed a bit by the dozen or so people who came up to welcome me personally to the church and to ask where I was from. "New York!" a woman said. "My! I had a cousin who went there once." In the chapel, Emma slipped off her high heels and played the organ as the others came in. Each member of the senior assembly stopped at the organ to greet Emma and then came over to me to say how pleased they were that I had come. Mr. Granger was the first to address the gathering. "I tell you, my wife is doing great," he said. "I knew last Sunday it was malignant, but I couldn't tell you, because the doctor had not confirmed it until Tuesday. I really have a heavy heart, but everything is being taken care of as far as I can tell."

From the rear of the chapel a woman said, "Ann McCoy is in Saint Joseph's Hospital in Savannah. She's havin' back problems."

Another said, "Sally Powell's sister died."

Mr. Granger asked, "Is there anyone else?"

"Cliff Bradley," several people said at once.

"Cliff went home yesterday afternoon, late," said Mr. Granger. "He seems to be doin' great."

"Goldie Smith needs our prayers," another woman said. "There's something the matter with her stomach. She's being fitted with a prosthesis."

A woman with pink lipstick and gold-rimmed glasses stood up to give a testimonial. "Me and my family weren't doing too good until I looked down and saw I had a God hole in my chest. We all have a God hole in our chest. You should all do what I did: Turn it over to Jesus."

When the assembly was over, Emma went to a small room off the chapel where she and a dozen other older women had their Sunday school class. Emma introduced me all over again, and the ladies chirped and mewed little hellos. The leader of the class said she would give a talk about God's People in a Changing World, but did anybody have any important announcements first.

"Myrtle Foster's incision is still draining," said a woman with glasses and a light green suit. "I talked to Rap Nelby last night, and they do not know when she will be able to come home."

"We'll have to put her on our prayer list," said the leader.

A woman with her hair in rows of small blue-white curls said, "Louise saw Mary at the beauty shop on Friday and it seems the two others are not doing well either, so we need to keep them on our list too." For the next few minutes, the health of several other members of the congregation was discussed, and the prayer list grew by three more names.

The leader then began her talk—"Jesus will never ask you to do anything he wouldn't do himself"—and Emma reached into her pocketbook and took out a small manila envelope with "Emma Kelly: $24" written across the top. She stood up quietly and put the envelope into a carton with the other ladies' envelopes. Then, motioning for me to follow, she tiptoed into the hall with the carton. I felt a tug at my jacket. "I hope you enjoyed it," a lady by the door whispered. "Come back and see us again."

Emma led the way down the hall. "Now we go to the little children two floors up," she said. First she went around to a windowless room and handed the carton to two men who were sitting behind a table piled high with little manila envelopes. "Mornin', Miss Emma," they said.

Upstairs, about twenty children were seated in a semicircle around an upright piano waiting for Emma. She accompanied them as they sang the titles of the books of the New Testament to the tune of "Onward, Christian Soldiers"—"Math-thew, Ma-ark, Lu-uke and John, Acts and the Let-ters to the Ro-mans. . . ." Then she played "Jesus Is a Loving Teacher" all the way through twice. "We can go now," she said, and we went back down the two flights of stairs and out into the parking lot.

"If the other lady who plays piano can't go to the nursing home, I go there now," said Emma. "But she's there today." So instead we drove directly to the Forest Heights Country Club, where Emma went to the buffet, put two fried chicken legs on her plate, and sat down at the piano in the dining room. For the next two and a half hours, she played background music and chatted with the diners who came up one by one or in family groups to greet her and pay their respects.

At two-thirty, Emma got up from the piano and said her good-byes. We walked out to the car and drove fifty miles into the bright afternoon sun to Vidalia, home of the sweet Vidalia onion. Emma had been hired to play for a wedding reception at the Serendipity Health and Racquet Club. Upon arriving, she went directly to the ladies' room and changed into a flowing black-and-gold kimono. The owner of the health club, a large lady with a bouffant blond hairdo, took us on a tour of the spa and showed us the new indoor-outdoor swimming pool and underwater grotto of which she was very proud. The wedding guests began to arrive from the church, but the bride and groom were late. Word had it that they had stopped at a 7-Eleven to get plastic glasses for the champagne they were consuming in the car.

When the wedding couple finally arrived, Emma found out that the name of the groom was Bill, and she announced she had a special song for the occasion. She sang, "Big Bad Bill is Sweet William now . . . married life has changed him . . . he washes dishes, mops the floor. . . ." The song was greeted with laughter and set everybody to dancing except the little boys who went out and put a bottle of champagne under the hood of the wedding couple's car next to the engine block so it would heat up and explode when they drove away.

At six-thirty, after Emma had played for two hours, we got back into her car for the drive back to Statesboro. If she was tired, she did not show it. She was not only wide awake but smiling. "Someone once wrote that musicians are touched on the shoulder by God," she said, "and I think it's true. You can make other people happy with music, but you can make yourself happy too. Because of my music, I have never known loneliness and never been depressed.

"When I was growing up, I used to put the radio under the covers with me at night. That's how I learned so many different songs. In fact, it was because I knew so many songs that I got to know Johnny Mercer in the first place. We met over the telephone twenty years ago. I was playing at a dinner party in Savannah, and a young man kept requesting Johnny Mercer songs. He was kind of surprised when I knew every one. Then I played some he hadn't heard before, and he was astonished. 'I'm Johnny Mercer's nephew,' he said. 'I want him to meet you. Let's call him now.' So he called Bel Air, California, and told Johnny he'd met this lady who knew every song he'd ever written. Then he put me on the phone. Johnny didn't even say hello. He just said, 'Sing the first eight bars of "If You Were Mine.' " Now, that's not a well-known song, but it was one that meant a lot to Johnny. I sang it without any hesitation, and we were friends from then on."

The sun was beginning to set. "To me, the words are as important as the music," said Emma. "Johnny and I liked to compare our favorite phrases. We both loved the lyric 'Too dear to lose, too sweet to last' from the song 'While We're Young' and the line from 'Handful of Stars' that goes 'Oh! What things unspoken trembled in the air.'

"Johnny's own lyrics are the best, though. It's hard to think of anything more beautiful than 'When an early autumn walks the land and chills the breeze and touches with her hand the summer trees. . . .' That's poetry. And 'Like painted kites the days and nights went flying by. The world was new beneath a blue umbrella sky.' "

It was because of Johnny Mercer that Emma started singing. Until she met him she played the piano and that was all. Mercer kept telling her, "Go ahead and sing." But she was afraid. She told him she had no range. "That's all right," he said, "just sing softly. You don't have to hit every note. Sing low and skip and cheat a lot. If you can't reach it or don't know it, skip it." He showed her how she could change keys instead of going up an octave for the second verse of "I Love Paris." He even helped her cheat with one of his own songs. She was having trouble with the line "I wanna be around to pick up the pieces when somebody breaks your heart"—she could not drop down for the second syllable of "somebody." Mercer told her to sing the same note for all three syllables.

She was still dubious about singing, though. Then one evening she started an engagement at the Quality Inn and found a microphone and sound system all set up. "Oh, look," Mercer told her, "you've got a mike. Now you can sing." And she did. Years later she found out that Mercer had arranged for the mike to be there and paid for it too.

Emma recalled how over the years she had played piano for plain folks and dignitaries, for three presidents, twenty governors, and countless mayors. She had jammed with Tommy Dorsey and accompanied Robert Goulet. She recalled the day, years ago, when playing piano every day of her life had become a necessity. It had happened on a Sunday morning when her youngest son, upset about having broken up with his girlfriend, dropped Emma and her husband at church and then drove into the woods, set a rifle butt against the floorboards, turned the barrel to his chest, and fired. He collapsed on the steering wheel, sounding the horn. Someone heard the horn and came running. The boy lost a lung, but his life was saved, at a cost of $40,000. Emma had to work day and night to pay the bills. The near tragedy only served to intensify her faith. "What if the bullet had gone just a fraction of an inch to the left or right? What if he had not fallen on the steering wheel? The Lord must have been with him," Emma said. "I have to go on believing for that reason alone." Even after she had paid the hospital bills, Emma continued her nightly appearances. It had become her life.

We arrived back in Statesboro shortly after seven-thirty. Before going home, Emma stopped at the home of her ninety-year-old aunt to bring her a box of food she had taken with her from the country club. Her aunt came to the door in her nightgown and nightcap; she'd been listening to the radio broadcast of the evening sermon at the Baptist church. Emma went inside for a few minutes and tucked her in bed. Then, more than twelve hours after her day had begun, she drove home.

"There's another wonderful thing about being able to play music," she said. "It's something Johnny Mercer told me. He said, 'When you play songs, you can bring back people's memories of when they fell in love. That's where the power lies.' "

—

On the basis of attendance alone, Emma's piano bar was an unqualified success. Financially, however, the bar did not do very well. Joe's inclination to give people free drinks was one reason. In addition to that, many of Joe's old creditors saw the bar as a chance to recoup some of the money he owed them. They would come in for an hour or so of drinking and then leave without paying. But even so, Emma's should have made more money than it did. Joe sought the advice of Darlene Poole, who knew the bar business inside out.

Darlene had worked as a barmaid in a number of local saloons and was engaged to the owner of a successful club on the southside. She and Joe sat at a table having a drink. "You got a nice setup here," she said. "The blue-rinse-and-foxtrot crowd finally have a place to go. Can't hardly go to the Nightflight, can't go to Malone's, can't go to Studebaker's. You got 'em all to yourself, honey. Nice going. Plus I see you've got Wanda Brooks coming in here. Broads like Wanda are what I call insurance. With her bumping into everybody and knocking drinks over left and right at three bucks a shot, you can't help but make it work. Now, if you can just keep the freeloaders out and stop giving away the liquor, you should do all right. Just make sure nobody's glass stays empty too long."

"Maybe that's the problem," said Joe. "Gotta get Moon to pour drinks faster."

"Moon?!" Darlene whirled around and looked toward the bar. Then she looked back at Joe. "Shit, Joe, you didn't tell me you had Moon Tompkins tending bar!" Darlene leaned closer to Joe and lowered her voice. "Moon's your problem, honey."

"Why do you say that?" Joe asked. "He seems okay to me. Maybe a little slow."

"Moon Tompkins has done three years for bank robbery," said Darlene.

Joe laughed. "Yeah-yeah," he said.

"And it wasn't just one bank, either. It was two."

"You're serious, aren't you?" said Joe. His laugh turned into a curious smile. He looked toward the bar, where Moon Tompkins was pouring vodka into a row of four tall glasses.

"Well, I'll be damned," he said. "I wouldn't have thought old Moon had it in him."

"How in hell did you ever let him in here as bartender?" Darlene asked.

"Emma hired him. I guess he didn't put the bank job on his résumé."

Darlene lit a cigarette. "I suppose you heard about the armed robbery at the Green Parrot restaurant last week?"

"Uh-huh."

"Moon did it."

"Oh, come on!" said Joe. "Are you sure about that?"

"Positive."

"But wait a minute," said Joe. "How could you know it was Moon? They haven't caught the robber yet."

"I know," said Darlene. "I drove the getaway car."

—

Joe had nothing against convicted bank robbers—or getaway drivers either—but he felt foolish entrusting his cash register to a dedicated thief. Moon was using the most rudimentary of all scams—making more drinks than he rang up—and when he did ring up drinks, he often propped the check on the cash register so it hid the numbers. "You can bet he's pushing the No Sale button whenever he does that," said Darlene, "and slipping twenty bucks in his pocket."

Joe decided that the wisest thing to do would be to catch Moon in the act, confront him quietly, and allow him to quit without a fuss. He would not tell Emma anything about it, because the idea that she had been in business with a bank robber might give her a heart attack. Joe asked two friends to come to the bar the following night and keep careful count of all the drinks Moon served. During the day, however, word leaked out that later that night Moon Tompkins would be caught with his hand in the till at Emma's, and by the time the bar opened a festive crowd was clamoring to get in and watch the sting unfold as if it were a sporting event.

"Good gracious, we're having a lively night," said Emma. Customers ordered drinks at a furious rate, hoping to encourage Moon to steal more than he had ever stolen before. The more drinks they ordered, the merrier the mood became, and by midnight it seemed that Emma and Moon were the only people in the bar who were unaware of the sting in progress.

The customers called out their orders:

"Hey, Moon! Gimme a *stinger*! Ha-ha! What better drink for a sting than a stinger!"

"I'll have a *Rob* Roy, Moon!"

A half hour before closing, Moon took the trash barrel out to empty it in the dumpster and never came back. When Joe stepped behind the bar and opened the cash drawer, it was empty. Moon had cleaned it out.

Moon's disappearance did nothing to dampen spirits at Emma's. It only served to heighten the level of hilarity. At closing time, there was nothing Joe could do but tell Emma what had happened, that Moon had taken all the money and run.

"My goodness me!" said Emma. "Did he really?"

"I'm afraid so," said Joe. "And I guess it's a good thing we're rid of him, because it seems he's done this kind of thing before. He's a bank robber."

"Oh, I know all about that," said Emma.

"You *knew*?"

"Why, of course," she said. "Moon told me about it when he first came looking for a job. He didn't try to hide it, and I told him I admired him for that. I thought he deserved a second chance in life. I think everybody does. Don't you?"

"Yes, ma'am," said Joe.

Emma got into her car and then pulled out onto Bay Street, headed for Statesboro.

As was his custom at this hour of the morning, Joe led a few friends back to his house, where, according to the fire captain's report later in the day, someone dropped a lighted cigarette into a wastebasket shortly before dawn and caused the fire that nearly gutted the house.

Joe was the first to smell the smoke. He ran through the house rousing people from beds and sofas and herding them into the street.

"Is everyone out?" the fire captain asked.

"Everyone I know about," said Joe.

"You mean there might be people in your house you don't know about?"

"Captain," said Joe, "there have been times when there were people in my *bed* I didn't know about."

It was widely assumed that Joe Odom had set his house on fire to collect the insurance money, even though he no longer owned the house. Joe's landlords asked him to vacate the premises at once, not so much because of the fire but because Joe had never paid them any rent. A week later, Joe took what furnishings he could salvage and moved into a large Federal-style brick townhouse at 101 East Oglethorpe Avenue, a few blocks away. His new next-door neighbors were Mr. and Mrs. Malcolm Bell. Mr. Bell was the retired chairman of the Savannah Bank, former president of the venerable Oglethorpe Club, and a respected historian. Mrs. Bell was an intellectual and a member of a distinguished Savannah family. In view of his august new neighbors, Joe's friends anticipated that life at his new home might perforce be a bit more modulated than it had been at 16 East Jones Street.

And perhaps it was. But before long, neighbors began to notice that visitors were passing through the unlocked front door of 101 East Oglethorpe Avenue in a steady stream, that tour buses were pulling up in front at noontime, and that pleasant piano melodies could be heard spilling out of the house day or night but especially at times when the city was otherwise utterly still.

Chapter 7

THE GRAND EMPRESS OF SAVANNAH

An unnatural calm descended over Jones Street after Joe Odom's move to Oglethorpe Avenue. No longer could Joe's sweet serenade be heard floating over the garden walls. In the stillness, it occurred to me that it was time to buy a car. I wanted to see more of the environs of Savannah, but I proceeded carefully in the matter of wheels.

Savannahians drove fast. They also liked to carry their cocktails with them when they drove. According to the National Institute of Alcoholism and Alcohol Abuse, more than 8 percent of Savannah's adults were "known alcoholics," which may have accounted for the disturbing tendency of motorists to run up over the curb and collide with trees. The trunks of all but one of the twenty-seven oaks that lined the edge of Forsyth Park on Whitaker Street, for instance, had deep scars at fender level. One tree had been hit so many times it had a sizable hollow scooped out of its trunk. The hollow was filled with pea-size crystals of windshield glass that glittered like a bowl of diamonds. The palm trees in the center of Victory Drive had the same sort of scars, and so did the oaks on Abercorn.

I had never owned a car. Living in New York I hadn't needed one, but the idea appealed to me now. If I was going to drive a car in this environment, though, it would have to be a very big and heavy one. It would probably have fins.

"I'm in the market for an old car," I said to Joe. "Something big and roomy. Nothing fancy."

An hour later we stood looking at a 1973 Pontiac Grand Prix. Its metallic-gold body was dented and flecked with rust. The windshield was cracked, the vinyl roof was peeling, the hubcaps were missing, and the engine was well into its second hundred thousand miles. But it ran well enough and it was big. It did not have fins, but its hood was so long it looked like the foredeck of an ocean liner. The man was asking $800.

"It's perfect," I said. "I'll take it."

Now I was completely mobile. I drove south of Gaston Street (breaking Joe's second rule). I took excursions into South Carolina. I sailed past the trees with the scars on them and shared the road with drivers who sipped from traveler cups and lurched from lane to lane. I felt perfectly safe in my rolling metal fortress, rusted and dented as it was. Nothing and no one could get to me, and nothing and no one did—with one very notable exception. Her name was Chablis.

—

When I first laid eyes on her, Chablis was standing by the curb, watching me intently as I parked my car. She had just come out of Dr. Myra Bishop's office across the street from where I lived. Dr. Bishop was a family practitioner. Most of her patients were conservatively dressed black women. Those whose gaze happened to meet mine usually nodded solemnly and moved on. But not Chablis.

She was wearing a loose white cotton blouse, jeans, and white tennis sneakers. Her hair was short, and her skin was a smooth milk chocolate. Her eyes were large and expressive, all the more so because they were staring straight into mine. She had both hands on her hips and a sassy half-smile on her face as if she had been waiting for me. I drew up to the curb and rolled to a stop at her feet.

"Ooooo, *child*!" she said. "You are right on time, honey." Her voice crackled, her hoop earrings jangled. "I am *serious*. I cannot *tell* you." She began moving slowly toward me with an undulating walk. She trailed an index finger sensuously along the fender, feeling the hollow of each and every dent. "Y-e-e-e-s, child! *Yay*yiss . . . *yay*yiss . . . *yay*yiss!" She walked on past me and continued all the way around the car, inspecting its condition and laughing. When she got back around to me, she leaned in the window. "Tell me somethin', honey," she said. "How come a white boy like you is drivin' a old, broken-down, jiveass bruthuh's heap like this? If you don't mind me askin'."

"It's my first car," I said.

"Oh! I hope I didn't hurt your feelings. If I did, I'm sorry. I truly am. I did not mean to do that. I just call it out, baby. Whatever way I see it, I just call it out."

"No, that's okay," I said. "I'm just practicing my driving skills before I go out and buy a Rolls-Royce."

"Aw *right,* honey, I can dig it! You are traveling in disguise, baby, you are incognito. Yes, I can dig that, child. I surely can. And you know, honey, when you drive a car like this, you don't get nobody fuckin' with it. Ain't no stereo for nobody to rip off. Ain't no fine paint job for nobody to scratch up with no key, honey."

"That's true too," I said, opening the door to get out.

"Oh, child, don't you be doin' that!" she said. "Don't you be haulin' ass with me standin' out here like this!"

"But I live here," I said.

"That's okay, baby. You can practice your driving skills some more on the way to takin' me home. Okay? 'Cause Miss Myra's shots is gettin' ready to kick in, honey. I can feel 'em. I am serious. And these feet are about wore out."

There seemed to be no doubt in the young woman's mind that I would take her home. I mumbled something on the order of "Well, sure," but it was unnecessary because she was already getting into the car when I did.

"I live downtown by Crawford Square," she said. "It won't take but a few minutes." She settled into the seat and looked at me. "Ooooo, child, you are some kinda handsome! If my boyfriend wasn't living with me I would hit on you for sure. I am serious. I like my white boys, and that's what I have plenty of waiting for me at home, thank goodness. My boyfriend is blond and beautiful. Hunk for days, honey. He satisfies my every need."

We pulled away from the curb.

"I'm Chablis," she said.

"Chablis? That's pretty," I said. "What's your full name?"

"*The Lady* Chablis," she said. She turned sideways in the seat, pulling her knees up and leaning back against the door as if she were sinking into a luxurious sofa. "It's a stage name," she said. "I'm a showgirl."

She was beautiful, seductively beautiful in a streetwise way. Her big eyes sparkled. Her skin glowed. A broken incisor tooth punctuated her smile and gave her a naughty look.

"I dance, I do lip sync, and I emcee," she said. "Shit like that. My mama got the name Chablis off a wine bottle. She didn't think it up for me though. It was supposed to be for my sister. Mama got pregnant when I was sixteen, and she wanted a little girl. She was gonna name her La Quinta Chablis, but then she had a miscarriage, and I said, 'Ooooo, *Chablis*. That's nice. I like that name.' And Mama said, 'Then take it, baby. Just call yourself Chablis from now on.' So ever since then, I've been Chablis."

"A cool white wine for a cool black girl," I said.

"Y-e-e-s, child!"

"What was your name before that?" I asked.

"Frank," she said.

—

We had stopped for the light at Liberty Street. I looked at Chablis again, very carefully this time. She had a small, feminine frame and delicate hands and arms. She carried herself like a woman; there was nothing masculine about her. Her big dark eyes were watching me.

"I told you I could dig bein' in disguise," she said. "I'm in disguise twenty-four hours a day. I am incognito."

"So you're really . . . a man," I said.

"No-no-no," she said. "Don't you be callin' me no man! Uh-uh, honey. Y'mama worked too hard to grow her titties. She ain't no man." Chablis unbuttoned her blouse and proudly revealed a medium-size, perfectly shaped breast.

"This is real, honey, it ain't silicone. It's what Dr. Bishop's shots do for me. Miss Myra gives me estrogen shots, female hormones, every two weeks. And in between, I take estrogen pills. They give me breasts and soften my voice. They slow down the growth of hair on my face. They make my body smooth all over." Chablis slid her hand from her breast down to her lap. "And my candy shrinks, honey, but I still have it. I ain't havin' no operation, child. I ain't studyin' that."

We were now crossing Liberty Street. Chablis's blouse was still wide open, exposing her breast not only to me but to half a dozen pedestrians. I had no idea how far she intended to go, but I feared the worst. I kept one eye on the traffic, the other on her. The back of my neck began to feel warm. "You don't have to show me your candy," I said. "Not here, I mean. I mean, not now. Or ever."

Chablis laughed. "Oh, I'm embarrassin' you. I'm makin' you all nervous."

"No, not really," I said.

"Child, don't lie to me. Your face is turnin' *ray*yid." She began to button up her blouse. "But don't worry, I ain't no stripper. At least now I know you ain't gonna be callin' me no man."

We pulled into Crawford Square, one of the two squares in Savannah that fell within the black section of town. Of the city's twenty-one squares, it was one of the smallest and most picturesque. It was surrounded by humble wooden buildings. In its center, instead of a monument or a fountain, there was a small playground. A huge, gnarled live oak spread its branches over a small basketball court where several boys were playing. Chablis pointed to a neatly restored four-story wooden house on the far side of the square.

"Y-e-e-e-s, child," she said. "Miss Myra's shots are startin' to do their thing. I'm feelin' that boost of energy. I'm gettin' that surge of femininity. Got to go and be with my boyfriend, now, 'cause in a couple of hours I'm gonna feel like the bitch of all time. That always happens too. I get to feelin' like the last bitch on earth, and until that passes I cannot stand to be touched."

Chablis stepped out of the car. "Thank you for bein' my chauffeur and everything," she said.

"My pleasure," I said.

"You should come and see the show sometime. I put my face on, and I get into my gowns."

"I'd like to see that."

" 'Cause, right now, y'see, I'm just little old Chablis. Just a simple girl. But when I get it together, I turn into *The Lady* Chablis. And I'm good, child, real good! I'm a beauty queen, you know. I been crowned in four beauty pageants. I've got titles. Lots of 'em. Right now you are lookin' at the Grand Empress of Savannah! That's who you had in your car today."

"Well, I'm honored," I said.

"Miss Gay Georgia, too, I won that one also. And Miss Gay Dixieland and Miss Gay World. I've been all of them, honey. I am serious, child." The Grand Empress turned and ascended the steps of her house. As she did, she put an extra measure of swing in her hips, an extra bounce in her stride.

—

It was not until I was halfway home that I realized Chablis had forgotten to tell me where it was she performed her act. If I had put the slightest effort into it, I could have found out. In a town the size of Savannah, there could not have been more than a couple of nightspots that featured drag shows. But I let it go. Not that Chablis didn't fascinate me; she haunted me. And she was definitely a she, not a he. I felt no tendency to stumble self-consciously over pronouns in her case. She had removed any trace of masculinity, and in that sexual limbo of hers she was a disturbing presence, one that challenged all the natural responses. A few weeks later, the telephone rang midmorning.

"Ooooo, child, I am some kinda mad at you! You ain't come to see my show!"

"Is this Chablis?" I said.

"Yes, honey! I just been to Miss Myra for my feminine booster shot."

"Would you like a ride home?" I asked.

"Well, *yay*yiss. I guess I done trained you right."

I came downstairs and we got into the car. "I would have come to see you," I said, "but you didn't tell me where you did your show."

"I didn't?" she said. "I'm at the Pickup, honey. That's a gay bar on Congress Street. Three nights a week. Me and three other girls. You may not be into drag shows, but you'll never know the real Chablis till you see me shake my butt and run my mouth up on that stage. And the way things are goin', you ain't gonna get the chance if you wait much longer."

"Why not?" I asked.

" 'Cause I'm fixin' to read my boss, and I might even do it during the show tonight. I always say whatever comes into my head, and I never know who or what it's gonna be about. Anyhow, my boss ain't on the top of my list right now. Him and me is about to have words."

"On the subject of what?" I asked.

"Money. My salary's two hundred and fifty dollars a week, but I ain't complainin' about that, 'cause it's for only three nights' work, and with tips it gives me just enough to live on. But I'm the only one that gets a regular salary. The other girls get twelve dollars and fifty cents a show, and that's damn pitiful. Last week, two shows had to be canceled when the D.J. didn't show up, and we were standing there with our faces all made up and our gowns zipped, and the boss didn't give those girls a dime. Oh, child, he's gonna hear from me!"

"And when he does?"

"There's no tellin'. My ass could be out the door."

"What will you do then?"

"Make guest appearances. I can get bookings in Atlanta,

Jacksonville, Columbia, Mobile, Montgomery—all those places. The South is one big drag show, honey, and they all know The Lady. They all know The Doll." Chablis looked coyly at me. "So, if I get my ass fired tonight, child, you're gonna have to travel if you wanna see me do my shit."

"Then I guess I'd better go to the Pickup tonight," I said.

"I guess you better had, honey."

Chablis touched my arm as we drew up in front of her house. "Look over there," she said. "There's somethin' I wanna show you."

A young blond man was leaning under the hood of an old car. He was stripped to the waist; his muscular torso was smudged with grease and glistening with perspiration. Two boys sat on the curb, watching him work on the car. "That's my boyfriend," said Chablis. "That's Jeff. He's the hunk I told you about. Come, I want you to meet him."

This, then, was the one who, as Chablis had put it, satisfied her every need. It was hard to imagine exactly what those needs might be, harder still to envision what sort of person would satisfy them. Yet, apparently, here he was. By all outward appearances he was normal, even wholesome. He broke into a broad grin when he saw Chablis.

"I think the trouble's in the alternator, Sugar," he said. He wiped his hands on his pants. "I'll get it workin' somehow, and then we can take a spin."

Chablis hooked a finger through his belt and pulled him toward her. She kissed his neck. "It's okay if you can't fix it, baby," she said. "We got us a new chauffeur and limo. Say hello."

Jeff smiled. "Hey," he said, extending his hand. "You better watch yourself, or Chablis is liable to start running your life too. But I guess worse things could happen to you." He slipped his arm around Chablis's waist.

Chablis put her chin on his shoulder and looked into his blue eyes. "You ready for lunch, baby?" she said.

Jeff cupped his hand around her buttock and squeezed it. "I already ate," he said.

She leaned into his body. "You *know* you ain't done eatin' yet, baby!"

"Soon as I get this engine running, I'll come in. I promise. You go ahead."

Chablis turned away with a mock pout. "My engine's already runnin', baby, but that's okay. You go play with your car. I'll be havin' lunch with my new chauffeur." She linked her arm in mine. "Come on, child, keep me company."

—

I was so taken by the situation at this point that I could not muster even a polite refusal. I gave in at once, and in a few moments we were sitting in Chablis's living room having a plate of tuna salad and a glass of Coca-Cola. The apartment was light and airy and comfortably furnished. The front windows looked out through the foliage of a magnificent oak into the square. There were two matador prints on the wall, a shag rug on the floor, and an Aretha Franklin record playing softly on the stereo. From the sofa where she sat, Chablis could look out a side window and see Jeff working on the car in the street below.

"My baby treats me like a goddess!" she said. "He leaves little notes all over the house sayin' how much he loves me. And I tell you, he is some kinda good up under them covers! The man is out to please, honey, and he does just that to The Doll!" Chablis stirred the ice in her Coke with her finger. "He's straight, you know. He's not gay. He attracts both men and women, but he's only into women. 'Course, my friends say, Well, how can he be straight if he goes with you? And I say, As long as I'm gettin' my fair share, I ain't gonna be askin' why."

She took a sip of her Coke and licked her lips.

"What sort of men do you attract?" I asked.

"That depends what's goin' on with me and my hormone shots. I've gone on them and off them, and they make a big difference. When I'm on them I attract very masculine men—men with girlfriends, men with wives and children. When I go off them for a while, my masculinity comes back a little and I get to feelin' like a tomboy. That's when I attract the gays. Parts of me get excited that usually don't. When I'm in my tomboy mood, watch out, 'cause I play with everybody, even the nelliest fags. If I think they're cute, I'm gonna tease and everything. There are times when I can be really butch."

As she said this, Chablis leaned forward and put her elbows on her knees. The cadence in her voice became more clipped, and the muscles in her face tightened. She moved her head and shoulders now with the jauntiness of a boxer. For the first time, the boy inside of her came to the surface.

"But then I go back to Miss Myra, honey," she said, "and I get a hormone refill. I become feminine again, and I attract the masculine men." She settled back into the sofa. The lines in her face softened as I watched, and her body became languid again. The boy vanished. Chablis was Chablis again. She smiled.

"I don't overdo the hormones," she said. "When I get too much of them, I don't climax. So I get off them now and then just to relieve the tension. I don't like to be lifeless down there. I take just enough hormones to give me that feminine glow and keep a chest on me."

Chablis went into the bedroom and came back carrying a black dress and a cigar box full of bugle beads. "You don't mind if I do a little sewin', do you, honey?" She threaded a short string of beads and stitched it to the dress. "A girl's gotta sparkle!" She shook the dress. Hundreds of bugle beads swayed and glittered. She strung some more beads, then looked up from her threading. "Ever put on a dress?"

"No," I said.

"Never even wanted to?"

"No."

"Well, honey, I never wanted to wear anything else! I been into women's clothes so long I have no idea what men's size I am. I'm serious. I gave up on men's clothes when I was sixteen. I started puttin' on makeup and wearin' little earrings to school, and slacks and blouses. For me it was the natural thing to do. I was always effeminate, and I was always called a sissy or a fag or a girl. So I didn't feel I had anything to hide. And I just liked girls' clothes."

"How did your family take all this?" I asked.

"My father and my mother were divorced when I was five.

I grew up with my mother, and I would visit my father up north every summer. He hated the way I was. His whole side of the family hated me. When he died, I went to his funeral in a dress, and I had this gorgeous white boy on my arm. They were appalled, honey, they were horrified! Especially my aunt. She started in on me at the funeral in front of everybody, and I told her to get out of my face or I'd say something about her own son she might not want to hear. So I stay away from that side of the family, honey. I don't clientele with them."

"Clientele?"

"Yeah, I don't have anything to do with them. I don't mess with them. Mama's different though. She has a big ol' photograph of me bein' crowned Miss World, and it's hangin' in her living room. She taught me not to worry about things that don't matter. She has a motto that I love: 'Two tears in a bucket. Motherfuck it.' That's Mama, she's a okay girl."

Chablis turned up the sound on Aretha Franklin and held the dress up to herself as she stood before a full-length mirror. She churned her hips in time to the music. The beads bounced. "*Yay*yiss, honey! When the drums roll, the bugle beads *floooowwww*! Look at them beads, baby! *Flaw*less!" She turned toward me again. "You *sure* you never wanted to put on a dress?"

"Yes, I'm sure," I said. "What makes you think I would?"

"Oh, nothin'. But you never can tell. That much I've learned, honey! I used to go to straight parties in Atlanta. They'd pay me a hundred dollars. I'd be announced at the door, you know, as Tina Turner or Donna Summer, and then I'd mix with the guests. Everybody knew I was really a drag queen. But I'd look like Tina or Donna, because I'd be wearin' a wig. I'd talk like Chablis, though, and I'd have a good time and so would they. Anyway, these gorgeous macho men would come up to me and ask for my phone number, and *ooooo!* I'd go home all excited. Then a couple days later they would call for a date. Well, honey, come to find out most of them really wanted me to dress 'em up in panty hose and walk all over 'em in high-heeled shoes!

"So you never can tell, child. You never know. When I see a gorgeous hunk, honey, I don't assume nothin'. More men are into dresses than you think. Us upfront drag queens is just the tip of the iceberg. Just the teeniest tip!"

"Do you ever feel like going out in the street in a suit and tie?" I asked. "Just for the hell of it?"

"If I went out without my drag, honey, those rednecks would clock me for the big sissy I am and kick my ass. I am serious. I'd be more paranoid out of drag than in it. But there's somethin' else that does worry me. Here in Savannah, I mean. Know what it is? Walkin' down the street as a couple with a white boy. *That* makes me paranoid in Savannah."

"Don't you ever date blacks? Don't you ever go to black bars?"

"No-no-no. I don't go up in there, child. That's something y'mama don't play. Uh-uh, I don't play up in them black bars, baby. Black boys will hit on you just like that the minute you walk in. They try to make a move on you and 'Hey, Mama!' you and 'Honey' you to death. I don't play that. Black boys are so aggressive, honey. It's nothin' for them to come up and start touchin' you and hittin' on you and stuff, even if you're with somebody.

"Oh, I know black boys have their points, honey. I had a white roommate in Atlanta once, a real girl, and she *loved* black men. You know how those white girls get when they get a piece of black dick, honey. Black dick will wear you out! It will make you wanna write all your checks."

Chablis stitched a string of beads onto the dress. "That's just another reason I like my white boys," she said. "Plus, when black boys find out my T, honey, they be ready to kick my ass."

"Your T?"

"Yeah, my T. My thing, my business, what's goin' on in my life."

"You mean, you've dated guys without telling them about yourself?"

"Y-e-e-e-s, honey. And when they find out, they either

kick my ass or they wanna *love* me. They reach down there to feel somethin' soft and wet, and they feel somethin' else that ain't so soft and ain't so wet. Know what I mean?"

"Then what happens?"

"One black guy put a gun to my head. We'd partied for hours, and he'd spent lots of money on me and showed me off to all his friends and everything. At the end of the night we went home and was lyin' in bed just huggin' and kissin' fully clothed, and he kept wantin' to touch me down there, and I kept sayin' no-no-no. And he kept sayin', 'Why won't you let me touch you down there?' And I said, 'I promise you, you don't want to be touchin' me down there, child.' And we went back to huggin' and kissin' again, and then he finally caught me off guard and touched me down there. And before I knew it, he pulled a gun and put it to my head. He said, 'I'll kill you, you sonofabitch! I'll fuckin' blow your damn brains out! You made a big fool out of me!' I told him nobody knew nothin'. I said, 'You didn't even know, and you were the closest thing to me, so let's just leave it at that. We had a good time, child, and if you're gonna blow my brains out, go ahead and blow 'em out and get it over with and get that gun out of my face because you're scarin' me to death.' When I made that comment he laughed. And he said, 'I'll admit I've had more fun with you than I've had with any bitch. I'm gonna let you slide this time. But you better not pull that shit with nobody else or you're gonna get hurt.' That's why I don't play up in them black bars, honey. I don't need no gun to my head."

"What do white men do when they find out about your T?" I asked.

"Jeff didn't know when he first met me. I was in this straight club. I had gone there with a bunch of my girlfriends. One of my roommates was a stripper—she was a real girl—and she would do her strip show and I would do my drag show, and then we'd meet and go out to the straight bars and have a good time. I was just sittin' at the bar havin' my cocktail and smokin' my cigarette, and I saw Jeff. He was tall and blond and gorgeous, and he just kept watchin' me.

I said to myself, 'No, Chablis, don't even try. Don't mess with this straight man, 'cause this man is too tall. He will wrap you in a knot, girl!' He sent a drink over, and I just nodded and thanked him. Then he came over and we started talkin'. He asked me to dance, and we danced. My girlfriends saw him and they all wanted to trade boys with me. Later we all went to my place and sat around and got high all night. Everybody was coupled off, just layin' on their boyfriends, but there was no sex at all. When Jeff got ready to leave, he asked for my phone number, and I gave it to him. I'd forgotten he didn't know, because I was carryin' on, sayin' 'Miss *Thing!*' and 'Yeah, *girl!*' So it didn't even occur to me he didn't know. He called the next day and asked me to go out.

"It was so romantic. I bought a new dress, and we went to a ballroom that had a live band. Afterward, we went back to my place and started kissin'. I realized I had to tell him, but I decided not to do it till the next night. Well, the next night he took me to a basketball game, and I ran into one of my old boyfriends. This old boyfriend was the insanely jealous type, which is why I had to leave him in the first place. So he started a bunch of shit, sayin', 'That's a drag queen you're with.' And that's how Jeff found out. He was so hurt he just walked off and left me there. I didn't hear from him for a week. Then he called me. He said he wasn't into men. I said, 'I'm not a man, bitch, don't call me no man!' Then he asked me, 'Well, what do you got between your legs?' I said, 'That's for me to know and for you to find out.' So he said, 'Well, whatever you are, I like you. I can't get you off my mind, and as long as we can be friends, I want to see you again.'

"I said that was fine with me. So he started comin' on my job and watchin' me do shows, and he got hooked. After a while, we started having sex, and we became lovers. I even went to see his parents. They live out on the southside. They're Baptists, honey, and they thought I was Jeff's girlfriend Chris. I had Thanksgiving dinner with them and Christmas too, and they liked me and had no earthly idea.

But after a few months, they realized I was not just a passing fling. Their son was really in love with me. That's when they had a problem: I was black. They started watchin' me very closely. I could feel it. They were lookin' to catch my ass in the slightest mistake. I really had to be on my guard. Then one time they acted very strangely toward me. They were givin' me funny looks, child. I could tell somethin' was wrong. Jeff's mama got me alone after dinner. She said, 'Chris, let's you and me just sit here in the living room and have a little talk.' Honey, the ol' girl was nervous as a cat.

"She said, 'Chris, there's something I've been wondering about. It's something that I know is very private with you, and I respect your privacy. But my son is involved with you, and I have to know. I want you to answer me truthfully.' Well, child, my heart nearly stopped. I looked around just to check out where the door was, in case I had to get outta there real fast. Then she said, 'Tell me. Honestly. Are you pregnant?'

"Well, I was so relieved. For the first time in my life I didn't have an answer. My mouth dropped open, and I grabbed my stomach. When I did that, she screamed and ran out of the room.

"I just sat there for a while, not knowin' what to do. I could hear all kinds of carryin' on at the other end of the house. I sat there alone for about ten minutes. Then Jeff walked in with the cutest little grin on his face. He said, 'Okay, Sugar. Everything's fine. Let's go.' "

"When we got outside, he was still grinnin', and I said, 'What the hell was goin' on in there? For a minute I thought your mama found out my T.' Jeff put his arm around me. 'Whatever you said, baby, you said it right. Look what we got!' Child, he pulled out the biggest wad of money I ever saw. He had eight one-hundred-dollar bills! 'It's from Dad,' he said. 'To pay for your abortion.' "

Chablis clapped her hands. "I took the money them white folks gave us to murder their unborn grandchild, and I bought that color TV sittin' over there and that videocassette player too. And with what was left over, I went out and got me the raunchiest little sequined dress I could find, so in case they ever do find out who I am, I can shake my ass in their face and tell them, 'Thanks from the bottom of our interracial baby's dead little heart!"

Chablis got up and went over to the window. "Ain't you finished yet, honey?" she called. Jeff looked up from the street below. He was standing in front of the car. The two boys sat in the front seat, gunning the engine. He made a V sign. "Be there in a second," he said.

Chablis turned back from the window. "Y-e-e-e-s, child! That abortion was some kinda good. I toyed with the idea of takin' Jeff's folks to court for attempted fuckin' murder. If you pay to have somebody spiked, honey, that's attempted murder, ain't it?"

"Could be," I said, "under the right circumstances."

"Well, I didn't do it, 'cause I didn't want to hurt Jeff. And also 'cause I wasn't finished with them two motherfuckers. No, baby! Six months later, we went back and convinced them I was pregnant all over again. That got us another eight hundred, which paid for a few more gowns and a *flawless* weekend up in Charleston. But that's gotta be the last of it. If we try it again, it'll dawn on them that it would be cheaper just to pay somebody to shoot me and throw me off the Talmadge Bridge."

Chablis put the dress aside and closed the cover on the bugle-bead box. "I don't see my in-laws anymore. But Jeff and me are closer than ever. Someday, he'll go back to wantin' girls, but I'm prepared for that. I just don't want him to leave me and go to a guy. I want him to go back to girls. If he goes to a guy, I'd feel awful bad. I dated one guy, and when we broke up he started goin' with men. That hurt me so bad, and he couldn't understand why. I tried to tell him: I'm a woman. Treat me that way, it's the way I treat myself. I want a man who wants a woman, not a man who wants a man."

Jeff appeared in the doorway.

"Well, thank goodness," Chablis said. "I was gettin' tired of waitin' on you. Another minute, and I was gonna start hittin' on my new chauffeur. I am some kinda ready for you, baby." Jeff lifted one of her feet and removed her sandal. She lay back on the sofa. " 'Cause Miss Myra's shots are startin' to kick in, honey," she said softly. He massaged her bare foot and stared into her eyes. "M-m-m-m-m. Y-e-e-e-s, baby," she said.

I got up quietly and took my leave. As I closed the door behind me, I could hear Chablis murmuring. "Yes, child. *Yaaaa*yyiss, baby! M-m-m-m-m-m-m!"

—

The Pickup occupied a loft building on Congress Street. I could hear the *thump-thump-thump* of disco music as I approached the club's front door. Inside, a short-haired woman wearing jeans and a work shirt sat on a stool chatting with a uniformed policeman. A handwritten sign on the wall read $15 MEMBERSHIP FEE, but she waved me in without taking any money.

The ground floor had a long, dimly lit bar and a dance floor with flashing lights and booming music. The place was crowded with young men in casual but, for the most part, conservative attire. A poster by the entrance announced the featured appearance of The Lady Chablis for two shows, at eleven o'clock and one. The three-dollar admission charge was collected by a thin man who wore a baseball cap over his stringy waist-length hair. "The overture's already started," he said.

The room upstairs was a narrow, low-ceilinged space with a bar at one end and a small stage and runway at the other. A revolving mirrored ball hung from the ceiling. About fifty people, including a number of couples, were taking their seats amid the din of the recorded overture—a scratchy, fast-paced medley of Broadway tunes played at extremely high volume in order to drown out the disco beat from below. As the overture ended, the room went black. The beat shifted to the pulsating rhythms of Natalie Cole's "Jump Start."

A spotlight hovered over the stage and then dipped. Chablis suddenly burst into view, looking like raging fire in a skimpy sequined dress with jagged red, yellow, and orange flamelike fringes hanging from it. She wore huge earrings and a wig of long black curls. The audience cheered as she strutted down the runway, working every nuance of the rhythm, shaking her behind like a pom-pom, whipping it from side to side. She looked over her shoulder with an expression of supreme sassiness. She was a minx, a temptress. She danced superbly, mouthing the words to the song and smiling as if tasting something delicious. The look in her eyes was lighthearted and outrageous. It seemed to say: If you thought that last bump was vulgar, honey, watch *this* one! One by one, her fans rose out of the audience and moved to the edge of the runway. They held out dollar bills folded lengthwise. Chablis accepted their offerings without missing a beat, taking the money in her hands or allowing them the campy pleasure of slipping it into her cleavage. As the song came to an end, she exited to cheers and whistles and stomping feet.

In a moment, Chablis's crackling voice came over the loudspeaker. "Hey, bitches!" she said.

Members of the audience called back, "Hey, bitch!"

Chablis returned to the stage carrying a microphone in her hand. She was dabbing perspiration from her neck and chest. "Ooooo, child! I am sweatin', honey! I truly am. And I'm not ashamed of it either. I want all you white folks to see how hard I'm workin' for you."

She wriggled as the audience cheered.

"I need another napkin, honey! Who's gonna give me one? Whoever gives me a napkin wins a prize, and I ain't sayin' what that prize is until you win it." A napkin was handed up from the audience. "Thank you, baby. You are a true gentleman. Yes, you are, honey. I am serious! And you win the prize. You get to eat my pussy for the rest of my life. Okay?"

The audience howled.

"Yes, honey. I am sweatin', but I'm gonna have to slow down soon. If I don't, the doctor says I'm gonna have me another miscarriage. Yes, honey, I am with child again! My due date is gettin' closer, and my young'un is droppin' lower and lower. It's tough dancin' in this heat when you're pregnant, you know. Have you ever tried it? Try gettin' pregnant, like me, and then come up here and dance, honey. Child, you'll be wore out! Are my feet swellin'? Can you see 'em? Are they swellin'? You know how your mama's did when she was pregnant with you? Do my feet look that way?"

The audience cried out, "No!"

"I hope not, child, 'cause your mama had some ugly feet when she was carryin' you." Hoots and whistles from the audience. "Just kiddin'," she said.

"I got a business deal to offer all you white boys. My husband's folks won't pay for no more abortions, and we're gettin' hard up for cash. Take me home to meet your mama and daddy, and tell them I am pregnant with your baby and see how fast they come up with the money. I'll split it with you fifty-fifty. You don't think they'd do it? Guess again, honey. My husband's daddy is a Baptist minister, and he's paid for it twice already. That's mass murder, child. I am serious!"

Chablis walked farther out toward the end of the runway, but after a few steps, the microphone cord snagged and stopped her short. She tugged at it, but it would not come any farther. She turned toward the D.J.'s booth. "Michael! Miss Thing!" She tugged again. "Miss Thing, you ain't fixed this cord yet?" She looked to the audience. "Now I ask you. Wouldn't you think Burt, the man that owns this damn club, would fix this cord so I could come all the way out into the audience and be closer to you? So I could touch you? So you could get those extra vibes?"

A chorus of scattered yeahs came from the audience.

"If y'all can't do better than that, you can take your damn tired asses on home. I'm serious. Now lemme hear you holler, 'Yeah, bitch!' "

"*Yeah, bitch!*"

"Must be somethin' wrong with my ears, child. I didn't hear nothin'."

"YEAH, BITCH!"

"That's better. Y-e-e-e-s, child! Now I can feel your presence." Chablis ran her hand down the side of her dress and shimmied. "Yes, I can feel you are here, child, even if I can't reach out and touch you the way I usually do and *would* do right now if it weren't for this sorry-ass cord."

Whistles and catcalls.

"Maybe Burt thinks I'll break down and get it fixed myself. Do you think I should? Do you? No way, baby! I ain't givin' up my coins for no cord, honey. Y'mama's gonna be shoppin' for *gowns*! Give me any length of cord you got, and I will play with her. Yes, girl. Long or short, I will play with your cord. Whatever size it *eeee*yiz, honey. 'Cause y'mama's gonna start actin' like the heterosexual pregnant white woman she is and keep her fuckin' money in her pocket!" The audience cheered. Chablis undulated in place. "Just kiddin', honey," she purred.

"Okay, gang, I want to thank you for coming tonight. If I offended anyone, two tears in a bucket, honey. Motherfuck it. Yes, child. We have a wonderful show lined up for you. We have a whole bevy of beautiful bitches, so I want you to put your hands together now and welcome to the stage, the—" Chablis looked down at a man and a woman sitting at a table by the edge of the runway.

"You two have been neckin' and carryin' on all through my number! No-no-no, that's all right, baby, I don't mind. Get it while you can, honey! But tell me somethin', girl, is he your husband or your boyfriend? He is? Well, I think I should tell you, him and me has been fuckin' since Christmastime. Yes, honey. He is the father of my baby. That's right, child. Where y'all from? Hilton Head! And what does the father of my baby do besides fuck real good? A lawyer! Ooooo, my young'un's gonna have a rich daddy! When you become a lawyer, honey, you get to have all that stuff after your name, don't you. Like 'Esquire.' And 'Attorney-at-Law.' I don't need nobody tellin' me about lawyers, child. You get messed up with reefer and the cops, honey, and you gonna know Esquires and Attorney-at-Laws. You gonna know lawyers. But your wife don't get none of that shit after her name, does she? She just gets to carry the baby, huh? Well, let me tell you something, child: I get something better after *my* name. I get applause, honey. And people yellin' 'Hey, bitch!' "

Chablis slinked along the runway as the audience cheered, "Hey, bitch!"

"And I get somethin' even better than that comin' after my *ass,*" she said. "I get some *fine* stuff comin' after my ass, child! I bet all you bitches wish you did too, don't you?" Chablis looked into the spotlight. "Miss Thing! Shine the light over there." Chablis pointed in my direction, and in a moment I was blinded by the spotlight.

"I want y'all to meet my new chauffeur!" she said. "Yes, child. My new white chauffeur, honey! He drives y'mama's black ass all over Savannah. Soon as he learns how to drive a little better, honey, we be gettin' a Rolls-Royce! That's right. Nothin's too good for The Lady! I am serious. Nothin's too good for The Doll. Okay, Miss Thing, that's enough with the light! Bring the light back to Mama! Thanks, honey. Now, I want y'all to enjoy the show. Have a good time. And don't let me catch none of you bitches layin' a hand on my new chauffeur. 'Cause if I catch you, child, you will have Chablis to deal with. That's right, honey. Me and my icepick." Chablis turned and undulated back up the runway. When she reached the curtain, she looked back over her shoulder and whispered into the microphone. "Just kiddin', honey!"

—

Chablis was followed by Julie Rae Carpenter, who was a foot taller and at least eighty pounds heavier. A curly-headed blonde, Julie Rae had a dimpled smile and wore a bright blue, ill-fitting taffeta dress that you could tell, from the puckered stitching, was homemade. She skipped and bounced and twice flung herself spread-eagle against the back wall for dramatic effect, but she did it without a hint of irony—and without a clue how embarrassing it was to watch her. About a dozen members of the audience gave

Julie Rae tips. An equal number got up and left. As I sat watching her, a waiter in a floppy straw hat tapped me on the knee. "Chablis asked me to bring you backstage," he said.

He led me around to a cramped dressing room shared by all the members of the show. They were adjusting their hair and makeup at a long dressing table. Chablis was wearing only panty hose. She caught my reflection in the mirror. "Hey, honey!" she said. "I hope you ain't mad at me after what I done to you out there, shinin' that light in your face and talkin' dirty and all."

"We're still friends," I said.

"That's good, honey. But I guess that lawyer from Hilton Head won't be comin' back soon. I was watchin' him the whole time, talkin' and neckin' with his fish while I was doin' my number, and, honey, I will not take that! Lucky for him he backed down when I got into his shit about it. 'Cause if he hadn't, I woulda got meaner." Chablis removed her wig and combed her natural hair into a pompadour. "I've gone as far as taken off my shoe and hit people over the head. To prove to them that, you know, don't let this dress fool you. Last weekend in Valdosta, a girl was talkin' real loud, and when I started in on her, she threw a beer at me. She was one of those real mean lesbians, honey; she was a pit-bull dyke. But what she failed to realize was that there was a whole pitcher of beer sittin' on her table. I baptized the bitch, honey! I baptized the bitch!"

"Well, how did your boss like being called a cheapskate?" I asked.

"Child, that was nothin'. I let him off easy, 'cause I remembered my pay envelope was downstairs at the bar. I was afraid he might not let me have it if I was too rough on him. I'll get him later though."

Julie Rae came off the stage and was followed by Stacey Brown, a tall, elegant black. Next up was Dawn Dupree, a statuesque blonde with long, straight hair and very modish clothes. Chablis told me Dawn was a professional seamstress. "She made the dress I just wore," she said. "Did you like it?"

"Very impressive," I said.

"It was perfect for my slut routine. But I'm doin' somethin' different for my second song. Somethin' just for you, honey, somethin' very demure. I'm gonna do my uptight pussy debutante number. In a floor-length gown. I'd wear pearls too, but I ain't that pure. Gonna have lots of rhinestones instead. The dress has a slit up the back too, all the way up to my ass. But I'm gonna move real slow and sedate, bein' the lady that I am. Slow dances are good for business. They make it easier for my fans to come up and give me tips. When you dance fast and dirty, it intimidates some of them. And it's hard for them to get to you, too, while you're jumpin' around. Fact, I gotta put that girl on quick, it's almost my turn."

Chablis riffled through a long rack of dresses.

"This is my drag, honey," she said. The rack held fifty or sixty dresses in a rainbow of colors, most of them sparkling with sequins and rhinestones. There were fluffs of marabou, ripples of velvet and satin, and clouds of tulle.

She held out a red strapless gown. "This is the dress I won Miss World in," she said. She pointed to a blue one. "And this one was my Miss Georgia dress. If you ever pass a dress shop and wanna be nice to The Doll, honey, just remember I'm a ladies' small, size six."

Chablis stood, virtually nude. Her torso was an ideal woman's shape, narrow-shouldered, full-breasted. Her hips were a bit on the slender side, but I noticed there were no bulges in her panty hose.

"Ooooo, *bayyy*by," she said. "I just clocked you checkin' out my pussy! You didn't see nothin', I hope."

"Nothing at all," I said.

"Good, 'cause if you ever see anything in my panties, child, you tell me. You say, 'Girl, your Kotex is showin!' and I will shift her, honey, 'cause I cannot *take* that! That is a ugly sight! That is a nasty-lookin' thing, honey, to be out there all painted with your dick showin'!"

Julie Rae looked up from her makeup. "Really, Chablis!" she said.

"That's why I wear a gaff," Chablis went on.

"What's a gaff?" I asked.

Chablis looked at me with genuine surprise. "You never heard of a gaff?"

"No, what is it?"

"A gaff is a girl's best friend," she said. "It holds her dick in place."

"Chablis!" Julie Rae blurted out through a mouthful of bobby pins.

"Sistuh hates it when I talk this way. Don't you, Miss Thing?" Julie Rae did not answer. She was piling her blond curls into a Gibson girl upsweep. Chablis turned back to me. "It's a trade secret, honey, and Miss Thing thinks I spoil the illusion when I talk about us girls havin' dicks and all."

Chablis picked up a small rectangle of pink cloth with two narrow elastic loops attached to it. "This is a gaff, honey. It's somethin' like a G-string. What you do is first you pull your stuff back between your legs, and then you step into the gaff and pull it all the way up. You shove your ovaries up inside you too—I call my testicles my ovaries, honey."

Chablis looked wide-eyed at me. "Child, you should *see* the look on your face!"

"I can't think of anything more painful than what you just described," I said.

"Then don't let me tell you what we do with duct tape!" Chablis did not wait for me to stop her. "Duct tape is for when you wanna be butt naked. You tape your stuff back inside the crack of your ass, honey, and nobody knows the difference. But you talk about pain! She is a painful girl to pull off! And gettin' a hard-on in that position ain't no picnic either."

Julie Rae slammed her hairbrush down and left the dressing room. "There goes Miss Thing all in a huff!" said Chablis. "She'll get over it though. She's a good girl and I love her and she knows it. And she's right, anyway. This bullshit ain't as easy as it looks. It takes me twenty minutes just to do a daytime face—eye shadow, eyeliner, mascara, rouge, lipstick. Twenty minutes, honey. And it takes a hour to get ready for the show."

Julie Rae came back into the dressing room. Chablis gave her a rueful look. "Okay, Miss Thing," she said, "I'm through talkin' that shit. I ain't givin' away no more secrets. I'm sorry I did it. Yes, I'm sorry, baby. All the way down to my real live pussy. Do you forgive me?" Julie Rae smiled in spite of herself. "Good, honey," said Chablis, " 'cause us girls has gotta stick together. Oh, child, there's my cue!"

Chablis took a midnight-blue evening gown off a hanger and slipped into it. The dress was high-necked and hung straight to the floor. A solid cape of rhinestones sparkled across her shoulders. "Zip me, honey," she said. I zipped her. There was, indeed, a slit halfway up the back. But the song was a slow-moving ballad, and Chablis swayed sinuously rather than bumped. She used her shoulders to express the emotion of the song, and her fans stood in a line to give her tips. When it was over, Chablis took the microphone again to thank the audience for coming. "If you liked the show," she said, "thank you from the bottom of my heart and just remember my name, The Lady Chablis. If you did not like the show, honey, my name is Nancy Reagan and go fuck yourself."

Chablis came backstage and took off the long gown. "My lawyer from Hilton Head learned his lesson," she said. "He tipped me twenty dollars." She put on a lime-green silk minidress with tiers of swaying beads. "Now it's time to go downstairs to the bar, pick up my money, and have an apple schnapps and a cigarette." She applied some lipstick. "Then I'll come back up for the second show, get into one of my nastiest bump dresses, and ream Burt's stingy ass from here to kingdom come!"

—

Downstairs, the disco music was deafening. I followed in Chablis's wake as she made her way through the crowd to the bar. She greeted her fans as they approached, turning her head so they could kiss her on her neck and not smudge her makeup or muss her hair.

"What, honey?" she said. "You missed the show? That's

okay. You can take that tip you was gonna give me and stuff it into my bosom right now. There you go. Ooooo, child! Thank you, honey. . . . Hey, baby, how y' doin'? . . . Okay, *girl*! Sistuh's lookin' *good*! . . . Oh, child, you still got that number you was here with last week? Yeah? Tell me quick! Pour the *tea,* girl. *Pour the tea!* Aw *right!* . . . No, honey, I did not bring my husband with me tonight. He's waitin' on me at home, savin' his big ol' hard-on just for me."

By the time Chablis reached the bar, her apple schnapps was waiting. She took it and raised her glass to the squat, thick-shouldered man standing next to her. "Hey, Burt," she said. "Two tears in a bucket!" She downed the drink.

Burt had a shiny bald head and sad eyes. "How you doing, Chablis?" he asked.

"Well, I ain't on food stamps yet," she said, "but I'm gettin' real close. It's a good thing y'all don't pay me any more than you do, or I might never qualify." Burt did not answer.

"Speakin' of which," she said, daintily holding out her hand, "may I have the envelope, please?" Burt gave her a small envelope.

"Thank you, honey," she said. "You comin' up to see the second show?"

"Yeah, I guess so," Burt said.

"That's good, 'cause I always do a better show after I've had my apple schnapps. And, honey, you *don't* wanna miss the second show tonight!" Chablis looked inside the envelope. "Where's the rest of it?" she said.

"The rest of what?" said Burt.

"My money. I'm a hundred dollars short. Y'all been takin' money out of my pay!"

"Oh, well, yeah," Burt said. "That was because of the two shows you didn't work. We didn't pay you for those."

A flash of anger sparkled in Chablis's eyes. "Burt, that's a buncha shit!" she said.

"What do y' mean?" said Burt.

"Maybe I wasn't in front of that spotlight, but I was in front of my makeup mirror, and that's work right there.

Then I caught a cab to come down here, and I got here on time. No one ever called me to tell me the shows were canceled. I get a salary. That's our agreement."

Burt gave Chablis a weary look. "If you don't work, Chablis, you don't get paid. That's the way it is."

"Burt, my rent is due, goddammit! How'm I gonna pay my rent?"

"You'll have to talk to Marilyn," said Burt. Marilyn was the bookkeeper.

"I ain't talkin' to nobody. I want my money!"

Burt sighed. "Chablis, I'm not going to argue with you. I'm tired. Fair is fair."

Chablis slammed her hand down on the bar. "Then fuck it," she said. "Watch this!" She turned and cut quickly through the crowd, pausing briefly for a whispered conference with Julie Rae. Then she charged up the stairs with Burt in close pursuit.

"Chablis!" Burt called after her. "What're you doing?"

"Give me my money!" she demanded.

"But you didn't work!"

"Yes, I did!"

In the dressing room, Chablis grabbed a handful of dresses off the rack. "I'm takin' my drag home," she said. "I'm quittin'!"

"Chablis, please don't," said Burt. He took hold of the dresses, and for a moment the two of them were locked in a tug-of-war.

"Don't you go pullin' my beads, child!" said Chablis. Burt, suddenly embarrassed, let go.

Julie Rae appeared in the doorway behind Burt. She was accompanied by a half dozen people she had brought up from downstairs. Chablis tossed the dresses over Burt's head. Julie Rae caught them and handed them out to the people in the hall. "Keep 'em coming, Chablis," she said. "We're with you, babe!"

Chablis took another handful of dresses from the rack, but this time Burt raised his arm to block her way. "Chablis," he said, "you're forgetting something. You borrowed a hundred dollars from us six weeks ago, and you haven't paid us back."

Chablis paused for a moment. "That's true," she said, "but you never gave me a deadline. You coulda warned me you were gonna cut my pay, especially when my rent was due. And somebody could have called to tell me the shows were canceled. I coulda got bookings somewhere else. I coulda went to Columbia. The tips in Columbia are *flawless*."

"Well, I'm sorry, Chablis," said Burt, "but I can't let you take anything out of here until you pay back the loan."

Chablis thrust a silver lamé dress at Burt. "Here!" she said. "Take this dress! It's worth a hundred dollars, and it'll make us even. Now I'm haulin' my shit outta here!"

Burt stared blankly at the dress. It was a piece of silver cloth no bigger than a tea towel. It hung limp in his hand. "What am I supposed to do with this?" he said.

"Wear it!" said Chablis. "And here's a little somethin' else, in case you wanna hide your dick while you got it on." She shoved a gaff into Burt's hand. Julie Rae squealed with delight.

Burt dropped the gaff with a look of disgust. "Chablis," he said, "the trouble with you is—"

"Don't start!" said Chablis, " 'Cause I know what the trouble with me is! The trouble with me is I buy a whole wardrobe of gowns, and then I spend hundreds of hours sewin' on beads and sequins and rhinestones, and I don't get paid for any of that. I buy records so I can learn new songs, and I get hormone shots for twenty dollars twice a month to maintain my feminine image, and nobody pays me for that either. Then I spend hours fixin' my hair and makin' my face and gettin' into my drag so I can come down to this filthy piss-hole of a place that looks like somebody's attic and do my best to create an illusion of glamour. Honey, the rafters in here are so low I'd be afraid to come out on that stage wearin' a tiara!" Chablis glared at Burt, her dark eyes blazing.

"Well, Chablis," he said, "if you—"

"The trouble with me is I work for a man who thinks he's doin' me a favor by lettin' me parade around on his stage. He thinks I have so much fun puttin' on dresses and shakin' my butt that I don't care if I get paid or not. Well, let me tell you somethin'. There are times I don't feel like puttin' on a dress or makin' my face. But I come down here and do it anyway, because it's my job. It's how I make my living. And I'll tell you somethin' else: It's damn hard work bein' a girl full time!"

"Chablis," said Burt. "You're not being fair. You know I think of you as family."

Chablis sighed. She had one hand on her hip and a sardonic smile on her face. "Sure, baby," she said softly. "I suppose that's why you got that sign down by the front door that says 'Fifteen Dollars Membership Fee.' The fee that only black folks are asked to pay, 'cause black folks are not welcome in this club as guests—only as the hired help. The hired help that don't always get paid."

Chablis took another handful of dresses off the rack. "Stand back, bitch," she said. "This member of the family is leavin' home!"

The hall outside the dressing room was now crowded. Chablis tossed out gown after gown. "Hold 'em up high, honey! Don't drag the drag! Hold 'em up over your head, baby!"

When the rack was empty, Chablis turned to Burt. He was still holding the silver lamé dress. "Don't forget your gaff, Burt," she said. "You're gonna need it to hide your dick when you wear that dress." Burt said nothing. Chablis shrugged. "Suit yourself," she said. "But when the time comes and you ain't got a gaff to wear, whatcha gonna do, huh? I'll let you in on a little trade secret. There's something else that works just as good as a gaff: Put on four pairs of panty hose. Do that, honey, and everyone'll swear you got a pussy!"

Chablis tossed the last dress to Julie Rae. "Okay, Miss Thing!" she said, "I am *ready*!" Then down the stairs she went, followed by a cascade of glitter and fluff. Chablis strutted out onto the dance floor, her long train of gowns floating behind her like a colorful, twinkling Chinese dragon. Other dancers joined the line, raising their arms to support the winding canopy of dresses. Chablis was radiant. "Ooooo, *child*!" she called out, "I wish my mama could see me now!" She bumped and wiggled and shook her butt. The gown-bearers fell into step behind her, hooting and hollering as Chablis led them snaking around the dance floor, into the bar, down its entire length, past the man with the baseball cap and the stringy hair, past the sign that read $15 MEMBERSHIP FEE and out into Congress Street.

She turned and headed east, still dancing to the music, her long train flowing out behind her. The streetlights glinted off the rhinestones and the sequins, igniting sparks of light in the billows of peach and red and green and white. "It's like I told you, honey," she called out as she passed me. "You're gonna have to travel if you wanna see me do my shit from now on. Macon, Augusta, Atlanta, Columbia. . . . They all know The Doll, honey! They all know Chablis!"

Traffic on Congress Street slowed to a crawl in order to take in the glittering procession. The air was filled with honks and whistles and shouts in a mixture of good-natured cheer and lusty derision. The motorists were unaware, of course, that the spectacle they were witnessing was that of the Grand Empress of Savannah parading every wig, gown, and gaff in her imperial wardrobe. Chablis waved to her subjects. "Sistuh's movin' out!" she shouted. "*Yay*yiss, honey! Mama's on the move! I am *serious,* child!"

Chapter 8

SWEET GEORGIA BROWN'S

"Lord, you Yankees are something else," said Joe Odom. "We do our best to set you on the straight and narrow, and look what happens. First you take up with folks like Luther Driggers, whose main claim to fame is he's gettin' ready to poison us all. Then you drive around in an automobile that ain't fit to take a hog to market in, and now you tell us you're hangin' out with a nigger drag queen. I mean, really! Your mama and daddy are gonna pitch a fit when they hear about this, and I reckon they'll blame it all on me."

Joe was seated at a table in a huge warehouse space that was soon to open its doors as Sweet Georgia Brown's, a piano bar with an 1890s atmosphere. Joe Odom was to be the proprietor, president, and featured performer in a three-man jazz combo. He was just now writing checks and handing them out to the workmen who were putting the finishing touches on the place. A carpenter was buffing the U-shaped oak bar to a lustrous sheen. In the center of the U, a white merry-go-round horse reared up over a hillock of liquor bottles. Mandy, who was to be part owner of the bar and a featured vocalist, stood on a ladder focusing spotlights on the bandstand, where Joe was having an afternoon scotch and signing checks.

Joe's parting from Emma's had been perfectly amicable. Under the circumstances, it had been the only gentlemanly thing he could have done. His part ownership of Emma's had drawn all of his creditors out of the woodwork, and they had pounced on the little bar with writs and lawsuits in the manner of depositors staging a run on a failing bank. Joe had become a liability to Emma's, so he withdrew and took the warehouse space across Bay Street. He was not really sure how Sweet Georgia Brown's would be any less a target of his creditors than Emma's had been. An indifferent shrug was the best answer he could give to that question.

Meanwhile, Joe and Mandy had been evicted from 101 East Oglethorpe Avenue for nonpayment of rent. They had taken up residence a few blocks away in a handsome white frame house on Pulaski Square. Joe's entourage followed him to his new house, and so did the tour buses. The only people who were unaware that Joe had moved into the house were the absentee owners and the real estate agent, John Thorsen, who had taken him through it. Joe had pretended to be undecided and in no particular hurry the afternoon Mr. Thorsen had shown him the empty house. The next day Mr. Thorsen departed for a six-month stay in England, and the day after that Joe moved in—furniture, piano, entourage, and all. He was a glorified squatter, but no one knew it at the time.

By the end of the first week, Joe was giving tours and lunches at three dollars a head. He greeted the tourists with a slightly altered version of the welcoming speech he had used at his other houses: "Good afternoon! My name is Joe Odom. I'm a tax lawyer, a real estate broker, and a piano player. I live in this house, which was built in 1842 by Francis Bartow, a Confederate general who died in what we like to call the War of Northern Aggression. Feel free to walk around and make yourselves at home. If you see a closed door, though, please don't open it, because you're likely to find dirty socks and unmade beds and maybe even people sleeping in them."

—

Mandy climbed down from the ladder. She was wearing a tight, floor-length beaded gown with a plunging neckline. A peacock feather was attached to her bejeweled headband. She had been trying on her Diamond Lil costume to go with the 1890s theme of the place.

"How do you like my look?" she said, striking a sexy pose against the piano.

"I like it just fine," said Joe.

"Marry it then," she said.

Joe gave Mandy a kiss. Then he went back to the business of writing checks. He gave one to the man who had installed the lights. He gave another to the carpenter and a third to the general contractor. Joe and the men bantered lightheartedly, as if all of them really believed the checks were good.

After the workmen had left, an old black man appeared beside Joe at the piano. He was leaning on a cane. He had been at the bar most of the afternoon, making coffee for the workers and keeping the place swept clean. "Quittin' time, Mr. Odom," he said. He cast a glance at the checkbook.

Joe shook his head. "Uh-uh, Chester. You don't want to fool with those things. Always insist on the real McCoy when you can get it." He pulled out his wallet and gave the old man the only bill in it, a twenty. The man thanked him and hobbled off.

"Now about these folks you've been consorting with," said Joe, turning his attention once again to me.

"I don't know," I said. "I kind of like the people I've been meeting in Savannah. I'll admit I might have to upgrade the car though."

"Then maybe there's hope after all," he said. He lit up a cigar. " 'Cause you know, Mandy and I are fixing to rent a house with a pool out in Hollywood for when they make the movie out of that book of yours. But it's starting to look like our costars are going to be nothing but a bunch of creeps. We need to do something about that."

"Who do you have in mind?" I asked. "The mayor?"

"Lord no, not him," said Joe. He thought for a moment. "We've got a lady staying with us at the house that you might be interested in. She writes a sex-therapy column for *Penthouse* magazine." He looked at me expectantly. "No? No."

I reached into my pocket and took out a note I had jotted to myself. "As it happens," I said, "I am about to widen my circle of acquaintances. See if you approve." I handed him the note. It read: "Jim Williams, Mercer House, 429 Bull Street, Tuesday 6:30 P.M."

Joe nodded with the solemnity of a jeweler appraising a rare gemstone. "Well now!" he said. "This is much better. So much better. Jim Williams is a stellar individual. He's brilliant. Successful. Much admired. A little arrogant, maybe. But rich. And the house ain't bad either."

Chapter 9

A WALKING STREAK OF SEX

And so it happened that I spent that extraordinary evening in Mercer House in the company of Jim Williams and his Fabergé trinkets, his pipe organ, his portraits, his Nazi banner, his game of Psycho Dice and—briefly but memorably—his tempestuous young friend, Danny Hansford.

"Well, what did you think?" Joe Odom asked me when I stopped in at Sweet Georgia Brown's afterward.

"I think I've met the young man you found in your bed," I said, "the one with the tattoos and the 'Fuck You' T-shirt. He works for Williams."

"So that's who it was," said Joe. "He must be the kid who drives that souped-up Camaro that's always parked in front of Mercer House. He hot-rods it all over town, whips around the squares like they were his own personal Indy 500."

Danny Hansford was unknown to most of the residents of Monterey Square. At best he was a nameless presence, someone seen entering and leaving Mercer House, parking and taking off in his black Camaro, wheels squealing. One of the few people who had met him was an art student named Corinne, who lived on the top floor of a townhouse just off the square. Corinne had soft white skin and a tumbleweed of auburn hair. She designed her own clothes, which were always black and usually emphasized her best features—her bosom and her buttocks. She breakfasted regularly at Clary's drugstore, and she was not ashamed to admit that she knew Danny Hansford. "He's a walking streak of sex," she told me.

Corinne had watched Danny from afar long before they had ever spoken. He was in his late teens, she surmised, roughly her own age. She was thrilled by his lean, muscular body, his tousled blond hair, and his tattoos. She was particularly taken with his walk, a cocky strut that said "Fuck you" as boldly as the T-shirt he wore so often. He was a motion study in energy and turbulence, never looking right or left or acknowledging the presence of other people on the street, except on one occasion that she vividly recalled.

She was crossing Monterey Square one afternoon when she heard the roar of Danny's Camaro coming down Bull Street. She quickened her step so as to put herself in front of Mercer House as he pulled up. He bounded out of the car and came face-to-face with her. He smiled shyly. Corinne congratulated herself on having put on a skintight jersey top and a skimpy skirt that morning. She stood squarely in his path and said hello. She asked if he lived in the big house.

"Yeah," he said, "I sure do. Wanna come in and see it?"

"You bet I did," Corinne told me months later in Clary's drugstore as she recounted in precise detail what happened after that.

She followed him up the walk, she said, her eyes fixed on the seat of his jeans, the back of his T-shirt, his arms. But when she stepped into the cool vastness of the entrance hall she forgot, momentarily, about all that and gaped in silence at the sight before her: the spiral stairs, the portraits, the tapestries, the crystal chandeliers, and the gleaming furniture.

"Good God," she murmured.

Danny stood with his hands in his pockets, rocking on his heels and eyeing Corinne. He had a boyish face, a pug nose, and sensuous lips that seemed to be fighting back a grin. "All this shit comes out of castles and palaces," he said.

"This *is* a castle," Corinne replied in an awed whisper.

"Yeah," said Danny, "and it's worth a couple million bucks too. Jackie Onassis tried to buy it off us once. She was the president's wife, y'know. But we told her, 'It ain't for sale, lady.' Man, we told that Jackie Onassis to fuck off." Danny laughed at the idea of it. He scratched his chest, hoisting his T-shirt slightly and revealing a glimpse of washboard stomach. "C'mon, I'll show you around."

They were alone in the house. As they walked from room to room, Danny gestured at the portraits on the wall. "All these guys are kings and queens," he said. "Every damn one of 'em. And the metal stuff is gold and silver too. Man, we got burglar alarms all over the place. Anybody tries to break in here, man, they're gonna get the shit kicked out of 'em. I hope I'm here when somebody tries it. *Yeahhhhhh!* 'Cause nobody fucks with me and gets away with it." Danny cut the air with a karate chop and then quick-kicked the imaginary intruder. *"Hung-GAH! Choong! Choong! Eat it, motherfucker!"*

They moved into the dining room, where Corinne paused before an oil portrait of a periwigged gentleman in a ruffled neck cloth. "Who's that?" she asked.

Danny looked up at the painting. "That fat sumbitch up there? He's a king, like I told you."

"The king of what?" she asked.

Danny shrugged. "The king of Europe."

Corinne started to say something in reply but caught herself. Danny glanced at her with a look of uncertainty and then abruptly headed back into the living room. "Hey," he said, "let's you and me have a drink. Then maybe we can go upstairs and shoot some roulette. Would ya like that?" He poured two tumblers of vodka and handed one to Corinne. Before she had taken three sips, he had drained his glass. He looked at her with an impish grin. "C'mon. Let's go upstairs."

In the ballroom on the second floor, they spun the roulette wheel a few times; then Danny pounded out a crude rendition of chopsticks on the pipe organ. Finally, he brought her into the master bedroom and took a plastic bag of marijuana out of his pocket. He rolled a fat joint.

"I got the best shit in Savannah," he said. "You can ask anybody. That's what they'll tell you. 'Danny Hansford's got great shit. It don't come any stronger.' I grow it in the garden out back and dry it in the microwave. It'll get you off for sure."

They smoked the joint. Corinne felt herself becoming lightheaded.

"Do you like me?" Danny asked, a note of tenderness in his voice.

"Uh-huh," she said.

He put his arms around her and stroked her back with both hands, caressing her throat lightly with kisses and sending a shiver down her spine. They tumbled onto the four-poster, and he began kissing her breasts while at the same time pushing her skirt up and pulling down her panties. She reached down to remove her shoes, but before she could do it, he was pressing against her, probing with his fingers, gently and insistently. With the other hand he unzipped his fly. He took her buttocks tightly in his hands and pulled her toward him as he thrust into her. She breathed the salty smell of his T-shirt and felt his belt buckle rubbing against her stomach. Their rising body heat enclosed them like a steamy towel.

It was over soon. He raised his head and looked at her. "That was great, wasn't it. Huh? You liked that, didn't you?"

"Uh-huh," she said. "Maybe next time we can even take our clothes off."

Corinne was not taken in by Danny's pretense of being the squire of Mercer House—she knew, as everyone in Savannah knew, that Jim Williams owned the house—but she played along, because the charade seemed to put spunk in Danny's swagger. Corinne sighed convincingly when Danny showed her the Jaguar XJ12 parked in the garage; she gasped when he opened a dresser drawer and showed her his "golden" watch and his "royal" cuff links. Corinne looked at him starry-eyed as they stood in the entrance hall saying goodbye. She told him she adored his castle and that he was a very handsome and sexy Prince Charming. Then the front door opened and Jim Williams walked in.

"Hey, Sport!" Williams said. He was in a cheery mood.

"We was just leavin'," Danny mumbled.

"What's your hurry? Stay for a drink. Introduce me to your pretty friend."

"We already had a drink," said Danny. His mood had turned sullen.

"Well, it won't hurt you to stick around a few minutes and be sociable," Williams replied amiably. "There's always time for that."

Williams introduced himself to Corinne and then walked into the living room with an air of such self-assurance that Danny and Corinne followed as if summoned by decree. Corinne told Williams she was a student at the Savannah College of Art and Design. Williams responded by telling several gossipy tales about various members of the SCAD faculty, much to Corinne's amusement. Danny sat on the edge of his chair, glowering.

Williams lit up a King Edward cigarillo. "I assume Danny has taken you on a tour of the house," he said. "Did he show you how to play Psycho Dice? . . . No? Ah! Then allow me!"

He took Corinne over to the backgammon table and sat her down. He explained the rules of the game and said that by concentrating on the dice, a person could improve the odds. He told Corinne about the scientists at Duke University and how their experiment had proved that if you really focused your mental energy you could make things happen—in dice or in just about anything. He glanced over at Danny, who was still sitting glumly in his chair. "Now, see, for example," Williams said slyly, "if we both put our minds to it, I mean really concentrate, we can probably get Danny to get up out of that chair and make himself useful by fixing us a drink." Danny got up wordlessly and left the room. Moments later the front door slammed with a house-shaking wallop.

Corinne jumped in her seat. Williams hardly flinched. He arched his eyebrows and smiled a bemused smile. "I guess the message was received," he said, "and returned to sender." He shook the dice and tossed them onto the green felt board.

Half an hour later, after having had a drink with Williams and played a few rounds of Psycho Dice, Corinne left Mercer House. Danny was standing by the curb, leaning against the fender of his black Camaro, his arms folded across his chest. Without taking his eyes off her, he reached down and opened the passenger door.

"Get in," he said.

It was late afternoon. Corinne had errands to do and plans for later on. She glanced at Danny's jeans, his T-shirt, his arms, and the smile that was beginning to creep across his face, and she got into the car. Danny made a ceremony of holding the door open and closing it politely. He walked around and got in.

Corinne patted his arm. "Okay, 'Sport,' " she said, "now, maybe you can tell me why you left in such a hurry."

Danny shrugged. "I don't like nobody making moves on a girl I'm with."

"Is that what you think Jim Williams was doing?"

"Yeah, and I don't go for that fuckin' shit."

"Let me tell you something," said Corinne. "I'm pretty good at knowing when somebody's making a pass at me. Jim Williams was not making a pass."

"He was bein' a wiseass."

"He was letting you know who's boss," she said.

Danny turned the key in the ignition. "Same difference. And, like I said, I don't dig that shit." He threw the car into gear and floored the accelerator. The car shot out from the curb with an ear-piercing squeal. Corinne grabbed the dashboard to brace herself. "Jesus Christ!" she said.

Danny swung around the corner of the square. A cloud of bluish-white smoke hung over the street in front of Mercer House.

"Buckle up!" Danny shouted. "You're gonna have the ride of your life!"

"No, I'm not!" Corinne answered. "Let me out! *Now!*"

"Later!" he said. "And don't worry. I ain't gonna kill ya. I'm a great driver, and this is the hottest damn car on the road. This baby is supercharged!" Danny was smiling triumphantly; his eyes were bright. His self-confidence had returned. If he was not exactly the master of Mercer House, at least he was king of the road.

Corinne breathed a sigh of resignation and settled back for the ride. "Okay," she said, "where are we going?"

"Out to Tybee," he said. "I want to show you something neat."

They sped east on the Islands Expressway toward the beach. Corinne looked at Danny, sizing him up. She preferred this cocky mood over the sullen one. "So tell me, what's your connection to Mercer House and Jim Williams?" she asked.

"I work for him," he said, "when I feel like it. Odd jobs and shit."

"Well, that sounds more like it," she said. "You didn't strike me as the stately homes type."

"I make good money, don't you worry. And if anybody hassles me, I'm gone, man. I don't take any shit."

"So I noticed."

"Yeah! Hey, I almost knocked that door off its hinges when I hauled ass, didn't I? I bet Jim was pissed."

"I wouldn't say that," said Corinne. "I think he got a charge out of it, which I thought was a little weird."

The bridge to Tybee Island lay up ahead. Danny suddenly gunned the engine and picked up a burst of speed. He swooped around the car ahead of him, leaving an open stretch of roadway to the bridge. "Hang on, now," he said. "This is where we really take off!" The car accelerated like a rocket. With a *whump* it hit a swayback bump in the road, and all four wheels lifted off the ground.

"Airborrrrrnnnne!!!!!" Danny howled.

"Jesus Christ," Corinne muttered as the car bounced back onto the road. "Is that what you brought me out here for?"

"Yeah! Neat, huh?" said Danny.

Corinne brushed the hair out of her face. "I need another drink."

They continued on to the DeSoto Beach Hotel, a somewhat seedy oceanfront motel that was popular with the young crowd. It had an open-air lounge with a pool, a rock band, and a tropical-style bar with a straw-hut roof. They ordered piña coladas and sat on the seawall to watch the surf and the people strolling on the beach. Within minutes, two good-looking young men came over, friends of Corinne's, fellow students at the Savannah College of Art and Design. While they talked, Danny remained silent. He became increasingly restive. He looked up the beach, down the beach. He fidgeted. He sighed. As soon as Corinne's friends said good-bye and walked away, he stood up.

"I got an idea," he said. "Bring your drink. We're goin' back into town."

That was fine with Corinne. She had things to do anyway. "You're not planning to fly over that bump again, I hope," she said.

"Nah, it only works in one direction." They got into the car and roared out of the parking lot, leaving a billowing back-blast of gravel and dust.

"Did I detect a teeny bit of jealousy back there?" Corinne asked.

"No, uh-uh."

"You didn't think they were 'making moves' on me, did you?"

"They were a couple of assholes is what they were."

Corinne did not answer. She was comparing Danny with her two friends. The other two were more clean-cut than Danny and better educated too; their families had money, and their futures were pretty much assured. Those two were probably not unlike the man she would eventually marry, whoever that might be. But neither one of them had a fraction of Danny's sex appeal. She looked at the Confederate flag tattoo on his arm, at his flat stomach, at the way he gripped the wheel with one hand and rested the other lightly on his upper thigh. He looked back at her and smiled.

"Hey," he said softly, "you know what? On the way back to town I'm gonna take you to the most beautiful place in Savannah. It's my favorite place to get high in the whole world."

He turned off Victory Drive and drove down a winding road through the gates of Bonaventure Cemetery. The late-afternoon sun filtered through the trees and cast soft, lengthening shadows. They walked down an avenue of oaks smoking a joint.

"Dreamy, isn't it?" said Corinne.

"Yeah," said Danny.

"What do you think about when you come here?" she asked.

"Dyin'," he said.

She laughed. "I mean, besides that."

"Bein' dead."

"That's horrible!" she said. "No, come on, really."

"I told you. I think about dyin' and bein' dead. What do *you* think about?"

"I think how peaceful it is. I think what a wonderful place this is to come to and escape from everything, to just cool out and relax and enjoy the serenity. But I never think about dead people. Looking at these old graves makes me think how generation after generation of the same family are all gathered together. And that makes me think about how life goes on, but not about dying. I never think about dying."

"Well, I do," said Danny. "I even think about what kind of grave I'm gonna be buried in. Like, see them big ol' tombstones over there? They belong to rich people. And see them other ones there—the little ones? Those are for poor people. If I die in Mercer House, I'll get to have one of the big ones."

"What a creepy thing to say."

"Jim Williams is rich," said Danny. "He'd buy me a big

tombstone." There was nothing joking or boastful in Danny's voice. He was simply speaking his mind.

"But you're not getting ready to die, are you?"

"Why not? I ain't got nothin' to live for."

"Everybody has something to live for," she said.

"Not if they're fucked up like me."

Corinne sat down on the moss-encrusted pedestal of a tall obelisk. She took Danny's hand and pulled him toward her. He sat down next to her. "We all have problems," she said, "but we don't go around bumming people out talking about dying."

"I'm different," said Danny. "I been on the street since I was fifteen. I quit school in the eighth grade. My family hates me. Bonnie, my girlfriend, won't marry me, 'cause I ain't got a full-time job."

"So you'd rather be dead, huh?"

Danny looked down at his feet and shrugged. "Maybe."

"Well, look at it this way. If you had died last night, you wouldn't have met me this afternoon. Right? And we wouldn't have fucked on that four-poster bed the way we did. That was something to live for, wasn't it?"

Danny took a long drag on the joint and handed it to her. She was sitting on the side of him that had the Confederate flag tattoo. He leaned against her and uttered a low growl.

"Well, was it?" she asked.

"Yeah, it was worth living for," he said, "but only if there's more where it came from." He slid his arm around her waist and kissed the back of her neck, growling softly and nibbling at her like a playful lion cub. She felt a tingle of pleasure. In a moment he was stroking her knee, rubbing her thigh, lifting her off the pedestal, and lowering her onto the ground. She squealed as he rolled on top of her. He lay lightly on her, supporting himself by his elbows to keep from pressing her too hard against the ground. Dried leaves crackled beneath them. She began to moan, louder and louder. Suddenly, he clapped his hand over her mouth and froze, motionless. Startled, she looked up and saw that he had lifted his head; he was peering out through the bushes. She could feel his heart pounding. He lay absolutely still, not moving a muscle. She heard voices. People were approaching. She turned her head and saw several pairs of legs walking along a path that would bring them to within a few feet of where they lay. She and Danny were only partly covered by the bushes. If the people looked in their direction as they passed, they would surely see them. She heard a middle-aged woman speaking in a complaining voice.

"Perpetual care means just what it says. It means taking care of things in perpetuity. Like pulling out weeds and sweeping up debris. Forever. I'm going to stop at the guardhouse and have a word with the groundskeeper before we leave."

They were twenty feet away now and coming closer. A man's voice replied. "They do a pretty fair job compared to most places. Anyhow, I can't imagine Granny minds a few weeds or a couple of twigs lying around."

"Well, I *do* mind," the woman persisted. "And I want to know that when I'm laid to rest, someone will tend the plot in perpetuity, as they've been paid to do."

The legs were walking right by them now. Corinne held her breath. "Suit yourself," said the man. "We'll wait for you in the car."

They had passed. They had not noticed. Danny relaxed his grip on Corinne's mouth and resumed having sex as easily as if he were picking up a conversation dropped in midsentence. Corinne was swept away by his staying power and by his ability throughout the entire terrifying interruption to maintain a rock-hard erection.

On the way back to the car he walked with a spring in his step. Corinne took his hand in hers. She had rescued him from morbid thoughts, and that pleased her. He was moody, all right, but what did that matter? She had found the perfect sexual playmate. He was aglow, and she was aglow—but for very different reasons, as she discovered when he turned to her in the car and asked, "Will you marry me?"

She was not so much taken aback as surprised at the absurdity of it. "But we just met three hours ago!" she said.

She started to laugh, but she realized almost at once, when she saw his expression suddenly turn grim, that his offer had been heartfelt. She had wounded him.

"You're gonna marry one of them two assholes at the beach, aren't you?" he said softly.

"No," she said. "I don't know them well enough either."

"Sure you do. They got money. They got an education. What else do you need to know?"

She had hurt him deeply, and she was crushed. She was touched that he was so desperate to be loved. "I had a wonderful time today," she said gently. "I really did. I—"

"But you won't marry me. You'll never marry me."

She struggled for words. "Well, but I . . . I certainly want to *see* you again. I mean, we can get together often and, you know, we can—"

She did not see the back of his hand coming at her until it struck her a glancing blow on the cheek. It would have landed with more force, but Danny had floored the accelerator at the same moment and swung sharply onto Abercorn Street, throwing her against the door and out of reach. They roared south on Abercorn, swerving from lane to lane, passing one car after another. It was getting dark.

Corinne cowered as far away from him as she could get. Her cheek felt numb. "Please take me home," she pleaded.

"When I'm goddamn good and ready," he snapped.

They sped south. Two miles, three miles, five miles. They sailed past the Mall, past Armstrong State College. Corinne felt dizzy. She could think only of Danny's death wish and that now he would kill them both. Surely the vodka, the piña coladas, and the marijuana had taken their toll. He would drive off the road; he would slam into another car. She was frightened just looking at him: He was so utterly changed. His jaw was set. A diabolical fire lit his eyes. He held the wheel in a ferocious grip. It all seemed like a horrible, surreal nightmare. Suddenly, his image began to flicker before her eyes—the back of his head, his shoulders, his arms, his face, his whole body—as if caught in the beam of a stroboscopic light. She was about to lose consciousness when she heard sirens. It was the police.

The rage drained out of Danny as quickly as it had flared up. He lifted his foot off the gas and pulled over onto the shoulder. Three squad cars quickly hemmed him in, blue lights flashing. The crackle of two-way radios filled the air. The policemen shouted at Danny and ordered him out of the car. He turned imploringly to Corinne, his face once again sweet, his voice childlike. "Get me out of this, will you?"

—

They did not see each other again after that. Corinne was still shaken by their encounter months later when she told me about it in Clary's drugstore. She had made mistakes before, she said, and she would make them again. But not like this, she hoped. She had watched Danny from afar for months—studied him, worshiped him, stalked him. In all that time, it never entered her mind that he might turn out to be so volatile. She had thought of him only as a walking streak of sex, and about that, at least, she had not been wrong.

Chapter 10

IT AIN'T BRAGGIN' IF Y'REALLY DONE IT

On the whole, the thirty-odd residents of Monterey Square regarded their neighbor Jim Williams with a respectful friendliness. Several were on his Christmas-party invitation list. Others were more wary and kept their distance. Virginia Duncan, who lived with her husband in a townhouse on Taylor Street, for example, still remembered the chill she felt when she came out of her house two years ago and saw the swastika hanging from Williams's window. John C. Lebey, a retired architect, had fought a number of acrimonious battles with Williams, all concerning what Williams described as Lebey's "destructive incompetence" in matters of architecture and historic preservation. So Mr. Lebey had no use for Jim Williams. But the Lebey-Williams feud was a mere quibble compared with the cold war that raged between Williams and his next-door neighbors, Lee and Emma Adler.

The Adlers lived in an elegant double townhouse that occupied the other of the two trust lots on the west side of Monterey Square. Their side windows looked directly across Wayne Street at Williams's parlor and the ballroom above. It was the Adlers' howling dog that had prompted Williams to play his thunderous version of César Franck's "Pièce Héroïque" on the organ. But the dog's bark was only one sour note in a whole medley of bitterness that existed between the two households.

Lee Adler, like Jim Williams, had played a central role in the restoration of Savannah's historic downtown. His approach was entirely different, however. While Williams's efforts had involved his own restoration of houses, Adler had been an organizer and fund-raiser who left the actual restoration work to others. Adler had helped create a revolving fund for the purpose of buying old houses that were in imminent danger of being razed; the houses were then sold as soon as possible to people who promised to restore them properly. Lee Adler's accomplishments had been so successful, and his participation so energetic, that he had emerged as a national spokesman for revolving funds and historic preservation. In recent years he had turned his attention to renovating old houses for poor blacks. He toured the country making speeches. He was elected to the board of the National Trust for Historic Preservation. He lunched at the White House. His name appeared frequently in *The New York Times* and in national magazines. Now in his mid-fifties, Lee Adler was probably the best-known Savannahian outside Savannah.

Lee Adler's national prominence inspired a fair amount of resentment in Savannah. It was widely felt, in Savannah at least, that Adler's manner was bombastic and peremptory, that he was an autocrat, and that he stepped on toes needlessly. He was accused, openly and behind his back, of taking more credit than was really due him for the renaissance of Savannah. It was said that he hogged the limelight, that he was insincere, and that his only interest in historic preservation was to use it as a means to gain fame and make money. Jim Williams was among those who felt this way about him.

Adler and Williams were outwardly civil, but just barely. Adler had been a member of the Telfair museum's board of directors when Jim Williams was president, and from time to time their animosity spilled out into the open at board meetings. On one occasion, Adler accused Williams of stealing furniture from the museum. Williams denied it and countercharged that Adler was trying to blacken the name of anyone who had more power over the museum's affairs than he did. Eventually, Williams engineered a plot that forced Adler off the board, and Adler never forgave him.

Williams was contemptuous of virtually everything about Lee Adler—his taste in art, his word of honor, even his house. A visitor once rang Williams's doorbell by mistake and asked if Mr. Adler was at home. Williams told the man, "Mr. Adler doesn't live here. He lives in *half* the double house next door."

Lee Adler was no less disparaging of Williams. He believed him to be fundamentally dishonest and said so. Furthermore, he suspected the Nazi flag episode was more than a lighthearted attempt to foil a crew of moviemakers. He let it be known that a letter addressed to Williams from the John Birch Society had once been delivered to his house. Adler was critical of Jim Williams's "decadent" life-style, but he was just curious enough about it to get out his binoculars and spy on one of Williams's all-male Christmas parties. Adler had clumsily forgotten to turn out the light behind himself and was silhouetted in the window. Williams saw him, waved, and drew his shutters.

In spite of all this, there were restraining factors that kept the two men on a civil footing most of the time. Lee Adler was Leopold Adler II, the grandson of the founder of Adler's department store, Savannah's answer to Saks Fifth Avenue, and his mother was a niece of Julius Rosenwald of the Sears Roebuck fortune. Emma Adler was the sole heir to the biggest block of stock in the Savannah Bank. She had been president of the Junior League and was an active member of several civic organizations. So, the reality of the situation was that both Jim Williams and the Adlers were prominent, influential, and rich. They lived in such close proximity and moved in so many of the same circles that they felt obliged to remain on cordial terms. Which was why, despite his loathing for them, Jim Williams always invited the Adlers to his Christmas parties. And why, even though they detested Williams in return, the Adlers always accepted.

—

Early one bright April morning, Lee Adler came toward me with a broad smile on his face and an arm outstretched in greeting. "Shake the hand that's going to shake the hand of the Prince of Wales!" he said.

Mr. Adler was making a jocular reference to an article in the morning paper announcing that he and his wife would be traveling to Washington at the end of the week to meet Prince Charles of England. The Adlers and the prince were to participate in a discussion of low-income housing. Adler assumed I had read the article, and of course I had. Most of Savannah had read it, and to judge from Mr. Adler's ebullient mood, he either did not know or did not care what certain people were saying about it.

"It's just another of Leopold's cheap, self-promotional ploys," Jim Williams said. But the rolling of eyes and clearing of throats was not limited to people who disliked Lee Adler. Katherine Gore, a lifelong friend of the Adlers, also found the news distasteful. "*I* would like to meet Prince Charles too," she said, "but I would never stoop so low to do it. Low-income housing, indeed!"

Adler and I were standing in Adler's office on the ground floor of his townhouse. This was the command post from which he directed his many projects in real estate and historic preservation. A telephone rang in another room. Somewhere a copy machine churned. The walls of his office were decorated with memorabilia of Adler's role in the remarkable renaissance of Savannah's historic district. The photographs documented parallel transformations that had taken place over the past twenty-five years: Savannah regaining the splendor of its youth and a youthful Lee Adler progressing by stages into silver-haired middle age.

Adler wore half-moon glasses and a pale, rumpled summer suit. His speech was a soft, cajoling drawl. We had met a week earlier at a garden party given by a local historian, and Adler had offered to take me on a tour of Savannah to show me, stage by stage, how Savannah had been saved from the wrecker's ball. As we got into his car, he let me know he was aware of all the carping going on behind his back.

"Do you know what the saying for the day is?" he asked. " *'It ain't braggin' if y'really done it!'* " He gave me a meaningful glance over the top of his glasses, as if to say: Never mind all the backbiting you've been hearing. It's sour grapes.

We pulled away from the curb and began moving through the streets at ten miles an hour. As we did, the visual treasures of Savannah flowed by in slow motion—townhouses, mansions, shadowed gardens, well-tended squares.

"Picture all of this deserted and empty," said Adler. "Imagine it run-down—windows broken, weatherboards unpainted and rotting, shutters falling off, roofs caving in. Think what the squares would look like if they were nothing but hard-packed dirt instead of grass and azaleas and beautiful landscaping. Because that's the way it used to be. That's why Lady Astor called Savannah 'a beautiful woman with a dirty face' when she came here after the Second World War. That's what Savannah had allowed itself to become. And what's frightening is that while it was happening, nobody gave one goddamn."

A truck behind us honked its horn. Adler pulled over to let it pass, then kept moving at a slow pace, continuing the story of Savannah's decline. Until the 1920s, he said, Savannah had remained basically intact—an architecturally exquisite nineteenth-century town. But the flight to the suburbs was just then beginning. People moved out of the lovely old houses downtown. They cut them into apartments, tore them down, or just boarded them up and left them empty. In those days all the money was being funneled into the development of the suburbs, which was fortunate for Savannah in one respect: It meant there was no clamor to bulldoze massive areas downtown for housing developments. Nor did Savannah have superhighways slicing through the center of it the way other cities did, because Savannah was not on the way to somewhere else. It was geographically the end of the line.

In the mid-1950s, almost a third of the old city was gone. Then in 1954, the owners of a funeral parlor announced plans to knock down a dilapidated tenement so they could use the space for a parking lot, and a number of concerned citizens rose up in protest. The tenement happened to be Davenport House, one of the finest examples of Federal architecture in America. It was a shambles at the time; eleven families were crowded into it. Seven ladies got together, Lee Adler's mother being one of them, and saved Davenport House and restored it. They then formed the Historic Savannah Foundation, and that was the beginning of Savannah's salvation.

In the early days, Historic Savannah had a vigilante committee that sounded the alarm when an old house was about to be demolished. But the committee had no power to prevent demolition of houses, or even to gain a stay of execution. All it could do was try to find some sympathetic soul who would buy the endangered building and restore it. Most of the time the house came down before the committee could find anybody to save it. It soon became clear that the only way to save old houses was to *buy* them. And that was when Lee Adler became involved.

"I was having breakfast one morning," he said. "It was December of 1959. I read in the newspaper that a row of four townhouses on Oglethorpe Avenue was about to be torn down. They were lovely. Built in 1855. They were known as the Mary Marshall Row. It was the same old story: A local wrecker had bought the houses in order to knock them down and sell the bricks. The *bricks*! You see, they're Savannah gray bricks, which are larger and more porous than ordinary bricks, and they have a very soft and beautiful color. They were kilned at the Hermitage Plantation on the Savannah River. They're not made anymore, and you can't duplicate them. They were selling for ten cents each at the time, more than three times the cost of an ordinary brick. Anyhow, the wrecker had already demolished the carriage houses, and the townhouses themselves would be gone in a matter of days."

Adler pulled over to the curb on Oglethorpe Avenue in front of Colonial Cemetery. Across the street stood a handsome row of four brick townhouses, each with a stoop of white marble steps leading up to the main entrance on the second floor. The bricks were a muted, grayish red. "There they are," he said, "fully restored. When I came to look at them that day, the windows were out, the doors were gone, and the steps were in bad shape. The bricks from the carriage houses were piled up in the backyard. I went into one of the houses and climbed up to the third floor and looked out at the magnificent view. And I thought, 'This can't be allowed to happen.' "

Adler paid a call on old Mr. Monroe, the wrecker, and told him he wanted to buy the whole row. Mr. Monroe told him he could get the bricks to him in six weeks. "I don't want you to *touch* those bricks!" Adler replied. "I want you to leave them right where they are." Mr. Monroe agreed, but said Adler would have to buy the land too; he could have the whole row, bricks and land, for $54,000. So Adler and three other men signed a note for it. Then they wrote a prospectus and took it to Historic Savannah Foundation, which had three hundred members at the time, proposing that the foundation buy the row—at a cost of $180 a member. "My idea," said Adler, "was that the foundation would resell the houses to people who would agree to restore them. Historic Savannah went along with it." That was the beginning of the revolving fund.

It happened that the poet Conrad Aiken had lived as a child in the house right next to Marshall Row—at number 228, the house in which Aiken's father had shot his mother and then himself on that terrible morning in February 1901. Having spent most of his life up north, Aiken wanted to come back and live his last years in Savannah. So a millionaire friend, a man named Hy Sobiloff, bought and restored the house on the end of Marshall Row for Aiken and his wife, Mary. It was number 230, the house next door to the one Aiken had lived in as a boy.

"When work was completed on the house," said Adler, "the contrast between it and the other three was startling. I went to the phone and called the newspaper and said, 'Do you want to see a miracle? Come on!' So they came over, and they did a big feature on it in their Sunday edition. That was in February 1962. We had an open house the day the story appeared. It rained, but something like seven thousand people came through the house. They wore the shellac off the banister. We let them go into the unrestored house next door, too, for a before-and-after comparison. And they saw for the first time how a dilapidated wreck could be transformed into something marvelous. When that happened, we started to get some interest. People began to see the potential. They began to think about moving back downtown. Of course, it didn't hurt one bit that Savannah's greatest man of letters, a Pulitzer Prize–winning poet, was leading the way."

We resumed our drive. Adler pointed out dozens of houses that had been saved, describing in detail their once-fallen condition. "The porch on that one was completely gone . . . that house had bright green asbestos siding and aluminum awnings . . . the roof on that one was rotted through. . . ." He was like a doctor reviewing the case histories of former patients, now fully recovered.

Adler's success with Marshall Row encouraged him to go out and raise money for a revolving fund to be used by Historic Savannah to save other houses in the same way. The concept was very simple: Historic Savannah would use the money to buy endangered houses, then resell them—at a loss, if necessary—to people who would sign a pledge to begin restoration within eighteen months. The foundation set a goal of $200,000 for the fund, enough money in those days to save a lot of houses if they were turned over quickly enough. And they were.

"But even with the revolving fund, it was a struggle," said Adler. "I'd come downtown every day and breathe in the air and plot out the day's fight. And it was indeed a fight, because the buildings were still coming down pretty fast. Sometimes we won. Sometimes we lost. And the voters of Savannah gave us no help at all. They rejected urban renewal three times because they thought it was a communist plot, and they defeated any number of proposals for historic-zoning ordinances. *That* monstrosity over there, for instance, was one of our biggest losses. The Hyatt Regency Hotel."

We were riding along Bay Street, passing in front of the Hyatt—a squat, modernist building next to City Hall. The Hyatt had been a great *cause célèbre* in Savannah. The building had taken a great chunk out of the row of nineteenth-century cotton warehouses along Factors' Walk, and its backside jutted out over River Street, interrupting the line of façades along the riverfront. The public battle over the hotel delayed its construction for ten years.

"You can see the hotel is all wrong for the site," said Adler. "We fought it in the courts, and let me tell you it was a bruising battle. Both of the developers were members of Historic Savannah Foundation. The sister of one of them was the acting director. The organization was split right down the middle. Practically destroyed. It was a very emotional time. I remember going to a wedding while all that was happening, and when I walked in I realized I was suing everybody in the room but the bride and the minister."

At about that time, restoration of the historic district was nearing completion. Over a thousand houses had been restored. The work had been done by affluent whites, but Adler insisted that blacks had not been displaced. Historic Savannah was buying empty buildings for the most part. But when the supply of unrestored houses in the historic district began to dwindle, the next logical step was to restore the houses in the neighboring Victorian district. And *that* would have been a different story.

We drove south on Abercorn Street. Within a few blocks, the restrained architecture of the historic district gave way to late-Victorian flights of fancy—big old wooden houses with romantic towers, gables, and elaborate gingerbread trim. A few were restored, but most were in very poor condition.

The Victorian district was Savannah's first streetcar suburb. It had been built for the white working class between 1870 and 1910. After World War II, when the whites moved farther out into the suburbs, absentee landlords took over, and by 1975 the area had become a black slum. The houses were in deplorable shape, but they were still beautiful, and in recent years speculators and upper-income whites started buying them. At that point, Adler became alarmed. "It would have meant gentrification and massive displacement of blacks," he said, "and I was determined to prevent that. I asked Historic Savannah to help find a way to restore this area without evicting the people who lived here, but Historic Savannah was still busted up over the Hyatt, and they weren't interested in the housing problems of poor people. That's when I quit Historic Savannah. I launched a nonprofit organization called the Savannah Landmark Rehabilitation Project, which has been a triumph, because the board includes everybody—black, white, you name it, rich and poor."

Adler's intention was to get houses out of the hands of the absentee slumlords and convert the Victorian district into a racially and economically diverse neighborhood. It occurred to him that the project might qualify for public assistance, and thus far, by using a combination of public and private funding, he had bought and renovated three hundred units. Tenants paid 30 percent of their income in rent, and the rest was made up by federal rent subsidies.

"I don't suppose I need to tell you," Adler said, "that not everyone is happy about what we're doing here. Some people complain privately about poor blacks living in subsidized housing so close to the historic district. A few people, like Jim Williams, have even spoken out publicly about it. Jim Williams says we're dealing with the 'criminal element.' I take it you've heard of Jim Williams."

"Yes," I said. "I've met him."

"Mmmmm. Do you know about the Nazi flag incident?"

"He told me about it," I said. "He said he draped it over his balcony to interrupt a film being shot in Monterey Square."

"That's right," said Adler. "He had all those little faggots hanging the swastika out there and moving it from window to window."

On Anderson Street, Adler stopped in front of a freshly painted gray-and-white house. "Now I'm going to introduce you to an example of our so-called criminal element."

We climbed the steps, and Adler rang the bell. A black woman in a flowered housedress came to the door.

"Morning, Ruby," said Adler.

"Morning, Mr. Adler," she said. Adler introduced me to Mrs. Ruby Moore.

"Ruby, I've brought this gentleman to see what life is like in the Victorian district. If you don't mind—"

"Oh, that'll be fine," she said pleasantly. "Come on in."

Ruby Moore's duplex was cool inside. It had three bedrooms, a modern kitchen, and high ceilings. There was a small garden in back. A portrait of John F. Kennedy hung over the living-room mantel. Adler led me on a quick tour, upstairs and down. Then we rejoined Mrs. Moore in the front hall.

"These houses was pitiful before they was fixed over," she said. "I never dreamed they would look like this after they got through. While they was redoing them, I was over here every day looking, 'cause I knew I was going to get one. I really do appreciate my apartment. I really do. It's got central heat and air."

"Is everything okay, Ruby?" Adler asked.

"Oh, yes," she said. Then she turned to me. "Would you sign my book, please?" A guest book lay open on a table in the living room. As I signed my name, I noticed that I was not the first outsider to be brought to this house by Lee Adler. A reporter from the *Atlanta Constitution* had signed a few spaces above.

We got back in the car. Adler told me that Ruby Moore qualified for one of his apartments because she was a longtime resident of the Victorian district, because she worked—she was a housekeeper at the Days Inn—and because her income was below a specified level. She paid $250 a month in rent, and federal subsidies covered the rest. Adler said that Mrs. Moore more than satisfied his inspection staff; her house was always immaculate, and she was the rule rather than the exception. "We're not interested in housing the whores or the gamblers or the dope dealers," he said.

We headed back into the historic district.

"I could show you another hundred apartments just like that one, but you probably get the picture. Once we got it going, private investors started buying houses, and property values began to rise. The Victorian district has been acclaimed as a national model for how to restore inner cities without uprooting the poor. We sponsored a national housing conference here in 1977, and four hundred people came from thirty-eight states. The next year, Rosalynn Carter came down and taped a segment of *Good Morning America* in one of our renovated apartments. And this Friday we're going to Washington to explain it all to Prince Charles."

We entered Monterey Square and swung around it counterclockwise, coming to a stop in front of Adler's house. "Well, there you have it," he said. "Historic preservation used to be an elitist hobby, something rich dilettantes dabbled in. But we've turned it into a grass-roots operation. In the process we created a $200 million tourist industry and brought people back downtown to live. Not bad, huh?"

"Quite an accomplishment," I said.

Adler looked at me over the top of his half-moon glasses. "It ain't braggin' if y'really done it."

—

A week later, the *Savannah Morning News* published an account of the Adlers' meeting with Prince Charles. Lee Adler was quoted saying that the prince "showed a keen interest in the problems of cities." Emma Adler said the prince had asked "marvelously intelligent, wonderful and apt questions." Four days later, the newspaper ran yet another article about the meeting, this one a first-person account written by Mrs. Adler. "It was a heavenly day in Washington," she wrote. "The sun was bright, the sky a deep blue. The weather was perfect for a suit. . . ."

Once again, the Adlers were the topic of conversation in certain circles. The talk was nowhere more animated than at the meeting of the Married Woman's Card Club on Tuesday night.

"Do you suppose," said a woman in a blue taffeta dress, "that the newspaper had to twist Emma's arm to get her to write that article? Or do you think Emma twisted the newspaper's arm to make them print it?" The woman's dress had a bow across the shoulders as big as wings.

"Julia, you're wicked," said a woman wearing a black velvet headband and single-pearl earrings.

"No, I'm not," the woman in blue replied. "The Adlers could have kept their audience with Prince Charles a private matter if they'd wanted to. But they've gone running to the newspaper as usual, and that changes things."

"True."

"I mean, Emma could have restrained herself a little, don't you think? She sounded so prissy and pleased with herself."

"Now, Julia," said the other woman, her voice dropping in volume, "I do believe you're jealous."

The two ladies had not yet begun to play cards. In fact, they were still standing outside Cynthia Collins's front door, waiting to be admitted. That was one of the unusual rituals of the Married Woman's Card Club.

Married Woman's (as it was known for short) was one of Savannah's most exclusive societies. No other city had anything like it. It was founded in 1893 by sixteen ladies in search of amusement during the day while their husbands were at work. There were always sixteen members—no more, no less. Once a month, always on a Tuesday, they would gather at one of the members' homes for two hours of card playing, cocktails, and a light supper. Thirty-two guests would be invited by engraved invitation so that the number of ladies in attendance always came to forty-eight—twelve card tables in all.

According to custom, the ladies would arrive a few minutes before four in the afternoon, wearing white gloves, long dresses, and huge hats adorned with flowers or feathers. They did not ring the doorbell. Instead, they waited outside, either in their cars or on the sidewalk, until the hostess opened the door punctually at four o'clock. The ladies would then enter, sit down at the card tables, and start playing at once. In the early years, they played whist or euchre or 500. Later the game became auction bridge, then contract bridge. But for many years there was always one table of whist, because Mrs. J. J. Rauers refused to learn how to play anything else.

Once the ladies had begun playing, events proceeded according to a strict schedule that began with the serving of a glass of water. Every member was given a printed copy of the schedule upon joining Married Woman's. It read as follows:

> Four-fifteen: water.
> Four-thirty: remove water.
> Four-forty: empty ashtrays.
> Four fifty-five: pass napkins.
> Five o'clock: cocktails.
> Five-fifteen: second cocktail.
> Five-thirty: third cocktail.
> Five thirty-five: last hand, pass linen.
> Five-forty: serve dinner plates.
> Five forty-five: high score and cut for aces.
> Six o'clock: prizes, ladies leave promptly.

Being the hostess at one of these affairs was a serious matter. It was viewed as reason enough to paint the house or redecorate the parlor. At the very least, one took the silver out of the vault. As for keeping to the printed schedule, there was always a cadre of maids who knew the sequence of events better than the members did, and they would be loaned to nervous hostesses in order to ease their burden. The importance of the schedule was that it enabled the married women to get home in time to greet their husbands when they returned from work. Husbands were as much a part of Married Woman's as their wives. They were, after all, the ones who footed the bill for the dinners and for refurbishing the house beforehand. And they were, of course, the major qualification for membership: A woman had to be married to belong. The rules stated that if a member obtained a divorce, she would be forced to resign and forfeit her dues. More than one marriage had been held together by that rule alone. In any case, three times a year the hour for Married Woman's was moved from four to seven-thirty so that the all-important husbands could attend. The men would wear black tie.

On the Tuesday following the Adlers' return from Washington, husbands were invited to Married Woman's. Mrs. Cameron Collins was the hostess for the evening. She and her husband lived with their three children in a townhouse on Oglethorpe Avenue. Men in black tie and women in long dresses began milling around in front of the house shortly before seven-thirty. I, too, had put on a black tie that evening, having been invited by Mrs. Collins.

"I am not jealous of Emma Adler," said the woman in blue. "Not at all. I'd be the first to admit that Emma does a great many worthwhile things. She is an asset to the community, and if anybody deserves to meet Prince Charles, she does. It's just this . . . this grasping for recognition. It's so undignified. They always do it. You'd think Lee restored Savannah single-handedly. Lee loves basking in the limelight, and so does Emma." The woman turned to a man with thinning blond hair, who was leaning casually against a tree with his hands in his pockets. "Darling," she said, "do you think I'm being unfair?"

The man shrugged. "If you ask me, Emma Adler is a vast improvement over her mother."

Emma Adler's mother was Emma Walthour Morel, a large and domineering woman known around town as "Big Emma." Big Emma was one of the richest people in Savannah, being the largest stockholder in the Savannah Bank, and she had a forceful personality. As one family friend put it, Big Emma was the sort of person who wasn't happy unless she had a table to pound on. Stories about her had become legend in Savannah. At home, she kept a padlock on the refrigerator to keep the help from stealing the food. She would get up from the table ten or fifteen times in the course of a dinner party to go into the kitchen and unlock and relock the refrigerator. Later on, after the guests had left, John Morel would slip into the kitchen and tip the help generously in an effort to soothe feelings bruised from an evening of Big Emma's abuse.

Well into her nineties, Big Emma could still be seen driving around Savannah at the wheel of her Mercedes limousine with her German shepherd sitting next to her on the front seat and an ancient black chauffeur, dressed in full livery, sitting in back. The chauffeur, who had worked for Mrs. Morel for more than thirty years (and for her mother before that), was permitted to drive her smaller car but not the Mercedes limousine. No one but Big Emma was permitted to drive that one; it was her exclusive domain. One recent noontime, she drove downtown to the headquarters of the Savannah Bank on Johnson Square to sign some papers. Before setting out, she had called ahead and told the bank's trust officer to meet her with the papers by the curb in front of the bank. She was in a hurry, she said, and did not want to be kept waiting. Twenty minutes later, Big Emma turned the corner into Johnson Square, the massive German shepherd sitting at her side and the old uniformed chauffeur cowering in back. She drew up to the trust officer, but never quite came to a complete stop. The trust officer trotted alongside the limousine, handing papers through the window, pleading, "For heaven's sake, Emma, stop the car!" Big Emma glided along at eight or ten miles an hour, scribbling on papers and handing them back, one by one. They were halfway around Johnson Square when she handed the last document back to the trust officer, rolled up the window, and sped off.

Of all the tales told about Big Emma Morel, the one most often repeated was her vociferous opposition to the marriage of her daughter to Lee Adler on the grounds that he was Jewish. Big Emma was vehement. She bellowed. She orated. She pounded on tables. She would not listen to arguments that John Morel, her own husband and Little Emma's father, was one-quarter Jewish himself. When Little Emma stood her ground, Big Emma turned sullen. She refused to take her daughter to New York to buy her a wedding dress. Lee Adler's mother took her instead. At the wedding rehearsal, Big Emma stood as far away as she could from the Adlers. Then at the reception after the wedding, she refused to let the Adlers join the receiving line. She froze them out. That episode was still remembered today, twenty-five years later. And it was the reason why the man standing outside Cynthia Collins's house with his hands in his pockets compared Emma Adler favorably with her mother.

At seven-thirty on the dot, a beaming Cynthia Collins opened her front door wearing a long black dress and carrying a black lace fan. "Come in, everybody," she said cheerfully. Her guests filed in and wandered among the card tables set up in the living room and the dining room. As soon as they found their place cards they sat down, and within minutes the tables were full. Conversation subsided to a muted hum, and the sound of shuffling cards swept through the house like autumn leaves blowing across a lawn.

Not being a bridge player, I joined two other nonplaying guests—a man and a woman—in a small library off the living room. The man had long white hair and a benevolent smile fixed on his face. He was, I gathered, a much-respected figure in the community. The woman was perhaps forty and smoked a pale blue cigarette. Across the room, two maids in crisp black-and-white uniforms stood beside pitchers of Manhattans, martinis, sherry-and-tea punch, and water. Cynthia Collins came into the room, flush-faced and smiling. "Well, the first rubber's started on time, so I can catch my breath for a moment. I hope y'all didn't wait outside very long in that awful heat."

"The curbside chatter was all about Lee and Emma," said the woman with the blue cigarette.

"You know, I thought about Lee this afternoon," said Cynthia, "while I was writing out place cards for tonight. You still have to be careful who you put with whom, because of the uproar over the Hyatt. Even now. We have Lee to thank for that, of course."

"Don't remind me," said the other woman. "It was dreadful. At the height of it, you couldn't go to cocktail parties. You couldn't do anything. People got into such awful arguments. It was easier to just stay home."

"My sister-in-law and I are not on speaking terms to this day," the white-haired man said solemnly. "However, I must say I'm rather grateful for that."

Cynthia Collins glanced discreetly at her watch. "Water!" she whispered to the maids.

"It's always all or nothing with Lee," said the other woman. "If he can't have his way, then nobody can. He follows a scorched-earth policy."

"And he does shout," said Cynthia.

"My dear, he does more than that. Don't you remember that business with the gun?"

"What gun?"

"Lee had a disagreement with one of the other members of the board of the National Trust and pulled a pistol on him at a formal dinner. I think it was in Chicago. A couple of years ago."

"Oh, that's right!" said Cynthia. "I'd forgotten. But it was a *toy* gun, as I remember. The way I heard it, Lee didn't actually accost the man. He presented the gun to him and suggested he shoot himself with it."

"Maybe that was it," said the other woman.

"People were aghast. There had apparently been some kind of shooting in the poor man's family not long before, which made it positively ghoulish. Jimmy Biddle was president of the National Trust at the time. He stepped in and told Lee he was completely out of line and to take his seat. It was all very tasteless and embarrassing."

"I guess that's what I was thinking about."

The white-haired man sat back in his chair, casting his

eyes from one woman to the other like a spectator at a tennis match.

Cynthia turned to me. "We must sound very catty to you," she said, "but years ago Lee was our hero. We were his disciples. Because of Lee, we all moved downtown when it was still slummy and not very safe. It was exciting. The Hartridges even bought a townhouse next door to a whorehouse on Jones Street. In those days, Lee was doing something magnificent. He was an idealist and a purist. He was saving downtown. Of course, he didn't actually *move* downtown until much later. He and Emma stayed out in Ardsley Park where it was safe, while the rest of us moved downtown and pioneered. The Cunninghams, the Critzes, the Brannens, the Rhangoses, the Dunns—the whole board of Historic Savannah lived downtown, except for Lee. The Adlers didn't stick their necks out. They talked one game and played another. And now all he seems to care about are those damned awards and cozying up to people like Prince Charles."

"What happened?" I asked.

"He became impossible to deal with," said Cynthia. "He was never much for democratic procedures in the first place. When he was president of Historic Savannah, he did just as he pleased and rarely consulted the board beforehand. It all came to a head with the Hyatt. We were all against the hotel. It was originally supposed to be a fifteen-story building that would have towered over City Hall. The whole board voted against it, including Lee. Then the board took a second vote on whether to make their opposition public. They voted to wait until they'd had a chance to talk with the developers. But Lee was adamant. He wanted a public confrontation right away. The board held firm. Since he didn't get his way, Lee decided to launch his own attack against the hotel. First he withdrew his annual contribution to Historic Savannah—seven thousand dollars, which he'd earmarked for the director's salary. That was typical of Lee, by the way, to specify some high-profile use for his donation instead of giving money with no strings attached the way other people did. That's Lee, the one-man show. If he can't run it, he doesn't want any part of it. You can hardly blame the board for throwing him out of Historic Savannah."

My ears pricked up at this. "I thought it was Lee Adler who broke with Historic Savannah," I said, "not the other way around."

"Lee was definitely voted out," said Cynthia, "and what made it so poignant was that the people who voted him out were his friends and disciples. And the vote was unanimous. The minutes of that meeting have disappeared from the files—mysteriously—but you can ask Walter Hartridge about it. He was president at the time. He and Connie are playing bridge in the next room."

"The saddest part," said the other woman, "was that things would have worked out a whole lot better if Lee hadn't stirred things up on his own. At one point, the developers offered a compromise that was better than what we finally ended up with."

"I had the impression," I said, thinking back to what Adler had told me, "that Adler quit Historic Savannah over a disagreement concerning housing for blacks in the Victorian district."

At this, the other woman stubbed out her blue cigarette. "I can't take it anymore!" she said. "It makes me so damn mad! Cynthia, I don't care where we are on the schedule. I'm ready for a drink." She went over to the table and poured herself a Manhattan.

"Lee Adler did not quit Historic Savannah! He was *thrown* out," said the woman. "That was in 1969. He didn't start Savannah Landmark in the Victorian district until something like five years later. One had nothing to do with the other. Savannah Landmark is nothing but an ego trip. Of course, he pretends it's more noble than that. He portrays himself as a preservationist with a social conscience. He says he's creating a racially mixed neighborhood. Bull! He's creating a new black ghetto. It's not true integration. It's segregation all over again.

"Lee was devastated when he was forced out of Historic

Savannah. He'd been president for six years. It was his life. He had to show Historic Savannah that he could do it on his own somehow, and he seized on the Victorian district as his vehicle. He hit on a scheme to use government money to buy and restore historic houses for subsidized tenants. It had nothing to do with pious social aims. It was just a way of financing a preservation project with himself at the head of it. He says he's restoring houses without displacing longtime residents—as if the Victorian district was historically black, or even mixed. Well, it wasn't. Until the middle of the nineteen-sixties, it was a white, middle-class neighborhood. If Lee hadn't been so damned stuck on himself, the private marketplace would have taken care of the Victorian district. And, believe me, blacks would still have been well represented downtown. Public housing is needed, I'll grant you, but the Victorian district is about the worst place for it."

The woman explained that the houses in the Victorian district were mostly wood-frame dwellings, which meant that the fire insurance was very high and that the houses had to be repainted every three years or so because the intense humidity made the paint peel quickly. "Costs like that are indefensible in publicly subsidized housing," she said.

"And Lee's not doing fine restoration work at all," she went on. "He's gutting the houses and ripping out nice little Victorian touches, like stamped-tin ceilings. And he's not keeping the houses in good shape. Take a look at them—*all* of them, not just the few he likes to show off. The paint is peeling, the porch railings are broken. Two or three years after they've been restored, his houses blend right in with the unrestored houses next to them."

Through the door I could see the maids moving from table to table, collecting the empty water glasses.

"And if I may be so bold," the woman went on, "what's so damned awful about gentrification? Gentrification was fine with Lee when it suited him in the historic district. He's stopped gentrification all right, and he's also killed real estate values in the Victorian district. It's a buyer's market, but there are no buyers. In the name of preservation, Lee Adler has stopped preservation cold."

But Adler had told me, I said, that restoration in the Victorian district had encouraged private investment there.

"That's a flat-out lie, and no one knows it better than Lee Adler. One of his sons bought a house on Waldburg Street and restored it magnificently. But when the time came to sell it there weren't any takers. His asking price was $135,000. Now it's down to $97,000, and still nobody wants it, because it is smack-dab in the middle of a black slum."

"Outside Savannah," said Cynthia, "people think the Victorian district has been a great success, because that's what Lee tells them. They all swallow his line. Prince Charles is just the latest in a long line of chumps."

"What's really irritating," the other woman said, "is the way the Adlers have set themselves up as moral arbiters. It makes me want to scream. I'm tired of Lee's noble pretensions. And I'm sick of Emma's Eleanor Roosevelt act. What have we done to deserve it?"

"Plenty," said the white-haired man.

The two women looked at the man in surprise. He was still smiling his benevolent smile.

"Lee is a prominent member of Savannah society, is he not?" the man asked gently. "He belongs to the Cotillion Club, which sponsors the debutante balls. He's one of the fifteen distinguished gentlemen in the Madeira Club, where he and the others deliver learned papers over epicurean dinners and fine Madeira wines. He belongs to the Chatham Club, where he can go for drinks and dinner and look out over the rooftops of the historic district he's been so instrumental in preserving."

The two women nodded cautiously, unsure what the man was driving at.

"He plays golf at the Savannah Golf Club," the man went on. "So Lee Adler is one of Savannah's elite. At least, you would think so. But he isn't really, is he? In Savannah we have our little way of drawing the line—of saying, You shall come this far and no farther, *you are not really one of us*. We have the Oglethorpe Club as our way of saying this. And we have the yacht club."

The man spoke softly, like a kindly professor. "Lee Adler

is Jewish. A great many of his good friends belong to the Oglethorpe Club and the yacht club, but he does not."

"But the Oglethorpe Club does admit Jews," said the woman. "Bob Minis is a member."

"Yes. Bob Minis is one of the oldest members of the Oglethorpe Club, and he's very well liked. He's also the great-great-grandson of the first white child born in Georgia, which makes him a living relic of Georgia history. He's Jewish, but not overly Jewish. Both of his wives have been Christians, and so have most of his friends, and his children have been raised as Episcopalians. Bob Minis gives good value as a member of the Oglethorpe Club. Apart from being delightful company, he enables us to say, as you have just said, 'But we *do* have Jews in the Oglethorpe Club.' "

The man folded his arms and looked at each of us in turn, as if to assure himself that his point had been received. "On the other hand," he went on, "there is Lee Adler. Cold-shouldered by the Oglethorpe Club and tossed out of Historic Savannah. What is he to do? He must do something brilliant, something absolutely ingenious. In my opinion, he succeeded beyond his wildest dreams. Through his work in the Victorian district, he has not only made a comeback as a historic preservationist, he has wrapped himself in a morally unassailable issue: housing for poor blacks. If you oppose him, you'll look like a racist. Lee's Savannah Landmark project may be unrealistically expensive. His restorations may be shoddy. He may have depressed real estate values in the Victorian district. He may have created a new black ghetto. He may even be in it, as some people suspect, for the money and the recognition. But nobody can stand up and say so, and that's why it's so brilliant. Lee Adler has achieved his objective: He has regained his position as one of America's leading preservationists, and in the process he has rubbed our noses in the issue of race."

"I don't believe he's sincere about blacks," said the woman with the blue cigarette. "Not one of the clubs Lee belongs to—at least none you've just mentioned—has ever had any black members."

"True," said the man, "and for that matter, I suspect the blacks themselves may wonder if Lee and Emma are sincere. For instance, if you read Emma's newspaper article about Prince Charles carefully, you will see something very curious. Emma twits the members of the Washington press corps who were present at the meeting for being interested only in 'frivolous speculation about Prince Charles,' rather than in the issue of housing. But then she carries on at great length about the sweet black cook she took with her and how the cook had made a basket out of pine needles for the prince and that she had worried for weeks about how to present it to him. Emma did not find fault with the cook's somewhat childlike preoccupation with her basket, though the basket didn't have anything to do with the issue of housing, either. Emma appears to have a double standard. One for educated journalists and one for simple black cooks. From this, one might draw the conclusion that Emma has a patronizing attitude toward blacks."

A satisfied smile spread across the face of the woman with the blue cigarette. "Mmmmm," she said.

"I think the blacks know where they stand with Lee and Emma," the man went on. "They also know, probably, that no one here tonight has renovated three hundred apartments for poor blacks or taken their black cook to meet Prince Charles. The blacks know that the Adlers are doing something for them, whatever their motives may be. And, in return, the blacks are doing something for the Adlers."

"What on earth are they doing for the Adlers?" asked the woman.

"They're giving the Adlers their vote," he said. "In the last election, you may remember that Lee and Emma supported Spencer Lawton for district attorney against Bubsy Ryan. The Adlers were among the largest contributors to Lawton's campaign. One can assume Lee passed the word to the black ministers that he was supporting Lawton. Presto, the black Ministerial Alliance, which had backed Ryan in the past, switched over to Lawton. Lawton won the black vote, and the black vote gave him his margin of victory. So whether he planned it or not, Lee Adler emerged from his crisis with a black-power base. And with the district attorney grateful to him for his help. This makes Lee a political power. It makes it *impolitic* for any city official to oppose Lee in any of his little housing ventures." The man raised his eyebrows as if to say, "I rest my case."

"Well, I do see your point," the woman said dryly.

The man then looked over at Cynthia Collins, but at that moment Mrs. Collins was stealing a glance at her watch. A flicker of concern crossed her brow. She caught the eye of the maid by the door. "Pass napkins," she whispered.

Chapter 11

NEWS FLASH

At this point in my experiment in bi-urban living, I found myself spending more time in Savannah than New York. The weather alone would have been reason enough for the tilt. By late April, New York was still struggling to free itself from the clutches of winter, and Savannah was well into the unfolding pageantry of a warm and leisurely spring. Camellias, jonquils, and paperwhites had bloomed in December and January. Wisteria and redbuds had followed, and then in mid-March the azaleas burst forth in gigantic pillows of white, red, and vermilion. White dogwood blossoms floated like clouds of confectioner's sugar above the azaleas. The scent of honeysuckle, Confederate jasmine, and the first magnolia blossoms were already beginning to perfume the air. Who needed the chill of New York?

So I lingered in Savannah. Its hushed and somnolent streets became my streets of choice. I stayed put, just as Savannahians did. Savannahians often talked about other places, as if they traveled a lot, but usually it was just talk. Savannahians liked to talk about Charleston most of all, especially in the presence of a newcomer. They would compare the two cities endlessly. Savannah was the Hostess City; Charleston was the Holy City (because it had a lot of churches). Savannah's streetscape was superior to Charleston's, but Charleston had finer interiors. Savannah was thoroughly English in style and temperament; Charleston had French and Spanish influences as well as English. Savannah preferred hunting, fishing, and going to parties over intellectual pursuits; in Charleston it was the other way around. Savannah was attractive to tourists; Charleston was overrun by them. On and on. In the minds of most Americans, Savannah and Charleston were sister cities. If so, the sisters were barely on speaking terms. Savannahians rarely went to Charleston, even though it was less than two hours away by car. But then Savannahians rarely went anywhere at all. They could not be bothered. They were content to remain in their isolated city under self-imposed house arrest. There were exceptions, of course, and Chablis was one of them.

Chablis took her act on the road via Trailways, just as she said she would—to Augusta, Columbia, Atlanta, and Jacksonville. She came back to Savannah between swings, long enough to freshen her wardrobe and avail herself of Dr. Myra Bishop's female hormone shots. When she was finished at Dr. Bishop's, she invariably called me up or threw pebbles at my window, and I would come down and drive her home. She came to look upon these rides as a ceremonial aspect of her sexual journey. The estrogen would be working its magic inside her, transforming the tomboy into a graceful empress even as we drove through the streets of Savannah.

One Saturday morning in early May, I was preparing to drive out to Fort Jackson to watch one of Savannah's traditional annual sporting events, the Scottish games, when the telephone rang. It was Chablis.

"It's the bitch, honey," she said. "It's The Lady. I ain't lookin' for a ride this time, though. I'm just checkin' to see if you've had a look at your morning paper yet."

"No, I haven't," I said. "Why?"

"Remember that antique dealer you told me you met? The one with the big house on Monterey Square?"

"Yes," I said.

"Didn't you tell me his name was Jim Williams?"

"Yes, I did. What about him?"

"*James A.* Williams?" she asked.

"Yes."

"Age fifty-two?"

"Sounds right," I said.

"Of 429 Bull Street?"

"Come on, Chablis. What happened?"

"She shot somebody last night."

"*What?* Chablis, are you serious?"

"I wouldn't joke about a thing like that. That's what it says right here in the paper. It says James A. Williams shot Danny Lewis Hansford, twenty-one. It happened inside Mercer House. They got a big ol' picture of your friend James A. Williams on the front page, but they ain't got one of the twenty-one-year-old, dammit, and that's the one I wanna see."

"Did Danny Hansford die?" I asked.

"He musta did, honey, 'cause they're chargin' Miss Williams with murder."

PART TWO

Chapter 12

GUNPLAY

Under the banner headline WILLIAMS CHARGED IN SLAYING, the story was very brief. It said that at 3:00 A.M., police had been summoned to Mercer House, where they found Danny Hansford, twenty-one, lying dead on the floor in the study, his blood pouring out onto an oriental carpet. He had been shot in the head and chest. There were two pistols at the scene. Several objects in the house had been broken. Williams had been taken into custody, charged with murder, and held on $25,000 bond. Fifteen minutes later, a friend of Williams had arrived at police headquarters with a paper bag containing 250 one-hundred-dollar bills, and Williams was released. That was all the newspaper said about the shooting. Williams was identified as an antiques dealer, a restorer of historic houses, and a giver of elegant parties at his "showplace" home, which Jacqueline Onassis had visited and offered to buy for $2 million. About Danny Hansford, the paper gave no information other than his age.

The next day's newspaper carried a more detailed account of the shooting. According to Williams, he had shot Danny

Hansford in self-defense. He and Danny had attended a drive-in movie, he said, and returned to Mercer House after midnight. Back at the house, Hansford suddenly went wild, just as Williams said he had done a month earlier. He stomped a video game, broke a chair, smashed an eighteenth-century English grandfather clock. Then—just as he had done before—he grabbed one of Williams's German Lugers. But this time he did not fire it into the floor or out into Monterey Square. This time he aimed it directly at Williams, who was sitting behind his desk. He fired three shots. All three missed. When he pulled the trigger to fire again, the gun jammed. That was when Williams reached into his desk drawer and took out another Luger. Danny was struggling to unjam his gun when Williams shot him.

Later in the week, Williams elaborated further in an interview in the weekly newspaper the *Georgia Gazette*. His tone was confident, even a little defiant. "If I had not shot Danny," he said, "it would have been my obituary that was published." Williams said the movie at the drive-in had been a violent horror film. "Lots of throats being slashed and that sort of thing. I told Danny we should leave and go play backgammon or chess or something, and we did."

By the time Williams and Hansford arrived back at Mercer House, Danny had smoked nine joints and consumed a half-pint of whiskey. They played a video game for a while and then a board game. At that point, Hansford launched into an irrational tirade against his mother, his girlfriend Bonnie and his buddy George Hill. Suddenly, in a flash of anger, he stomped the video control panel. "Games!" he screamed. "It's all games. That's what it's all about!" Williams stood up to leave the room. Hansford grabbed him by the throat and threw him up against a doorjamb. "You've been sick," he screamed. "Why don't you just go off someplace and die?" Williams wrenched himself out of Hansford's grip and went into his study, where he sat down at his desk. He heard loud crashing noises—the grandfather clock falling to the floor, glass breaking, and other sounds of destruction. Danny came into the room carrying a German

Luger. "I'm leaving tomorrow," he said, "but you're leaving tonight!" With that, he took aim at Williams and fired. Williams said he felt a breeze as one of the bullets passed his left arm. Then Danny's gun jammed. Williams grabbed his own gun and fired.

After Danny fell, Williams put his gun down on the desk, walked around the desk, saw that Danny was dead, then went back behind the desk and called a former employee, Joe Goodman. Williams told Goodman he had just shot Hansford and to come to Mercer House right away. After that, Williams called his lawyer. Then he called the police.

Williams's lawyer, the police, Joe Goodman, and Joe Goodman's girlfriend all arrived at Mercer House at the same time. Williams was standing at the open door. "I just shot him," he said. "He's in the other room."

The first policeman to arrive on the scene, Corporal Michael Anderson, recognized Danny immediately. Corporal Anderson was the same policeman who had come to Mercer House a month earlier to take Danny into custody after his previous rampage. On that occasion, he had found Danny upstairs stretched across the bed, fully clothed. This time he found him lying on a Persian carpet in Williams's study with his face in a pool of blood. His right arm was outstretched above his head, his hand cupped lightly over a gun.

Toward 7:00 A.M., the police escorted Williams to headquarters. They fingerprinted him, booked him for murder, and set bond at $25,000. Williams went to a telephone and called Joe Goodman, who was still waiting back at Mercer House. "Joe, now listen carefully," he said. "Go upstairs to the tall cabinet outside the organ room. Stand on the chair next to it, reach up, and take down a paper sack that's sitting on top." Fifteen minutes later, Goodman arrived at police headquarters with a brown paper bag containing 250 one-hundred-dollar bills, and Williams went home.

A few days later, the police announced that certain lab tests would show whether or not Danny Hansford had actually fired a pistol as Williams claimed. A crucial test would be the presence, or absence, of gunshot powder on

Hansford's hands. If gunshot residue could be detected, it would mean Hansford had fired his gun before Williams killed him; the absence of residue would mean he had not fired. Police said the results would be ready in a week or so and could make or break the case against Williams.

Despite the heavy charges hanging over him, Williams went calmly about his affairs. On Wednesday, four days after he shot Hansford, he asked the court for permission to fly to Europe on an antiques-buying trip. The judge raised his bond to $100,000 and let him go. In London, Williams stayed in his favorite suite at the Ritz and played roulette at Crockford's Club. Then he flew on to Geneva to attend a sale of Fabergé. He returned to Savannah a week later.

Soon afterward, the police announced that the lab tests would be delayed because of a backlog of work at the Georgia Crime Lab in Atlanta. A month later, the police were still awaiting results.

In the meantime, people in Savannah were coming to conclusions on their own without benefit of lab results. Facts about Danny Hansford were beginning to circulate, and they lent credence to Williams's claim of self-defense. Hansford had been in and out of juvenile homes and mental hospitals. He had dropped out of school in the eighth grade and had a history of violence and getting into trouble with the police. Williams himself had bailed him out of jail nine times in the past ten months. Skipper Dunn, a horticulturist, who had once lived in the same rooming house as Hansford, described him as a dangerous psychotic. "He was a berserker," Dunn said. "I saw him run amok twice, breaking things, reaching for knives. It took two people to pin him down. You could look into his eyes and see there was no person left, only rage and violence. It was easy to see that he might try to kill someone some day." Hansford had once torn a door off its hinges in an effort to get at his sister and beat her up. His own mother had sworn out a police warrant against him, declaring that she was afraid he would do bodily harm to her and her family.

In his interview with the *Georgia Gazette,* Williams described Hansford as severely disturbed. He said Hansford had once told him, "I'm alone in this world. No one cares about me. I don't have anything to live for." With a strange sort of detachment, Williams saw himself as Danny Hansford's savior rather than his nemesis, much less his murderer: "I was determined to save him from himself," he said. "He had given up on being alive." Though Williams's view was unabashedly self-serving, it was compelling in its detail. Hansford had developed a fascination with death, he said. He would frequently go to Bonaventure Cemetery with friends and point to the grave markers and say that the small ones were for poor people, and the big ones were for rich people, and that if he died in Mercer House he would get a big one. Hansford had twice tried to commit suicide at Mercer House by taking drug overdoses. The second time, he had written a note: "If this stuff does the job, at least I'll get a decent tombstone." Williams had rushed him to the hospital both times. All of that was a matter of record.

Beyond saying Danny Hansford was an employee, Williams never fully explained their relationship. But it soon became known that Hansford had been a part-time male hustler who loitered in the squares along Bull Street. Most people did not need to have the rest of the story spelled out for them. A few of Williams's friends, however—society ladies for the most part—discovered they had been completely in the dark. Millicent Mooreland, an Ardsley Park hostess and a blue blood, had known Williams for thirty years. Yet when a friend called her to say, "Jim Williams has just shot and killed his lover," she was dumbstruck for two reasons, not just one. "That statement left me absolutely gasping," Mrs. Mooreland said. "My friendship with Jim had been based on antiques and parties and social things. I simply wasn't aware of his other interests in life."

Most of the social set were more worldly than Mrs. Mooreland. "Oh, we knew," said John Myers. "Of course we knew. We weren't aware of the details, naturally, because Jim exercised discretion, which was the right thing to do. But all along we'd congratulated ourselves about Jim's social success because of what it seemed to say about us. We thought it proved Savannah was cosmopolitan, that we were sophisticated enough to accept a gay man socially."

Mrs. Mooreland remained loyal to Williams, but there were certain things that did trouble her, apart from the shooting itself. She was perplexed by a seemingly small detail in the rush of events that happened that night. "Joe Goodman," she said. "Who is he? I don't know him. I've never seen him in Jim's house, and yet he was the first person Jim called."

Mrs. Mooreland's consternation about Joe Goodman arose from the fact that she had lived her entire life within the reassuring confines of what was known as Old Savannah. Old Savannah was a sharply circumscribed, self-contained world. The supporting roles for all of its dramas had been cast long ago. In times of crisis, one turned to the relevant figures in the community—the legal authority, the moral pillar, the social arbiter, the financial titan, the elder statesman. Old Savannah was well structured for dealing with crises. Having spent a lifetime in this comforting environment, Mrs. Mooreland was surprised that in his moment of need Jim Williams had reached out to someone completely unknown—rather than to Walter Hartridge, for instance, or to Dick Richardson. It was a signal to her that something was terribly off kilter.

With so much talk centering on Jim Williams—his origins, his career, his exploits, his everything—the incident of the Nazi flag came in for a good bit of rehashing. And now a shooting with a German Luger, no less.

Some people, even a few Jews like Bob Minis, dismissed the Nazi flag episode as insignificant—"It was stupid," said Minis. "Jim acted quickly, without thinking." But others were not inclined to let Williams off so easily. "I'm sure he doesn't actually think of himself as a Nazi," said Joseph Killorin, an English professor at Armstrong State College. "But come on, Nazi symbols are not totally bereft of meaning. They still carry a very clear message, even if they're displayed under the guise of 'historic relics.' The message is *superiority,* and don't think for a minute Jim Williams isn't aware of it. He's too smart not to be. In the South, among extreme chauvinists, you sometimes find a strange affinity for Nazi regalia. It has to do with a sense of once having been treated for what one was worth and now being treated merely as an equal. There is a terribly social gentleman here in Savannah who sometimes wears Nazi uniforms to costume parties—anyone can tell you who I'm talking about; he's known for it—and he says he does it for shock value, but the deeper meaning is still there. In Jim's case, it may not be anything more than apolitical arrogance. If a man lives in the grandest house in town and gives the most extravagant parties, he could easily come to believe he was superior. He might also think the rules for ordinary people no longer applied to him. Displaying a Nazi flag would be one way of demonstrating that."

All in all, if a straw poll had been taken in Savannah in the first few weeks after the shooting, it would most likely have shown that the public expected the case to be dropped. By all appearances, the shooting had been self-defense or, at worst, a spur-of-the-moment crime of passion. Matters like these were traditionally settled quietly, especially when the accused was a highly respected, affluent individual with no criminal record. Savannahians were well aware of past killings in which well-connected suspects were never charged, no matter how obvious their guilt. One of the more colorful stories involved a society spinster who claimed that her gentleman lover had shot himself with a rifle while sitting in a wing chair in her living room. The woman "found" her lover's body, cleaned the rifle, put it back in the rifle case, and then had the body embalmed. Only after having done all that did she call the police.

"Oh, Jim Williams will probably get off," said Prentiss Crowe, a Savannah aristocrat, "but he'll still face a few problems. There is bound to be a certain *resentment* about his having killed that boy—that boy in particular, I mean. Danny Hansford was a very accomplished hustler, from all accounts, very good at his trade, and very much appreciated by both men and women. The trouble is he hadn't quite finished making the rounds. A fair number of men and women were looking forward to having their turn with him. Of course, now that Jim's shot him they never will. Naturally, they'll hold this against Jim, and that's what I mean when I say 'resentment.' Danny Hansford was known to be a good time . . . but a good time not yet had by all."

At the bar in the Oglethorpe Club, Sonny Clark put it more bluntly: "You know what they're saying about Jim Williams, don't you? They're saying he shot the best piece of ass in Savannah!"

The entire city was captivated by the sensational shooting, and for weeks afterward curious Savannahians drove their cars into Monterey Square and circled around and around. Dog-eared copies of the March 1976 issue of *Architectural Digest*, the one with the feature on Mercer House, were passed from hand to hand. People who had never been inside the house came to know it as if they lived there. They could tell you that Danny Hansford had died midway between an oil painting attributed to the nephew of Thomas Gainsborough and a gold-encrusted desk that had been owned by Emperor Maximilian of Mexico. They could recite, with malicious glee, the now-ironic concluding sentence of the article: "The charm of the city and its way of life have found expression in [Williams's] careful and loving restoration of Mercer House—a house once ravaged by war and neglect but now a center of harmony and quiet living."

There was one major imponderable in the case against Jim Williams: Spencer Lawton, the new district attorney. Lawton was too new at the job to be predictable. Also, he owed a debt of gratitude to Lee Adler, whose support and beneficence had helped put him in office—and whose long-running feud with Jim Williams was well known. Lee Adler was uniquely positioned to influence the course of events, if he chose to do so. He could, in private conversation, encourage Lawton to prosecute Williams. Or, as seemed less likely, he could urge lenience. To people who were bold enough to ask if he was pressuring Lawton in any way, Adler stoutly replied, "Spencer Lawton is his own man."

For more than a month after the shooting, Lawton kept a remarkably low profile. His name was never mentioned in press coverage of the case. All public statements from his office were made by his chief assistant. A preliminary hearing was set for June 17, at which time Lawton would decide whether or not to seek an indictment.

Five days before the hearing was to take place, Lawton went before the Chatham County grand jury and presented his evidence in secret session. The grand jury acted quickly. It indicted Williams for first-degree murder—premeditated and with malice aforethought. The severity of the charge raised a few eyebrows. If there was to be an indictment at all, involuntary manslaughter had seemed a more likely charge than murder, given what was known of the case. Lawton would not discuss the evidence publicly except to say that the lab tests had been only partially completed. Jim Williams would have to stand trial.

A few days after the indictment, Danny Hansford's mother sued Williams for $10,003,500. She charged that he had killed Danny in an "execution style" shooting. The $3,500 was for funeral expenses.

Even now, Williams maintained an air of unruffled calm. His trial was not scheduled to begin until January, more than six months away. He asked the court for permission to go back to Europe on another buying trip, and permission was granted. When he returned, he kept to his old routines. He had his hair cut by Jimmy Taglioli on Abercorn Street, he shopped at Smith's market, he ate dinner at Elizabeth on 37th. He was not even slightly remorseful. He had no reason to be, he thought. As he had told the *Gazette*, "I haven't done anything wrong."

Chapter 13

CHECKS AND BALANCES

"Sometimes I think you Yankees only come down here to stir up trouble," said Joe Odom. "I mean, look at Jim Williams. A model citizen. Minds his own business. One success after another. Then you come along, and the next thing we know he's killed somebody. I mean, really!"

It was three in the morning. Joe was moving out of the house on Pulaski Square exactly six months after having moved in. The unsuspecting real estate agent, John Thorsen, was due back from England the next day, and Joe intended to restore the house to the condition in which Mr. Thorsen had left it: locked and empty. Joe had found another house to move into on Lafayette Square. And now, in the dead of night, he dumped a last armload of clothes into the van parked out front.

"All right," he said. "So now we have a murder in a big mansion. Goddamn! Well, let's see where that puts us. We've got a weirdo bug specialist slinking around town with a bottle of deadly poison. We've got a nigger drag queen, an old man who walks an imaginary dog, and now a faggot murder case. My friend, you are getting me and Mandy into one hell of a movie."

Joe went back inside to search for telltale signs that he had been living there for six months. In the past half year, the supposedly unoccupied house had played host to a maelstrom of humanity. Over a thousand tourists had traipsed through, peering into every nook and cranny and pausing to have a buffet lunch before leaving. At the same time, the never-ending parade of Joe's friends flowed in and out, with Jerry the hairdresser operating an all-but-full-time beauty salon in the kitchen. These diverse activities merged and mingled, sometimes with comical results. More than a few elderly ladies who came to the house for lunch got back on the tour bus with their hair completely restyled, and nearly everyone emerged clutching handbills advertising Sweet Georgia Brown's.

As always, new faces joined the cast of characters in Joe's entourage. Some hung on for a week or a month, others longer. As adroit as he was at gathering a crowd around him, Joe was utterly unable to cast anyone out. That task fell to an inner circle of friends who took it upon themselves to weed out unsavory hangers-on, with or without Joe's knowledge. In recent months, the primary target of this group had been a well-dressed man who had arrived in Savannah purporting to be a Palm Beach millionaire. In actual fact, he was a small-time entrepreneur who had opened a whorehouse on the road to Tybee. Before anyone knew it, he was quietly soliciting business from the men in the tour groups at Joe's. The inner circle called on a retired policeman, Sarge Bolton, to get rid of him. One glimpse of the revolver in Sarge's shoulder holster, and the man was gone.

Joe's friends had nothing against whorehouses, but they were worried that this one might complicate matters for Joe, who was just now coming under the scrutiny of the authorities because of the bad checks he had written before the opening of Sweet Georgia Brown's. The checks had begun to arrive at the prosecutor's office on the average of one a week: the carpenter's check, the electrician's check, the plumber's check, the check for the antique merry-go-round horse on top of the bar. When the total reached $18,000, two sheriff's deputies came to Sweet Georgia Brown's and served Joe with a summons. He was directed to appear for a hearing in court. Depending on the outcome of the hearing, he might or might not be indicted for writing worthless checks—a felony punishable by one to five years in prison.

On the day of the hearing, Joe strolled calmly into the courtroom twenty minutes late. Before taking his seat, he ambled over to the bench where the plaintiffs were sitting and greeted each of them.

"Howdy, George," he said to the carpenter.

The carpenter managed a wan smile. "Hey, Joe," he said.

Joe moved on to the electrician, the plumber, the general contractor, the man from the linen supply, and on down the line. "Howdy . . . Afternoon . . . Hello . . ." He spoke without a hint of sarcasm or irony. His voice was cheerful. His eyes were bright, his smile broad and easy. It was almost as if he were greeting patrons at Sweet Georgia Brown's. Joe's affability contrasted with the discomfiture of the men on the bench. Their embarrassed, almost sheepish expressions made them seem more like the accused than the aggrieved—as if by being there they had been caught in an act of disloyalty against their genial friend. They smiled meekly and mumbled hellos. At the end of the row, Joe came to a tiny, sparrowlike man with silver hair and bushy black eyebrows. It was an antiques dealer from Charleston who had sold him the merry-go-round horse and other pieces of furniture. Joe brightened.

"Why, Mr. Russell!" he said. "What a surprise! I didn't know you were coming."

Mr. Russell shifted nervously in his seat. "Believe me, Joe, I would rather not have come. I really hate this, but you know. I . . . uh . . ."

"Oh, that's all right," said Joe. "I can't say I blame you. It's just that if I'd known you were coming I'd have asked you to bring that pair of sconces I liked so much."

"Oh, did you?" the man said. "I mean, did I . . . I mean, did we . . . uh." Mr. Russell blinked, as if trying to clear his head. "Oh, now I remember," he said. "We did talk about those sconces, didn't we. You're right. I'd forgotten all about that. Well . . . uh. Now that you mention it, Joe, I guess I could have brought them with me—"

"Well, don't worry about it," said Joe. "We can discuss it later." He walked over and took his seat alone at the defense table.

The hearing judge gaveled the room to order.

"Mr. Odom, are you being represented by counsel?"

"Your Honor," said Joe, "as a member in good standing of the state bar of Georgia, I'll be representing myself."

The judge nodded. "Well then, let's proceed."

An assistant prosecutor read off the list of Joe's bad checks. Then one by one the plaintiffs took the stand and described the work they had done or the goods they had supplied and how, no matter how often they tried to cash Joe's checks, they always bounced. When Mr. Russell took the stand, the prosecutor and the judge conferred at the bench for several minutes, riffling through papers. The judge then rapped his gavel and informed Mr. Russell that in filing his complaint he had not followed the proper procedure; therefore his claim would be disallowed, at least for the time being. This would reduce the bad-check charges against Joe by the sum of $4,200. A red-faced Mr. Russell came down from the stand and took his seat.

"Your Honor," said Joe, "with your permission, I'd like to have a word with Mr. Russell."

"No objection," the judge replied.

Joe motioned for the antiques dealer to come over and sit next to him. He took the man's file and spread the papers on the table. Then, while the courtroom looked on, Joe read through the papers, speaking to Mr. Russell in a quiet, confidential tone. After a few minutes, he looked up at the judge.

"Your Honor," he said, "if you will allow me, I think we can remedy this situation in twenty minutes or so, and once we've done that you can reinstate Mr. Russell's claim against me."

The judge looked warily at Joe, uncertain whether he was merely having a laugh at the court's expense, or whether he might actually be slipping a fast one by him.

"The court appreciates your offer," the judge said, "but I

doubt there's any precedent for a defendant acting as counsel for the plaintiff. One could worry that counsel might place his own best interests ahead of those of his client, if you see my point."

"I do, Your Honor," said Joe, "but in this case it's really just a matter of filling out forms. This gentleman has come all the way from Charleston to claim money that's rightfully his, and it doesn't seem fair to turn him away just because he messed up on some minor clerical procedure."

"True," said the judge. "Well, all right. Go ahead."

"One more thing, Your Honor," said Joe. "I would like to add for the record that I am doing this on a *pro bono* basis . . ."

"Good of you," said the judge.

". . . forgoing my normal legal fee of forty-two hundred dollars." In the laughter that followed, Joe turned toward Mandy and me and winked.

The hearing went into recess while Joe rewrote Mr. Russell's claim against him. When he was finished, Mr. Russell's $4,200 was added back onto the total, and Joe took the stand. He told the court that he had written the checks in the expectation that the developers of City Market, where Sweet Georgia Brown's was located, would come through with several thousand dollars they owed him, but they had not. Therefore the checks were unintentional overdrafts. The judge and the prosecutor appeared to doubt Joe's explanation, but they agreed to drop the charges if he made good on the entire $18,000 in one month's time. Failing that, he would almost certainly be indicted. The judge, the prosecutor, and the plaintiffs all expressed the hope that Joe would settle the matter before it came to that.

And he did. But it was not through the cash flow of Sweet Georgia Brown's. Joe was saved this time by a loan of $18,000 from a rich young couple, who had recently moved to Savannah and had fallen under the spell of Joe Odom and Sweet Georgia Brown's.

Joe's good luck extended to the matter of finding new quarters to live in before John Thorsen returned. At the last moment, he had arranged to occupy the spacious and elegant parlor floor of the Hamilton-Turner House a few blocks away on Lafayette Square. The landlord was an old friend who lived in Natchez and knew all about Joe's bus tours and the tourist lunches and Joe's entourage and Jerry the hairdresser. All of that was fine with him.

Joe finished his sweep of the Pulaski Square house, removing the last traces of his occupancy. Then he came back outside to sit on the front steps and have a cigarette. He had to admit things were not so bad after all. His bad checks had been made good. He was about to move into a beautiful old mansion. The prosecutor was off his back, and there was nothing for him to do now but smoke his cigarette and wait for Mandy to do one final load of laundry. When she was finished, he would disconnect the electricity and the telephone, turn off the water, lock the front door, and move on.

It was daybreak when Joe went to bed in his new house. He slept until early evening. Then he rose and went to Sweet Georgia Brown's, where the first person through the door was Mr. Russell, the antiques dealer from Charleston. He was carrying the sconces—ornate brass fixtures with tall hurricane lamps. Joe put them up on either side of the big mirror over the bar and lit the candles. The light danced and flickered.

"Will you take a check for them?" he asked.

"Why certainly," said Mr. Russell.

"I'd be much obliged," said Joe, "if you'd . . . uh . . . hold on to it until the first of the month."

"I'd be happy to," Mr. Russell said.

Joe turned to go back to the piano and found himself looking into the grinning face of the real estate agent, John Thorsen.

"I'm back!" Mr. Thorsen proclaimed. "If you still want that house on Pulaski Square, you can have it. I saved it for you the whole time I was gone."

"I know you did," said Joe, "and I appreciate it more than I can say."

Chapter 14

THE PARTY OF THE YEAR

Engraved invitations to Jim Williams's black-tie Christmas party began arriving in the mailboxes of Savannah's better homes the first week in December. They were received with surprise and consternation, for it had been assumed that under the circumstances Williams would not be giving any party at all this year. Faced with the invitations, Savannah's social set grappled with the realization that the crowning social event of the winter season was going to take place at the scene of a notorious shooting and that barely a month later the host would go on trial for murder. What to do? Savannah was a place of manners and decorum, first and foremost. It had been the birthplace, after all, of Ward McAllister, that self-appointed social arbiter of late-nineteenth-century America. It was Ward McAllister who had compiled the list of New York's elite "Four Hundred" in 1892. This son of Savannah had codified the rules of conduct for ladies and gentlemen. The lively debate already raging over Williams's guilt or innocence shifted focus, moving to the question of whether it was proper for him to give his

Christmas party and whether (since he was indeed going to give it) it was proper to attend. This year, instead of asking, "Have you been invited?" people wanted to know "Are you going to accept?"

Millicent Mooreland had counseled Williams not to give his party. "It wouldn't be the thing to do, Jim," she told him, and she thought she had talked him out of it until her invitation arrived. For Mrs. Mooreland, the party posed an agonizing dilemma. After many sleepless nights, she decided not to go.

Williams refused to acknowledge that his party might be a manifestation of poor taste. He and his lawyers, he said, had decided that not to have the party would be an admission of guilt. Therefore, he was going to have it. He would, however, skip the all-male party the night after. "The only person who's really going to miss that one," Williams said, "will be Leopold Adler. He won't be able to get out his binoculars and spy on it."

Williams was convinced that Lee Adler had prodded the district attorney into charging him with murder instead of a lesser crime, while outwardly pretending to be concerned for him. Two days after the shooting, Emma Adler had written Williams a note expressing her sorrow and offering to help in any way possible. She had signed the note "Fondly, Emma."

"The use of the word 'fondly,' " said Williams, "proves the letter was an exercise in insincerity. Emma Adler is no more fond of me than I am of her, and we both know it." Williams did not invite the Adlers to this year's party.

As in years past, Williams set about making elaborate preparations well in advance. His assistants went out and gathered three truckloads of fresh palmetto fronds, cedar boughs, and magnolia leaves, and spent a full week decorating the seven fireplaces and six chandeliers in Mercer House. On the day of the party, Lucille Wright arrived with roasts of ham, turkey, and beef; gallons of shrimp and oysters; tureens of dips and sauces; and quantities of cakes, brownies, and pies. She arranged the bountiful repast on silver platters and placed them around a mound of pink and white camellias in the center of the dining-room table. A sixty-foot garland of flame-throated orchids hung in swags along the spiral stairway. The scent of cedar and pine accented the air.

At seven o'clock sharp, Williams opened the front door of Mercer House and stood with his mother and his sister, Dorothy Kingery, to receive his guests. The two women wore evening gowns. Williams had on black tie and dinner jacket with Russian imperial Fabergé cuff links gleaming in the cuffs of his dress shirt. He took a deep breath. "Now I'll find out who my real friends are." He did not have long to wait. The first arrivals were already coming up the walk.

And they kept coming. Dozens, scores, over a hundred. Each greeted Williams with warm expressions of support and then left their coats with an attendant in the study. If the mood was subdued at first, it picked up quickly as more and more guests arrived. White-jacketed butlers circulated with trays of drinks and hors d'oeuvres ("Pour with a heavy hand," Williams had told the bartender). Soon, the laughter and hilarity rose to such a pitch it drowned out the cocktail pianist at the grand piano. Williams had invited 200 people and set a goal for himself of 150 acceptances. It was clear that he had made his goal. In his own mind at least, he had won a plebiscite of the social set. After an hour, he left his post in the receiving line and mingled with his guests.

"What sort of people have come?" I asked him. "And what sort have stayed away?"

"The holier-than-thou set has stayed home," he said, "the ones who have always been jealous of my success in Savannah and who want to let me know they disapprove. In addition to them, some of the people who honestly wish me well but are afraid to admit it publicly have also stayed home. The people you see here tonight are the ones who are secure enough to ignore anyone who might question their decision to come. Like that lady over there, Alice Dowling; her late husband was the U.S. ambassador to Germany and Korea. She's talking with Malcolm Maclean, the former mayor of Savannah and head of one of Savannah's leading law firms.

The little old lady immediately to Maclean's right is one of the seven women who founded the Historic Savannah Foundation: Jane Wright. She's descended from the third royal governor of Georgia. Now, to her right, you see a distinguished-looking man with a white mustache. He's Bob Minis, one of the most brilliant and influential financiers in Savannah. His great-great-grandfather was the first white man born in the state. He's Jewish—a blue-blood Georgia Jew, the only Jew in the Oglethorpe Club. To his right, the two men talking in the doorway are George Patterson, the retired president of the Liberty National Bank, and Alexander Yearley, the former chairman of Robinson-Humphrey, the big Atlanta investment bankers." Williams had the look of a poker player holding four aces.

"Now, over there by the piano," he went on, "the lady in the bright red dress and the contralto voice. She's Vera Dutton Strong, talking nonstop as usual. She's the heiress to the Dutton pulpwood fortune, and she lives in a giant palace in Ardsley Park. It's fit for an embassy. Vera raises champion poodles. She's got about a dozen, and at least seven of them sleep right in the bedroom with her and her husband, Cahill. Vera's audience at the moment happens to be the director of the Telfair museum, Alexander Gaudieri, which is a blessing because she won't give him a chance to get a word in, and nobody wants to hear what *he* has to say anyway."

As we walked past Vera Strong and the museum director, we caught a snippet of their conversation. "The bloodlines on both sides are magnificent," Mrs. Strong was saying. "You should see the way she carries herself. She has an even temperament and bright eyes. She's very intelligent."

"Not another dog!" Williams cut in.

"Who said anything about a dog?" Mrs. Strong replied.

"Now don't be coy, Vera," said Williams. " 'Magnificent bloodlines . . . even temperament.' No one begrudges you another poodle. Come, come. Fess up!"

Vera Strong suddenly gasped. "My God! How embarrassing! I was talking about Peter's fiancée. I'm going to be a mother-in-law!" She threw her head back and laughed; then she clutched Williams by the arm. "You must *swear* you'll never tell anybody what I just said!" Having sworn Williams to secrecy, she turned to the couple standing next to her. "Did you hear that? Jim overheard me talking about Peter's fiancée, and it's simply *too* mortifying, I was saying . . ."

Williams turned aside. "Well, that's Vera Strong. One of her many saving graces is her sense of humor.

"Now those two," he said, nodding toward a handsome middle-aged man and woman, "are Roger and Claire Moultrie. He was president of the Savannah Gas Company until about fifteen years ago, when they got involved in a bit of a scandal. One night they drove out to a secluded spot along the river and parked their car. A night watchman came by and told them to leave, because they were trespassing on the grounds of some shipyard or other. They refused to budge. The watchman called the cops. A cop came and demanded identification. Roger became belligerent and scuffled with the policeman. At that point, Claire grabbed a pistol out of the glove compartment and shouted, 'Duck, Roger, I'll kill the sonofabitch.' The cop dragged her out of the car and pummeled her so badly she spent a week in the hospital. Both were charged with trespassing, drunkenness, disorderly conduct, and resisting arrest—she with threatening the life of a policeman, he with striking a police officer. Roger refused the judge's suggestion that he pay a small fine and be done with it, so they went to trial. At the trial Roger said they had driven to the moonlit spot to inspect the installation of gas lines and that therefore, in so many words, they had been on company business. The most respected citizens of Savannah lined up to serve as character witnesses, and the jury delivered its verdict in twenty-five minutes: innocent of all charges. Those two don't feel they have to answer to anybody. That's probably why they're here tonight."

Williams looked around the room. "That man over there in the formal hunting outfit is Harry Cram. He's a legend." Williams was speaking of a patrician gentleman, about seventy, who was wearing a scarlet tailcoat with gold embroidery over one pocket. "Harry Cram has never worked a day in his life," said Williams. "He's one of the first remittance men to come to the low country. His family sends his monthly checks from Philadelphia with the understanding he'll never go back there, and he leads a life of high style—traveling around the world, hunting, drinking, and playing polo. He's a wild man, completely charming. The woman standing next to him is his fourth wife, Lucy. They live out on Devil's Elbow, a huge, wooded island off Bluffton, South Carolina. There's a John Singer Sargent portrait of Harry's grandfather in the dining room." In his formal hunting togs, Harry Cram looked a fit subject for a Sargent portrait himself.

"Harry used to amuse himself by flying over friends' houses in private planes and bombing them with bags of flour, aiming for the chimney," said Williams. "One time he rode into the old DeSoto Hotel on horseback. He's a daredevil and a superb marksman. When he was living out at Foot Point Plantation, he'd invite people for Sunday lunch and tell them, 'Now, be sure to arrive by noon.' And he meant it. At quarter to twelve, he'd take a drink and his rifle and climb into a tree, where he could watch his guests coming up the long driveway. At the stroke of noon, he'd take aim through the telescopic sights and shoot the hood ornaments off the cars of the latecomers, just to let them know they were late."

Williams caught Harry Cram's eye from across the room, and we started moving in his direction. "One last story before we say hello to Harry," Williams said. "About five years ago, two Parris Island marines swam over to Harry's island in frogmen's suits and broke into the house. They took Harry's sixteen-year-old son, Peter, at bayonet point, down the hall to Harry's bedroom door. Peter called out, 'Dad, there's two men here with bayonets. They say they're going to kill me unless you give them some money.' Harry called back through the door, 'All right, just let me get the money.' Peter knew what to expect, so the moment Harry flung the door open, he ducked. Harry fired two shots with his thirty-eight and hit both marines between the eyes."

At this point, Williams and I were standing in front of the Crams. "I didn't hear you ask for a *ginger ale,* did I, Harry?" Williams asked in mock alarm.

"I'm afraid you did," said Cram. "Isn't it shameful! I'm on the wagon, believe it or not. It's been about a year now." Cram had bright, darting eyes and wispy hair that stood straight up on the top of his head like the crest of a snowy egret. "Lucy brought me to the Veterans Hospital in Charleston drunk as a fiddler's bitch. Apparently, they asked me who the president was. They always ask drunks that. I hadn't the vaguest idea. So they put me in something called 'the Tank.' I was there a week, and I haven't wanted a drink since. I have no idea what they did to me. I've been meaning to ask."

Mrs. Cram nodded. "The time had definitely come," she said. "Harry wanted to play William Tell and shoot an apple off my head."

"I must say, though," said Harry, "I never shot badly during my drinking years, and I don't think I was ever sober from the age of sixteen. I've gone on the wagon quite a few times in my life, but I always got off it in a hurry. This dinner jacket is proof of that. See this little hole?" Cram pointed to a small hole just below his breast pocket. "One time, years ago, I stopped drinking and locked all the liquor in the closet. The next day I decided I'd been sober long enough, but I didn't have the patience to look for the key. So I just shot the lock off the door. The bullet went through every suit on the rack." Harry turned around. There was another bullet hole in the back.

A couple standing next to the Crams joined the fun inspecting the bullet holes in Harry's jacket. Williams drifted toward the living room. "And that's Harry Cram," he said. "I imagine he's here tonight because it would never occur to him that he shouldn't be. Now, see that lady standing over by the window, talking to the bald-headed man? She's Lila Mayhew. Her family's one of the oldest in Savannah; they've lived in two of Savannah's most important historic houses. She's a little dotty though, so it's possible she doesn't even know that I've shot anybody."

Williams left me and went back to the entrance hall, and I drew closer to Mrs. Mayhew. She was speaking to the bald man.

"Now, exactly where did Jim shoot the young man?" Mrs. Mayhew asked, her voice sounding like that of a little lost girl.

"I think it was in the chest," the man said.

"No, I mean where in this house?"

"Oh, ha-ha. In the study. Across the hall, where you put your coat."

"And what did they do with the body?" she asked.

"I suppose they buried it. Wouldn't you?"

"That's not what I mean," said Mrs. Mayhew. "Did they cremate it first or bury it whole?"

"That I couldn't tell you."

"Because you know what happened to Grandmother, don't you?"

"I certainly do," said the man.

"Grandmother's body was sent to Jacksonville to be cremated."

"Yes, I remember that well," he said. "That's a famous story—"

"And the crematorium sent her ashes back to us in an urn. We put the urn in the parlor until it could be interred at Bonaventure. But Father was a chemist, you know."

"And a very good one too," said the man. "The very best."

"Father was feeling downcast and at loose ends. After supper, he took the urn downtown to his laboratory and performed tests on the ashes. That's when he found out they were not Grandmother's at all. The ashes were pure oak. They'd sent us the ashes from an oak tree. We never did find out what happened to Grandmother. When Father passed on, we took no chances. We buried him just as he was when he died, in his raincoat. That's why I wondered if they cremated the young man Jim shot and, if they did, whether they know for certain they got his ashes back . . ."

Lila Mayhew trailed off into a sort of reverie, and the bald man peered out the living-room window. "My God," he said, "here comes that Dawes woman! She's all in green, from head to toe!" Serena Dawes was just then coming up the walk on the arm of Luther Driggers. She was wrapped in a green feather boa, and her fingernails, toenails, and eye shadow were green to match.

Williams greeted them at the front door. "Our emerald bird has arrived at last!" he said.

"I need a drink and a place to rest my ankles," Serena said, blowing a kiss and sweeping past him into the living room. She settled herself in an armchair, arranging her ostrich feathers with one hand and scooping a martini from a passing tray with the other. Her eyes swept the room. *"Boy!"* she called to a short man with a camera. "Come over here and take a picture of a real lady!" Once the afterimage of flashbulbs had cleared from Serena's vision, her gaze came to rest on a pretty young blond woman.

"I don't believe I've had the pleasure," Serena said sweetly. "I'm Serena Dawes."

"My name is Anna," the blond woman said. "I'm visiting from Sweden."

"Isn't that nice," said Serena, "and what brings you to Savannah?"

"Well, it's such a beautiful city. I love to come here to . . . to look at it."

"Really! Just to look? Is that all?"

"I love architecture, and you have such beautiful houses here."

"But do you have friends in Savannah?" Serena persisted.

"Oh yes," said Anna.

"Do tell me who!"

"Colonel Atwood."

"Well!" said Serena, fluffing her feathers. "Why didn't you just say you've come to Savannah to fuck? We'd all have understood completely!"

A dark-haired gentleman bowed and kissed Serena's hand. "Serena, how lovely to see you out of bed."

"Colonel Atwood, you're too kind. I'd get out of bed for you anytime."

Colonel Jim Atwood was a man of varied interests. He was the first person in America to cultivate water chestnuts on any considerable scale, having planted fifty acres of them in a former rice paddy south of Savannah. But that was just a hobby; Atwood was primarily an entrepreneur and a trader who dealt in everything from storage tanks to damaged merchandise. He had been known to produce his American Express card and buy, sight unseen, the contents of entire warehouses and oceangoing freighters. He had bought and sold 119 water-damaged sports cars in one deal and 400 tons of squashed dates in another. One of Colonel Atwood's many interests was the subject of his book *Edge Weapons of the Third Reich*. At the time the book came out, he had cornered the market in Nazi daggers, swords, and bayonets. He had bought sixty German arms factories together with their stocks of abandoned Nazi weapons. He also owned Hitler's personal silverware, heavy oversized pieces with AH engraved in a slender sans-serif.

Serena batted her eyes at Colonel Atwood. "Are you carrying any of your Kraut daggers tonight, Colonel?"

"Nope. Only my trusty sidearm," said Atwood. He took a small revolver out of his pocket and held it in his palm. "Know what this is?"

"Of course I do," said Serena. "My late husband blew his brains out with one of those."

"Oh!" said a bone-thin woman standing next to Serena. "So did mine! I'll never forget it." The woman was Alma Knox Carter, a convenience-store heiress who lived across Monterey Square. "I was fixing myself a drink in the kitchen. *Gunsmoke* was on TV, and I heard a shot. Naturally I didn't think anything about it. I thought it was part of the TV show, but then I walked into the foyer and saw Lyman sprawled out on the floor with a pistol in his hand."

Colonel Atwood's revolver caught the attention of Dr. Tod Fulton. "Twenty-two Magnum, huh? Not bad. I carry this little number." Dr. Fulton reached in his pocket and took out a black leather wallet. The wallet had a hole through the middle. The crescent curve of a trigger could be seen along one edge of the hole. "It's a twenty-two Derringer in disguise," he said. "If a mugger holds me up and demands my money, all I have to do is pull out this wallet and . . . payday!"

"My word!" said Mrs. Carter.

Dr. Fulton pocketed his wallet. "My wife carries a thirty-eight," he said.

"So do I," said Anna brightly.

"I'll tell you one thing," Mrs. Carter said. "If I'd so much as touched that gun in Lyman's hand, they'd have charged me with murder as surely as I'm standing here!" Mrs. Carter was so frail one might have doubted she had the strength to lift a gun.

"Someday I *will* shoot a man!" said Serena. "God knows I've already tried!" She lifted a pearl-handled revolver out of her purse and held it daintily by its chrome-plated muzzle. "Just ask my former sweetheart, Shelby Grey. I wanted like hell to shoot him! I begged him to let me do it! I didn't want to kill him, of course. I only wanted to shoot him in the toe, just to give him something to remember me by. But the coward wouldn't hold still! I blew a hole in the air conditioner."

"You . . . shot him?" Mrs. Carter said, wide-eyed.

"I missed."

"How fortunate."

Serena sighed. "Not for dear Shelby. Now he has nothing of any permanence to remind him of my love. Still, I am very much afraid I will have to shoot a man one day, and it won't be in the toe. My husband left me priceless jewels, as everybody knows, and certain individuals would love to get their hands on them. I live in fear of burglars day and night. That's why I always have this little beauty close at hand. When I'm home I keep it by my bed." Serena glanced at Colonel Atwood. "And when I leave the house I put it in my purse. But anytime I feel the bastards are about to spring, I just stash it between my boobs." Serena tucked the revolver into her bosom and lifted a fresh martini from a passing tray.

Feeling in need of a drink myself at this point, I intercepted the waiter as he came in my direction. Two other guests, a man and a woman, stepped up and helped themselves too.

"It was a *crime passionnel,*" the woman was saying, "so I don't think it counts. You know, a lovers' quarrel. These things happen. It isn't the same as murder."

"My dear," said the man, "it may have been a crime of passion, but I know three people who served on that grand jury. They've seen the evidence, and I gather it's going to be sticky for Jim."

I turned my back and looked in the other direction, but at the same time I moved closer to the couple in order to hear them better. The man lowered his voice.

"First of all," he said, "I'm told the Crime Laboratory came up with some troubling results. There was no gunpowder residue on Danny Hansford's hands. That means he couldn't have fired the gun at Jim, as Jim claims he did."

"Good Lord!" the woman gasped.

"The location of the bullet wounds also appears to be at odds with Jim's scenario of self-defense," the man said. "One bullet entered the chest, which sounds all right, but another hit Hansford in the back. A third one hit him behind the ear. So the way it looks, Jim shot him once in the chest and then stepped around the desk and shot him twice more as he lay facedown on the floor, in a sort of coup de grâce."

"How dreadful," the woman said. "You mean it wasn't self-defense?"

"I'm afraid it doesn't look that way. The fingerprint analysis is even more damaging. The gun found under Hansford's hand had no fingerprints on it at all, even though it had been fired. This means somebody wiped them off. So it begins to look as though Jim shot Danny and then got a second gun and fired a few shots from where Danny had been standing, to make it look as if Hansford had fired at him. Then it seems he must have wiped his fingerprints off the gun and put it under Danny's hand."

"I'm feeling faint," the woman said. "What do you think will happen to Jim?"

"Just what I told him when I arrived here tonight. He'll get off."

"But how is that possible?" the woman asked.

"A good lawyer can challenge the evidence, maybe even turn it around to the defendant's advantage. And Jim has good lawyers. That's why I think he'll get off. That, and because of his standing in the community."

Having delivered his private assessment of the case, the man changed the subject, and I drifted into the hallway, where Williams and his mother were standing with a small circle of guests.

Blanche Williams had driven in from Gordon, Georgia, where she had lived all her life. Now in her late seventies, she was a tall woman, thin as a stork. Not a hair was out of place in the arrangement of tight white curls that covered her head like a snowy cap. She stood shyly with her hands clasped in front of her. One of the other women was admiring her evening gown.

"Why, thank you," Mrs. Williams said politely. "James gave it to me. Whenever he has a big party, he likes to make sure I have a pretty new dress and that there's a flower waiting for me when I get to Savannah." She glanced at her son, as if to reassure herself that she had said the right thing.

"Mother is always the belle of the ball!" Williams said heartily.

Mrs. Williams took this as a sign of approval and was emboldened to continue. "James has given me so many pieces of jewelry until finally I got to where I told him one day, I said, 'James, I don't know how I'll ever wear them all!' And he said, 'Well, Mother, I'll just have to give more parties so you can come to Savannah more often and wear all the things you've got.' James is real good about taking me places too. He's taken me to Europe five times, and *oh!,* one time he called and said, 'Mother, we're going to leave in three days for London on the Concorde,' and I said, 'Now, James, don't tell me that. We're not going to fly anywhere on the Concorde!' And he said, 'Oh yes, we are. I've already got the tickets,' and I thought, 'My Lord, what did they cost!' But then pretty quick I knew James was serious, and I had to stop fussin' and get busy. I had to get ready in three days, and I did, and sure enough we went to London on the Concorde."

Mrs. Williams spoke in a quiet rush of words, as if wanting to finish quickly and not trespass on the conversational terrain any longer than necessary. Her erect posture and the alert look in her eye suggested that despite her apologetic manner, she was a lady of considerable fiber and determination. In a few moments, Williams was drawn into a conversation with new arrivals, and Mrs. Williams and I found ourselves facing each other. I uttered a pleasantry about the festive party, and Mrs. Williams nodded in agreement.

"James has always had a crowd around him," she said, "even when he was little. One time, he got him a little picture machine—the kind that flashes pictures on a wall—and he'd give little picture shows, and the other children would come over and have the best time, and he'd charge them a penny apiece. 'Course I had to have a little something for them to eat or drink, you know, just to munch. That was when he was eleven or twelve. When he was thirteen, he used to ride around the countryside on his bicycle, buying antiques to sell. That's how he started out. At first he went to the colored people's houses, and he'd buy little oil lamps and things they didn't want. He'd pay a quarter for them and then fix them up and sell them for fifty cents. Then he bought better things, like mirrors and furniture and whatnot, and he'd fix them in his woodworking shop. He put a little ad in the paper, 'Antiques for Sale,' and you'd be surprised. The ladies from Macon would come to Gordon and get him out of high school! The superintendent was so impressed. They were high-class ladies—doctors' wives and so forth—and James would bring them to the house, and they'd buy things right out of his bedroom! He worked his way up. Bit by bit, all by himself.

"It got to where a few years ago I thought, Isn't life grand! My children have turned out fine. My daughter teaches at the university, and James is doing so well in Savannah. My work is done. The Lord can take me now. But He didn't. And when James got in this awful mess, I thought this must be what God has been saving me for."

The din of the party surged in volume, but Mrs. Williams did not raise her voice. She kept speaking in her quiet way, looking straight into my eyes—in fact, she seemed to be looking through me.

"James called me on a Saturday, right after lunch I believe it was, and he told me, 'Mother, I've got bad news. I had to shoot Danny.' Well, I just froze. I said, 'Sugar, you come right straight home,' and he did, and when he got there I didn't question him. I just let him talk when he felt like it, because he was so keyed up and hurt and everything else, and before long people found out he was there, and I tell you people started calling. Goodness, there were so many calls I just put them on a slip."

Mrs. Williams paused as two guests stopped to say goodbye. "Y'all be sure and come back again next year," she told them. Then she turned back to me.

"I never did trust that boy. He was kind of vague, the way he looked at you. I wouldn't tell James this, but to me that Danny Hansford was just b-a-a-ad news. James brought him to the house one time. In a little bit, James went out in the back to wash his car, and I didn't see the boy, and I said, 'James, I don't see him,' and James said, 'Oh, that's all right, Mother. He told me he was just going to walk around out front.' Well, when it came time to eat, the boy was still not there, and James said, 'Mother, I'll tell you what: If Danny takes a notion to go somewhere, he won't tell anybody about it, he'll just go. He's done it before.' Well, right then I understood what the boy had done. Don't ask me how I knew. Something just told me. I had an idea he was downtown huntin' dope. Gordon's only a small town, but I figured he saw something down at the filling station on the way to the house, and he wanted to go back there and buy some dope. James found out the next day that the boy had hitchhiked all the way back to Savannah."

Mrs. Williams looked down briefly as she rearranged the wadded handkerchief she'd been clutching in her hands.

"Now, I'll just be frank with you," she said. "Sometimes James is too good to people. I don't know, maybe he got it from me. I can get feeling sorry for people too quick, and that's not good, because a lot of people know how to play you and get your sympathy. I know some people do James that way, and he'll get to where he feels sorry for them. He'll try to help 'em, like he tried to help that boy. There were times I felt like maybe I should talk to James, but being a mother I was afraid I might be interfering. You don't want to overstep the line, so I never did talk to him like I wish I had.

"James would help anybody, and that's the reason I just hate to see him in this mess. Why, when James sold Cabbage Island and made a bunch of money, the first thing he did was he fixed up my house, and then he gave my church a check for ten thousand dollars to buy an electric organ. I just don't know. Maybe this mess is going to be a lesson. I believe it's going to make James realize that he's got to think of himself sometimes. . . ."

Mrs. Williams smiled as her son reappeared at her side.

"Well, I'll hush now," she said.

"What have you two been talking about?" he asked.

"I was saying how everything is going to work out just fine, James." Mrs. Williams's answer was drowned out by the convivial hubbub around her.

"I'm sorry, Mother, I didn't hear."

Mrs. Williams took a deep breath, and for the first time all evening she raised her voice a little. "I said, 'Everything is going to work out . . . just . . . fine!' "

"Of course it is, Mother," he said. "It always has, and it always will."

Chapter 15

CIVIC DUTY

"Hell, I'd have shot Danny Hansford too," said Dr. James C. Metts, the coroner of Chatham County. "This guy was just a badass. He scared Williams to death. You know, hell, it's three o'clock in the morning, and here he is having a temper fit because Williams won't play an Atari game." Dr. Metts, a generally soft-spoken man, had spent several hours investigating the scene at Mercer House the night of the shooting. It was he who had signed the death certificate and ordered the autopsy. A week before Jim Williams's trial was to begin, one of Williams's lawyers, John Wright Jones, paid a call on Dr. Metts in his office to discuss the case.

John Wright Jones was one of Savannah's better-known criminal lawyers. A burly bear of a man, he was assisting in Williams's defense. He had seen the autopsy report and the police photographs taken in Mercer House after the shooting. He was concerned about the bullet hole in Danny Hansford's back and the one behind his ear. He asked Dr. Metts if it was possible to reconstruct the shooting in such a way that Danny Hansford was *not* lying facedown when those two shots hit him.

"Yes," said Dr. Metts, "you could do that. The first shot hit him in the front left side of the chest. When you get shot in the chest, it's like a punch; you rotate, you spin around. So the next shot hits you in the right side of the back, and you keep rotating, and the next one hits you behind the ear. It's possible, if the ballistics work out, that Danny Hansford was not shot lying down. He could have been standing up."

"That's what I was hoping," said Jones. "So the bottom line is that you don't really know whether or not he was shot when he was lying on the floor, do you?"

"That's correct."

"All right. And if you are called to testify, that's what you're going to say?"

"Yes," said Dr. Metts. "But, John, you've got another problem. The hand lying on top of the gun has blood all over it, and there's no blood on the gun itself. Now, there are only two places where blood was flowing from Danny Hansford—his head and his chest. The boy, when he fell, must have fallen on his right hand. And I guess maybe for artistic license Williams might have moved his hand out and put it over the gun where, you know, it looked better."

"You sure about that?"

"Positive. You see, the blood on Hansford's hand is smeared, like somebody dragged it out from under the body. If I were you, I'd say Williams panicked and checked Danny Hansford's pulse—reached in there and pulled his arm out and checked his pulse and then put it on the gun so it would look better or something."

Dr. Metts's suggestion was not an acceptable option. Jim Williams had already put his version of the story on record with his interview in the *Georgia Gazette*. In the interview, Williams had made no mention of ever touching the body.

"Damn, if you don't brighten up my day," said Jones.

"Then there's one other thing," said Dr. Metts, "something else that shows Mr. Williams rearranged the scene. He moved furniture to make things look a little bit better, I guess, but he got a little careless doing it."

"In what way?"

"He picked up a chair and put it down on top of the guy's britches leg." Dr. Metts chuckled.

"Oooh, I bet y'all got pictures of that, ain't you?"

"Color prints," said the coroner.

"It shows the pants leg underneath the chair?"

"Uh-huh."

"Well, that sure is nice." Jones shook his head ruefully. "What else you got?"

"I tell you what," said Dr. Metts. "I believe I know when that bastard got shot."

"When was that?" asked Jones.

"When he stubbed out his cigarette."

"His what?"

"I found a cigarette butt that had been stubbed out into the leather desktop. It was still sitting on its end. I think when the guy did that, Mr. Williams got pissed off and shot him."

"Like I said, Doc, you really brighten up my day," said Jones.

"Quite frankly, though, my sympathies lie with Mr. Williams," said Dr. Metts. "It did occur around three in the morning. Mr. Williams presumably had to get up and work, and this kid was being an obnoxious bastard, wanting to play games and bust up the furniture."

"Any other kind words of encouragement?" Jones asked.

"Not that I can think of, John," he said. "You've got your work cut out for you, though. I would think your jury selection is going to be key. You have a problem there in that it was obviously a homosexual-type situation. You'll have to play it so the jury is sympathetic to Mr. Williams and don't think too bad of him for shooting this guy."

Jones picked up his briefcase. "Well, as we all know, Doc, juries in Savannah don't seem to mind seeing homosexuals get killed. I mean, you can stomp a homosexual to death in our community, and that doesn't seem to make a difference."

"No, I know," said Dr. Metts. He walked Jones to the door of his office. "Well, John, all I can say is Mr. Williams probably did his civic duty shooting this sonofabitch."

—

John Wright Jones's remark about stomping homosexuals to death was a reference to a murder case that had come to trial only a few months earlier and deeply shocked Savannah.

The murder victim in that case had been a thirty-three-year-old man from Columbus, Georgia, who had come to Savannah to judge a beauty pageant. Married and with two children, he was stomped to death in a darkened parking garage by four U.S. Army Rangers. Rangers were reputed to be the toughest men in the army. There was a squadron of them out at Hunter Army Airfield on the southside. They were trained to endure harsh punishment and to dish it out as well. Early on the evening of the stomping, a witness saw the four Rangers strolling on Bay Street, bending parking meters to the ground with their bare hands. Later, the four went into Missy's Adult Boutique, a pornographic bookshop off Johnson Square, where they encountered the beauty-pageant judge. The man made a sexual advance. They enticed him into a parking garage and beat and kicked him so brutally that an expert in trauma injury testified that when the victim arrived at the hospital he was "probably the most mutilated person I have ever seen still alive." He had suffered multiple fractures of the skull, cheeks, jawbone, and eye sockets. The expert said it had taken two people to pry his eyes open. "He was almost unrecognizable as a human being."

At the trial, the attorney for the Rangers asked the jury to "place responsibility where it lies." The defendants, he said, were young, foolish, clean-cut, and honest. They had been the victims of a homosexual advance. The jurors were sympathetic to the Rangers and rejected the charge of murder. Still, each man had admitted kicking the victim, so the jurors felt compelled to declare them guilty of something. They chose the lightest possible count: simple battery. Simple battery is a misdemeanor; it can mean that one person merely touched another. The sentence was one year in jail with the possibility of parole in six months.

The Ranger verdict provoked a bitter public outcry. Letters to the newspaper condemned the jury for its callousness and for sullying the name of justice in Savannah. One of the nurses who had treated the victim wrote: "If this is a misdemeanor, may I never see the victim of a felony."

The trial had been the courtroom debut of Chatham County's new district attorney, thirty-seven-year-old Spencer Lawton, Jr. The verdict had been a crushing defeat, and it left observers wondering whether Lawton was capable of discharging the responsibilities of his new office.

The Lawtons were a distinguished old Savannah family. Spencer Lawton's great-great grandfather, General Alexander R. Lawton, had been in charge of defending Savannah during the early part of the Civil War and later became quartermaster general of the Confederate Army. After the war, General Lawton was one of the ten men who founded the American Bar Association; he served as its president in 1882. Later, Grover Cleveland appointed him ambassador to Austria. The Lawton family plot at Bonaventure Cemetery was one of the largest. A white marble figure of Christ stood by a towering Gothic arch on a bluff by the river.

Another of Lawton's forebears, Spencer Shotter, amassed a fortune in the naval-stores business at the turn of the century and built one of the most grandiose estates in the South on the grounds of Greenwich Plantation, immediately adjacent to Bonaventure Cemetery. Shotter hired the renowned architectural firm of Carrère and Hastings, designers of the New York Public Library building on Fifth Avenue, to build the house. It had forty rooms and a double colonnade of gleaming white marble columns that wrapped around all four sides. There were twelve master bedrooms, ten baths, a ballroom decorated in gold leaf, a dairy farm, a covered swimming pool, and magnificently landscaped grounds. Palm trees were imported from the Holy Land, a weeping willow from Napoleon's tomb on Saint Helena, and statues from the ruins of Pompeii. The estate was the setting for exquisite balls and yachting parties. Movie scenes starring Mary Pickford and Francis X. Bushman were filmed there.

By the time Spencer Lawton came along, however, the grandeur of the Lawton family had all but vanished. The

Shotter mansion had been destroyed by fire in the 1920s, and the grounds became an extension of Bonaventure Cemetery known as Greenwich Cemetery. The prestigious law firm of Lawton & Cunningham had been absorbed by another law firm, and the imposing Lawton Memorial Hall on Bull Street had been converted to a Greek Orthodox church.

Spencer Lawton was a soft-spoken, mild-mannered man with gentle blue-gray eyes and dark hair combed in a pompadour. Chubby cheeks and a ribbon-bow mouth gave him a cherubic look. He had been, bv his own admission, an indifferent student at the University of Georgia Law School. Afterward he returned to Savannah to practice law. He did largely *pro bono* work. A woman who encountered him when he was a hearing officer for the Savannah Housing Authority remembered him as being highly principled. "He was a decent man," she said. "He more than did his job; he showed concern and compassion for the poor. But he was a little timid, as I recall."

For the past thirty years, the Chatham County prosecutor's office had been the private domain of Joe Ryan. Ryan's son, Andrew "Bubsy" Ryan, had succeeded his father and had served one term when Spencer Lawton decided to run against him.

Bubsy Ryan was a good ol' boy. He liked to go fishing, hunting, and drinking. He had a full head of tousled brown hair, long reddish sideburns, and bags under his eyes that made him look permanently hung over. He got along well with the police; he was good at horse-trading and had a folksy, drawling courtroom manner. Bubsy argued every major murder case himself, but it was no secret that his management of the prosecutor's office was casual at best, just as it had been under his father. A backlog of over a thousand untried cases stretched back twenty-five years. Bubsy enjoyed being D.A., but he admitted it did have its drawbacks. "You're limited in some ways," he said. "You can't go out drinkin' with your wife, 'cause you'll read about it in the paper the next day."

The Ryans were not accustomed to having opposition at

election time. But when Bubsy came up for reelection, one of his assistant D.A.s announced he would challenge him in the Democratic primary. The two began sniping at each other almost immediately, and on the last day of filing, Spencer Lawton saw an opportunity for himself and made it a three-way race. "I ran for a lark," Lawton said later. While the other two tore into each other, Lawton took the high road and spoke about case management and other sensible-sounding things. He tiptoed through the wreckage of Bubsy and the other man.

When Bubsy and Lawton found themselves in a runoff, Bubsy took aim at Lawton. He hooted that Lawton had been a failure as a lawyer, that he had never tried a felony case, never had appellate experience, never argued a case before the Georgia Supreme Court, and that as a direct result of his laziness and incompetence he had exposed a law firm he had worked for to a malpractice suit. Two days before the election, Bubsy went one step further. He took out a half-page ad in the *Savannah Morning News* and quoted from a statement made in divorce proceedings by Lawton's former wife. Mrs. Lawton said that Spencer had told her many times that "he would be happier staying at home and keeping the house and reading than he would be working." The underlying message in the ad was that Spencer Lawton was not man enough for the job. Bubsy's crowd referred to Lawton as "the Pillsbury Dough Boy." But then on the night of the primary, Bubsy Ryan watched in disbelief as the returns from the black precincts went against him and gave the nomination to Lawton. Lawton went on to defeat the Republican candidate in the general election.

Doubts about Lawton's ability grew after he took office. Disgruntled staff members, holdovers from Bubsy Ryan's era, passed the word that Lawton did not know the law. "He's asking for memos on things he should know," one assistant D.A. complained, "like extradition. He wanted a memo on insanity defense, too, which you could write a book about." Then came the stunning defeat in the Rangers case. As it happened, the Rangers verdict was handed down a few days after Jim Williams shot Danny Hansford. Lawton drew a bead on the Williams case. It would be a means of redeeming himself, if he won. But it would be a difficult fight.

To handle his defense, Jim Williams retained Bobby Lee Cook of Summerville, Georgia. Cook was a famous character in criminal courts throughout the South. His specialty was murder. Over a span of thirty years, Cook had defended 250 people accused of murder and got 90 percent of them off, sometimes against substantial odds. Cook would take the untouchable cases, cases nobody thought could be won, and he would win them. He was famous for his lacerating cross-examinations. "I've seen him take a fellow before lunch," said a federal judge, "examine him awhile, comment at lunchtime that he was playing his witness like a bass, and then come back after lunch and finish destroying the man." In an article extolling his technique and his daring, *People* magazine had once declared that "if the Devil ever needed a defense, Bobby Lee Cook would take the case."

Being from the mountains of north Georgia, Cook knew that a Savannah jury would perceive him as a slick, out-of-town lawyer. Therefore, he wanted a local lawyer to assist him, and in filling that position he selected the attorney most likely to unnerve Spencer Lawton—the lawyer who had just beaten him so badly in the Rangers case: John Wright Jones.

Chapter 16

TRIAL

The Chatham County Courthouse was one of a half dozen modern buildings in downtown Savannah. It was made of precast concrete. Flat, blockish, and bland, it sat at the western edge of the historic district. A companion building stood next to it and was linked to it by an underground tunnel. This other building, also made of concrete, was a vaultlike cube with vertical slits for windows—the Chatham County Jail.

The benches at the rear of Judge George Oliver's courtroom were filled to capacity on the first day of Jim Williams's trial. The windowless room had bright fluorescent lighting and sound-absorbing tiles that removed all tone and timbre from the human voice. Retired businessmen, housewives, and Williams's high-society friends sat side by side with courthouse flacks, newspaper and television reporters, and a fair number of local trial lawyers who had come to watch the famous Bobby Lee Cook take on the new district attorney. Jim Williams sat at the defense table, and his mother and sister sat a few feet behind him in the first row.

Danny Hansford's mother, Emily Bannister, also attended the trial, but she was not permitted inside the courtroom. Bobby Lee Cook feared she might create a scene and prejudice the jury against Williams. He did not have her banned outright; instead he listed her as a defense witness, which had the same effect. Witnesses were not allowed to watch the proceedings until after they had testified. Cook, of course, had no intention of ever calling Mrs. Bannister to the stand, but his ploy would keep her out of the jury's sight. She came to the trial anyway and sat outside in the corridor.

"Don't look now," one of Williams's socialite friends murmured to a female chum as they arrived on the first day, "but there's Danny Hansford's ten-million-dollar mother."

Emily Bannister, not yet forty, looked surprisingly youthful for a woman with a twenty-one-year-old son. She had light brown hair and angular, childlike features. Her expression, which one might have expected to reflect anger and resentment under the circumstances, was merely one of sadness. She spoke only to the woman who sat next to her, an assistant in the district attorney's office. When reporters approached, she turned away in silence.

—

It was nearly lunchtime when the bailiff called out, "Order in the court! Extinguish all cigarettes! Please rise!" Judge Oliver entered from a door behind the bench and took his seat in a high-back swivel chair. An imposing man, he had a mane of snowy white hair and a handsome, craggy face. He was a steward of the Wesley Monumental Church and had been in Mercer House many times, but never as a guest of Jim Williams. He had gone there in the forties and fifties, when the house was the Shriners' Alee Temple. Oliver brought his gavel down and in a deep drawl called the courtroom to order. "All right, gentlemen, let's begin."

In his opening statement, Lawton spoke earnestly and in a soft voice. He told the jury that in the coming days he would prove that James A. Williams had shot Danny Lewis Hansford in cold blood and with malice aforethought and that afterward Williams had engaged in elaborate efforts not only to cover up what he had done but to make it appear that he had done it in self-defense.

Bobby Lee Cook then rose. He had long white hair, a square-cut goatee, and piercing eyes. He bore a striking resemblance to the image of Uncle Sam in James Montgomery Flagg's I WANT YOU FOR THE U.S. ARMY recruiting poster. Cook's habit of pointing his forefinger at the jury as he spoke only underscored the similarity. Cook said the defense would disprove everything Spencer Lawton had just told them. They would learn, said Cook, that Danny Hansford was "a violent and tempestuous character" and that he was the aggressor in this case.

When the introductory remarks were over, Judge Oliver called a brief recess before beginning the parade of witnesses. In the corridor, a man in a short-sleeved shirt and slicked-down hair approached me. "I see you've been taking notes," he said. "You doing legwork for the defense?"

"No," I said, "it's just for myself." The man was carrying a rolled-up newspaper. He had been sitting in the row in front of me, perched sideways in his seat with one arm slung over the back of the bench. Every so often he would laugh silently to himself, and his body would jerk in spasms of suppressed mirth. Then his head would roll back, and he'd peer through his grimy glasses at the proceedings. I took him to be a courthouse regular.

"Spencer Lawton's as much on trial here as Williams," he said. "They tell me he's been in hibernation for two months preparing his case. He's turned his office into a bunker. Won't take telephone calls, staff can't get in to see him. He and Depp—Deppish Kirkland, his chief assistant—they're trying to keep stuff away from the defense at all costs. They want to surprise 'em, turn it into a trial by ambush. They're paranoid about things leaking out. That's what I hear. It's strictly bush league. The bottom line is Lawton's scared to death."

"Who tells you all this?" I asked.

"I hear things. People talk." The man looked from one

end of the hall to the other. "I'll tell you one thing. Lawton's overplaying his hand in this case. See, it's not a murder case. Nobody thinks it is. The facts don't add up to it. It's manslaughter. Williams and Hansford argued. Somebody grabbed a gun. Maybe Williams panicked afterward and tried to rearrange things. But it wasn't premeditated."

Then why was Lawton going for a murder conviction?

"Could be politics," he said. "Could be he wants to win big after losing the Rangers case. Could be he doesn't want to appear to be too soft on hermaphrodites."

"On what?" I asked.

"Hermaphrodites," the man said. "That's what this whole thing's about, you know. Or haven't you heard?"

"Oh. Right," I said. "That's what I've heard."

—

Lawton opened his case by calling the police dispatcher who had been on duty the night of the shooting. The dispatcher said that at 2:58 A.M., she received a call from Jim Williams reporting that he'd been involved in a shooting at his residence. That was all she had to say. Next, Lawton called Joe Goodman to the stand. Goodman said that Williams had called him between 2:20 and 2:25 A.M. to say he had shot Danny. That left a gap of more than thirty minutes between the shooting and Williams's call to the police. The rest of Lawton's witnesses gave testimony bearing on what might have happened up to and during those thirty minutes. Their combined testimony brought out the prosecution's theory of what had happened:

Williams had fired once across his desk at an unarmed Danny Hansford. Hansford clutched his chest and fell to the floor facedown. Williams then walked around the desk and fired at Hansford twice more at point-blank range, hitting him behind the ear and in the back. Then he put his gun down on the desk, picked up a second gun, and fired "at himself" from Hansford's side of the desk to make it look as though Hansford had shot at him. One bullet passed through some papers; another bullet struck a metal belt buckle that had been lying on top of the desk. Williams wiped his fingerprints from this second gun, pulled Hansford's right hand out from under his body, and placed it over the gun. Then he called Joe Goodman. While Goodman and his girlfriend were on their way, Williams went around his house, smashing bottles, overturning the big clock in the hall, and creating a scene of general mayhem. Thirty minutes after calling Joe Goodman, Williams dialed the police.

According to the prosecution, the physical evidence showed that Williams had made a series of blunders. When he fired the shots "at himself," Williams had stood in the wrong place. He had stood where Danny's head lay; he should have stood where Danny's feet were. Second, police photographs of the top of the desk showed tiny paper fragments lying *on top of* the German Luger that Williams said he had used to shoot Hansford. This could only mean that Williams had already fired his gun at Hansford and laid it down *before* any bullets came from Hansford's side of the desk and hit the pile of papers, creating the paper fragments. Third, a bullet fragment was found on the seat of the chair that Williams had claimed he was sitting in when Danny shot at him. Fourth, the blood on Danny Hansford's hand was smeared, suggesting Williams had pulled Danny's hand out from under his body to place it on top of the gun. Strangest of all was the chair straddling Danny's legs; one of the chair legs was resting on the cuff of his blue jeans. It could only have been placed there after Danny had died. The prosecution suggested that Williams had unintentionally put it there while rearranging the scene.

Dr. Larry Howard, director of the state crime lab, summed up the prosecution's case. "The scene," he said, "appears contrived."

Throughout the four days of prosecution testimony, Bobby Lee Cook rose repeatedly to challenge the state's witnesses in blistering cross-examinations. At one point, Cook seized on an apparent inconsistency in the state's theory that Hansford was lying facedown on the floor when he was shot in the head. With a dramatic flourish, he lay down on the courtroom floor and asked Detective Joseph Jordan to position his head as Danny Hansford's had been.

"Am I now lying on the floor as the body of the deceased was lying when you saw it?" Cook asked, looking up at Detective Jordan.

"Tilt your head over to your right," said Detective Jordan. "A little bit more. That's close. Yes, sir."

"Are you aware," Cook asked, "that the point of entry of the head wound was on the right side above the ear?"

"Yes, sir," said the detective.

"And is it not true that the right side of my head is lying securely upon the floor?"

"That's correct."

"Then the shot to the head could not have been fired as the victim lay on the floor," said Cook. "It would have been impossible unless you got up under it to shoot."

"That's basically correct," said the detective.

"In fact, it would be completely illogical," Cook crowed. "It would be like telling someone that you could pour water uphill, wouldn't it!"

"Yes, sir," said the detective.

As for the absence of fingerprints on Danny's gun, Lawton himself elicited the comment from Detective Jordan that the textured surface of the Luger handgrip was a type that rarely yielded fingerprints. "It would not be conducive to a good fingerprint," said the detective. "It's too rough."

The most damning feature of the state's case was the negative test for gunshot residue on Danny's hands. Detective Joseph Jordan testified that he had taken great care to preserve whatever residue had been on Hansford's hands. He had placed paper bags on the hands and fastened them with evidence tape. Randall Riddell, the technician who performed the gunshot-residue tests at the state crime lab, testified he had found no gunshot residue at all on Danny's hands. Cook bore into him.

"You are familiar, of course, with antimony and lead and barium," said Cook. "You deal with these elements on a continuous basis in your specialty of gunshot-residue analysis, do you not?"

"Correct, sir," said Riddell.

"What is the atomic weight of antimony?" Cook asked.

"I don't recall," said Riddell.

"What is the atomic weight of lead?"

"I don't recall exactly," said Riddell.

"What is the atomic weight of barium?"

"I don't recall."

"What is the atomic number of lead?"

"I'm not familiar."

"What is the atomic number of barium?"

"I don't recall."

"Of antimony?"

"I don't recall," said Riddell, his face reddening.

"What method of analysis did you utilize in examining the swabs from Mr. Hansford's hands?" Cook asked.

"Atomic absorption," Riddell replied.

"And you got negative results?"

"Yes, sir."

"Are you aware," Cook asked, "that in the Atlanta area the atomic-absorption test yields negative results sixty percent of the time when it is done on the hands of persons *known to have committed suicide with a gun*?"

"I would ask to see your figures, sir," Riddell answered.

"You would like to see some figures on it?" said Cook. "Do you know Dr. Joseph Burton?"

"Yes, sir," said Riddell. "He's the medical examiner in Atlanta, I believe."

—

Bobby Lee Cook called Dr. Joseph Burton as the first defense witness. As a medical examiner in Miami and Atlanta, Burton had performed some seven thousand autopsies. At the time of Jim Williams's trial, he was working on the well-publicized Atlanta child-murder case of Wayne Williams. Dr. Burton had autopsied nine of those murders. Cook was counting on him now to challenge the state's interpretation of much of the evidence in the case against Jim Williams.

"Dr. Burton," Cook began, "what, in your opinion, is the significance of a negative result for gunshot residue on an atomic-absorption test?"

"A negative result has relatively little significance to me," said Dr. Burton. "A gun may give you a positive result on one firing and a negative result on another. It's an unreliable test. Virtually everyone in my profession of forensic pathology would like to see this test discontinued." Dr. Burton went on to say that it was he who conducted the study of gunshot-residue tests on suicides and found that fewer than 50 percent tested positive.

"Then in your opinion," said Cook, "does a negative result indicate that the deceased did not fire a weapon?"

"No, sir, it does not."

Dr. Burton said he had visited Mercer House several times to reenact the shooting, and it was his belief that all the shots had been fired from behind the desk. "It would be physically impossible to walk around and shoot either the head shot or the back shot and have them go through the body and end up in the floor the way they did." Burton interpreted the evidence just as the coroner, Dr. Metts, had suggested: The first bullet struck Hansford in the chest and spun him counterclockwise, accounting for the second and third bullets entering from the rear. Burton called attention to small particles of skull and hair that had been found in the southwest corner of the room, several feet from Danny's head. "They were knocked out by the bullet passing through the body," he said, "and they follow the same line the bullet follows." So, Williams did not deliver a coup de grâce, said Burton. He fired three shots in rapid succession: "Bam, bam, bam—fast as the body fell to the floor. It accounts for the pieces of bone, the hair, the holes in the floor, the blood spatters, and the angles through the body."

Dr. Burton offered an explanation for the presence of smeared blood on Hansford's hand: After the first shot hit him, Hansford might have dropped his gun and clutched his chest. "Then as the body hit the floor the hand might simply have sprung out to the side. Then the blood would have been smeared as the hand came out from under the bodv."

The chair on the pants leg? "The chair doesn't really concern me in the case," said Dr. Burton. "It doesn't indicate a contrived scene. In fact, it would go against someone trying to set this scene up, because it seems to be somewhat out of place sitting on his leg."

By the time Dr. Burton was finished testifying, the defense had responded to most of the prosecution's arguments. In addition, over Lawton's objections, the defense had called several witnesses who testified that Danny Hansford was an extremely violent young man. A psychiatrist at Georgia Regional Hospital told of treating Hansford after he had broken furniture in his mother's house and "threatened to kill someone." The doctor said Hansford had to be subdued and secluded because he was "dangerous to the hospital staff and to himself." A nurse at the hospital on that occasion said that when she admitted Hansford she classified him as "homicidal" on the admission form. A week after his death, in fact, Hansford had been due to appear in court on a charge related to a fist fight with a neighbor. Williams had paid the $600 bond to get him out of jail that time too.

The prevailing opinion in the corridors of the courthouse was that Bobby Lee Cook had raised just enough doubt about the state's case to enable jurors to vote "not guilty" in good conscience. The groundwork had been laid for an acquittal. Now it was up to Jim Williams to take the stand and win the sympathy of the jury. It was a jury composed of six men and six women. They were plain, middle-class people—a secretary, a teacher, housewives, a nurse, a plumber. One of the women was black; the rest of the jury was white.

Williams took the stand dressed in a pale gray suit. He leaned forward respectfully as Bobby Lee Cook guided him gently through a narrative of his modest childhood in Gordon, Georgia. Williams told about his arrival in Savannah at the age of twenty-one, his restoration of houses, his success in business, and his rise in Savannah society. He spoke with a confident, somewhat lofty tone. He explained that twice a year he attended the international Fabergé sales in Geneva.

"You've heard of Fabergé perfume?" said Williams. "We're not talking about that. Karl Fabergé was the court jeweler to the czar of Russia and to most of the other European courts. He made some of the finest works of art that anyone has ever created. I collect Fabergé in a small way."

Williams recalled how he had met Danny Hansford. "I was getting out of my car in front of the house and this fellow rode up on a bicycle. He said somebody told him I hired people to work in my workshop who had no experience. I said, 'Well, that is true, but I only hire people who are capable of learning things.' Danny started off by stripping the finishes off furniture. He worked on and off for two years. Part time. He would leave town and then come back."

In precise and chilling detail, Williams described Danny's rampage through the house on April 3, a month before he died. Danny stood in the bedroom, having fired a shot into the floor, glaring at Williams, gun in hand. "How damn mad do I have to make you before you'll kill me?" he said. Then he went outside and fired into the square. When Williams called the police, Danny ran upstairs and pretended to be asleep in bed.

It was shortly after that incident that Williams asked Hansford to go with him on his buying trip to Europe. Williams explained that his health had begun to suffer and that he had blacked out several times from hypoglycemia. He needed someone to accompany him. "I didn't want to pass out somewhere en route without somebody with me for two reasons, healthwise and moneywise." Williams would be carrying a large quantity of cash, he said, "because you get a far better rate of exchange on your money if you take it in cash." He had asked Danny to go along "because I thought I could control him."

But in mid-April, Hansford told Williams he was planning to take marijuana on the trip, and Williams said in that case he could not go. "Danny and I agreed we'd ask Joe Goodman to go instead," said Williams. "We were both happy with that arrangement. Danny could smoke his dope in Savannah, and I'd have somebody to go on my trip with me."

A week later, on the night of the shooting, Danny had exploded in a fury. As Williams told it, Danny had carried on about how his mother put him in detention centers and how she had hated him because he looked like his father, whom she had divorced. He raged on about his friend George Hill wanting his car and about his girlfriend Bonnie, who wouldn't marry him because he didn't have a steady job. Then he turned on Williams. "And *you* took away my trip to Europe!" Hansford stomped the Atari game. Williams stood up and walked out of the room. Hansford grabbed him by the throat and threw him up against the door. Williams pulled away and went into his study to call the police. Danny came into the study after him. "Who are you calling?" he demanded.

"I had to think real quick," said Williams. "I said, 'I'm calling Joe Goodman to tell him the European trip is off.' " Williams dialed Joe Goodman, and both he and Danny spoke to Goodman on the phone. That was at 2:05 A.M. The call had lasted a few minutes.

Williams continued his story as the packed courtroom listened in silence. "Danny sat down in the chair opposite me and leaned back. He picked up a silver tankard and held it in his hand and just looked at it. Then he said, 'You know, this silver tankard has about made up its mind to go through that painting over there.' It was an English painting, about eight and a half feet by ten feet, of the Drake family in the eighteenth century. Danny had that crazed look on his face.

"I stood up and put my finger straight out, and I said, 'Danny Hansford, you're not going to tear my house up anymore! Now, you get out!' That's when Danny got up and went out into the hall, and there were crashing sounds. He came back with a gun in his hand and said, 'I'm leaving tomorrow, but you're leaving tonight.'

"The minute I saw that Luger," said Williams, "I reached into the drawer. As I was coming up from my seat, a bullet was fired at me. I felt the breeze go by my right arm."

Some time between 2:20 and 2:25 A.M., Williams called Joe Goodman again, this time to tell him he had shot Danny.

—

Spencer Lawton stepped up for the cross-examination. He began by asking Williams to describe the guns he kept in Mercer House: the gun in the downstairs hall, the gun in the rear parlor, the gun in the study, the gun in the living room. Williams sat back in his chair with his chin slightly raised. He stared at Lawton with a look of icy disdain and answered his questions in clipped syllables. Lawton led Williams once more through the events on the night of the shooting, to the point when Williams said he felt the breeze of the first bullet go by his right arm.

"Do you recall," Lawton asked, "having told Albert Scardino of the *Georgia Gazette* in the interview four days after the incident that you felt the first bullet go by your *left* arm?"

"Mr. Lawton," said Williams, "under those conditions, I was not taking notes."

"Could it be," said Lawton, "that you have some doubt as to which side of you the bullet went on because you were standing on the other side of the desk when you fired the bullet into the paper?"

"I never fired any bullet into any paper on any desk. What are you talking about?"

"And that therefore, thinking about yourself from this position, you would get the arms mixed up?"

Williams looked down from the stand with an expression of loathing. He was obdurate and imperious, not even slightly defensive. For all the world, he could have been the czar in his Fabergé cuff links, the emperor Maximilian sitting at his gold-encrusted desk. Williams assumed the haughty boredom of all the monarchs and aristocrats whose portraits and baubles he now owned.

Lawton moved on to another topic. "You've testified at considerable length concerning your relationship with Danny Hansford. Other than the fact that, as you tell it, he attacked you, did you have any reason to want to see him dead?"

"None whatsoever."

"You had no particular resentment or dislike for him, no anger at him?"

"If I had, he wouldn't have been around me. I was trying to straighten him out. I was trying to help him, and he made progress."

"I have to say," said Lawton, "that from what you've said of it, you do seem exquisitely solicitous of his needs. You had some *unusual* feelings about him, didn't you, because—"

"What *unusual* feelings?" Williams cut in.

"I get the impression you considered it somewhat your personal charge to save him from himself."

"It's just that I was trying to help him make something of his life. Danny said to me on more than one occasion, 'You're the only person that's ever really tried to help me. You're the only person that hasn't used me.' "

"Well, now," said Lawton, "again I don't want to seem picky, but I do want to understand the nature of the relationship and—"

"Fine," said Williams.

"What exactly did he do for you? He drove?"

"Yes."

"I think you testified that he was employed by you in two other capacities, one as a part-time worker in your shop and the other to look after you because of your health condition. Is that right?"

"Yes. He would come by and check on me. Sometimes he would spend the night in the house, sometimes he and his girlfriend would both spend the night in the house."

"Did you ever pay him for any other work or service that he did other than what we've just described?"

"He used to move furniture for me in my pickup truck."

"But in no other capacity and for no other work or anything did you pay him?"

"How do you mean?" Williams asked coldly. "What other work would there be?"

"I'm just asking you. I just want to be sure that I've got it right."

At this point, it was Spencer Lawton who was playing his witness like a bass. The more stubbornly evasive Williams became, the more Lawton seemed to encourage him. His intention was not to hook Williams at all but to tease him along and draw out the play. One more time, he asked Williams if he had anything to add about himself and Danny.

"Does the situation we've just been outlining *fully* describe your relationship with Danny?"

"Uh-huh."

"Indicating 'yes'?"

"Yes."

Williams appeared to be holding back a smile. He felt he was winning this test of wills. He had not broken under Lawton's insistent probing. He had made it through to the end of his testimony with his good name still intact. From here on, it would be all in his favor. He was to be followed on the stand by seven unimpeachable character witnesses, seven of Savannah's most upstanding citizens. They were waiting in the corridor, out of hearing of the proceedings. There was Alice Dowling, the widow of the late Ambassador Dowling; the silver-haired George Patterson, a retired bank president; Hal Hoerner, another retired banker; Carol Fulton, the pretty blond wife of Dr. Tod Fulton; Lucille Wright, the cateress. They and others were waiting to tell the jury about Jim Williams's peaceable nature and his good character. Williams stepped down from the stand to await the endorsement of his friends and the conclusion of the trial.

But those endorsements would have to wait. Spencer Lawton announced that he had two witnesses to call in rebuttal to Williams's testimony. "If it please the court," he said. "I'll call as the state's next witness: George Hill."

George Hill was twenty-two years old. He had curly dark hair and a hefty build. He took the stand and identified himself as a deckhand on a tugboat in Thunderbolt. He had been Danny Hansford's best friend. He also knew Jim Williams. Lawton asked him if he could identify Williams anywhere in the courtroom. Hill pointed to him at the defense table.

"Do you know whether or not Danny Hansford had any sort of relationship at all with Jim Williams?" Lawton asked.

"Yes, I do," said Hill.

"What, if anything, do you know about that relationship?"

"Well, Mr. Williams was giving Danny money when he needed it. He bought him a nice car and give him fine clothes, in exchange for going to bed with him."

"In exchange for who to—I'm sorry?"

"For Danny to sleep with him."

"How do you know that?"

"Me and Danny talked about it a few times. Danny told me he liked the money and everything. He said it was fine with him if Mr. Williams wanted to pay him to suck his dick."

George Hill's words were framed in silence. Lawton paused so as not to crowd them or diminish their effect. Members of the jury stole glances at one another. Blanche Williams looked down at her lap. The courtroom flack sitting in front of me laughed his silent laugh.

Bobby Lee Cook sat in stony silence. Earlier in the day, in a session in the judge's chambers, he had lodged formal objections to Lawton's stated intention of bringing George Hill to the stand to say what he had just said. Cook had told the judge that any testimony based on statements made to Hill by Danny Hansford would constitute inadmissible hearsay. He urged Judge Oliver to be wary. If George Hill were allowed to cross the line, it would be impossible to tell the jury to ignore what it had heard. "You can't unring the bell," he said. "You can't throw a skunk in the jury box and then tell them they didn't smell it." But Lawton argued that George Hill's testimony would introduce a motive for the killing, and Judge Oliver ruled that he could testify.

"Did Danny ever tell you of any disagreements that he had with Mr. Williams?" Lawton continued.

"Well, a few times when I was over there," said Hill, "they had a few small ones, whenever Mr. Williams wouldn't give Danny the money he wanted. One time—I wasn't there when the argument took place—Danny started dating a girl named Bonnie Waters, and Mr. Williams wasn't too happy about it. He bought Danny a four-hundred-dollar gold necklace, with the agreement Danny would quit seeing this girl. Danny gave the necklace to Bonnie and then took her over to the house with it on. Williams got pretty mad and told him he'd have to pack his stuff and leave. Danny was real worried that he'd just lost his meal ticket."

"When was this?"

"About two nights before he died."

For his cross-examination, Bobby Lee Cook took a kindly-uncle tone. He asked Hill to tell the jury about his fondness for guns—Hill had two pistols and four rifles—and about the time he had assaulted another boy and the boy's father and knocked their door down. Cook asked Hill to tell how he and a friend had once been arrested for shooting out fifteen streetlights.

Cook also wanted to know why George Hill had not told the authorities about the necklace and Danny Hansford and Jim Williams for more than six months, until just before the trial. "When you finally told someone," Cook asked, "who did you talk to?"

"Well," said Hill, "Danny's mother got in touch with me and asked me to please talk to her attorney or one of the district attorneys."

"Oh, Danny's mother got in touch with you?" Cook assumed a look of surprise.

"Yes, sir."

"She got in touch with you, because she told you she had a lawsuit against Jim Williams, didn't she! And she wanted to collect ten million dollars and would give you part of it, *didn't she!*"

"That's a lie," said Hill, "and I don't think it's very polite of you saying things like that."

It was Bobby Lee Cook's turn to pause and let the silence in the courtroom emphasize the point he had just made.

Spencer Lawton's second rebuttal witness was another young friend of Danny Hansford's, Greg Kerr. Kerr was twenty-one and blond and worked in the pressroom of the

Savannah Evening Press. He wore wire-rimmed glasses and was visibly nervous. Knowing that he would probably be confronted with it anyway, he blurted out every bad thing about himself he could think of. He had been arrested for possession of drugs and obstruction of justice; he had been involved in "the homosexual scene" ever since he was seduced by a high school teacher. But his last homosexual encounter had been three weeks ago, he said, and he was out of it for good now.

"Do you, of your own knowledge," Lawton asked, "know anything of any relationship that Danny Hansford may have had with Jim Williams?"

"Yes, I do," said Kerr.

"How do you know?" asked Lawton.

"I went to their home to play backgammon, and Danny stepped out of the room or something to go to the rest room. I said, 'He's a nice-looking young man,' and Mr. Williams said, 'Yes. He's very good in bed. And also, he's well endowed.' "

"Did Danny use drugs?" Lawton asked.

"Yes, he did," said Kerr. "He had marijuana at the house when I was over there one time."

"Did he ever say anything to you about where he got it?"

"Yes, he did. He said, 'Jim buys all my drugs.' "

Bobby Lee Cook leaped to his feet. "Your Honor, this is the rankest and purest sort of hearsay!" Judge Oliver overruled the objection.

On cross-examination, John Wright Jones brought out the fact that once, in the middle of a backgammon game, Jim Williams had accused Greg Kerr of cheating and had then hit him over the head with the backgammon board. So Kerr's testimony might have been motivated by spite. But Kerr insisted it was not. He said that upon reading a copy of the *Evening Press* earlier in the week, during the trial, he learned that Danny Hansford had been described in court as having a violent temper. Having read that, Greg Kerr decided it was his duty to come forward.

"Mr. Williams had assured me numerous times that he

was innocent," said Kerr, "and he bragged to everyone that he would just appeal and appeal again. So I felt that, you know, Mr. Hansford is dead, and after I read how everybody was cutting him down, I decided to come up here. I called Mr. Lawton, I would say, around ten-thirty that night."

"Why didn't you come forward sooner?" Jones asked.

"I'd thought about doing it many times, but I was scared, because I was still involved with the homosexual scene, and I just felt I shouldn't."

"And when did you say you extracted yourself from 'the homosexual scene,' as you put it?"

"Well, I've been trying for three or four years. I did have one homosexual experience, the last one was three weeks ago, which I barely remember, but up until that point it had been a month and a half. I am doing good, and I will never go back to that type of life again, 'cause it's wrong, it's in the Bible that it's wrong, and I urge all homosexuals to please get out of it while they can, because they're going to end up just an old fuddy-duddy, and nobody's going to want them. I'm lucky. I'm just a young man, and I'm out of it."

"You're out of it about three weeks at this stage."

"I'm out of it."

"No further questions," said Jones.

Greg Kerr stepped down and left the courtroom.

Bobby Lee Cook stood up at the defense table. "Call in Mrs. Dowling, please," he said.

Alice Dowling, the late ambassador's widow, walked into the courtroom with a pleasant smile and not the slightest idea what had been going on while she and the others had been waiting in the corridor. She said she had known Jim Williams ever since he had been a consultant on the restoration of her house on Oglethorpe Avenue.

"Have you had occasion to visit with Mr. Williams at his home at parties and festivities and social occasions?" Cook asked.

"Yes," said Mrs. Dowling politely. "For many years we have attended his Christmas parties."

"On any of those or other occasions, have you noticed

anything that would indicate the use or approval of drugs by Mr. Williams?"

"Never," said Mrs. Dowling.

Spencer Lawton then cross-examined Mrs. Dowling.

"Mrs. Dowling, have you heard anything of a relationship that Jim Williams may have had with a young man named Danny Hansford?"

"No, sir," Mrs. Dowling said. "I know absolutely nothing about Mr. Williams's private life."

"Thank you," said Lawton. "That's all I have."

One by one, the highly respected friends of Jim Williams entered the courtroom and took the stand to vouch for his good character. One by one, they all said they had been at his lovely Christmas parties, never saw drugs either being used or approved of by him, and knew nothing of Danny Hansford.

The parade of witnesses over, the judge called a recess for the weekend, admonishing the jurors not to talk about the case to anyone and not to look at newspaper and television coverage of it. On Monday, the trial would resume for closing arguments and the judge's instructions to the jury.

On Sunday—perhaps intentionally, perhaps not—the *Savannah Morning News* published a story about the grim living conditions in the Chatham County Jail. A federal judge had toured the facility and pronounced it "filthy." He was amazed and appalled, he said, by the lack of sanitation. Inmates were "crowded, ill-fed, dirty and lacked medical attention." The building was only three years old, a modern concrete structure with a fringe of neatly landscaped lawn. At night it was spotlit and looked as clean and tranquil as a branch bank in Palm Springs. But the inside was a different story. Chaos reigned, to hear the federal judge tell it. "There is no supervision," he said. "Food is terribly handled."

On Monday morning, the mood in the courtroom was tense. The revelations about the jail seemed to raise the stakes in this trial. Spencer Lawton rose to make his closing argument. "There's a lot more wrong with Jim Williams than hypoglycemia," he said. "Jim Williams is a man of fifty years of age. He is a man of immense wealth, of obvious sophistication. He lives in an elegant home, travels abroad twice a year. He has many powerful and attractive and influential friends. There's something else about Williams too. He has a houseful of German Lugers, cocked and loaded all the time. He has a Nazi hood ornament on the desk in his study. He has a Nazi officer's ring with the skull and crossbones on it.

"Danny Hansford was an immature, undereducated, unsophisticated, confused, temperamental young man, preoccupied with feelings of betrayal and rejection, even at the hands of his mother, says Jim Williams. I suggest to you that Danny Hansford was a young man who was a great deal more tragic than evil. Can you not imagine how easily impressed a young man like that would be, living in a house, being friends with a man of Jim Williams's stature?

"Danny Hansford was never someone that Jim Williams really cared for. He was a pawn, nothing more or less than a pawn in a sick little game of manipulation and exploitation. Danny maybe thought of himself as a bit of a hustler. Well, he was in way over his head. He was playing for keeps with a pro, and he turned out to be the ultimate loser. I don't think he was a hustler. I think he was being hustled. I think he was what amounts to a prisoner in a comfortable concentration camp, where the torture was not physical but emotional and psychological.

"There is abundant reason to wonder why in the world Jim Williams would keep somebody around that he knew to be an unskilled, undependable, highly emotional, depressed psychotic, to protect and serve him in his hour of greatest need, when he collapsed in fainting spells and became comatose. And there is every reason to wonder why Jim Williams would voluntarily take to Europe somebody who, he says, was felonious, violent, and psychopathic."

Lawton was eloquent and venomous. He spoke softly, as he had throughout the six-day trial, but his righteous anger rang throughout the courtroom like a shout.

"What happened was an act of murder," said Lawton.

"The self-defense was a coverup. It did not occur. Thomas Hobbes is often quoted as having said that life is nasty, brutish, and short, and surely it must have seemed so to Danny Hansford during the last fifteen or twenty seconds of his life, while his life was oozing out onto Jim Williams's Persian rug."

It was during his closing argument, in the final moments of the trial, that Lawton introduced a new and diabolical element into the state's theory of what had really happened. Lawton suggested that the earlier episode of violence at Mercer House—Danny's rampage on the evening of April 3, when he had stormed through the house and fired a gun into the bedroom floor—was all a hoax. Williams had staged it, Lawton suggested, as a prelude for murdering Hansford a month later. "Could it be a setup?" he asked. "Could Jim Williams have known that about now he would be testifying in court that he had been forced to kill Danny Hansford in self-defense? Did Williams want to create some evidence of Danny's violent nature, get something into the police records, set it up while Danny was asleep upstairs?"

Lawton was proposing that the shooting of Danny Hansford was neither self-defense nor a crime of passion but a carefully planned murder. He was suggesting that on April 3, while Danny Hansford lay sleeping upstairs, Williams was downstairs stomping a marble-topped table, slamming a cut-glass pitcher into the floor, smashing eighteenth-century porcelain objects, and firing a German Luger into Monterey Square—all with the intention of calling the police afterward and blaming it on Hansford. Why didn't the shot into the bedroom floor wake Danny up? Because, according to Lawton's theory, nobody fired a bullet into the bedroom floor that night; the bullet hole in the bedroom floor was an *old* bullet hole. Lawton had persuasive evidence of that. Corporal Michael Anderson, the police officer who had come to the house that night, had testified about that earlier incident. "We pulled up the carpet, and we did see a bullet hole in the floor, but we couldn't find no bullet. I couldn't determine if that was a fresh bullet hole or an old one." Now, in his closing comments, Lawton told the jury, "Obviously, Corporal Anderson didn't believe that bullet hole was created by Danny Hansford." Bobby Lee Cook, having already made his closing statement, could not respond to Lawton's startling allegation.

When Lawton was finished, the judge called a recess for the day. In the morning, the benches were once again filled to overflowing. Judge Oliver read a long list of instructions and then excused the jury to consider its verdict.

Three hours later, word spread through the courthouse that the jury was returning to the courtroom. The bailiff called the court to order, and the jury filed in.

"Mr. Foreman, have you arrived at a verdict?" asked Judge Oliver.

"Yes, sir, we have," said the foreman.

"Would you give it to the clerk that he may publish it?" The foreman handed a piece of paper to the clerk, who stood up and read from the paper:

" 'We, the jury, find the defendant guilty of murder.' "

A gasp of surprise sounded throughout the courtroom.

"The sentence is life imprisonment," said Oliver.

Two bailiffs approached Williams and escorted him to a small door at the end of the jury box. Before going through the door, Williams paused briefly and looked back, his expression blank, his dark eyes as impenetrable as ever.

The spectators flowed out of the courtroom into the corridor and formed a crowd around Bobby Lee Cook, who stood in the glare of television lights, expressing his disappointment and saying he would file notice of an appeal within a few days. While he spoke, a solitary figure walked around the fringe of the crowd and stepped into an elevator, unnoticed by the reporters. It was Emily Bannister, Danny Hansford's mother. She turned as the elevator door started to close. It was not really a smile that crossed her face so much as a look of quiet satisfaction.

Chapter 17

A HOLE IN THE FLOOR

Jim Williams had begun the day in the spacious grandeur of Mercer House and ended it in the cold confines of the Chatham County Jail. His glittering social life was over. Never again would the cream of Savannah society pray to be invited to his extravagant parties. He would spend the rest of his life in the company of burglars, muggers, rapists, and other murderers—the very people, as Lee Adler pointed out, who represented the "criminal element" Williams had publicly disdained.

The enormity and suddenness of Williams's downfall shocked Savannah. It was a tribute to Williams that the public found it difficult to believe he had really been brought so low. Barely twelve hours after he had been escorted from the courtroom, rumor had it that he was rearranging life behind bars to accord with his personal tastes.

"He's having his meals sent in," said Prentiss Crowe. "I hear that's already been arranged. His lunches will be catered by Mrs. Wilkes's boarding house, and he'll be getting supper from Johnny Harris one night and Elizabeth's the next. He's even written a list of the pieces of furniture that he wants moved into his cell—a firm mattress, I'm told, and a Regency writing table."

Prison officials denied that Williams was receiving any special favors. They insisted he would be treated like any other inmate at the Chatham County Jail. And, as everyone knew, that was bad news for Williams. Even more ominous, however, was the possible fate that awaited him at the Reidsville State Penitentiary, where he was likely to be transferred to serve out his term. Reidsville was a hard-core prison seventy miles west of Savannah. At the very moment Judge Oliver was pronouncing Williams's sentence, the inmates at Reidsville were rioting and setting the prison on fire. On his first morning in the Savannah jail, Williams was greeted by a newspaper account of the riot. He could hardly have missed it. The story appeared on page one, along with coverage of his own conviction. The following day, Reidsville was back on the front page. Three black inmates had killed a white inmate by stabbing him thirty times. After the stabbing, prison officials had conducted a shakedown inspection of the jail and confiscated a small arsenal of weapons, including a homemade bomb. Under the circumstances, the real question was not who would cater Jim Williams's meals in the Chatham County Jail, but whether his lawyers could manage to keep him out of the Reidsville penitentiary.

Speculation about Williams and his fate came to an abrupt halt after two days when Judge Oliver released him on a $200,000 bond pending appeal. A swarm of reporters and TV cameras buzzed around Williams as he walked from the door of the jail to his blue Eldorado. "Will it be business as usual, Mr. Williams?" a reporter called out.

"Business as usual. Damn right!" he said. Minutes later he was back in Mercer House.

—

On the surface at least, Williams's life did return to something approaching normal. He went back to selling antiques, and with the court's permission he traveled to New York to attend a black-tie party for the Cooper-Hewitt Museum's exhibition of Queen Elizabeth's collection of Fabergé. His manner was calm; his conversation had lost none of its sharp edge. But now he was a convicted murderer and, despite the wit and the light humor, there was an aura of quiet desperation. His black eyes seemed darker than ever now. He still received invitations to dine, but the invitations became fewer. Old friends called, but less often.

In private, he expressed bitterness. What galled him most was not his conviction or the harm done to his reputation or even the cost of his defense; it was the indignity of having been charged with any crime at all. From the outset, he had assumed that his word as a gentleman would be accepted and that the whole affair would be settled quietly, the way Savannah had settled past incidents involving prominent suspects—the mysterious bludgeoning of a socialite at the beach not long ago, for example, or the tumble down a flight of stairs that killed a rich man who was about to divorce his wife, or the case of the spinster who embalmed her lover's bullet-riddled body before calling the police.

"At least I did call the police," Williams told me shortly after being released from jail. "You should have seen them that night. When word went out over the police radio about what had happened and where it had happened, they started arriving in droves. They wandered through the house like little children on a tour of Versailles. They looked at everything and whispered among themselves. They stayed for *four hours*. Now that's unheard of. If a black man kills another black man in Savannah on a Friday night, two policemen might drop by for thirty minutes, and that would be the end of it. But the police were having a ball in my house. When the police photographer was finished taking pictures, she went into the kitchen and made tea and coffee and served it to the others with cookies. I thought, Well, this is a damned nuisance, but I guess it's the price I have to pay. I'll just let them have their fun, and then it will all be over. They were exquisitely polite. It was 'Mr. Williams this' and 'Mr. Williams that' and 'Can we help you, sir?' One particularly obsequious cop came up to me and told me that he had doused the carpet with club soda so Danny's blood wouldn't cause a permanent stain. I thanked him for being so thoughtful. Later, down at the police station, we went through what I thought was a routine signing of papers. The police were so congenial I had no idea I'd been charged with murder until I read it in the newspaper the next day."

Williams's deepest resentment was not directed at the police, however. It was directed at Savannah's society and the power structure that it dominated.

"Men from Savannah's good families are born into a pecking order they can never get out of," he said, "unless they leave town forever. They've got to go to a proper secondary school—Savannah Country Day or Woodberry Forest—then to a good enough college, and then come back home and join the team. They've got to work for a certain company or a certain man and move up gradually. They've got to marry a girl with the right background. They've got to produce a proper little family. They've got to be a member of Christ Church or Saint John's. They've got to join the Oglethorpe Club, the yacht club, and the golf club. Finally, when they're in their late fifties or early sixties, they've arrived, they've made it. But by then they're burned out, unhappy, and unfulfilled. They cheat on their wives, hate their work, and lead dismal lives as respectable failures. Their wives, most of them, are little more than long-term prostitutes, the main difference being that when you factor in the houses, the cars, the clothes, and the clubs, Savannah's respectable wives get a lot more money per piece of ass than a whore does. When people like that see somebody like me, who's never joined their silly pecking order and who's taken great risks and succeeded, they *loathe* that person. I have felt it many times. They don't have any say-so over me, and they don't like that at all."

Despite his bitterness, Williams was confident that his appeal would be successful. If it was not, he had an idea or two how he might seek revenge on Savannah. He would use Mercer House as the instrument. "I might turn the house over to a charitable society," he mused, "to be used as a drug-rehabilitation center. It's big enough to handle several hundred addicts a day, wouldn't you say? The addicts could use Monterey Square as an outdoor waiting room. It would drive the neighbors wild, especially the socially conscious Adlers. But they could hardly object to such a public-spirited gesture."

And what if Danny Hansford's mother won her $10 million lawsuit against him? Would the house not fall into her hands? "Danny's mother will never live in Mercer House," Williams declared, "because I will destroy it first. It won't be easy, because the house is very solid; the interior walls are made of brick. What I would do is this: I would cut a large hole in the ceiling of each of the four corner rooms on the main floor, all the way through to the second floor. Then I would put acetone in each of the cutout holes and blow the place to bits. I've been assured I could demolish the entire house that way. In Georgia, arson is a crime only if it's done for the insurance. Mercer House is not insured. Danny's mother might get a nice piece of property, but there won't be a house on it."

—

At the same time Jim Williams was calculating where to drill the holes in the floor of Mercer House, the Georgia Supreme Court was focusing its attention on a hole that was already there—the bullet hole in the bedroom floor upstairs. This was the hole allegedly made by Danny Hansford during his rampage through the house a month before he was killed. It was the hole about which the arresting officer, Corporal Anderson, had testified, "I couldn't determine if that was a fresh bullet hole or an old one." Seizing on that remark, Spencer Lawton had suggested that the bullet hole was an old one and that Williams had faked the incident to lay the groundwork for killing Hansford in "self-defense" a month later.

Some weeks after the guilty verdict was handed down, Bobby Lee Cook received an envelope from an anonymous source in the district attorney's office. Inside was a copy of the police report written by Corporal Anderson on the night of the earlier incident. The report contained the statement: "*We did find a fresh bullet hole in the floor.*" It contradicted his sworn testimony at the trial.

The defense had obtained an edited copy of Anderson's written report by court order before the trial, but Lawton had whited out that particular line. When Bobby Lee Cook saw the complete text, he immediately realized that Lawton's excision amounted to prosecutorial misconduct. He made it the central argument in his appeal before the Georgia Supreme Court. The court responded angrily. It cited the "patent inconsistency" of Corporal Anderson's two statements about the bullet hole and denounced Lawton's attempt to cover it up. "We cannot and will not approve corruption of the truth-seeking function of the trial process," the unanimous ruling read. "*Judgment reversed.* A new trial must be ordered."

Chapter 18

MIDNIGHT IN THE GARDEN OF GOOD AND EVIL

For all the commotion over the reversal of Jim Williams's conviction, the Georgia Supreme Court's ruling appeared to be little more than a temporary reprieve. The hole in the floor had been an unimportant detail in the trial; the main points of evidence in Spencer Lawton's case against Williams still remained intact. It seemed obvious that Williams would have to mount a stronger defense in his second trial, or the outcome would likely be another conviction.

Williams was exultant nonetheless. He boasted that the reversal had vindicated him completely. He gloated that the wording of the ruling proved that Spencer Lawton and the police were liars. Williams dropped hints that, indeed, his defense would be stronger the second time around. "Things will be going my way from here on," he would say with a wink and a sly look. "Certain 'forces' are at work." He deliberately left his listeners wondering whether he meant to say simply that public sympathy had shifted in his favor or, more darkly, that the fix was in.

One evening, Williams invited me to drop in at Mercer

House. I found him sitting at his desk in his study having a vodka and tonic. He regaled me with stories about two of his latest pet subjects—the "corrupt" Spencer Lawton and the "biased and stupid" Judge Oliver. Then he came around to the subject of the mysterious forces working on his behalf.

"You know, I never had any doubt that the Supreme Court would throw out my conviction," he said. "I knew all along they would do it. I was absolutely sure of it. Do you know why? Because I refused to allow myself even to *think* they would reject my appeal. If I had thought about it, if I had dwelt on it, if I had become depressed and imagined the worst, then the worst would have happened." I could feel Williams watching me closely, weighing my reaction.

"Concentration," he went on. "That's what it was. Just like the little experiment I told you about at Duke University, with the dice. I improved the odds in my case the same way the men at Duke did with the dice, the same way I do when I play my little game of Psycho Dice—through mental kinetics.

"You may think all this is nonsense," he went on. "Most people do, and all I can say to them is: Fine, don't believe it, I'm not out to prove anything—but you're overlooking a valuable power available to anyone." Williams smiled enigmatically, but I could tell he was not joking.

"Of course, I have had help," he said. "I'm not the only person who has been concentrating on my behalf. I've had the assistance of someone very expert in these things. And I can tell you that when my second trial comes up, the judge, the D.A., and whoever gets to sit on that jury will be at the receiving end of some very powerful vibrations."

Williams took a handful of dimes out of his pocket and put nine of them in a neat stack on the desk blotter.

"I use the word 'vibrations' for want of a better word," he said. "These vibrations, these thought waves—whatever you want to call them—will be generated by me and by a woman named Minerva. She's an old and very dear friend. She lives in Beaufort, South Carolina—about forty-five minutes from here. I am going to pay her a visit tonight."

Williams opened a drawer and took out a bottle of water. "This is rainwater," he said. "Minerva told me to bring it with me tonight. She also told me to bring the dimes. These things will be coming into play later on tonight." Williams looked up at me. "If you're game, you're welcome to come along. It will take two or three hours at most. Interested?"

"Sure, why not?" I said. As soon as I had said it, I thought of a dozen reasons why not, but it was too late. Half an hour later, we went out through the back of Mercer House to the carriage house, where a green Jaguar sports car was parked on an oriental carpet. Williams set his vodka and tonic on the control panel and eased the car out into Wayne Street. In moments we were gliding through the quiet streets of Savannah, up and over the Talmadge Bridge and into the darkness of the South Carolina low country.

The light from the dashboard cast a pale glow on Williams's face. "If I told you that Minerva was a witch doctor or a voodoo priestess, I'd be close," he said. "She's that and more. She was the common-law wife of Dr. Buzzard, the last great voodoo practitioner in Beaufort County. Whether you know it or not, you are in the heart of voodoo country. This whole coastal area has been loaded with it since the slaves brought voodoo with them from Africa.

"Dr. Buzzard died a few years ago, and Minerva carries on his practice. For years, Dr. Buzzard was king of the low-country root doctors. He was a commanding presence—tall, erect, and rail thin. He had a goatee, and he wore purple-tinted glasses. No one who saw those eyes staring through those purple lenses ever forgot them. He was especially effective 'defending' clients in criminal cases. He'd sit in the courtroom and glare at hostile witnesses as he chewed the root. Sometimes they'd change their stories when they got on the stand and saw Dr. Buzzard staring at them. Either that or they'd just turn tail and run. Dr. Buzzard would focus his energies on the jury and the judge too. I know a judge in Savannah who says he can tell when rootworkers are involved in a case, because his bench will be dressed down. He'll find roots and herbs and bones arranged around it.

"Dr. Buzzard made a good living. People would pay him to put curses on their enemies, or to remove a curse that their enemies had put on them. In some cases, he was paid by both parties. The money piled up. Dr. Buzzard built two big churches on Saint Helena Island and always drove around in big flashy cars. He was quite a ladies' man, too, and in his last years Minerva became his mistress." Williams took a sip from his drink, then set it back in its holder on the control panel.

"When Dr. Buzzard died, Minerva put on his purple glasses and set herself up as a root doctor. She uses some of his techniques and some of her own too. She gets her special status—and some of her spiritual powers—by having direct access to Dr. Buzzard in perpetuity. She goes to his grave and calls on his spirit constantly."

Williams said he did not, himself, believe in voodoo. "I don't put much stock in the hocus-pocus part of it, the herbs and roots and powdered bones and frogs' tongues and all that. They're only props. But I do have respect for the spiritual force behind it. Minerva told me to bring nine shiny dimes tonight and some 'fresh water that ain't run through no pipe.' The dimes were easy, but her instructions about the water meant I either had to get it from a stream or find some rainwater. There happened to be rainwater in a basin in my courtyard. That's what's in the bottle."

"Would she know the difference if you had just filled it with tap water?" I asked.

"Not from the look or the taste," he said. "But she'd know in an instant just by looking at my face."

—

The town of Beaufort was dark and still. Williams drove along the main street, passing the great old houses that faced across the harbor toward the Sea Islands—eighteenth-century mansions of brick, tabby, and wood. Halfway between Savannah and Charleston, Beaufort had once been a major shipping center, but it was now an almost forgotten, perfectly preserved, gemlike little village. We cruised along the narrow streets, passing rows of handsome white houses gleaming in the darkness. The tidy, well-manicured section of town gave way shortly to unpaved streets and tiny run-down cottages. We pulled up in front of a wooden shanty with a swept-sand front yard. The house was unpainted except for the door and windows, which were a light blue. "Haint blue," said Williams. "It keeps the evil spirits out." The house was dark. Williams knocked lightly and then pushed the door open. The flickering light from a TV set was the only illumination in the cluttered front room. Pungent cooking smells, of pork and greens, filled the air. A man lay asleep on a daybed. He stirred as we entered. A young black woman came into the room through a curtained doorway carrying a plate of food. She nodded toward the back of the house without saying a word, and we walked on through.

Minerva was sitting in a small room under a bare light bulb. She was like a sack of flour. Her cotton dress was stretched tight over her round body. Her skin was a pale brown, and her face was as round as a tranquil moon. Her gray hair was pulled back in a bun except for two little pigtails, one hanging over each ear. She wore a pair of purple-tinted, wire-rimmed glasses. The table in front of her was piled high with bottles, vials, twigs, boxes, and odd bits of cloth. The floor was littered with shopping bags, some bulging, some empty. When she saw Williams, she broke into a broad, gap-toothed smile and motioned for us to sit down on two folding chairs.

"I been waitin' on you, baby," she said in a half-whispered voice.

"Well, how've you been, Minerva?" Williams asked.

Minerva's face clouded over. "I been dealin' with a lot a graveyard dirt."

"Not again!" said Williams.

Minerva nodded. "Mm-hmmm. There's a lot a grudgefulness and deceitfulness." Minerva spoke in a faraway voice. It came from so deep within her that the words sounded as if they had been uttered eons ago on a distant planet and were just now reaching the earth through her.

"My son's ex-wife. She had three children with him. She drive by and throw graveyard dirt on my porch. I gets it by the bucketful. That's how come I be blocked a lot. Business gets po'. Then my boy gets in trouble with the po-lice. I can't sleep. And I been raisin' hell with my old man that's dead."

"Dr. Buzzard?"

"Yeah, him," said Minerva. "I need to git me some money, and I been playin' the numbers, so I can git some. I always go to him and I pay him a dime for him to give me a number. But he won't give me one for shit. I cuss he ass out. I don't know why he don't want me to git no money."

Minerva put aside a small wax doll she'd been working on. "Well, it looks like we're back in business again, you and me, don't it?"

"Yes," said Williams. "Now we've got a second trial to work on."

"Yes, I know that." Minerva leaned forward and brought her face close to Williams. *"He's workin' hard against you, baby!"*

"Who is?" Williams was startled. "Not Dr. Buzzard!"

"No, no," Minerva said. "The boy. The dead boy."

"Danny? Well, it doesn't surprise me. He planned this whole thing. He knew I was getting tired of his damn games. He knew I had twenty-five thousand dollars in cash at the house that night, because I was going to Europe on a buying trip. It was his big chance. He could kill me and take it."

Minerva shook her head. "That boy is workin' hard against you."

"Well, can you do something about it?"

"I can try," she said.

"Good. Because there's something else I want you to do too," said Williams.

"What's that, baby?"

"I want you to put a curse on the district attorney."

"Well, of course. Tell me his name again."

"Spencer Lawton. L-A-W-T-O-N."

"Yeah. I worked his name before. Tell me what's goin' on with him since we got you off."

"He's desperate. He's been district attorney now for two years, and he's never won a case himself in court. He's mortified. People are laughing at him."

"They gonna keep on laughin'. Did you bring them things like I told you to?" Minerva asked.

"Yes," said Williams. "I did."

"Water that ain't run through no pipe?"

"Uh-huh."

"And did you put it in a quart jar? With no label on it? And no metal cap?"

"Yes."

"And those nine shiny dimes?"

"They're in my pocket."

"Okay, baby. Now I want you to sit down and do somethin' for me." Minerva gave Williams a quill pen and a bottle of red ink labeled Dove's Blood. "Write Spencer Lawton's name on this piece of paper seven times. Connect the two names as one. Dot no *i*'s and cross no *t*'s. Now, you do that while I do some work over here."

Minerva began filling a plastic shopping bag with odd items—two trowels, pieces of cloth, some bottles. Somewhere on the table, under all the piles of stuff, a telephone rang. Minerva dug out the receiver.

"Hello. Uh-hunh. Okay, now listen to me." She spoke in a half-whisper. "She want you back, but she want you runnin' behind her, beggin'. Remember what I told you. Before you sleep with her again, put a tablespoon of honey in the bath and take a honey bath. After you have sex, dry yourself off with that piece of muslin cloth I gave you. Hang it up to dry. Do not wash it. Later on, wrap it around a purple onion and tie the corners with a square knot. Huh? I say, a square knot. That knot I showed you. Two knots makes one. Okay. Then all you got to do is bury the cloth where she will walk over it or pass by. Uh-huh. Now, darlin', don't you depend on her to give you too much money. 'Cause she won't give you none. That's why her and her husband don't git along. Uh-uh. She ain't gonna be issuin' out no money. And listen, be careful about your personal belongings—your dirty socks, your dirty undershorts, your hair, pictures of your head. She might try to take them to someone like me. Put a picture of her in your wallet in a secret place, between things, with her head upside down. Do that for me. Uh-hunh. That's right. And let me know. Bye-bye."

Minerva looked across the table at Williams. "You done, baby?"

"Yes," he said.

"Okay. Now, you know how dead time works. Dead time lasts for one hour—from half an hour before midnight to half an hour after midnight. The half hour before midnight is for doin' good. The half hour after midnight is for doin' evil."

"Right," said Williams.

"Seems like we need a little of both tonight," said Minerva, "so we best be on our way. Put the paper in your pocket where the dimes is, and take your bottle of water. We goin' to the flower garden."

—

Minerva picked up her shopping bag and headed out the back door. We followed close behind as she made her way down the lane with a slow and ponderous stride. As she approached the next house, an old man got up from a chair on the porch and went inside. A window in another house closed. A door shut somewhere. Two men standing beside an oleander bush parted when they caught sight of Minerva and withdrew into the darkness. In a few moments, we reached the end of the lane. The sliver of a new moon hung like a slender cradle over a grove of tall, dark trees. We were at the edge of a graveyard. On the far side, a hundred yards beyond the trees, a floodlit basketball court cast a pale gray light into the graveyard. A boy was bouncing a ball and taking shots at the basketball hoop. *Thunk, thunk, thunk . . . proinnng.* Otherwise, the graveyard was deserted.

"A lot a people does this kind of work," Minerva said. "But it look like we got the garden all to ourselves tonight."

We walked single file into the graveyard, taking a winding route and stopping finally at a grave under a large cedar tree. My first thought was that this was a new grave, because unlike the others the soil appeared to be freshly spread on top of it. Minerva knelt by the headstone. She reached into the shopping bag and gave Williams a trowel.

"Go to the other end and dig a hole four inches deep with this spade," she said. "Drop one of the dimes into it and cover it up." Williams did as she said. The earth came up with no effort at all. The grave had clearly been dug into and churned so often that the soil was as loose as sand in a sandbox.

I stood a few yards back and watched. Minerva and Williams were like two people kneeling at the opposite ends of a picnic blanket. They faced each other over the bones of Dr. Buzzard.

"Now's the time for doin' good," said Minerva. "First we gotta get that boy to ease off a little. Tell me somethin' about him."

"He tried to kill me," said Williams.

"I know that. Tell me something before that."

"Well." Williams cleared his throat. "Danny was always getting into fights. He got mad at his landlord once and threw a chair through the man's window. Then he went outside and tore up his car with a brick. Another time, he got angry at an exterminator who'd been hired to spray his apartment, so he punched him in the eye, banged his head on the pavement and then later, after the man had sworn out a police warrant against him, took a baseball bat and chased him around Madison Square, screaming that he was going to kill him. He bragged to me once that he'd fired five shots from a pistol at some guy on a motorcycle because the guy was trying to date the same barmaid Danny was seeing at the time. One bullet hit the guy in the foot. His mother had to get police protection from him. She took out a peace warrant against him, which meant if he came within fifty feet of her he'd be arrested."

Minerva wrapped her arms around herself and shivered.

"It ain't doin' no good," she said. "That boy is still workin' hard against you." She thought for a moment. "Tell me somethin' good he done."

"I can't think of anything," said Williams.

"All he ever done was bad things? What made him happy?"

"His Camaro," said Williams. "He loved that Camaro. He used to zoom around in it and see how many wheels he could get off the ground at once. If he turned a corner real fast, he could usually get two wheels in the air. When he drove out to Tybee, he liked to shoot up over that bump in the road leading onto the Lazaretto Creek Bridge, because if he hit it just right he could get all four wheels off the ground at the same time. He loved doing that. He wouldn't let anybody touch that car. It was his pride and joy. He painted it with a spray can, flat black, just the way he wanted it. He'd spend hours fixing it and cleaning it and painting those racing stripes on it. And he was very good at that, painting those stripes and the little curlicues. He was very creative. That's something most people didn't understand about Danny. He was an artist. He flunked every subject in school but art. He always got an A in art. Of course, his talent wasn't developed. He didn't have the patience. I have a couple of his paintings. They're full of fantasy and they're wild, but you can see he had talent. I used to tell him, 'Danny, *do* something with this. You're *good* at it.' But he could never apply himself to anything. He never got past the eighth grade, but he was quick-witted and bright. One time I paid him to dismantle two crystal chandeliers at Mercer House and clean them. When he was just about finished reassembling them, I noticed he'd attached all the little prisms backwards. There were hundreds of them. I explained that each of the prisms was like a diamond ring and that the flat surface had to face out and the pointed surface had to face inward, otherwise it wouldn't sparkle. I told him he'd have to take them all off and put them back on the right way. I said I'd pay him for the extra time it took. Well, he looked at that chandelier. He looked at it real long like it was a rattlesnake. Then he climbed down from the ladder and said, 'The hell with it. I'm outta here. I ain't servin' no *prism sentence*!' I laughed at his pun. I thought it was delightful. He turned around and stormed out of the house, but I could see the corner of his mouth was turned up in a little grin. It pleased him that I'd laughed at his joke."

Minerva smiled. "I felt him backin' off a little," she said.

"What do you mean?" asked Williams.

"I felt it just as you was sayin' those things about him. I felt that boy ease up some."

"Why do you suppose that happened?" Williams asked.

"He heard you say you loved him," Minerva said.

"What?! But that's . . . he tried to kill me!"

"I knew he was workin' against you, baby, and now I know what he was tryin' to do! He was tryin' to make you hate him. He wants you to show the world you hate him. That way, they'll think you hated him bad enough to kill him in cold blood. If you do that, you will surely go to jail, and he knows it."

"I have every right to hate him," said Williams. "He tried to kill me."

"And he paid a heavy price for it. Now he's tryin' to make you pay a heavy price too!"

Minerva turned her shopping bag upside down and hurriedly spread its contents in front of her. "We ain't got time to argue! That was the openin' I was lookin' for. Now I can get to work. Quick, we ain't got much time left. It must be nearin' midnight. Dig another hole and put another dime in it, and this time *think about that boy's Camaro!* Come on! Do it! Think about them pretty stripes the boy painted on it and how good he done it."

Williams silently dug another hole and dropped another dime in. Minerva dug a hole at her end and slipped a root into it. Then she covered it up and sprinkled it with a white powder.

"Now dig another hole, and this time think about that boy's two paintings you got. Think how good they was. We tryin' to keep him off your case. He's backin' off. Oh, he's backin' off. I feel it."

Minerva took a twig and poked it into the ground several times, mumbling and chanting as she did. She sprinkled some more powder and then drew a circle in the dirt. "You through, baby? Now do it another time and think about that 'prism sentence.' Think how it made you laugh. And think how your laughin' made the boy smile. Do that for me."

Minerva continued her ministrations over the head of Dr. Buzzard, while down at the old man's feet Williams silently dug yet another hole.

"Now do it one more time," said Minerva, "and this time drop the rest of the dimes into the hole and think about all them things together. And think about anything else that was good about that boy that maybe you ain't told me yet." Minerva watched as Williams followed her instructions. "Now take that bottle and pour a little water on each of the covered-up holes, so your kindly thoughts about that boy will take root and flower and come back to bless you."

Minerva closed her eyes and sat in silence for several minutes. A church bell began to chime the hour of midnight. She opened her eyes again and quickly picked up a pink plastic purse. She scooped a trowel of dirt into it. "Graveyard dirt works best when it come from a grave right at midnight," she said. "This ain't for your job, though, baby. This is for my private use." She sighed. "Black magic never stops. What goes from you comes to you. Once you start this shit, you gotta keep it up. Just like the utility bill. Just like the grocery store. Or they kill you. You got to keep it up. Two, five, ten, twenty years." The purse was now bulging with dirt. She put it back into her shopping bag.

"It's after midnight now," she said. "Time for doin' evil. I'm gonna work on the D.A. He's a man, so I will cross sex with him and go to nine different dead women. Nine. I will call them three times. I can't guarantee they will all be in your favor. But somewhere down the line there will be an opening, and the dead will settle with him the way they did the last time. Take that piece of paper out of your pocket, the one with his name written on it, and lay it flat on the ground with the writing up." Williams did as he was told.

"Now fold the paper over once, and then fold it again. Then put it back in your pocket. Okay. Now you just sit quiet while I call on the dead."

Minerva spoke unintelligible words in her dreamy, half-whispered voice. All I could make out were the names of the dead women: Viola, Cassandra, Serenity, Larcinia, Delia. Minerva used every prop she had brought with her—roots, charms, powders, squares of cloth. She put them on the ground in front of her and stirred them with two sticks as if mixing a voodoo salad. Then, one by one, she put all the items back into her shopping bag. When she was done, she looked at Williams.

"Walk to the edge of the graveyard and wait for me there," she said. "And don't look back. I got some more work to do here."

Williams and I walked away. After a few steps, I ducked behind an oak tree where I could still see Minerva. She began to mutter. Her muttering became moans, the moans turned into wailing, and the wailing grew louder and louder. Minerva's arms fluttered and wheeled like small propellers. When she was finally out of breath, her hands fell to her lap. She bowed her head in silence for a moment. The only sound in the graveyard was the *thunk, thunk, thunk* of the basketball bouncing in the distance. At length, Minerva spoke in an urgent whisper.

"Listen to me, old man! Why you doin' me this way? Tell me why! I give you dimes and ask for a number, but you won't give me one for shit! You lay there night after night just laughin' at me. Didn't I do right by you? Didn't I wait for you in the bed when you was old and tired and your teeth was rotten? Dammit, *listen* to me!" Minerva poked the ground with her trowel. "Give me a damn number! *Give it to me!*" She poked the ground again. "I ain't givin' you no peace, old man, till you give me a number. Look at me havin' to wear this nasty dress. I need to buy me a new one. The roof is leakin'. The boy's in trouble with the po-lice. I gits graveyard dirt on my porch. I be blocked. Business gits po'." With each complaint, Minerva jabbed the ground in the vicinity of Dr. Buzzard's ribs. Finally, she dropped the trowel into her shopping bag and pulled herself to her feet with a sigh.

I slipped away and joined Williams at the edge of the graveyard. Moments later Minerva approached us, muttering. "Stubborn old man," she said. "I cuss he ass, but he still won't give me a number."

"Haven't you won that damn numbers game by now, Minerva?" Williams asked.

"Yes, I won it," she said. "One time I put thirty-six dollars on triple three. And that was the number."

"How much did you win?"

"I should have won ten thousand dollars, but I didn't git one dime."

"Why not?"

"The bookie changed the number!"

"How could you let him get away with that?"

"He didn't git away with nothin', baby. I fixed it so he don't work no more. I went to the garden and gave him back his kindness. Now he's sickly, and we got us a new bookie."

As we walked up the lane from the graveyard, Minerva gave Williams his parting instructions. He was to put the paper with Spencer Lawton's name on it into a jar filled with water that had not run through any pipe. He was to place the jar in the darkness of his closet, where it would not be touched by the light of the sun or the glow of the moon, until the trial was over. He was to cut a photograph of Lawton's face out of the newspaper, black out his eyes with a pen—first the right eye, then the left—draw nine lines across his lips as if sewing him up, put the photograph in his coat pocket, and make sure a preacher touched his coat. Afterward, he was to burn the photograph in the exact spot where Danny Hansford had died.

"Do that," said Minerva, "and Spencer Lawton will lose your case. But you must do one more thing too. Once a day, every day, you must close your eyes and tell that boy you forgive him for what he done to you. And deep in your heart you must truly forgive him. You hear?"

"I hear," said Williams.

Minerva stopped at a turnoff to another road. "Now, you go on back to Savannah and do like I say," she said.

"Aren't you going home?" Williams asked.

Minerva patted her shopping bag. "Baby, I never takes graveyard dirt into my own house. I will deliver it first, and I must do that alone."

—

Williams was silent as we began the drive back.

"Are you going to follow Minerva's instructions about Spencer Lawton's picture?" I asked.

"I might," said Williams. "It's a little corny, but it could end up being good therapy—sewing up his mouth, blacking out his eyes. Yes, that's something I might be able to get into."

"How about the daily message of forgiveness to Danny Hansford? Are you going to do that too?"

"Definitely not!" he said. "Danny was nothing but a would-be murderer." Williams picked up his glass and drank what was left of his vodka and tonic.

"My case has come down to one thing and one thing only," he said. "Money. Danny knew I had twenty-five thousand dollars in cash in the house. When my lawyer, Bob Duffy, arrived at Mercer House that night, he walked around inspecting the merchandise, picking up little objects and turning them bottom side up. When I asked him what he was going to charge to represent me, he said, 'Fifty big ones.' Later, when I realized I needed a good criminal lawyer, I hired Bobby Lee Cook. Bobby Lee brought his wife to the house, and she picked out fifty thousand dollars' worth of antiques. That was his fee. His expenses were in addition to that. He was assisted by John Wright Jones, who got twenty thousand dollars. And now I will have to pay all over again for another trial.

"But Danny's mother takes the prize with her ten-million-dollar lawsuit against me. After all the anguish and grief Danny had caused her, after she'd thrown him out of the house and gotten police protection from him, Danny was suddenly her beloved dead son, miraculously transformed from a dangerous liability into an asset worth ten million dollars. Lord knows what it will cost me to defend myself against her lawsuit.

"So, you see, it's all about money. And that's one of the reasons I love Minerva. You can laugh at that voodoo stuff if you want, but she only charged me twenty-five dollars tonight. I don't know whether or not you got her point, but no matter how you look at it, she's a bargain."

I did not answer, but it occurred to me that, yes, I did get Minerva's point. I got her point very clearly. What I wondered was, did Williams?

Chapter 19

LAFAYETTE SQUARE, WE ARE HERE

Glass in hand, Joe Odom stood on the roof of his new home and looked down at the floats and the marching bands passing through Lafayette Square below. It was a perfect spot for watching the St. Patrick's Day parade. From the rooftop, Joe could see green-tinted water bubbling out of the fountain in the center of the square. He could see crowds lining the streets wearing green hats and carrying big paper cups full of green beer. St. Patrick's Day in Savannah was the equivalent of Mardi Gras in New Orleans. It was an official holiday; the whole town turned out for it. There were to be more than two hundred marching units today, plus forty bands and thirty floats. A cheer rose up from the crowd as the Anheuser-Busch team of eight shaggy-hoofed Clydesdale horses trotted around the square, past the front of the house.

Like most St. Patrick's Day parades, Savannah's was an ecumenical affair. Blacks, Scots, and Germans marched along with the Irish, but this parade had a distinctly southern flavor. At one point, that flavor took a bitter turn. A column of marchers dressed in gray Confederate uniforms came into the square, with a horse-drawn wagon bringing up the rear. The wagon had low wooden sides, and from the street it would have appeared empty. But from the roof we could see a blue-clad Union soldier sprawled motionless on the floor of the wagon. It was a chilling tableau, the more so because it was meant to be surreptitious.

"Poor damn Yankee," said Joe. "Look at him down there, all bloody and dead."

"The Civil War's been over quite a while," I said. "Isn't it time all that was forgotten?"

"Not if you're a southerner," said Joe. "But you know, that dead Yankee isn't just about the Civil War. He's sort of a symbol of what could happen to any Yankee, even a modern-day Yankee, who comes down here and gets folks all riled up." Joe looked at me and lifted his glass in tribute. "He could be some fella from New York who decided to write a book about us and started filling it with drag queens and murderers and corpses and bottles of poison and—what's that you were telling me about just a minute ago? Oh yeah, voodoo! *Voodoo!* Witchcraft in a graveyard! Damn!"

"I'm not making any of this up, Joe," I said.

"I'm not saying you are."

"So I take it you don't really disapprove."

"No. As a matter of fact, when I think about it, it suits me fine. See, with all these weirdos you got filling up your book, I figure somebody's gonna have to play the good guy, and it's beginning to look like it'll be me."

—

Joe Odom's new residence was by far the grandest of the four he had occupied in the short time I'd known him. It was an ornate four-story mansion, a Second Empire château built by a former mayor of Savannah in 1873. It was the only house of its kind in Savannah, and it stood out. People often referred to it as "The Charles Addams House," because it had a mansard roof topped by a lacy ironwork cresting. The Hamilton-Turner House was its proper name, and it was so fine an example of its type that it was featured in *A Field Guide to American Houses*. Tall, paired windows opened onto elegant balconies, and a cast-iron picket fence embraced the site. All in all, the Hamilton-Turner House was so imposing and yet so fanciful a structure that passersby often stopped in front of it for no other reason than to marvel at it. Joe was not one to let such an opportunity slip through his fingers; he posted a sign on the gate a few days after he moved in: PRIVATE RESIDENCE: TOURS 10:00 A.M. TO 6:00 P.M.

Knowledgeable Savannahians were taken aback by the sign, because they knew that the outside of the Hamilton-Turner House was the only part worth looking at. The interior had been gutted and cut up into apartments long ago. Joe had taken the parlor floor for himself, and it was only this portion of the house that was open for viewing. The space did have tall windows with dramatic views of the square, but the once-stately progression of beautifully proportioned rooms had been sacrificed to make bathrooms, bedrooms, closets, and a kitchen. Walls had been moved and open archways filled in. And yet, because of its vastness, the parlor floor still did retain the aura of a grand *piano nobile.* It had old chandeliers and mantels and pier mirrors (though none were original to the house), and Joe did manage to fill the place appealingly with what was left of his own furniture plus antiques borrowed from friends or taken on consignment from local antique shops.

Joe had, in fact, created something new in Savannah: the only private house that was operating as a full-time tourist attraction. Seven other houses were also open to the public, but they were all museum houses, all important architectural specimens authentically restored and staffed by professional curators and operated on a nonprofit basis. Joe's made-over parlor floor had, in effect, gone into competition with the museums. And he did get his share of tourists. At least fifty people would walk in off the street every day, and half a dozen or more tour buses would stop by. One busload usually stayed for lunch, and in the evenings Joe made the dining room available for private dinners by candlelight.

To help handle all this traffic, Joe hired a short, indomitably cheerful black housekeeper and stationed her at the top of the front steps in a crisp black-and-white maid's uniform. Her name was Gloria, and she had big eyes and little corkscrew curls hanging down over her forehead. Knowing that half the money she collected at the door was hers to keep, Gloria flagged down virtually everybody who came near the house. On slow days, she was not above offering a cut-rate deal—one dollar per person instead of the usual three. ("It may only be but a dollar," she would say later, "but it sure looks like a lot sittin' next to nothin'.") Gloria gave her customers a glass of lemonade and led them through the parlor floor, blinking her eyes in wonderment as she recounted the historical highlights of the house. She explained that it was the first house in Savannah to be electrified (the mayor who built it had also been head of the power company) and that it had served as the center of the city's social and cultural life in the latter part of the nineteenth century. "This house is the center of a lot of things now too," she would add with a big smile. If "Mr. Joe" happened to be home, he would play a few old standards for the guests, and then Gloria would sing the few lines she knew from "Stormy Weather" while doing a dance that resembled the hula.

Joe netted an average of $500 a week from the house, most of it in cash, which suited his needs perfectly since there was not a single bank left in Savannah that would give him a checking account. Even the bank account at Sweet Georgia Brown's had been taken out of his hands. It was now in Mandy's name, and it was her signature, not his, that appeared on all the checks made out to employees and suppliers of the bar.

Joe and Mandy were no closer to marrying. In fact, his attentions toward other women had become more frequent and more open. On several occasions Gloria found the door to Joe's bedroom locked while she was leading tours through the house. She was never at a loss for words. "Beyond this door lies the mansion's master bedroom," she would say, "and today the editors of *Southern Accents* magazine are photographing it for publication, and we cannot disturb them. So I am very sorry, but we will not be able to see this room today." Her explanation might or might not be thrown into question by the sounds of laughter and giggling on the other side of the door.

Mandy was aware of Joe's flirtations. "I swear Joe Odom is going to drive me into being a feminist," she said. "Two years ago if anybody had told me that, I'd a died." But Mandy began to display a new assertiveness. She snatched up the checkbook at Sweet Georgia Brown's and stationed herself at the cash register, thereby shutting off Joe's supply of easy money. So the cash flowing into Joe's pocket from the tour business provided a much-needed lifeline. But there was a hitch: It was illegal.

The Hamilton-Turner House was zoned for residential use. Private tour houses were not permitted.

Lafayette Square was a quiet, conservative corner of Savannah. It was surrounded by stately townhouses and free-standing mansions. The townhouse where the writer Flannery O'Connor had lived as a child stood catty-corner from Joe on Charlton Street. Directly across the square the magnificent Andrew Low House, a pink Italianate villa with a Greek Revival portico, sat in all its architectural and historic splendor; Juliette Gordon Low had founded the Girl Scouts of America there in 1912, and it was now the Georgia headquarters of the Colonial Dames. Of all Joe's neighbors, however, none was more reproachful a presence than the Lafayette apartment house, that monument to Joe's financial debacle of just a few years back. The Lafayette stood on the far side of the square in silent rebuke to Joe. Within its walls there were half a dozen people who had still not recovered from the shock of having their apartments foreclosed (and then having to sue to get them back) when Joe defaulted on his construction loan.

The noise and the fumes of the buses irritated the residents of Lafayette Square, but the wedding parties nearly drove them to distraction. For these affairs, Joe literally annexed the square as his own front yard. He put a Dixieland band on the portico over his front door and pitched tents in the square without bothering to obtain a permit. The square reverberated with blaring music and the shrill chatter of a hundred wedding guests milling about. "Everybody loves a wedding," said Joe, grievously miscalculating the tolerance of his neighbors. After enduring three such weddings, the neighbors formed a committee and sent a spy into the Hamilton-Turner House on a fact-finding mission.

The spy was a dowdy middle-aged woman who lived on the southside. Posing as a walk-in tourist, she entered the Hamilton-Turner House at three in the afternoon for what was supposed to have been a twenty-minute tour. She emerged two hours later with her hair frosted and spiked and her face made up to look like Cleopatra. She declared that Joe Odom was a heartthrob, that the housekeeper, Gloria, was so cute she could just eat her up, and that she did not have time to discuss it any further because she needed to rush home, change clothes, and get to Sweet Georgia Brown's in time for happy hour.

Exasperated, the committee selected a second spy, also a middle-aged woman, but this one was a bit more savvy, having been a docent in one of the museum houses. This second spy came back to report that there was a lot more going on in the Hamilton-Turner House than tours. "Joe Odom, charming as he is, seems unable to distinguish between his private and his business lives. His many friends pop in and out and mingle with the paying guests in a most familiar way. They converse, they make drinks, they raid the refrigerator, they use the telephone. Four men were playing poker in the dining room, and I could swear I saw one of them on the evening news not long ago—he was very fat, that's why I remember him—and he'd been arrested for embezzlement, or maybe it was drug-running. There was a woman curled up on a sofa sleeping off what Mr. Odom laughingly described as 'a marathon binge.' In the kitchen we came upon an extremely talkative young man giving an elderly woman a permanent wave. He had the cheek to suggest that *I* should be next, that I could use a comb-out, I think it was. When you add to these activities the constant comings and goings of the tenants who live in the upstairs apartments—they must all walk through Mr. Odom's entrance hall to reach the stairway—you have an idea of the chaotic atmosphere that prevails.

"Mr. Odom's tours are an out-and-out con job," the spy went on. "Three dollars is a lot to pay for a glimpse of a thrown-together apartment with no historic interest. Most of Mr. Odom's artifacts are bogus—General Oglethorpe's snuffbox and that sort of thing. Often Mr. Odom simply lapses into a parody of a real house tour. He referred to a pair of oil portraits as his 'ancestors-by-purchase,' because he said he'd found them in a flea market and they seemed to want to come home with him. The furniture is an ungainly combination of styles—some reproductions, some period pieces—almost all of it in deplorable condition. One loveseat had an overturned slop bucket in place of a missing leg. Knowing of Mr. Odom's precarious financial situation, I was not surprised that he made several allusions to the fact that everything in the house was for sale—carpets, paintings, furniture, bric-a-brac. He sang a few songs, which was pleasant enough, but he then made a blatant pitch for Sweet Georgia Brown's, fliers for which lie in stacks on every table. It seems clear that this whole tawdry enterprise is nothing but a promotional come-on for Mr. Odom's nightclub. By contrast, the museum houses give far greater educational value, and the fees they collect are used for the worthwhile purpose of maintaining important remnants of Savannah's heritage. Mr. Odom's tours merely cheapen the concept."

Shortly after this visitation, the Department of Inspections notified Joe by certified letter that the tour business at the Hamilton-Turner House violated the zoning code and must cease immediately.

Joe ignored the order. "The best response is always no response," he said. "It buys you two or three months' breathing time, six if you're lucky." In the meantime, he quietly persuaded friends on the Metropolitan Planning Commission to propose a zoning amendment allowing private tour houses. When the Downtown Neighborhood Association got wind of it, they voted to oppose it, and the amendment went down to defeat. A few weeks later—the day before the St. Patrick's Day parade—the Department of Inspections again ordered Joe to stop the tours at once or face legal action. This time the *Savannah Morning News* picked up the story. Joe's breathing time, it seemed, was over.

—

The wagon carrying the dead Union soldier turned the corner and continued up Abercorn Street.

"I don't know, Joe," I said. "I get the feeling you might end up in that wagon before I do."

"Now, don't you start frettin' about your friend Joe," he said.

"You're going to obey the court order, aren't you?"

"Me? The Host of Savannah? Close my doors? It's not my nature to be antisocial. Goes against my grain. Besides, I'm getting filthy rich being so hospitable. I'd have to be crazy to become unfriendly all of a sudden." Joe looked out over the square, scanning the buildings ranged around him as if they were enemy fortifications. "I have a plan."

"What is it?"

"I thought I'd enlist the help of some of your new friends. That Minerva woman, for instance. I thought we might drive over to Beaufort around midnight and have a little chat with her. See if she'll cast a spell on some of the folks who want to shut me down. Or maybe we could get your buddy Luther Driggers to poison 'em. Or your pal Jim Williams to shoot 'em . . . in self-defense, of course."

"Poor taste," I said.

"No good, huh? Well, I have another idea. I really do, and this one is serious. Come on downstairs. I'll show you what I mean."

Joe worked his way down the stairs shaking hands and calling out greetings. Parade-watching parties were in full swing on every floor of the house. Friends shouted expressions of support. "Keep up the fight, Joe!" "Don't let 'em close you down." "Hell with 'em, Joe, they ain't got no right." And Joe told them again and again, "Don't worry. We're staying open. We're staying open."

The crush of people on the parlor floor was so dense it was difficult to make our way through it. This was the first time Joe had lived in a house on the actual parade route, and as a result his St. Patrick's Day party was an even bigger draw than usual. In the midst of it, Gloria, the housekeeper, was gamely showing tourists through the house at three dollars a head, perhaps for the last time. Three middle-aged couples stood clustered around her, cupping their ears in order to hear her over the din of the jostling crowd. "In the olden days," Gloria was saying, "the ladies used to sit by this fireplace shielding their faces behind these beaded heat screens. You see, in those days, ladies' makeup was made out of wax, and if it got too hot it would run down their pretty faces. . . ."

Joe led me into a small, cluttered room at the rear of the house. He took a sheaf of papers out of a desk drawer. "Now, here's my plan," he said. "I've had to come out of retirement to draft it—had to put on my lawyer's hat. Anyhow, tomorrow morning I will go over to the courthouse and dump this legal rigmarole in their lap." He handed me the papers. They were the incorporation documents for "The Hamilton-Turner Museum Foundation," which was described as "a nonprofit corporation whose purpose will be to restore the interior of the Hamilton-Turner House through proceeds generated by a private, not-for-profit tour business on the premises—Joseph A. Odom, president."

"So that's it, plain and simple," he said. "After we deduct salaries and expenses, I can't say there will be any proceeds. But at least we won't be in violation of any zoning code. As of tomorrow morning, the Hamilton-Turner House will not be a private house; it will be a museum. So, if they still want to close me down, they'll have to close the others too."

"Do you think it will work?" I asked.

"It'll work until they figure out how to get around it. But by the time they do, I reckon it won't matter because I'll be rich and famous as the hero of your book."

At that moment, appropriately enough, a flourish of trumpets and a crash of cymbals was heard from the passing parade.

Chapter 20

SONNY

Two weeks before his second trial was to begin, Jim Williams stood in the street outside his antiques shop watching three men unload a heavy piece of furniture from a large van.

"Easy now," he said. They were lowering a carved sideboard. "Up a little on the right."

"How's it going?" I asked.

"Business as usual," he said.

"I mean that other bit of business."

"My trial? I haven't the vaguest idea. I leave all that to my lawyers. To me it's a giant bore. Now *that* interests me." Williams nodded at the sideboard. "That's a very rare example of Georgian furniture. Black walnut. Early nineteenth century. The Regency details are extremely unusual. I've never seen anything like it before."

He spoke as if the furniture coming off the truck was his sole concern. In fact, the defense arrangements for his upcoming retrial had been in turmoil only a few weeks earlier, necessitating a change of lawyers. Bobby Lee Cook, for all his guile and resourcefulness, had not been able to free himself from a conflict in court dates. He was committed to represent another client in a federal case, and the federal calendar always took precedence over state-level cases. Williams, suddenly finding himself without a lawyer, turned to Frank "Sonny" Seiler, a prominent Savannah attorney and a partner in the law firm of Bouhan, Williams and Levy. Seiler was already involved in the case peripherally, having been retained by Williams in his defense against the $10 million civil suit brought by Hansford's mother. That suit would come to trial once the criminal case was settled. Now, in Cook's absence, Williams asked Seiler to take over the criminal case as well.

At fifty, Sonny Seiler enjoyed a position of considerable stature within the Georgia legal community. He was past president of the State Bar of Georgia. He was listed in the book *The Best Lawyers in America* as one of the top civil litigators in the country. He was also a native Savannahian, and that was a major plus for Williams. Juries, especially Savannah juries, were instinctively suspicious of out-of-town lawyers. Bobby Lee Cook had been from Summerville, Georgia, a hundred miles north of Atlanta, far enough away to make him a foreigner in Savannah. Seiler was not only homegrown, he had earned a place in Savannah lore. Thirty years earlier, at the age of twenty-two, he had dived into the Savannah River at the foot of East Broad Street and swum eighteen miles out to Tybee in six hours against rough water and the threat of a hurricane.

"Sonny Seiler's been busily at work on my case," said Williams. "He calls to tell me about it, but I only half listen. He sends me letters, but I just scan them. If you think it would amuse you, go see him yourself and let him explain it to you. Then you can tell me, in a few well-chosen words, how you think my case is going. It'll save me the trouble. His office is right around the corner in Armstrong House, that big gray mansion I used to own at Bull and Gaston. I'll tell him to talk to you. Just make sure you see him after five o'clock. Any earlier would be during office hours, and he'd probably bill me at his hourly rate. I've come to know the ways of lawyers." The corners of Williams's mouth drew downward. "Tell him to give my best to *ugh*-uh."

"*Ugh*-uh?"

"U-G-A. Uga. Uga's a big white bulldog. He's the University of Georgia mascot. Sonny Seiler is the proud owner." Williams said this with a disdainful look. "Sonny is very gung-ho. He's the university's number-one football fan. He's owned the school's mascot since he was in law school in the nineteen-fifties. The current Uga is the fourth in the Uga dynasty. Twenty-five years of Ugas and football. Sonny drives Uga up to Athens for all the home games in a big Georgia-red station wagon. The license plate reads 'UGA IV.' "

—

The entrance hall of Armstrong House was a cavernous space with marble floors and a baronial fireplace. A full-length oil portrait of a British nobleman in a crimson cape dominated one wall. Beneath it, old Mr. Glover, the porter, sat sleeping in an armchair. A receptionist at the foot of a sweeping stairway whispered that I should go right on up.

Sonny Seiler's office was a large, elegant room that had once served as the mansion's master bedroom. Tall French windows looked out across Bull Street toward the Oglethorpe Club. On the walls, where one might have expected to find portraits of the firm's founders, there were portraits of Uga I, Uga II, and Uga III. Each of the bulldogs wore a bright red football jersey over massive shoulders; a black *G* for Georgia was centered on the dog's chest. Seiler was sitting at his desk in a white short-sleeved shirt. He was solidly built and had big shoulders. When I came in, he bounded up from his chair like a halfback breaking out of a huddle. We shook hands. He wore a ring big enough to be brass knuckles. It sparkled with two rows of diamonds that spelled out in big block letters GEORGIA—NATIONAL CHAMPIONS—1980. I sat down across the desk. It was quarter to six, but I got right to the point, thinking Seiler might have the clock running anyhow.

"Will your approach to this trial be any different from the first one?" I asked.

"Hell, yes," he said. "We're gonna have a whole new game plan. The biggest mistake the defense made in the first trial was not facing the homosexual issue head-on. Bobby Lee Cook thought he had an agreement to keep it out of the trial altogether, so he settled for a jury of old-maid schoolteachers and it was a disaster. He was double-crossed when the judge allowed those two punk friends of Hansford's to testify about Jim and Danny having sex. So I sat Jim down and said, 'Look, we can't make that mistake again. If we do, Lawton will bring those guys back and send the jury into orbit the way he did last time. You've got to come right out with it yourself this time, *in your own words*. Phrase it gently and get the shock of it over.' Well, Jim was dead set against it. He flatly refused, said absolutely not. He said he'd never expose his mother to that kind of talk. So I said, 'For God's sake, Jim, she was sitting right there during the first trial! She's already heard it!' 'Not from me, she hasn't,' he said. So I thought a minute and I said, 'How about if your mother is *not* in the courtroom when you testify? Then she won't hear it from you.' Jim finally came around. He agreed to do it. I told him not to worry, we'll back him up by picking a jury that's not biased against homosexuals."

"How do you plan to do that?" I asked.

Seiler leaned forward, putting his elbows on the desk. "Well, Coach, this is what we're gonna do. When we interview prospective jurors, we're gonna ask 'em, 'Would you have a problem if you learned that a defendant was a homosexual?' They'll all say, 'Oh, no! No problem at all.' Then we'll ask 'em, 'Would you want a homosexual teaching your children at school?' Right there, we'll trap a lot of 'em: 'Well . . . no,' they'll say, 'I wouldn't want that,' and we'll strike those people for cause. If they slip past that question, we'll hit 'em with 'Are there any homosexuals in your church?' Then: 'Would you mind if your minister was a homosexual?' If there's any bias, we'll dig it out sooner or later."

Seiler was not interested in seeking a change of venue.

"We might be very sorry if we got it," he said. "There's no telling where we'd end up tryin' this case. We'd have no control over it. We could find ourselves in Ware County." He rolled his eyes. "All they got there are a bunch of damn rednecks. I mean, hell, people over there think it's a sin to have sex with the lights on. They'd lynch Jim before they ever got around to convicting him. So I think we're better off right here in Savannah. The D.A.'s case isn't as strong as he makes it out to be, and it's gettin' weaker all the time."

"How?" I ventured to ask.

"Well, I'll tell ya. Lawton likes to talk about the 'overwhelming' physical evidence against Jim. That's bullshit. He's got two pet theories: the gunshot-residue theory and the coup de grâce theory. He claims the absence of gunshot residue on Danny's hands proves he didn't fire a gun, and he says Danny was lying on the floor when Jim shot him in the back. Well, we've come up with brand-new evidence that knocks hell out of both those arguments. I don't mind telling you what we've got, 'cause we've had to share it all with the D.A.

"Last month, we got a court order that allowed us to have our own experts conduct laboratory tests on the two German Lugers—Jim's and Danny's—and the shirt that Danny was wearing. We lined up one of the top forensic pathologists in the country to do the tests, Dr. Irving Stone of the Institute for Forensic Sciences in Dallas. He's the guy who analyzed the clothing worn by President Kennedy and Governor Connally for the congressional committee that reexamined the Kennedy assassination. In other words, he's no slouch.

"Now, we were stickin' our neck out, 'cause we didn't know whether Stone's findings would help us or hurt us, and we were under court order to give the results to Lawton. In fact, the D.A. sent his man with us to Dallas—Dr. Larry Howard, the director of the Georgia Crime Lab. Ol' Doc Howard carried the guns and the shirt down there.

"Well, when Dr. Stone stepped up to test-fire Danny's pistol, something unexpected happened. It wouldn't fire. At first, Stone thought the safety was on. But it turned out that the trouble was that the gun had an unusually heavy trigger pull—twenty pounds. A normal trigger pull is four to six pounds. Stone had to squeeze hard to pull the trigger, and as he did, the gun jerked around drastically. Right there we had an unlooked-for explanation for why Danny missed Jim and shot into the desk. It was a bonus. It just fell into our lap.

"Then Dr. Stone went ahead and tested the gun to see if it was consistent in the way it threw off gunpowder. Get this: Stone found that when he held Danny's gun in a downward angle and fired it, as Danny would have, the gunshot residue was diminished by more than half. Not only that, the gun was erratic in the amount of residue it threw off! Well, ol' Doc Howard was breathin' heavy right about now.

"Then Dr. Stone ran an analysis of Danny's shirt. Hell, there wasn't any gunpowder on it at all! According to Stone, that proves Jim had to be standing at least four feet away from Danny, because that's how far Jim's gun ejects debris out the front of the barrel. Stone says that means there's no way Jim could have come around the desk to fire the last two shots, because there'd be gunpowder on Danny's shirt if he had. So much for Lawton's coup de grâce theory. I thought ol' Doc Howard was gonna pass out."

Seiler pulled a manila envelope out of his desk drawer. "Now, I'm gonna show you a little surprise we have in store for Lawton. After the police got to Jim's house, they photographed the room where the shooting took place. Those pictures showed all sorts of supposedly incriminating details. Right? A chair leg on Danny Hansford's trousers, particles of paper on top of the gun on the desk, smeared blood on Danny's wrist. Bad stuff. Lawton introduced about twenty photographs in the first trial, but the police photographer testified she took *five rolls*. That means there were over a hundred pictures we hadn't seen. A couple weeks ago we asked to have a look at the rest of them. We didn't know what we were looking for, and frankly we didn't think we'd find anything.

"Well, we got the full set of photographs a couple of days ago. Okay. Now, look at this one."

Seiler handed me a photograph showing the chair behind Williams's desk. A leather pouch lay on the carpet against a leg of the chair.

"Now compare that photograph . . . with this one." In the second shot, the leather pouch was no longer touching the chair leg; it was several inches away. "You can tell from the designs in the carpet that both the chair and the leather pouch have been moved. I don't know who moved them or why, but nobody is supposed to touch anything at the scene of an alleged crime until photography is completed and measurements are taken. If the police do move anything, they're required to photograph it actually being moved, and they didn't. When we looked through the rest of the pictures, this is the sort of thing we found."

Seiler laid out several other photographs showing objects on the top of Williams's desk. "Notice the position of the pink box, here . . . and here." The pink box, too, had been moved. So had a copy of *TV Guide*, a stack of envelopes, rolls of paper, and a telephone directory.

"When you look at all the pictures—and not just the twenty the D.A. used for the first trial—you can see that things were being shuffled around all over the place. That means the scene of the shooting was never properly secured. There's not supposed to be anybody in the room when the police photographer is shooting pictures, but just look at these photographs: You can see feet, arms, legs, civilian shoes, uniform shoes, black shoes, felt shoes. The police were swarming all over the house that night. It was a convention. And now we discover they were moving the evidence. That's crazy. It violates rudimentary police procedure. What's more, *it taints all the evidence in the room!*"

Seiler beamed. "I tell ya, we're in good shape. The only thing out of our control is Jim's arrogance on the witness stand. But hell, we ain't never gonna get around that. We're just gonna have to live with it."

Seiler tilted back in his chair and clasped his hands behind his head. "Lawton's in trouble, but it's his own fault. He made a terrible blunder playing keep-away with the evidence in the first trial. Lawton's articulate and smart, no question. But he doesn't have the experience a D.A. oughta have. Believe me, I know what I'm talking about. I've been practicing law for twenty-five years, been in court dozens and dozens of times. Spencer Lawton hasn't handled but two court cases in his life—the Rangers case and Jim's first trial—and he hasn't won one yet, now that Jim's conviction has been reversed. He's anxious and he's green, and we're gonna take advantage of that. We've been keeping the pressure on him, swamping him with pre-trial motions, distracting him with details. There's nothing we can do about the horrendous publicity, of course, but this time we're gonna sequester the jury to shield them from it. I hate to do it to 'em, but we'll try to speed things up a little by having Saturday sessions in court." Seiler shook his head. "Right in the middle of football season too. That oughta prove I didn't make the decision lightly. I've been to every Georgia home game for the last twenty-five years. I figure I'll miss at least one game, maybe two this year because of the trial. But we'll be at the opener against UCLA this Saturday."

"You and Uga?"

"Yup," said Seiler. "Ever seen Uga?"

"No, but I've heard about him."

"People *love* Uga!" he said. "He's the most famous animal in Georgia!" Seiler gestured toward a bank of file cabinets next to his desk. "That whole thing is full of nothing but Uga." He began rolling out the drawers. They were crammed with clippings, photographs, posters, letters.

"Last year, Uga went to the Heisman Trophy award dinner in New York," he said. "Did you hear about that? Here, look." Seiler pulled out an AP Wirephoto of himself and Uga IV with Herschel Walker, the Georgia halfback who had won the Heisman Trophy that year. The three of them, the dog included, were wearing black tie. "Uga's the only dog ever to be invited to a Heisman dinner," he said brightly.

He continued wading through the files. "Uga's correspondence is amazing. When he had an operation on his knee, he got *hundreds* of get-well cards from all over the country. There's a file of them somewhere in here. He even got a card from Mike the Tiger."

"Who's Mike the Tiger?" I asked.

Seiler looked up from the cabinet, surprised at my ignorance. "LSU," he said. He pressed the intercom. "Betty, you got that file with Uga's get-well cards? I cain't find it."

Seiler's secretary came into the room with a worried look. "It should be in there, Sonny," she said. She opened another drawer and looked through it. Then she left the room. Seiler went on rummaging, thoroughly engrossed. Meanwhile, I glanced around the room. A life-size porcelain bulldog lounged on the hearth. Above it, a procession of carved bulldogs prowled across the mantelpiece in bas-relief. Scattered here and there were other objects of bulldogiana—framed snapshots, a brass paperweight, figurines, needlepoint pillows. Betty came back into the room.

"I think this is it, Sonny," she said. She gave him a file labeled "Knee Injury." Scores of cards and letters fell out onto the desk. Seiler began to paw through them.

"Here it is," he said. "Mike the Tiger. And here's one from the Boston College Eagle . . . the Kentucky Wildcat . . . Mrs. Willingham's fourth-grade class in Macon." Some of the letters ran to several pages. Seiler held up a handful. "I tell ya, Uga's a phenomenon. Uga III even made it into *The Animals' Who's Who*. He was the mascot when we won the national championship a couple years ago."

Seiler went over to the bookshelf and took down the book. Indeed, Uga III was immortalized in it, along with Rin Tin Tin, Man o' War, Moby Dick, Toto, and The White Rabbit. I put the book down on Seiler's desk, which was now awash in Uga memorabilia.

"You know," said Seiler, looking up from the pile, "you oughta try to make it up to Athens this weekend. We're playing UCLA. Oughta see at least one game while you're here. If you do, come on by the hotel suite around noon. We always have a little gathering before the game. That's when Uga gets dressed."

—

On Saturday morning, traffic flowed north toward Athens with the exuberance of a cavalry charge. Red-and-black pennants fluttered from aerials. Homemade signs flashed messages of common cause: GO BULLDOGS! BEAT UCLA! HOW 'BOUT THEM DAWGS!

At noon, a dozen guests were gathered in Sonny Seiler's hotel suite. A radio on the dresser was tuned to a pregame call-in question-and-answer show. Seiler sat on the edge of the bed talking on the telephone. He wore a red sweater, black slacks and a white baseball cap inscribed with the letter *G*. He was shouting into the receiver.

"That you, Remer? Can you hear me? We all up here listenin' to the damn talk show, but you ain't called in yet! . . . They got a bunch a crackers callin' in. Huh? Oh, hell, they just askin' dumb questions like, 'When do we wear white pants and when do we wear red?' and 'How many conference games has Georgia lost in red trousers?' You gonna call in? . . . It's that 800 number I gave you. You got it? . . . Okay, Coach, we'll be listenin' for ya."

Sonny got up from the bed. "That was Remer Lane. He's back in Savannah. Gonna call that radio show with a question about Uga." At this moment, Uga himself was reclining on a blanket in the shower stall, an enormous heap of furry white wrinkles surrounded by a cluster of admirers including Seiler's daughter, Swann. "Hey, baby, hey, sweetie," a woman cooed. "You gonna pull us through today, Sugar?"

Sonny went to a makeshift bar on the dresser and poured several drinks. "I tell ya," he said, "I got every bit of faith in this team. We gonna have another winning season, but I sure do miss Herschel."

"Amen," said a man in a red blazer. Herschel Walker had played his last season the previous year and was now a rookie with the New Jersey Generals.

"We'll do okay," another man said, "but I'm already beginning to sweat the Florida game. Not the outcome of the game, mind you. The tickets. Everybody wants tickets. I'm usually pretty good at finding 'em, and everybody and his brother seems to know that. But I mean, Jesus, it's only September and it's already started."

"September!" said a tall man in a red-and-black windbreaker. "My phone usually starts ringing around the middle of July, and that's no exaggeration. Then come August, it really heats up. I get phone calls, I get interoffice memos, I get telegrams, I get letters. I'm the most popular man in Georgia when it comes to the Georgia-Florida game."

Most of the men in the room were well-connected football fans, and now they traded stories about getting tickets for friends. "Hey, Sonny!" one of them called out. "What about that Williams murder case? You figure you're gonna win it?"

Seiler looked at the man. "Is Georgia gonna beat UCLA?" Georgia was heavily favored. "I tell ya, Coach," said Seiler, "don't go placing any bets against us yet. We got a couple of surprises up our sleeve. New evidence, a couple of new witnesses. It's gonna be a . . . Oh, *wait*! There it is!" Seiler reached over and turned up the volume on the radio.

"*. . . of course, Uga has a big appetite,*" the announcer was saying, "*and our caller from Savannah wants to know: 'What brand of dog food does Uga eat?'* "

"Attaboy, Remer!" said Seiler. Everyone in the room knew the answer: Jim Dandy dog ration. Uga not only ate Jim Dandy dog ration, but he officially endorsed it too. Plastic cups were raised in a toast to Uga IV and Jim Dandy. Swann Seiler poked her head in the door. "Daddy, it's time to dress Uga."

"Ah, the Dressing of the Dog!" intoned a portly man standing by the window.

Seiler held up a red jersey and called out, "*Heeeeeeyuuhhhhh!*" Uga came trotting into the room, wriggling and wagging his sixty-five-pound body. Seiler slipped the jersey over his head and fastened a spiked collar around his neck. "If we have a defeat," said Swann, "then we don't ever wear that jersey again. Sometimes, if things aren't going well, we change jerseys in the middle of a game."

"We've got five or six with us today," said Sonny. "We can change if we have to. I hope we don't."

"Mom used to make them," said Swann. "We've got some historical jerseys that Uga wears when we've won bowl games. Uga's got a bigger wardrobe than I do."

The guests started putting on their coats as Seiler brushed the dog and sprinkled talcum powder on the top of his head to cover a grayish spot. "That's for the cameras," he said. "He's supposed to be a picture-perfect, all-white dog. Well, let's go." He opened the door, and Uga surged down the hall, straining on his leash and leading the procession to the elevator and out through the lobby.

In the parking lot outside Sanford Stadium, Seiler lifted Uga onto the roof of his red station wagon, the one with the "UGA IV" license plates. Thus enthroned, Uga accepted the adoration of his fans. Thousands of spectators waved, called his name, patted him on the head, and took snapshots on their way into the stadium. Uga wiggled and panted and licked as many hands as he could reach.

Shortly before kickoff, Seiler took Uga down from his perch and led him around to the open end of the U-shaped stadium. He and Uga paused just outside the end zone in front of three marble tombstones set into a landscaped embankment. This was the Uga memorial plot. Bunches of flowers had been placed at the foot of each tombstone, and each bore an inscription to a late Uga:

"UGA. Undefeated, Untied. Six bowl teams. 'Damn Good Dog' (1956-1967)."

"UGA II. Five bowl teams. 'Not bad for a dog' (1968-1972)."

"UGA III. Undefeated, Untied, Undisputed, and Undenied. National Champions of College Football 1980. 'How 'bout this dog.' "

The band was assembling in the end zone. The Georgia cheerleaders came to take Uga from Seiler and put him into his official doghouse, which was shaped like a big red fire hydrant on wheels. It was air-conditioned, the Georgia heat being less than ideal for Uga's breed of English bulldog. The hydrant was wheeled out to midfield for the opening ceremonies. Just before kickoff, Uga jumped out and trotted to the sidelines. A roar went up from the crowd. "Damn good dog! Damn good dog! Damn good dog! *Rooff! Rooff! Rooff! Rooff-rooff-rooff-rooff-rooffrooffrooffrooff!*"

—

Later that evening, I called Williams to tell him about my conversations with Seiler.

"It sounds as if he's come up with strong new ammunition for you," I said.

"I would think so," said Williams, "considering the rates he charges. What did you think of him?"

"Smart, energetic, committed to your case."

"Mmmmm," said Williams, "and to the money he's making from it." I could hear the clinking of ice cubes at Williams's end of the line.

"Do you want me to explain what he's got?"

"No, not especially. But tell me—not that I really care about this either—who won the game today?"

"Georgia. Nineteen to eight."

"Good," said Williams. "That means Sonny will be in high spirits. It's all so childish. When Georgia loses, it absolutely destroys him. He goes into shock and can't function for days."

"In that case, I think you'll get a vigorous defense out of him. It was a solid victory."

"Not too big a victory, I hope. He might regard my trial as an anticlimax."

"I don't think the game was that important," I said. "It wasn't a Southeastern Conference game."

"Wonderful," said Williams. "I wouldn't want him to be all distracted and daydreaming. I want him to be frisky. Yes. That should work." Williams paused. The ice cubes clinked. "Yes, that should work very well."

Chapter 21

NOTES ON A RERUN

This is not a happy jury. Six men, six women—seven black, five white. When Judge Oliver told them to go home and come back in the morning with enough clothes for a two-week stay, four of the women burst into tears. One of the men jumped up and shouted, "I refuse it! I refuse it! I'll lose work. *It will make me hostile to the case!*" Another man bolted for the door and had to be restrained by the bailiffs. "You can take me to jail!" he screamed. "I'm not serving!" The judge summoned the six recalcitrant jurors to his chambers and listened to their complaints. Then he told them to go home and pack.

—

Spencer Lawton leads off with the police photographer, Sergeant Donna Stevens, who gives a photographic tour of Mercer House, using huge blowups on an easel. "This is an outside shot of the house," she says. "This is the living room. . . . This is the hallway, and that's a grandfather clock dumped over. . . . This is the doorway to the study, showing the victim laying on the floor. . . . This is a shot of blood on the carpet. . . ."

When she is finished, Seiler steps up for cross-examination.

"Do you remember photographing a pouch and a chair leg?" he asks.

"Yes," she says.

"Did you photograph it when you first got there?"

"Yes, sir, I did."

"And did you photograph it again after the detectives and other people had been stirring around in there?"

"Yes."

Seiler holds up the two photographs showing the pouch and the chair leg in different positions. "I'm interested in the traveling pouch," he says, raising an eyebrow. Sergeant Stevens concedes that the chair has been moved, but she denies that the pouch has been moved. Seiler asks if by looking at the designs on the carpet she can see that indeed the pouch, too, has been moved. No, she does not see any such thing. Seiler keeps at it. "Well, let's look at the first picture and count the dots in the carpet," he says. "One . . . two . . . three . . . four . . . five . . . six! And in the second picture there are only *two* dots, right?"

Sergeant Stevens grudgingly admits that the pouch has also been moved.

—

The jury is entertained by Seiler's self-assured courtroom manner. He strides back and forth, impeccably groomed in custom-tailored suits, French cuffs, highly polished shoes. He thunders and growls. His tone shifts from curiosity to sarcasm to outrage to surprise. Lawton is dull by comparison. He stands flat-footed in a rumpled suit. His manner is shy and unassuming. He flinches whenever Seiler shouts "Ob*jec*tion! Mr. Lawton is leading the witness again." Seiler does this repeatedly to unnerve Lawton and send a message to the jury that the D.A. lacks a grasp of basic courtroom procedure.

—

At Clary's drugstore, Ruth wonders out loud whether this trial will be as "juicy" as the first. Luther Driggers says he thinks Williams made a mistake after shooting Hansford. "He should have taken Danny's body out west, pulled his teeth, dissolved them in nitric acid, peeled off his skin, and fed it to the crabs."

"Why such a complicated cover-up?" Ruth asks.

Luther shrugs. "It beats leaving the body on the floor of Mercer House."

"Well, whatever Jim Williams should have done with the body, he's going about his defense the wrong way," says Quentin Lovejoy, putting his coffee cup down gently. Mr. Lovejoy is a soft-spoken classics scholar in his mid-sixties; he lives with his maiden aunt in a high-Victorian townhouse. "All this talk about Danny Hansford being a violent, brutal criminal! Jim Williams does himself no credit blaspheming the boy that way."

"But Quentin," Ruth protests, "Danny Hansford beat up his sister! His mother took out a police warrant against him. He'd been arrested umpteen times. He'd been in jail. He was a common criminal!"

"Not at all," says Mr. Lovejoy in a voice slightly louder than a whisper. "The only crime that boy ever committed was turnin' twenty."

—

Seiler objects to the repeated use of the term "crime scene" by prosecution witnesses. "It has not yet been established that any crime has been committed here," he says.

Judge Oliver apparently does not hear Seiler. In fact, the judge appears to be dozing. His eyes are closed, his chin is resting on his chest. The judge has made it abundantly clear, by heaving deep sighs and becoming increasingly cranky, that he is bored with this retrial. His apparent catnaps are causing comment in the courthouse. At any rate, he does not respond to Seiler's protest. Less than a minute later, a prosecution witness says "crime scene" again, and Seiler lets it pass.

—

In the corridor during a recess, a pair of purple glasses catches my eye. Minerva is sitting on a bench with a plastic shopping bag on her lap. I sit down next to her, and she tells me she has been asked to appear as a character witness for Williams. The defense hopes she will appeal to the seven blacks on the jury. She will identify herself as a laundress, which is her part-time profession, but from the witness stand she'll be in a position to make direct eye contact with the D.A., the judge, and the members of the jury. This will enable her to put a curse on every one of them.

While she waits, she sits out in the hall, humming and gurgling softly to herself. Occasionally, she cracks open the door and peers into the courtroom.

—

Danny Hansford's mother, Emily Bannister, also sits in the corridor. Sonny Seiler has listed her as a defense witness, just as Bobby Lee Cook did, in order to keep her out of the courtroom. She is quiet and composed, and it strikes me that Seiler's main concern is not that she will cause a disturbance in front of the jury but that her waiflike appearance will win their hearts. In any case, she still refuses to talk to the press (or to me). As the trial progresses, Mrs. Bannister sits in the corridor just outside the courtroom door reading, writing notes in a journal, and needlepointing.

—

The first Saturday in court, both Sonny Seiler and Judge Oliver appear to be on edge. They are worried about the Georgia–Mississippi State game, which is taking place concurrently in Athens. Seiler stations an associate in the corridor listening to the play-by-play on a portable radio. Oliver, a past president of the University of Georgia Club, asks Seiler to keep him advised of the situation. Seiler does so during whispered conferences at the bench. Georgia wins, 20 to 7.

—

Monday morning. Williams testifies. Standing outside the courtroom beforehand, he appears relaxed. "Sonny called me last night to tell me to act humble and remorseful," he says. "I don't know if I can manage that, but I am making a sincere effort to look impoverished. I'm wearing the same blue blazer I wore on Friday. It will give the jury the impression I haven't got anything else to wear. What they won't know is that it's a custom-made Dunhill jacket, and that the buttons are eighteen-carat Georgia gold."

Seiler puts his new game plan into effect. Before Williams takes the stand, his sister escorts his mother out of the courtroom. On direct examination, Seiler asks Williams to explain his relationship with Danny Hansford.

"He was a nice fellow," Williams says. "He could be charming. He had his girlfriend, I had mine. But to me, sex is just a natural thing. We'd had sex a few times. Didn't bother me. Didn't bother him. I had my girlfriend, and he had his. It was just an occasional, natural thing that happened."

The expressions on the jurors' faces suggest they do not find this arrangement natural at all.

—

Lawton steps up to cross-examine Williams. Williams regards him with undisguised contempt.

"You indicated that you and Hansford had sex from time to time," says Lawton. "Is that right?"

"Mm-hmmm."

"And that you feel that sex is a perfectly natural thing."

"Well, you see, it's not only just natural. At the time, Danny was a hustler on Bull Street selling himself to anybody who wanted to pay for it."

"Exactly," says Lawton. "Right. So he was a street kid and had been since fourteen years of age, I think you indicated?"

"Oh, yes."

"An eighth-grade dropout, and something on the order of twenty years old, is that right?"

"He was twenty-one. He was no child."

"I wouldn't, of course, dispute your right to have any relationship you wanted to. But you were fifty-two and he was twenty-one. Was that a natural and normal relationship?"

"Mm-hmmm. I was fifty-two years old, but he had fifty-two years' worth of mileage on him."

"I don't have anything else," said Lawton. "Thank you very much."

Williams's choice of words may not have been what Seiler had hoped for, but his frankness has made it unnecessary for Lawton to call Hansford's two friends in rebuttal. That, Seiler believes, has spared Williams major damage.

—

During a recess, Seiler tells me Judge Oliver is old and tired. He is also terrified of being reversed by the state supreme court again, so he is allowing the defense to bring in a lot more evidence about Danny Hansford's history of violence than he did in the first trial. "We wouldn't get half that stuff past a younger, more able judge," says Seiler.

—

Barry Thomas, the foreman of Williams's shop, is one of the people permitted by Judge Oliver to tell a story about Hansford's violence. A slightly built Scotsman, Thomas recalls how, without warning and for no apparent reason, Hansford physically attacked him at Mercer House two months before he died.

"It was the end of the workday," Thomas says, "and I was getting ready to leave through the front door of Mercer House when I heard these footsteps behind me. I looked around and saw Mr. Hansford charging toward me. He just went at me and kicked me in the stomach. Jim grabbed him and pulled him off me and said, 'You better get out of here. Danny's gone crazy.'

"Well, a couple of days later, Mr. Hansford apologized for kicking me. He said he didn't know why he did it. He wanted me to kick him in the stomach in return, but I said no. I thought he was sick. I have no idea why he attacked me, other than it was just his nature."

—

Thomas steps down after testifying. As he goes out into the hall, a hand reaches up and grabs his ear. He lets out a sharp *"Aiieee!"* as the door closes behind him. I slip into the corridor and see that the hand clutching his ear is Minerva's.

"*Why did you say that?*" she hisses.

"Say what?" says Thomas, grabbing hold of her arm.

"About the dead boy," she says, giving his ear a sharp yank. "Why did you say that?"

" 'Cause it's true," says Thomas. "He kicked me in the stomach for no good reason."

"That don't matter," she says, letting go of his ear. "You got the boy angry again. Now we gotta calm him down."

"What do you want me to do?"

"Git me some parchment. I need a pen too. One that's got red ink in it. And let me think . . . scissors! Gotta have a scissors. And a candle and a Bible. I need 'em quick!"

"Parchment?" Thomas asks. "Where am I gonna fi—," Minerva grabs him by the ear again.

"I know where you can get a Bible," I say, stepping forward. "At the motel across the street."

Five dollars coaxes a Bible and a candle out of the desk clerk at the motel. At Friedman's art supply shop, Thomas buys a red felt-tip pen and a package of heavy vellum tracing paper, which is the closest thing they have to parchment. When he starts to pay, Minerva puts her hand on his arm and stops him. "Lay the money down on the table first," she says. "That way the lady can't work with your hand. Kiss it before you lay it down, so it will come back to you." Thomas obediently kisses the money and lays it on the counter.

Back in Thomas's car, Minerva spreads out her paraphernalia on the backseat and says, "Take us close as we can git to water." Thomas drives down the steep cobblestone street leading from Factors' Walk to River Street. We move slowly along the River Street esplanade—the docks on one side, the old warehouses on the other. Minerva points to an old three-masted schooner. "Right there."

Thomas pulls to a stop at the ship's bow, and Minerva lights the candle and begins to chant. With the red pen, she scribbles phrases from the Bible onto the vellum. When she is done, she cuts the vellum into small squares and sets them on fire one by one. Glowing ashes float around like black snowflakes inside the car.

"Take these three pieces I ain't burned," she says to Thomas, "and tell Mr. Jim to put them in his shoes."

Suddenly, I become aware that there are four of us present, not three. The fourth is a policeman who is looking in the window about a foot from my face.

"Ma'am?" he says.

Minerva holds the burning candle in front of her face and stares at the policeman through her purple glasses. She opens her mouth wide. "Ahhhhhhhhhhhhhhh!" she says. Then she puts the candle in her mouth and closes her lips around it. As she does, the light sets her cheeks aglow like a jack-o'-lantern. The glow goes out with a sizzle. She hands the extinguished candle to the policeman. "We ain't burnin' no more," she says softly. She taps Thomas on the shoulder, and as we pull away, I can see the policeman in the side-view mirror. He is still holding the candle and looking blankly in our direction when we turn the corner.

—

Back in the courtroom, a psychiatrist testifies that as a child Danny Hansford was a breath holder. What he means by that, he says, is that Danny used to torment his mother by holding his breath until he turned blue and passed out.

—

Minerva will not testify after all. She has suddenly realized that she knows one of the jurors, and he knows her.

"I done some black magic on him," she says. "He's still mad as hell." She will not say what she did to him or why.

—

Dr. Irving Stone, the forensic pathologist from Dallas, takes the stand and makes forceful arguments for the defense about the gunshot residue and other aspects of the shooting, as Seiler said he would. His comments are supported by Joseph Burton, the medical examiner from Atlanta who testified in the first trial and has returned for this one. More compelling than their testimony, however, is the casual shoptalk they engage in while waiting in the corridor to take the stand.

"I identified 357 bodies in that Delta crash we had in Dallas the other day," says Stone. "Got thirty a day. It took twelve days."

"Jeez," says Burton. "Nice going. How many did you get from fingerprints?"

"Seventy-four percent."

"How about dental records?"

"Can't remember. Ten percent, maybe. My favorite was the one I got from a pacemaker. Noted the serial number. Called the manufacturer. Got the name that way."

—

Seiler has saved his two surprise witnesses for late in the trial.

Vanessa Blanton, a brunette in her mid-twenties, is a waitress at the 1790 restaurant and bar. She says she used to live in a townhouse on Monterey Square, and she remembers seeing a young man fire a pistol into the trees about a month before Danny Hansford was killed. She did not know that this incident had any bearing on Williams's trial until recently, when a law associate of Sonny Seiler's happened to overhear her mentioning the incident to another waitress at the restaurant. Seiler subpoenaed her. She takes the witness stand.

"We closed the bar at two-thirty, and I got in my car and went straight home. I was going up the stairs, when I heard a gunshot. I looked over my shoulder towards Mr. Williams's house. It sounded as if it had come from that direction. There was a young man in blue jeans and a T-shirt, holding a gun, pointing it towards the trees. He fired another shot."

"What did you do after that?" Seiler asks.

"I opened the front door to go into my apartment, and when I looked back I noticed the young man was going back up the front steps to Mr. Williams's house. Then I collected my thoughts for a minute and I thought about calling the police, but when I looked out the window again, a police car was pulling up to the house."

Spencer Lawton sees Miss Blanton as a serious blow to his April 3 scenario. He challenges her ability to see the figure in front of Mercer House clearly at that distance and in the dark of night. But she sticks to her story.

Seiler's second surprise witness is Dina Smith, a blond woman in her mid-thirties. On the night Danny Hansford was shot, she was visiting Savannah from Atlanta and staying with her cousin just off Monterey Square. Sometime after two o'clock, she went out to sit on a bench in Monterey Square and enjoy the night air. "After I'd been in the square for some minutes, there were several loud gunshots fired all at once. It was very loud. It seemed to be coming from all around. I kind of just sat there frozen. I looked around and remained in the square for twenty to thirty minutes and then walked back across to the apartment."

"Were there any police cars in front of Mr. Williams's house at that time?" Seiler asks.

"No, sir. The front door was standing open. The lights were on."

"All right," says Seiler. "Did you see anyone?"

"No, sir."

"Did you call the police then?"

"No, I didn't."

"Why not?"

"I wouldn't have known what to tell them. I didn't know what I had heard."

The next morning, Mrs. Smith left her cousin's house to

go to the beach and saw a TV news van in front of Mercer House. She read about the shooting later and only then realized what had happened. Mrs. Smith says she was introduced to Williams by her cousin on a subsequent visit to Savannah, while Williams was appealing his conviction. She told Williams what she had heard, and he asked her to speak to his lawyers.

The import of what Dina Smith has to say is that all of the shots, as she heard them, were fired in rapid succession, just as Williams said. There were no pauses—no time, if she is to be believed, for Williams to get a second gun and fake the shots from Hansford's side of the desk.

—

The final day in court, a Saturday. On tap for today: closing arguments, the judge's instructions to the jury, the Georgia-Mississippi game.

In his summation, Sonny Seiler puts heavy emphasis on the clumsiness of the police at Mercer House, comparing them to the Keystone Kops. "They had so many people in Jim Williams's study while they were investigating the scene they can't count them," he says. "First Corporal Anderson comes, and he brings a rookie cop along. Following them is Officer Traub, as I recall, and then they started coming out of the woodwork. In they come, one after another—I don't know how many, something like fourteen in all—and it wasn't a matter of just coming. It was 'Come and join the party!' because you don't have many things like this happening in Savannah, in a historical mansion with an environment of antiques and fine things and an air of mystery and intrigue. And they all go into the study at one time or another. Anderson, White, Chessler, Burns, Traub, Gibbons, Donna Stevens. All of them, back and forth, in and out, all around the room. Everybody's curious, you see. They're picking things up and they're putting them down. And every expert on the stand, including their own, says that is not good investigative procedure. Yet they want you to believe they had some sacred veil over all the stuff while they took photographs. They tell you they secured the scene. Baloney! You've seen the pictures."

—

Lawton, in his closing statement, will not give up on the idea that Jim Williams staged the April 3 incident, in spite of what Vanessa Blanton says she saw. Lawton tells the jury, "If you believe Vanessa Blanton really saw Danny Hansford out there shooting in Monterey Square, then okay. But I will suggest to you that it may be very difficult to tell, down there in those shadows, whether what you're looking at is Danny Hansford . . . or *Jim Williams*. We have to entertain the possibility that it was practice, a dry run that sets up Danny Hansford's violent nature within a month of when he gets killed."

Of Dina Smith and the shots she heard on the park bench a month later, Lawton makes it clear he does not believe her. "I will suggest to you that she was a friend trying her best to help out in a pinch."

Toward the end of his summation, Lawton engages in a bit of stage business concerning the twenty-pound trigger pull on Danny's gun: "The defense tells us that when Danny Hansford fired at Williams and missed, it was because the trigger pull on his gun was so strong. So strong, indeed, that Dr. Stone—an ex-FBI agent and obviously no weakling—had to use two hands to fire it. I'd like to show you something if I may." Lawton hands Danny's gun to his petite female assistant and asks her to point it toward the wall and pull the trigger. She does so with no effort at all and without jiggling the barrel a millimeter. Seiler objects to the demonstration, but Oliver overrules him.

—

After the closing arguments, Judge Oliver reads the jury its instructions. He offers three choices: guilty of murder, guilty of voluntary manslaughter, and not guilty. It is 5:30 P.M. when the jury retires to consider its verdict. Williams and his family head back to Mercer House. Seiler goes to his office in Armstrong House; on the way out, he gets good news from his man in the corridor: Georgia has beaten Ole Miss, 36-11.

I ask Minerva if she wants to go have something to eat while we wait. She shakes her head and rummages in her shopping bag. "I got work to do here."

—

Three hours later, the jury sends word that it has reached a decision. Seiler returns to the courtroom, clearly worried. "It's too soon," he says. "The case has too many issues. They can't have reached a well-thought-out verdict yet. Maybe they just wanted to get it over with and go home." Blanche Williams, too, has a sense of foreboding. "We hadn't sat down to dinner when they called us," she says. "I made a caramel cake, that's James's favorite, and I was just getting it ready. Before we left the house, I saw James slip something into his sock. Maybe it was cigarettes. It makes me think James must feel he's not coming back home."

I sit down next to Minerva and notice almost at once that there is a thin trail of white powder on the floor in front of the jury box. There are also twigs and pieces of root in front of the judge's bench. Minerva is chewing slowly. The jury files into the jury box. She glares at them through her purple glasses.

Upon the judge's order, Williams rises. The foreman hands a piece of paper to the clerk, who reads the verdict aloud:

"We find the defendant guilty of murder."

Judge Oliver bangs his gavel. "The sentence is life imprisonment. That's mandatory."

The courtroom is silent. Williams calmly takes a sip of water from a paper cup. Then he walks across the floor and is escorted by the bailiffs through the door that leads to the tunnel that will take him to jail.

I feel Minerva's hand on my arm. She is gazing straight ahead at a group of people milling around Spencer Lawton, and she is smiling.

"What is it?" I ask, wondering what she could be smiling about.

She points a forefinger at the district attorney, whose back is turned to us. He is gathering up papers and accepting the murmured congratulations of his staff, unaware of the footprint-size smudge of chalky white powder on the tail of his suit jacket and the seat of his trousers.

"Did you put that white stuff on the D.A.'s chair, Minerva?" I ask.

"You know I did," she says.

"What is it?"

"High John the Conqueror. A powerful root."

"But what good can it do now?"

"By gettin' where it got, that powder means Delia still be workin' on the D.A.," she says. Delia was one of the names Minerva had called out in the graveyard. "And she got him by the seat a his pants too! She ain' done settlin' with him."

"What do you think will happen?" I ask.

"You mean if Delia don't leave go?"

"Yes. If she hangs in there."

"Why, the D.A.'s gonna have to turn Mr. Jim loose. It's just that simple. If I was the D.A., I wouldn't be thinkin' about no celebration. Not with Delia hangin' on he ass like she be. When she was livin', she was bad. Dead she's worse! And now she 'bout to raise all kinda hell!"

"What happened to the other eight dead women you called in the graveyard?"

"Didn't git no reply from the first three. Delia was the fourth."

"And Dr. Buzzard? Is he involved?"

"He gave Delia the okay."

"Has he given you a number yet?"

Minerva laughs. "Shit, no. He likes me po'. That way I gotta keep workin' and goin' to the flower garden to see him. That way he keep a hold on me." Minerva picks up her shopping bag and gets ready to leave. The bag opens momentarily, and I catch a glimpse of what looks like a chicken foot. Minerva waves good-bye and slips into the crowded corridor.

I make my way out of the courthouse, past Sonny Seiler, who is standing in front of the television lights, talking about an appeal. The courthouse flack sidles up, looking slyly amused as usual. "With good behavior," he says, "Williams will be out in seven years."

"I'm told he might be out even sooner," I reply, "if a certain lady named Delia has anything to say about it."

"Who?" The flack cups his ear.

"Delia."

"Who is Delia?"

"You mean who *was* Delia," I say. "That's all I know about her. She's dead."

Chapter 22

THE POD

The posthumous powers of the late Delia, if she had any, were apparently not the sort that took effect immediately. This became clear the day after Jim Williams's conviction, when his lawyers went before Judge Oliver to ask for his release on bond and were curtly turned down. The judge did relent on one point, however: Williams would not be transferred right away to the much-feared state penitentiary at Reidsville. He could remain in Savannah at the Chatham County Jail so that his lawyers could consult with him while they worked on his appeal—and that could take a year or more. This concession displeased the county commissioners, who voted to sue Williams for room and board while he remained at the county facility—$900 a month. (The suit was dropped when the county attorney advised the commissioners it would not stand up in court.)

In the absence of its master, Mercer House assumed a ghostly air. The interior shutters of its great windows remained closed against the outside world. The gala parties were over. The elegant guests coming up the walk in evening clothes were only a memory now. But the hedges remained neatly clipped, the front lawn was mowed, and in the evenings slits of lamplight shone though the louvered windows. In fact, Blanche Williams had moved into the house from her home in Gordon. She lived alone in the house, biding her time. She polished the silver and dusted the furniture, and every week she baked a fresh caramel cake in expectation of her son's return.

The shop in the carriage house stayed open for business and was tended by Williams's shopkeeper, Barry Thomas. From time to time, Thomas could be seen standing in the street outside the shop taking Polaroid pictures of a plantation desk or a chest of drawers being off-loaded from a truck. Thomas would then deliver the photographs, together with catalogs of upcoming sales and auctions, to the jail a few blocks away so that Williams could see his new purchases and make selections of what to buy or bid on next. It was common knowledge that Williams was running his antiques business from jail.

He was aided in this effort by the lucky chance that there was a telephone in his cell. Ordinarily, an inmate serving a life sentence would not have ready access to a telephone; however, Williams's cell housed not only convicted criminals but men who were still awaiting trial and therefore had a need—and also the right—to talk to lawyers and family. The phone was set up to make outgoing calls only, and all the calls had to be collect. It would have been unthinkable, of course, for Williams to make business calls that began with an operator announcing bluntly, "I have a collect call from Jim Williams at the Chatham County Jail"—but he got around that easily enough. He would make a collect call to Mercer House, and then his mother or Barry Thomas would accept the charges and use three-way calling to put his call through. By routing his calls through Mercer House, Williams stayed in touch with major figures in the world of antiques without ever having to reveal that he was calling from jail. He chatted with Geza von Habsburg at Christie's auction house in Geneva and placed a bid for a pair of imperial-presentation Fabergé cuff links made for a Russian grand duke. He spoke with the editor of *Antiques* magazine about an article he had promised to write on the eighteenth-century portrait artist Henrietta Johnston. Williams followed up each call with a short note, dictated over the phone to Mercer House and typed on his engraved personal stationery—"It was good talking to you today. Hope to see you soon. . . ."

The pretense that he was calling from the dignified confines of Mercer House was a difficult ruse for Williams to carry off, as I discovered the first time I spoke with him. A television set blared in the background, and I could hear raucous shouts and an occasional high-pitched scream. Williams had been placed in a cell for homosexuals and the mentally unstable. He and his cell mates were segregated from the general jailhouse population for their own safety. The cell was known as the "pod." It was twenty feet by twenty feet and held eight inmates. The mix of personalities confined in it created an unpredictable atmosphere.

"It all depends who's here at any given time," Williams explained. "Right now, there's one other white inmate and five *garçons noirs*. Three of the five *noirs* play cards all day, but whenever there's any music on TV they get up and dance and sing at the top of their lungs. That happens a lot, because the TV's on from eight in the morning till two or three at night, with the volume turned up to scorch. I wear earplugs, and over that I clamp earphones so I can listen to tapes. But the noise from the TV cuts right through, and when they get to singing and stomping, I can barely hear my own music. I dread it when *Soul Train* comes on.

"The other two *noirs* are a pair of long-lost lovers who were reunited in here last week. There was much wailing and carrying on when they recognized each other—accusations of betrayal, declarations of love and forgiveness, weeping, laughing, screeching. It went on for hours. As we speak, they're braiding each other's hair into corn rows. Pretty soon they'll be into face-slapping, and then they'll probably have sex. The white inmate is a little weak in the head. They put him in here this morning, and he's been rubbing the walls and preaching out loud ever since. We can't make him stop. It's a zoo.

"Things usually quiet down at feeding time, though. The menu usually consists of stale peanut-butter-and-jelly sandwiches or a small slice of rancid meat. It's completely inedible, of course, but my cell mates don't know it, and it calms them down for a while. That's when I make my phone calls. At other times, if I need to, I can usually bribe them into shutting up with cigarettes and candy bars I buy from the commissary cart."

Williams discouraged his friends from coming to see him at the jail. "The visitors' room is a long, narrow hall with a row of stools facing plate-glass windows," he said. "Whole families come to see their criminal loved ones. Babies are crying, everybody is shouting to be heard, and nobody can hear anything. It's bedlam." Williams clearly preferred not to be seen in such humbling circumstances. The telephone suited his purposes far better. He generally made his social calls in the evenings. There were no ice cubes clinking in his glass, but he was allowed to smoke his cigarillos, and I could hear him puffing on them as he spoke.

"We've had a little excitement in here," he told me one night in mid-November. "We have a new cell mate who crawls around on his hands and knees and barks like a dog all day long. Once in a while he lifts his leg and pees on the wall. We've complained, but nobody does anything about it. Yesterday afternoon while the man was asleep, I bribed the others into turning down the TV and being quiet so I could make a few quick business calls. I was in the middle of a conversation with an important art dealer in London about a painting I was offering for sale when the new inmate woke up and started barking. I kept right on talking. 'Oh, that's my Russian wolfhound,' I said. But then the barking moved up an octave and turned into yapping. 'What's that one?' the dealer asked. 'A Shar-pei?' 'No, no,' I said, 'that's a Yorkie,' and then I cupped my hand half over the phone and shouted, '*Won't someone please put the dogs out in the gar-*

den?' At that point I nodded at my other cell mates, and they tackled the madman and clapped their hands over his mouth. The dealer and I went on politely discussing the niceties of the English landscape tradition while my cell mates scuffled at my feet. There were grunts and muffled strangulation noises. I don't know what the dealer thought, but in the end he bought the painting."

Although Williams spoke with his customary self-assurance, he made no attempt in our conversations to conceal the grimness of his existence. He had no visual contact with the outside world. The cell's six narrow windows were fitted with a muddy brown translucent glass, and the lights inside the cell stayed on twenty-four hours a day. Williams said he could not eat the food and lived mostly on peanuts and candy bought from the commissary. A hard bump had appeared on his forehead, and there was a ringing in his ears and a rash on his arms and back. When the rash worsened, he went to the doctor and found five other inmates in the waiting room with the same rash. "Neither the blankets nor the mattresses are cleaned between inmates," he said, "and I have no confidence in the doctor here." Several crowns had fallen off Williams's molars, and there was no dentist at the jail. A trip to his own dentist could have been arranged, but he would have been forced to go in chains, shackled at the waist, so he dropped the matter.

Williams continued to maintain his innocence. He was convinced that the jury in the second trial had simply rubber-stamped the first conviction. They had all been familiar with the case beforehand because of its great notoriety, and they were under the impression that the first conviction had been reversed on a technicality. Williams was contemptuous of the jury, the witnesses, the district attorney, Judge Oliver, and the local newspaper. But he saved his sharpest scorn for his own lawyers.

"I loathe them," he said. "They have meetings and conferences, supposedly to discuss my appeal, but they accomplish nothing and then send me bills for the time they've wasted. They are five- and ten-thousand dollaring me to death. The last thing they want to do is settle my case. It would cut off their supply of money. They've cost me four hundred thousand dollars so far, and I've had to sell truckloads of valuable antiques out of my house to pay them. Alistair Stair came down from Stair and Company in New York and bought a lacquered Queen Anne desk and a rare Charles II cabinet made in Charleston. He also bought the grandfather clock in the hall that Danny Hansford knocked over. I mean *fine* things. The most beautiful silver coffee urn I had ever seen. A pair of marble Fu lions that came out of the Imperial Palace in Peking during the Boxer Rebellion. They were my treasures. I sold the Early American four-poster bed out of my bedroom, the finest bed of its type I'd ever seen. I sold an Irish linen press that's featured in a book on Irish furniture by Desmond Guinness. Carpets. Portraits. I sold a pair of Irish Chippendale chairs—one of them was the chair that I supposedly placed on Danny's trouser leg. Every penny from the sales goes into the bank and then straight out again to lawyers, investigators, and expert witnesses. I have no choice. I have to do it. Money is ammunition, and as long as I have some I'll use it. Spencer Lawton has an unlimited budget, full-time investigators, free use of state laboratories. But I'm forced to pay for every move my lawyers make to counter them.

"People think I'm rolling in money. They think I've lived a luxurious life with lots of servants and breakfast in bed. But that's all an illusion. I have a maid three times a week, but no cook. I make my own breakfast. I eat a sandwich for lunch and go out for supper, usually to the Days Inn coffee shop. But most people don't want to believe that. In Savannah, all you have to do is pay your bills and people will say you're rich."

And how were the lawyers progressing with his appeal?

"Mmmmm," he said. "Whenever I call to talk to Sonny Seiler, he's either in Athens at a football game, or on vacation, or just nowhere. I finally got him on the phone the other day, and I said, 'Hey, Sonny. How's it going?' Sonny said, 'Not well, Jim. Not well at all.' He sounded very down, so of course I assumed the worst. I said, 'Why? What happened?' And Sonny said, 'Jesus, Jim, don't you read the newspapers? The Dogs lost last Saturday!'

"I told him, 'Sonny, let's get one thing straight. The only game I'm interested in is the one I'm playing.' "

—

In fact, no progress could be made with Williams's appeal until the trial transcript had been typed by the court stenographer. The trial had been long and involved, and the transcript would run fifteen hundred pages. It would take months to complete. Meanwhile, Williams remained optimistic. "I *will* get out of here," he said. "The Georgia Supreme Court will reverse my conviction, and when I get out I will see that Spencer Lawton is charged with prosecutorial misconduct, suborning perjury, and denying me my civil rights."

"How do you propose to do all that?" I asked.

"The same way I restore houses," said Williams. "Step by step. Inch by inch. I learned an invaluable lesson from my old mentor, Dr. L. C. Lindsley. Did I ever tell you about him? Dr. Lindsley was a college professor who restored and lived in one of Georgia's great houses, Westover. It was built in Milledgeville in 1822 in the grand style. It had spiral stairs and a pair of white double-height columns on each side of the front entrance.

"Dr. Lindsley told me that an old house will defeat you if you try to restore it all at once—from roof to windows, weatherboarding, jacking it up, central heating, wiring. You must think of doing one thing at a time. First you say to yourself: Today I am going to think about leveling off the sills. And you get all the sills leveled. Then you turn your mind to the weatherboarding, and gradually you do all the weatherboarding. Then you consider the windows. Just one window at a time. That window right there. You ask yourself, 'What's wrong with that *part* of that window?' You must do it in sections, because that's the way it was built. And then suddenly you find the whole thing completed. Otherwise, it will defeat you.

"That's how I will get out of here. Step by step. First I will work on Sonny Seiler. Get him moving on the appeal. Then I'll concentrate on the seven justices of the state supreme court. Send them mental messages, just as I did after my first trial. Get them to see things my way."

I heard Williams draw on his cigarillo. I pictured him tilting his head back and sending a stream of smoke ceilingward.

"One way or another," he said, "I will get out. You can rely on that. And I'm not talking about suicide, although I've contemplated that option. My conviction will be reversed. You'll see. It may seem impossible to you, but let me point out something else—something else I learned from Dr. Lindsley. One day he said, 'You know, robins move houses. Little birds with orange tummies can move a house. In fact, they tried to move Westover.' I said, 'All right, I give up. How do they do it?' And he said, 'They eat chinaberries, and then they drop the chinaberry seeds near the foundation of a house. A chinaberry tree grows there and uproots the house.' And he was right. I've seen it happen. Chinaberry trees grow very rapidly, and they will tear up the foundations of a house. That's how I intend to undo all the work Spencer Lawton has done to put me here. I will shake him to his foundations. It just might take a little time."

Chapter 23

LUNCH

Rather than arrive early for Blanche Williams's luncheon party, Millicent Mooreland drove around Monterey Square several times. Then she moved on, two blocks north, and drove around Madison Square. She went back and forth, circling one square and then the other, taking her time, driving very slowly.

Mrs. Mooreland hardly knew Blanche Williams. She had met her briefly at Jim Williams's Christmas parties, and in the eight months since Williams went to jail she had made a point of calling Mrs. Williams every few weeks to see how she was getting on. After all, Mrs. Williams was nearly eighty and had moved into Mercer House all alone without any family or friends nearby.

Mrs. Williams appreciated the gesture and told her son she wished she could thank Mrs. Mooreland and many of his other friends for being so thoughtful. "Why not have them all to lunch?" he had suggested. The idea terrified Mrs. Williams, but her son reassured her. "You won't have to do anything at all," he said. "I'll take care of everything."

From his jail cell, Jim Williams organized every detail of his mother's luncheon party. He drew up the guest list. He ordered stationery for the invitations and wrote out a sample for his mother to copy. He telephoned Lucille Wright, the cateress, and asked her to prepare a buffet of low-country food. He selected the menu—shrimp, smoked ham, roast lamb, okra, squash, sweet potatoes, rice, cornbread, cookies, and cakes—and told Mrs. Wright to plan for twenty guests (he later expanded the list to forty-five) and to serve the meal on the Duchess of Richmond's porcelain with Queen Alexandra's silverware, both of which she would find in the breakfront cabinet in the dining room. Williams hired his usual bartender and urged his mother, who did not drink, to allow her guests at least half an hour for cocktails before serving lunch. "That will give them a chance to loosen up," he said. "We don't want them to be too glum and serious." Finally, he told Barry Thomas to fill the house with fresh flowers on the morning of the party and to be sure to go into the garden before the guests arrived and turn the fountain on.

Mrs. Mooreland was doing more than simply whiling away the time as she drove around the squares. She was peering into the parks in a way she had never done before—scrutinizing the people sitting on the benches, particularly the young men. She was surprised at herself for doing it, but she could not resist. Conflicting emotions were battling inside her today. It had all started with the headline in the morning paper: NEW WITNESSES IN WILLIAMS CASE. Two new witnesses had come forward, both of them favorable to Jim Williams. Such good news! And on the very day of Mrs. Williams's luncheon party! It was the first glimmer of hope for Jim Williams in nearly a year. Before she had even read the story, Mrs. Mooreland rushed to the foot of the stairs and called up to her husband to tell him about it. Then she went back to the kitchen and sat down to read.

Both of the new witnesses were young men, one eighteen, the other twenty-seven. They did not know each other. They had come forward independently to say that Danny

Hansford had approached them in the weeks before he died and tried to enlist them in schemes to kill or injure Jim Williams and then steal cash out of his house. Both of the young men said they had met Danny Hansford while hanging out in the Bull Street squares hustling gay men.

A flush of embarrassment came over Mrs. Mooreland as she read, but she kept reading.

One of the young witnesses had been enrolled in a drug-rehabilitation program. The other had a string of convictions and was currently being held at the Chatham County Jail on auto-theft charges. Both men said Hansford had wanted them to lure Williams into a "sex scene" as part of the plot. They had refused. Later, when Hansford himself was killed, one of the young men said he had thought to himself, The dumb ass tried to pull it off. The newspaper quoted Sonny Seiler saying he would use the affidavits of the two young men in his appeal.

Mrs. Mooreland was in turmoil. Happy as she was for her friend Jim Williams, she was nonetheless appalled. She had been unaware of the details of Williams's private life until his trials had so rudely awakened her, and she had finally come to terms with all of that, mainly by putting it out of her mind. But now this sordid business about the squares. And these new witnesses! Who *were* they? Male prostitutes! Burglars! Thieves! Mrs. Mooreland unburdened herself to her husband over breakfast. He attempted to put the new developments in perspective for her. "You wouldn't expect this Danny Hansford, this unsavory little punk, to discuss his murderous schemes with someone on the order of Mac Bell, would you? Or Reuben Clark?" The names Mr. Mooreland mentioned were two of Savannah's most esteemed gentlemen, bank presidents both.

Well, that did make some sense, Mrs. Mooreland had to admit. But she was still dazed by what she had learned about the nefarious goings-on in the squares, and as she drove around them this sunny noontime in May, she did a little timid sleuthing. Maybe that's one of them, she thought, casting her eyes on a shaggy-haired boy lounging casually on a bench in Madison Square. But then it crossed her mind that he could have been one of those art students from the Savannah College of Art and Design. How could anybody tell anymore? Mrs. Mooreland shuddered and checked her watch. It was time to go to the party. But she had still not resolved her biggest dilemma: what to say to Mrs. Williams about the news. She could hardly exclaim, "Isn't it wonderful!" because a plot involving sodomy, murder, and theft could in no way be described as wonderful. There was nothing in those horrid little stories that was even slightly discussable at a polite luncheon party. She told her husband she thought she might just feign ignorance and pretend she had not read the newspaper at all that day. But he pointed out that a tactic like that could backfire. "It might just force Mrs. Williams to tell you all about it herself," he said. "Better to say something noncommittal like 'We're all keeping our fingers crossed.' " And that is what she finally did.

In fact, in one way or another, that was how all of the guests handled the matter. Mrs. Williams stood at the door of Mercer House in a light blue chiffon dress, accepting obliquely worded congratulations as her guests arrived.

"I feel the tide is turning," said Mrs. Garrard Haines, giving Mrs. Williams a kiss on the cheek.

"Isn't *this* a sunny day!" said Lib Richardson.

Alexander Yearly put it another way: "I expect it won't be long before Jim will be among us again."

Mrs. Williams beamed. "It's just like James said. Everything is going to work out just fine."

The double doors at the end of the center hall were open to the courtyard, giving a view all the way through the house to the opulent greenery of the courtyard garden. The rear of Mercer House was distinctly different from the Italianate façade in front. The back of the house had the look of an antebellum mansion. Tall columns supported a wide porch shaded by dense swags of overgrown wisteria. Several of Mrs. Williams's guests came out to sit in the wicker chairs and look at the sunken garden, the grove of ten-foot-high banana plants, and the lily pond while they ate their lunch.

Betty Cole Ashcraft sat beside Lila Mayhew. Mrs. Mayhew poked absently at her tomatoes and okra. "I suppose we'll have another Christmas without Jim's lovely party," she said in a wistful voice.

"Good gracious, Lila," said Mrs. Ashcraft, "it's only May. So much can happen before Christmas, and anyway it does look as though it isn't all over for Jim just yet."

"Jim always had his party the night before the debutante ball," Mrs. Mayhew went on. "That was his night. Friday. I can't remember what on earth we used to do in the days before Jim started having his parties. I've tried, but I can't recall. My memory is failing, you know."

"Well, never mind, Lila," said Mrs. Ashcraft. "Before you know it, Jim will be right back here giving his parties again. They'll just have to let him out now. I feel sure of it, what with all these ruffians popping up at long last and saying how they were getting ready to kill him. It's a wonder Jim didn't shoot them all. He would have been within his rights, you know."

Mrs. Mayhew put down her fork. "Every year, Beautene made a new dress for me to wear to Jim's party. Beautene is my colored seamstress. I think sometimes she just redecorated an old dress so it looked new. I wouldn't have known the difference anyway. But last Christmas when Jim was in jail, I said, 'Beautene, let's don't bother this year. There won't be anything to do in Savannah the night before the Cotillion anyhow.' "

"Now, Lila," Mrs. Ashcraft said gently.

"And do you know what Beautene told me? She said, 'Miss Lila, there may not be anything for you folks to do that night. But that night—the night before Cotillion—that's the night of *our* debutante ball.' "

"Lord in heaven!" said Mrs. Ashcraft. "You don't mean it."

"Yes. The colored girls. They have a debutante ball the night before Cotillion. When Beautene told me that, I thought, How lovely for them. And I knew right then and there that I would miss Jim Williams's Christmas party more than ever."

Mrs. Mayhew took a sip of her iced tea and gazed into the garden.

As the two ladies lapsed into silence, I became aware of a conversation taking place sotto voce between a man and two women seated on the divan across from me. They were speaking like ventriloquists, barely moving their lips so as not to be overheard. When I tuned in to what they were saying, I understood why.

"It won't work?" one of the women asked the man. "Why not?"

"For several reasons, one of which is that those statements sound as if they were bought and paid for by Jim."

"Would Jim do that?"

"Of course he would," said the man, "and so would I in his position. Sonny Seiler's had both of the boys checked out by a private detective—Sam Weatherly, an ex-cop, good man. Sam says one of the boys may be telling the truth. The other one is poison; he has a reputation for selling testimony to the highest bidder."

"Why can't Sonny just use the one who's telling the truth?"

"Because no jury is going to believe a street hustler, and anyway what he has to say is irrelevant. Danny Hansford's motives are not the issue. He may have wanted to kill Jim, but there's no evidence he tried to do it. There's no evidence he even had a gun in his hand that night. No fingerprints. No gunpowder residue. The physical evidence is the issue. Now, if Jim could pay someone to discredit the physical evidence, *that* would be money well spent."

Mrs. Williams came out onto the porch with a Polaroid camera in her hand. "All right now," she said, "everybody get ready to look pretty!" Her guests looked up from their plates, and Mrs. Williams snapped their picture. The camera made a whirring sound and churned out a black rectangle of film. Mrs. Williams went back inside and laid it on the sideboard with the others. "Later on," she said, "I'm gone carry all these pictures over to James. I just know when he sees them he'll feel like he's been at the party too. I really do.

Whenever something important happens, I take a picture to show him. I took him one of the wisteria when it blossomed over the front door, and he called and said, 'Thank you, Mother. Now I can tell it's spring.' "

Faces were beginning to emerge in the photographs on the sideboard. There was Emma Kelly sitting between Joe Odom and Mandy in the rear parlor. Upon arriving at the party, Emma had told Mrs. Williams that every day for the past eight months, she had played "Whispering" on the piano because she knew it was Jim's favorite song. Joe Odom remarked with an ironic smile that the way things seemed to be going lately, he and Jim might be trading places before long.

Two people whose faces were just now coming into full color on the sideboard had caused other guests to stare in disbelief when they arrived at the party: Lee and Emma Adler.

"Now I've seen everything," Katherine Gore had said when the Adlers appeared in the entrance hall.

The antagonism between Lee Adler and Jim Williams had gained a new dimension because of Adler's close association with Spencer Lawton. Lawton had recently announced he was running for reelection, and Adler had cosigned a $10,000 bank loan for his campaign. That check had made Adler responsible for more than two-thirds of all Lawton's campaign money. Adler made no effort to conceal his closeness to Lawton; on the contrary, he put a large RE-ELECT SPENCER LAWTON poster on the fence in front of his house. Lawton's smiling face could be seen from the windows of Mercer House. If anything, Adler seemed to revel in Williams's predicament. He hosted a Lawton fund-raising party at which he stood up and read a telegram from "a Lawton supporter" who had been unable to attend. It turned out to be a joke telegram signed "Jim Williams, Chatham County Jail," and it wished Lawton the very worst of bad luck. Adler's audience was not amused. "It was tacky," said one guest. "It made us all uncomfortable, especially Spencer Lawton, who was present."

Meanwhile, Williams waged war against Lawton's re-election campaign from his jail cell, quietly channeling money to Lawton's opponent. A series of full-page anti-Lawton ads appeared in the Savannah newspaper bearing the headline DISTRICT ATTORNEY LAWTON CHARGED WITH CORRUPTION AND MISCONDUCT. The ad reminded voters that in reversing the first Williams conviction, the Georgia Supreme Court had accused Lawton of "corrupting the truth-seeking function of the trial process." The ads had been written and paid for by Jim Williams.

For their part, the Adlers were as perplexed as everyone else as to why they had been invited to Mrs. Williams's lunch. After signing their names in the guest book, Emma Adler wrote the word "neighbors" in parentheses, as if to make the point that their connection to the party was purely geographical.

Mrs. Williams slipped the snapshot of the Adlers into the middle of the stack. "James has his reasons, I'm sure," she said in her quiet way, "but, oh, that Lee Adler made me so mad one day. I would never tell James this. It's been about three months ago, I guess. One afternoon he came to make a courtesy call, and I thought, Well, the man knows James is in a bind now, and he's come to have a look around. He thinks there won't be a thing on the walls and that all the furniture will be sold. So he came in, and he was very polite and everything. But I could see right through him. I knew it wasn't in him to be nice to James. He told me, 'Mrs. Williams, I saw Mr. So-and-so from Sotheby's in New York and this, that, and the other, and if I could do anything for James, or if there's anything he wants to sell, just let me know.' *Well!* I'm gone tell you, right about that time I was fixin' to blow up, but I didn't say a word. I was just as calm as I could be. And I said, 'I appreciate that very much, Mr. Adler, but even where he is now, James has got connections. He can call New York. He can call London. He can call Geneva.' I wasn't ugly to him or anything. But, honey, inside I was boilin' over, 'cause I knew he came to have a look around."

Lee Adler's attachment to Spencer Lawton was the very reason Jim Williams had told his mother to invite him. In Williams's view, Lee Adler controlled Spencer Lawton. "Leopold is the power behind the throne," he said. "He's like the vizier in the Turkish court, the man who stands behind a silken screen and whispers in the sultan's ear. Lawton doesn't dare make a move without instructions from Leopold. That makes Leopold dangerous, particularly to me. I've given him plenty of reasons to hate me. I engineered throwing him off the board of the Telfair museum when I was president, and I'm quite sure he pushed the D.A. into charging me with first-degree murder instead of involuntary manslaughter, though he denies it. He's dangerous. No question. But I understand him. I can talk his language if I have to. Honor among thieves, you know. It's never too late to hold out an olive branch. With my new witnesses, my case is going to break wide open. I can feel it. And when that happens, I don't want Leopold skulking around behind that silken screen making mischief."

Williams clearly had some irons in the fire—an appeal in progress, possible new witnesses, and a candidate working to unseat Spencer Lawton. None seemed particularly promising, but if Williams was able to take comfort in them, what was the harm? It was unlikely that an invitation to a congenial luncheon party would convert Lee Adler to his cause. Still, Williams had summoned all the influence he could muster in the effort—the guileless charm of his mother, the delectation of Lucille Wright's cooking, the company of friends in common, and not least of all, the mysterious powers of Minerva. Minerva had come in from Beaufort and was dressed for the occasion in a maid's costume. For the first hour or so, she stood quietly in the dining room while the guests served themselves from the buffet. Later on, she circulated with a pitcher of iced tea. At one point she poured two tall glasses for the Adlers, while munching on a root and fixing them with a penetrating stare through the purple lenses of her wire-rimmed glasses.

Williams kept informed of the party's progress through periodic telephone calls during the course of the lunch. He reminded Barry Thomas to turn on the fountain (Thomas had forgotten), and he gave instructions to his mother and Lucille at each stage of the lunch. When the last of the guests had left, Mrs. Williams and Barry Thomas reported to Williams that the lunch had been a success. Mrs. Williams said she would be leaving shortly to bring the snapshots over to the jail so he could see for himself.

After she hung up, she lingered at the desk for a moment. The morning paper lay on the desk in front of her.

"Barry?" she said.

Barry Thomas turned back at the doorway. "Yes, Mrs. Williams?"

Mrs. Williams paused uncertainly. She glanced down at the paper and the story about the new witnesses.

"I . . . I've been wondering," she said. "All these things they've been saying about James . . . and that Hansford boy . . . and now these other boys." Mrs. Williams gestured at the paper. "I try not to pay any mind. But I don't know. Seems like I remember hearing people say the same thing about King James of England. You know, the King James that had them to write the King James Bible? Do you know if that's true? Have you ever heard anybody say that about King James?"

"Well, yes, as a matter of fact, I have," said Thomas. "King James did have favorites among the men at court, if that's what you mean. He had his special friends. I think he had several."

The hint of a smile appeared at the corners of Mrs. Williams's mouth. "Well," she said softly, "all right then."

Chapter 24

BLACK MINUET

In mid-August, despite the statements made by Jim Williams's new witnesses, Judge Oliver denied Williams's motion for a new trial. Sonny Seiler promptly announced he would take the appeal to the next level, the Georgia Supreme Court. A few weeks later, Spencer Lawton won reelection as district attorney, ensuring that he would be in a position to fight the appeal every step of the way.

When the bad news reached Williams, he picked up the telephone and called Christie's in Geneva to place a bid on a Fabergé cigarette case that had once belonged to Edward VII. "It cost me fifteen thousand dollars, which I can ill afford," he said, "but it makes me feel better. I'm the only person in the world who's ever bought Fabergé from a jail cell."

Increasingly, Williams used little tricks to convince himself and others that he was not really in jail. He continued routing his phone calls through Mercer House and dictating letters that were typed at home on his engraved stationery. He sent several such letters to newspapers and magazines. One was published in *Architectural Digest*. It was a note praising the magazine for having run an article by the New York socialite Brooke Astor. "Delightful!" Williams's note read. "Brooke Astor has given us a delicious treat by recounting her early experiences with formal dining. Her recollections will serve as a lasting guide in the art of living well. My best wishes to our hostess.—*James A. Williams, Savannah, Georgia.*"

Williams would not submit to the notion that he was in jail. "It's a matter of survival," he said. "I hypnotize myself so that, in my own mind at least, *I am not here.*"

Wherever Jim Williams's mind had taken him, it was clear by early fall that his body would still be in jail at Christmastime. Once again, there would be a gap in the social calendar on the night before the Cotillion ball, the night formerly reserved for his Christmas party. I recalled Lila Mayhew's lament back in May that she would have nothing to do that night. I also remembered what her black seamstress had told her—that the night of Jim Williams's party was the night the blacks had their debutante ball. The more I thought about it, the more I began to feel the urge, as an observer of the local scene, to know more about the black debutante ball and, if possible, to be invited to it.

—

Savannah's blacks had been presenting debutantes at formal balls for nearly forty years. The ball was sponsored by the graduate chapter of Alpha Phi Alpha, a black fraternity at Savannah State College. Nationally, Alpha Phi Alpha was the oldest black college fraternity in the country, having been founded at Cornell at the turn of the century. The fraternity was intended to be more than just an undergraduate social club, as its slogan "Bigger and Better Negro Business" suggested. In fact, the graduate chapter in Savannah, with sixty-five members, was more active than the undergraduate chapter, which had fifteen.

The graduate Alphas were representative of the upper level of Savannah's black community. Their membership included teachers, school principals, doctors, ministers, owners of small businesses, and lawyers. Notably absent were bankers, partners of the city's most influential law firms, directors of big corporations, and people with inherited wealth. The Alphas, unlike the members of the Cotillion, did not belong to the Oglethorpe Club, the golf club, or the yacht club. One of Savannah's three black city councilmen was an Alpha, but it could not be said that the Alphas—or the black community as a whole—were part of Savannah's power structure. The annual activities of the Alpha graduate chapter included a voter-registration drive, a dance to raise money for scholarships, and a series of social events leading up to the debutante ball.

The debutante ball had been the brainchild of Dr. Henry Collier, a gynecologist and the first black doctor to perform surgery at Candler Hospital. Dr. Collier got the idea for the ball in the 1940s when he heard that a group of black businessmen in Texas had sponsored a cotillion. He suggested to his fellow Alphas that they sponsor a similar ball in Savannah, and the Alphas agreed.

Dr. Collier lived on Mills B. Lane Boulevard, several miles to the west of downtown. He had built his house in the 1950s when no one would sell him property in the exclusive white enclave of Ardsley Park. It was a rambling brick structure that had been added on to over the years without any apparent plan. A modest front door opened on a double-height entrance foyer with a grand circular stairway and a bubbling, two-tiered fountain in the center. A buoyant man in his late sixties, Dr. Collier greeted me warmly and ushered me into the family room off the kitchen, where we had coffee while with great enthusiasm he told me about his brainchild, the debutante ball.

"Our first ball was in 1945," he said. "We presented five girls that year, and we set up a system that we've used ever since. The members of the fraternity nominate the girls, and then we check them out to make sure they meet our criteria. The girls have to be of good moral character. That's most important. They have to have finished high school and be matriculated in a school of higher learning. We interview their neighbors, their high school teachers, and people in their church. For a girl to be disqualified, somebody has to have definite knowledge of misconduct—that she has left home, or that she frequents lounges or nightclubs, or has been in trouble with the police. If a girl has had an abortion, for instance, that would rule her out.

"Once the debutantes have been approved, we require that they attend what we call Charm Week so that they will know how to be gracious and the like. The Alphabettes take charge of that. That's what we call the wives of the Alphas—Alphabettes."

Dr. Collier opened a photo album of memorabilia from past debutante balls. "This was our first ball," he said. "We had it at the Coconut Grove, which was a black dance hall. In those years, of course, public facilities were segregated, so none of the hotels would rent their ballroom to us, and the newspapers acted as if we didn't exist. We got coverage in the black press only. That all changed with integration. In 1965, for the first time ever, we presented our debutantes in the ballroom of the old DeSoto Hotel—the same room where the Cotillion had its ball the very next night. About that time, too, the *Savannah Morning News* finally decided it could call blacks by the courtesy titles—Mr., Mrs., and Miss—and they began to publish the names of our debutantes. I wouldn't say we've reached absolute parity with the Cotillion yet, though. The society pages always report on all the coming-out parties that precede the Cotillion ball—the mother-daughter luncheons, the barbecues, the lawn parties, the oyster roasts, and what have you. But when we submit photographs from our coming-out parties, they don't use them. However . . ." Dr. Collier waved his hand. "In time, that, too, will come."

As Dr. Collier flipped through the pages of the photo album, year after year of debutantes flowed by. Midway through, around 1970, I noticed that a change in complexion had come over the girls. Almost all of the early debutantes had been light-skinned; now there were darker faces too. The change coincided with the emergence of Black

Pride, and it seemed that the Alphas had responded by expanding the range of skin tones deemed acceptable for debutantes.

Dr. Collier continued turning the pages. "You know, some people say our debutante ball is just a copy of the Cotillion ball. Sure it is. But you know, in one way our ball is better than the Cotillion ball. And it tickles me every time. See this picture?" Dr. Collier pointed to a photograph of fifteen debutantes in a procession, their left hands resting daintily on the raised right hand of their escorts. "Know what they're doing here?" he asked. "They're dancing the minuet! They don't do that at the Cotillion." Dr. Collier laughed a delighted, cackling laugh. "That's right. We have 'em dance the *minuet*!"

"How did you happen to choose the minuet?" I asked.

Dr. Collier threw up his hands and laughed. "I don't know! I think I must have seen it in the movies. We do it very properly too. We hire a string quartet to play the minuet from Mozart's *Don Giovanni*. And let me tell you, it's quite a spectacle. I'd like you to come as my guest. Then you'll see."

—

"Ooooo, *child*!" Chablis cooed when I told her I was going to the black debutante ball. "Take me with you as your date, honey!"

I would have been hard-pressed to imagine a more demented faux pas than to appear at the ball with a black drag queen on my arm. I was hoping to be as inconspicuous as possible and had already decided to go alone. "Sorry, Chablis," I said. "I'm afraid not."

Chablis saw nothing at all outlandish in the idea of accompanying me to the ball. "I promise I won't embarrass you, baby," she pleaded. "I won't cuss or dance dirty or shake my butt. I won't do any of that shit. I promise. I will be The *Laaaayyy*-dy Chablis all night long. Just for you. Oh, I've never been to a real ball. Take me, take me, take me."

"It's out of the question," I said.

Chablis pouted. "I know what you're thinkin'. You're thinkin' I'm not good enough to clientele with them fancy-ass black folks."

"I hadn't even thought about that part," I said, "but now that you mention it, the debutantes are all rather proper young ladies from what I've been told."

"Oh?" Chablis looked at me archly. "And what does that mean, if you don't mind me askin'?"

"Well, for one thing," I said, "none of them has ever been caught shoplifting."

"Then they must be real good at it, honey. Or else they don't know what shoppin's all about. I am serious. I can't believe you're tryin' to tell me that out of twenty-five bitches not one of 'em has ever stolen a bra or a pair of panty hose, 'cause I will not fall for that shit. All right, now tell me what else is so proper about them?"

"They're all enrolled in college," I said.

"Uh-huh." Chablis studied her fingernails.

"They do volunteer work for the community."

"Uh-huh."

"They go to church regularly and are known to be women of good character."

"Mm-hmmm."

"None of them has ever been seen hanging out in bars or lounges."

"Child, you are beginnin' to work my nerves! Next you're gonna be tellin' me they've all had their pussies checked out, and they're virgins."

"All I know, Chablis, is that they have spotless reputations. That much has been checked out. And not one of them has ever been known to be guilty of 'misconduct.' "

Chablis shot me a sideways look. "Are you sure these girls are black?"

"Of course."

"Then all I can say is they must be *reeeeeal* ugly."

"No, Chablis, they're pretty good-looking actually."

"Well, maybe, but anytime I wanna see a bunch of stuck-up nuns parade around in white dresses, I can take my ass to church. I don't need to go to no ball to see that. So, you can forget about askin' me to be your date, honey, 'cause I ain't goin'."

"Well," I said, "I guess that settles that."

—

The twenty-five debutantes had been culled from an original group of fifty nominees. Some of the nominees had declined the offer for lack of interest or because they could not afford the $800 that being a debutante would cost, including the entrance fee, the price of a gown, the expense of hosting a social event, and incidentals. The prospective debutantes were invited to a meeting at the Quality Inn, where they were welcomed by members of the Alphabette Debutante Committee and told what lay in store for them in the months preceding the ball.

They would be expected to perform ten hours of community service or write a three-page paper on an approved topic. They would be required to appear at four minuet classes. And they would be obliged to host a coming-out party with several other debutantes to which all the debutantes, parents, escorts, and members of the Alpha Debutante Committee and their wives would be invited. Charm Week was the centerpiece of the debutantes' indoctrination. The Alphas' wives, the Alphabettes, taught classes in beauty and the social graces—how to plan a party, send out invitations, set a table, introduce people properly, and write thank-you notes. There was a session on table manners ("Butter only the piece of bread you are about to put in your mouth. . . . If food drops to the floor, let it stay there; call for the waiter. . . . If you happen to put a piece of gristle in your mouth, take it out with whatever put it in—a fork, a spoon, not your fingers"). The debutantes were taught ways to improve their speech ("Never say 'aks,' say 'ask.' *Aks* should be *axed* from your vocabulary . . . and get rid of words like 'um' and 'well.' ") They were taught how to curtsy ("Don't pop up—come up slowly"), how to sit gracefully ("Keep your legs straight together or crossed at the ankles, never crossed at the knees"), and how to walk like a lady ("Back straight, shoulders up, arms to your sides, and *no bopping!*").

There was a set of criteria for the debutantes' escorts too. It boiled down to two requirements: They had to be high school graduates currently in college or the military, and they could not have been convicted of a felony. Lining up escorts was not an easy matter. Boys tended to regard being an escort as more a chore than an honor. They balked at attending the dance classes, renting a tailcoat, and going to so many parties where the chaperons tended to outnumber the young people. It was not unusual, therefore, for a debutante's boyfriend to beg off and for the debutante to be escorted by someone who had been pressed into service—an older brother, the son of a graduate Alpha, or one of the current undergraduate Alphas.

—

At noon on the day of the ball, the twenty-five debutantes arrived at the Hyatt Regency for a dress rehearsal, carrying their gowns in garment bags. They went upstairs to a suite of rooms reserved as dressing rooms, and after changing, they came down to the ballroom, where their fathers and their escorts were waiting to rehearse the waltz and the minuet.

The Alpha ball was to be a more modest affair than the Cotillion ball the next night: There would be two cash bars instead of five open bars; there would be a breakfast served at 1:00 A.M. instead of both a dinner and a breakfast, and there would be minimal decorations. Nonetheless, the impending affair was not going unnoticed in the hotel. During the dress rehearsal, a cluster of curious onlookers peered through the door, captivated by the sight of so many young black girls in flowing white ballgowns. One of the observers, a man in a gray suit and tan shoes, called attention to the cases of wine and liquor being unpacked at the far end of the ballroom. "Don't kid yourself," he said with a knowing air. "Blacks drink better whiskey than whites do. Dewar's,

Johnnie Walker, Seagram's, Hennessy. All the high-priced brands. I have a theory about why that is." The man cupped the elbow of his pipe-holding arm and rocked back on his heels, glancing to his right and left to satisfy himself that the people standing in his immediate vicinity were paying sufficient attention. He then delivered himself of a peculiarly homespun theory: "Remember when the black athletes at the Mexico City Olympics won a lot of medals and raised their fists in the black-power salute? Well, that's when blacks in Savannah started drinking Dewar's scotch, Seagram's gin, and Smirnoff vodka. If you look at those bottles, you'll notice that all the labels have medals on them. Blacks had suddenly begun to identify with medals because of the Olympics, and that's why they bought those brands. At about the same time, they also started drinking Hennessy cognac. The Hennessy label has a picture of a hand holding a mace—something like the black-power salute. Johnnie Walker scotch has a man with riding breeches and a top hat, which represents the 'good life.' It all has to do with the symbol on the label. The best example of that was when school integration was taking place. That's when blacks started drinking Teacher's scotch, which has a label showing a professor wearing a mortarboard. They go for the symbol, y'see. At least that's the way I figure it."

Toward nine o'clock, the Hyatt's vast atrium lobby began to fill with guests arriving for the ball. A long, steep escalator carried a stately stream of formally dressed black couples high above the potted plants and trees to the ballroom on the second floor. Inside the ballroom, a string quartet played chamber music as four hundred guests mingled briefly before quietly taking their places at tables around the dance floor. One table of guests, knowing that no dinner would be served, brought a carton of take-out snacks, which they started eating as soon as the lights dimmed.

The president of the graduate chapter of Alpha Phi Alpha stepped to the podium dressed in the fraternity's colors—a black-and-gold tuxedo, a gold dress shirt, and a gold bow tie. He welcomed the gathering and bade the ceremonies begin. With the string quartet playing background music, an Alphabette took the microphone and read the name of the first debutante. The debutante, escorted by her father, walked to a small platform, mounted the steps, turned toward the audience, and curtsied. The announcer called out the names of her parents, her high school, her college, and the subject in which she was majoring. Then her escort approached from the other side, took her hand, and led her down from the platform as the announcer read his name and those of his parents, his school, and his major. One by one, the debutantes and their escorts were introduced in this manner. The girls each held a bouquet of yellow flowers dotted with twinkling pin lights powered by batteries in the handle of the bouquet. The escorts were dressed in black tie, wing collar, tailcoats, and white gloves. They held their left hands behind them at the small of their backs, palm outward.

At the end of the presentations, the debs and escorts stood facing each other in two long rows that filled most of the dance floor. The hall was silent for a moment; then the string quartet struck up again. The escorts bowed in unison, and the debutantes curtsied, their gowns sweeping the floor in a foamy surf of white ruffles and lace. The couples then joined hands and moved forward in a graceful promenade, dancing a lilting minuet to the strains of *Don Giovanni*. The room seemed to rise and fall with each gliding step; it was almost as if they were skating. A current of exhilaration coursed throughout the room. Women held their breath, men stared in wonder. At the table of honor, Dr. Collier smiled from ear to ear, his joy shared by all.

When the minuet was done, the debutantes danced two waltzes, first with their fathers, then with their escorts. After that, the string quartet packed up and left, and the Bobby Lewis band began setting up for ballroom dancing.

Dr. Collier had put me at a table with several Alphas and Alphabettes. In the afterglow of the minuet, the Alphas were beaming with pride. One of the women mentioned that the local chapter of the Links, the most prestigious black women's civic and social organization in the United States, had expressed a desire to preside over the Savannah debutante proceedings, as they did in Atlanta and other cities. But the Alphas would not give it up.

"The AKAs want to sponsor it, too," another woman said, referring to the Alpha Kappa Alpha sorority. Although the woman was an Alphabette, she was also an AKA, and it was clear she had mixed feelings on the issue. "This has been a long-running battle," she said. "We women feel the matter of debutantes should be our prerogative. It should not be left to a male fraternity."

The three Alphas at the table laughed contentedly. "If we gave it up," one of them said, "we'd lose our status. We can't do that."

The women exchanged silent looks. One of them pointedly changed the subject. "My, isn't *that* a lovely gown," she said, gazing across the room.

I turned and looked in the direction she was facing. An elegant black woman was standing at the entrance to the hall, peering uncertainly into the room as if looking for someone. She wore a slim-fitting dark blue evening gown with a solid mass of rhinestones glittering across the top. I turned back to my table, but something about the figure in the doorway—something about the rhinestones and the way the woman held her head haughtily in the air—made me take a second look. Sure enough, it was Chablis.

At the moment I saw her, she saw me. She took a deep breath, raised her chin a little higher, and started walking toward me at an exaggeratedly regal pace. Her eyes were locked on to mine, and her lips were pursed in a fashion-model-style pout. She was playing The Lady Chablis, The Grand Empress of Savannah. The crowd parted for her as she approached, all eyes on her. I felt a sudden throbbing in my head and a ringing in my ears. She was not more than five steps away from me when she reached out a slender gloved arm. I saw it as the Grim Reaper's scythe, swinging toward me. At the last moment, she turned to the right and clasped the forearm of a muscular teenager standing next to my chair.

"Young man," she said, "can you help me?" She looked

plaintively into his eyes. "I am a damsel in distress. I surely am."

The young man broke into a handsome smile. "I can try, ma'am," he said. "What's the problem?"

Chablis turned her shoulders slightly so she could see me as she spoke. "I am here alone," she said. "I do not have the slightest idea who invited me. I am serious. My social secretary took down the information and wrote it on a piece of paper, but I left the paper in the limousine and sent my driver away. He won't be back till midnight."

Chablis entwined both of her hands around the young man's biceps. "And you know how it is with us ladies," she purred. "We must never be alone. That is not acceptable in polite society. We must always have a *may*yin by our side."

"I know what you mean, ma'am," he said.

"So I was hopin' you would stay by me till I can find my host," she said. "And you can quit callin' me 'ma'am.' My name is Chablis. What's yours?"

"Philip. I'm an escort."

"Ooooo, child! An escort! You mean you work for one of those dating services?"

"No, no," he said. "See, all the debutantes here have escorts. I'm here with a debutante."

"Oh, I see. Which one is yours?"

"She's standing in that group over there. It's my sister."

Chablis drew back in surprise. "Child, you have got to be kiddin'! You mean to tell me you're doin' it with your *sister*?"

"No, no, no," Philip said. "You got it all wrong. See, Gregory—that's my sister's boyfriend—he flat refused to come to this thing. He said, 'No way. I'm not going.' So I got roped into coming instead. That's how it works sometimes."

"Oh, now I understand," said Chablis, "you're just fillin' in, huh? You ain't got a real date tonight, do you?" She leaned closer to him, her hands gently stroking his arm.

"Well, that's sorta true," he said.

"Tell me something, child. Are you carryin' a gun?"

"A gun? Naw, I don't mess with that stuff."

"That's good. I didn't think you did, honey. But you see, one time I was out with a very high-class gentleman, and he put a gun to my head. So I always like to ask."

"I don't think you'll run up against any guns in this ballroom," said Philip. "Everybody here is pretty law-abiding."

"You've never even been arrested? Not even once?"

"Well . . ." Philip smiled shyly. "One time, sorta."

"Ooooo! Tell me, tell me, tell me! What was it for? Drugs? Reefer? 'Cause I am simply dyin' for a drag on a—"

"Naw, it wasn't much. Me and a couple of guys had a few too many drinks one night and we kinda, you know, disturbed the peace a little."

"Ooooo, I bet you did! I bet you could disturb that peace real *bayy*id if you wanted to. I can see it now. *Yay*yiss." Chablis shuddered with pleasure. She was now massaging Philip's arm. "Oh, look," she said, "here comes Mother Superior headed this way!"

"That's my sister," said Philip.

Chablis loosened her grip on the young man's arm as a tall debutante in a lace gown approached. "Chablis, this is my sister LaVella," he said. "LaVella, this is Chablis." LaVella wore her hair in bangs and a pageboy cut.

Chablis offered her hand. "We was just talkin' about you," she said. "I understand y'all goin' to college."

"Yes, I'm a freshman at Savannah State," LaVella said with a perky smile. "I'm majoring in electrical engineering."

"Really, child! Electrical engineering! See now, that's something I wish I knew how to do. Last week my TV broke down right in the middle of *The Young and the Restless,* and all I could think to do was kick it. That didn't help none at all. 'Course I never got to go to college. I had private tutors from kindergarten right on up. It doesn't matter now, though. I'm in show business, and I go on tour most of the time."

"Oh!" said LaVella. "That sounds so glamorous! You get to travel to so many places."

"Travel does have its points," said Chablis. "See this little handbag?" Chablis held up a beaded clutch purse that twinkled in the light. "I got it in London."

"Oh! It's so beautiful!" said LaVella.

"And my shoes are from Rome. And, let's see . . . the gloves are from Paris, and the gown is from New York."

"Gosh!" said LaVella. "We've all been admiring your gown. It's exquisite."

"Well, honey, you, too, can have clothes like this if you play your cards right."

"I guess I better start saving up right now!" said LaVella.

"Oh, no! Uh-uh!" Chablis waved a finger. "That is not the way to do it. Never spend any of your own hard-earned money on clothes and accessories. You need to get yourself a *may*yin to buy all of that for you." Chablis put her hands on Philip's arm again. "You need to have a talk with that boyfriend of yours—what's his name, Gregory, the one that refused to come with you tonight. And you need to tell Gregory to get ready to shake loose some of his coins and buy you gowns and finery."

"I can try," LaVella said with a rueful smile, "but I don't think it will work."

"Then, I guess you'll just have to get all this shit the way I did," said Chablis. "Shoplifting."

Before LaVella could respond, Chablis took Philip by the arm and led him toward the dance floor. " 'Scuse us, Miss Thing," she said, "me and Philip is about to disturb the peace a little."

My first thought was to flee immediately before Chablis had a chance to make it known that I was more-or-less responsible for her presence. She had a devilish smirk on her face. She was in her glory. She pressed against Philip's body as they spun around the floor. They moved as one, not so much dancing as writhing to the beat. The rhinestones on Chablis's dress sparkled in the light and set her face aglow. I recognized it as the dress I had zipped her into backstage at the Pickup, the one with the slit up the back. Every so often the slit parted, revealing a whole haunch of calf, thigh, and buttock.

So far, Chablis's antics had gone unnoticed, but I doubted they would remain unnoticed for long, considering the deep backward dips she was now executing, not to mention the full-throttle bumps and grinds. I got up from my chair and headed for the door, but my path was obstructed by an exuberant Dr. Collier.

"There you are!" he said. "I've been looking for you! What did you think of the minuet?"

"It was stunning," I said, "and I want to thank you so much for inviting me. It was very kind of you. I've had a lovely time . . ."

Dr. Collier had me firmly by the arm. He was looking around the room. "I want to introduce you to the man that taught 'em how to do it. He's the athletic director at Savannah State. John Myles. He taught 'em the waltz too. I don't see him just now, but that's okay . . . we'll catch him a little later."

I now had a choice of slipping away and insulting my host or staying and becoming entangled in Chablis's inevitable denouement. I withdrew to the bar nearest the door to figure out what to do next. From that vantage point I had a view of the dance floor and a clear shot at the exit. I ordered a double scotch.

"And *I'll* have an apple schnapps!" said Chablis, suddenly materializing beside me. She was breathing heavily and dabbing her face with a napkin.

"What happened to your friend Philip?" I asked.

"His sister cut in on us," she said with a look of extreme distaste. "But that's all right, honey. I'll get even with her. And anyway, I don't mind. The Doll has her eye on a couple of the other escorts now. Soon as she gets a little liquid fire in her belly, she'll be gettin' into the cuttin'-in business herself. Big time." The bartender set a shot glass of apple schnapps in front of Chablis. She drank it in a single gulp and coughed. Her eyes blazed. She looked out over the dance floor, and her mouth twisted in a leer. "Eeenie, meenie, mynie, mo . . . catch an escort by the toe. Isn't that how the little ditty goes, honey? Did I get it right? Did I? Hey, Mr. Chauffeur, are you listenin' to me?"

"Forgive me, Chablis," I said, "but I think you have a hell of a nerve busting in here like this."

"*Ooooo,* I have made you angry, baby. You are some kinda cute when you get *may*yid, child. But you see, baby, The Doll felt like bein' a little uppity tonight. And this ballroom happens to be the uppitiest place in Savannah at the moment. That is why she is here."

"Well, let's not argue," I said. "I have no intention of insulting these people, and if you're planning to pull any more pranks, I'd appreciate it if you'd stay well away from me. Better yet, why don't you just leave now? Before things get out of hand. You've had your fun. Why ruin it?"

"Oh, but the fun's just startin', honey."

"Well, it's all over for me," I said. "I'm leaving."

"Oh no, you ain't, child. 'Cause if you do, I will read your beads right here in public, I promise you. I will scream and carry on. I will go up to that old man in the blue ruffled shirt you was just talkin' to, and I will tell him that you brought me here, and that I am carryin' your baby, and that you have just walked out on me."

Every hair follicle on my head began to tingle. I was too respectful of Chablis's sense of drama to dismiss her threat out of hand. She smiled and moved closer to me. "This is what you get for not bringin' me as your date," she said. "But if you are a good boy, I promise I won't say nothin'."

"Just behave yourself, Chablis," I said.

"I'll try, honey," she said. "But it ain't gonna be easy. Whenever I'm around high yellas, I get jumpy. Know what I mean? And this place is loaded with 'em. Just look around." Chablis leaned on an elbow and scanned the crowd, panning slowly from one end of the hall to the other. "What you are lookin' at is 'black society,' " she said. "And now you know the big secret about black society: The whiter you are, the higher you get to rise in it."

"But the debutantes don't all have light skin," I said. "They represent a pretty broad mix if you ask me."

"They can make debutantes in any color they want," said Chablis, "but it won't make any difference. The girls with the light skin are the ones the successful black men are gonna marry. It gives them status. Black may be beautiful, honey, but white is still right when it comes to gettin' ahead in this world, in case you didn't know. I ain't got nothin' against high yellas. Their color ain't their fault, but they do tend to clan together. You oughta see 'em at Saint Matthew's Episcopal Church on West Broad Street. That's the black status church here in Savannah. People say they got a comb over the front door, and they won't let you in unless you can run the comb through your hair without breakin' it. Inside the church the real light-skinned people sit in the pews up front, and the darker ones sit in back. That's right, honey. Just like it used to be on the buses. Y'see, when it comes to prejudice, black folks are right up there with white folks. Believe me. It's no big deal, but when I see black folks start actin' white, honey, it brings out the nigger bitch in me." A sly smile crept across Chablis's face. She peered seductively over her shoulder at me.

"Behave yourself," I said.

Chablis ordered another apple schnapps and drank it down. "We gotta stop talkin' now, child. It's time for The Doll to go play with the boys."

Chablis walked demurely onto the dance floor and tapped the shoulder of the first debutante who passed. She and the debutante exchanged polite smiles and traded places. In a moment, Chablis was nestled against the chest of her new dancing partner. I watched from the bar, my anxiety tempered somewhat by my double scotch. Five minutes later, Chablis disentangled herself from her new partner and cut in on another couple. She did this several times in the next half hour, working the room and rubbing up against all the best-looking young men. She took care, as she made her rounds, not to neglect the feelings of the debutantes. "*Love* the gown!" she would say as she cut in. Chablis's mouth was moving as fast as her body. She whispered to her partners, she gossiped with the girls.

At one o'clock, the dancing came to an end, and a breakfast buffet was laid out. Chablis filled her plate with eggs and sausages and then, as people began to sit down at their appointed tables, she floated around the room looking for a place to alight. Before long I noticed she was floating in our direction. She scooped up an empty chair from the next table and dragged it over to ours, squeezing it in between the two matrons who were sitting opposite me. They obligingly made room for her.

"Oh, pardon me," said Chablis. "Is it all right if I join you?"

"Why, certainly," said one of the women. "I must tell you I have not been able to take my eyes off your beautiful gown all night. It makes you look like a movie star."

"Thanks," said Chablis, settling into her seat. "As a matter of fact, I wear it on stage a lot."

"Oh, are you in the theater?" the woman asked.

"Yes, I'm an actress," said Chablis.

"How fascinating. What sort of acting do you do?"

"Shakespeare. Broadway. Lip sync. I'm based in Atlanta, but I came to Savannah tonight so I could see my cousin become a debutante."

"Oh, how nice," said the woman. "Which one is she?"

"LaVella."

"Oh, LaVella's a lovely girl! Don't you think so, Charlotte?"

"Oh, my yes," said the other woman, nodding and smiling broadly.

"I think so too," said Chablis, a saccharine sweetness creeping into her voice, "and she's always wanted to be a debutante. Ever since I can remember." Chablis ate her food with exaggerated gentility, both pinkies raised.

"Isn't that sweet," said the woman. "LaVella's so delicate and pretty. And so intelligent."

"She's wanted it so bad. We used to talk about bein' debutantes when we was kids," said Chablis. "I'm so glad she got to be one. She was afraid she wouldn't make it, though."

"Well," said the woman, "I can tell you LaVella had nothing to worry about. She's a first-class young lady."

"She was worried anyhow. She'd say to me, 'Oh, Cousin Chablis, I'll never make it. I know I'll never make it.' And I would say, 'Now listen, girl. You got nothin' to worry about. If Vanessa Williams can get to be Miss America in spite of all the checkin' up they do at the Miss America pageant, you ought to be able to slide right by that two-bit debutante-screening committee in little ol' Savannah."

The two matrons glanced across Chablis at each other.

" 'Besides, LaVella, honey,' I said. 'You are always so careful to save your whorin' around for when you come to Atlanta. No one in Savannah has a clue.' "

The two women stared wordlessly at Chablis, who continued to eat her breakfast daintily while she talked.

"I wanted to be a debutante too," she went on. "Oh, yes, I really *deeyid*. But like I said to LaVella, if I am gonna be a debutante, let me be a *real* debutante. Let me be a Cotillion debutante. I am serious.' "

One of the women coughed; the other looked away from the table in desperation, as if searching the horizon for a rescue ship.

" 'Oh, sure, LaVella,' I said, 'The Alpha ball is very beautiful and glamorous. Don't get me wrong. But, LaVella,' I said, 'what are you gonna do this summer when you get off from school? Huh? You're gonna work at the Burger King on West Broad Street. Right? Well, honey, Cotillion debutantes do not work at the Burger King. No way, child. They take bicycle trips through France and England. I am serious. They go to Washington and work for a United States senator who happens to be a friend of the family. They sail on a yacht. They fly to a spa and lay on their asses all summer. That's what they do. And that's what *I* want to do as a debutante.' "

Chablis pretended not to notice the discomfort she was causing the women. She glanced at me briefly and pursed her lips. Then she went right on talking.

"So I said, 'Go ahead and laugh, girl. But you know I really *could* be a Cotillion debutante if I wanted to be. 'Cause I'm so good at passin'. I can be whatever I choose to be, and if I choose to be a rich white girl, honey, that's what I will be. God knows I'm halfway there already. I have plenty of blond hunks to play with, honey, and I'm workin' on havin' me a white baby.' "

The women gave me pained glances, embarrassed that I—the only white person in the ballroom—should be forced to hear such talk. The temperature in the room seemed to rise by sixty degrees. I was sure my face was bright red. Suddenly Chablis put down her knife and fork.

"Oh, my goodness!" she said. "What time is it?" She grabbed the hand of the woman next to her and looked at her watch. "Half past one! My driver's been waitin' for me since midnight." She glanced around the room, then pushed her chair away from the table and stood up. "Well, it's been nice meetin' you," she said. "I gotta say good-bye to some people before I go. If you ladies happen to see my chauffeur, would you tell him I'm still here and not to leave without me? Tell him we'll be takin' my cousin with us—my *other* cousin, that is. Philip. Tell him Philip and me haven't finished disturbin' the peace yet. He'll know what that means."

"Yes, why certainly," one of the women mumbled.

"And you won't have any trouble spottin' my chauffeur," said Chablis, casting a glance my way. "He's white."

Then she set off around the room, table-hopping and slipping her telephone number to several of the boys. Now, I figured, was the time for me to leave. Quickly. I nodded good-bye to my table mates and headed toward the door, giving Chablis a wide berth. I knew that if she saw me she would draw me into whatever stunt she was about to pull. I approached Dr. Collier and hurriedly thanked him for inviting me. Dr. Collier did not sense the urgency of my departure and introduced me to the man standing next to him, the man who had taught the debutantes how to dance the minuet. I smiled and uttered pleasantries but barely heard a word that either of the two were saying; my eyes were darting around the room for signs of Chablis. When at last it was possible to take my leave, I withdrew, ducked around the bar, slipped through the ballroom doors, and bounded down the escalator two steps at a time. I managed to make it across the lobby without incident and dashed out the front door into a calm, untroubled misty night on Bay Street.

Chapter 25

TALK OF THE TOWN

Midway through Jim Williams's second year in jail, Savannah more or less forgot about him. The city turned its attention to other topics. There was a good deal of talk, for example, about the divine intervention allegedly visited upon George Mercer III.

George Mercer III was a prominent businessman and the nephew of the late Johnny Mercer. Mr. Mercer was leaving his house in Ardsley Park one evening to go to a dinner party when he suddenly realized he'd forgotten his car keys. He went back inside to get them. In the front hall he heard a voice say loud and clear, "George, you drink too much!"

Mr. Mercer looked around, but the hall was empty. "Who are you?" he asked. "And where are you?"

"I am the Lord," said the voice. "I am everywhere."

"Well, I know I drink more than I should," said Mr. Mercer, "but how do I know you're the Lord? If you really are, show me. Show me now. If you can prove to me you're God I'll never drink again." Suddenly, Mr. Mercer felt himself being lifted high in the air. Up over his house. Up over Ardsley

Park. He was lifted so high he could look down and see all of Savannah—the downtown squares, the river, Tybee Island, and Hilton Head. And the voice said, "Have I proved to you that I am real?" Mr. Mercer declared then and there that he did believe, and the Lord put him back down in the front hall. George Mercer III never took another drink after that.

Even people who doubted the truth of that story had to admit that on a spiritual level at least something very strange was happening to Savannah's upper crust. How else could one explain the charismatic services Thursday nights at Christ Episcopal Church? Christ Church was Savannah's oldest and most tradition-bound house of worship. It was the Mother Church of Georgia, John Wesley having served as its rector in 1736. But now the charismatics had a foot in the door, and they were gathering in the basement on Thursday nights, speaking in tongues, strumming guitars, banging on tambourines, and waving their arms in the air whenever the spirit moved them. The more conservative parishioners were appalled; some simply refused to believe it.

Spiritual matters were not Savannah's only preoccupation, however. There was concern about the city's economy as well. Savannah's renaissance had crested, and a decline had begun. The city seemed more isolated than ever. Northern businesses were relocating in the South, but they were putting down roots in Atlanta, Jacksonville, and Charleston, not in Savannah. Downtown real estate values, after rising sharply for twenty years, had softened. Retail stores were abandoning Broughton Street and moving out to the Mall and elsewhere on the southside. More ominous yet, it seemed that Savannah's most lucrative source of income—the shipping business—was on the verge of being choked off by, of all things, the old Talmadge Bridge. As tall as the bridge was, it was not quite tall enough to allow the huge new superfreighters to sail under it to the docks upriver. Several medium-size containerships had already clipped off aerials and radar masts on the underside of the bridge, and port officials dreaded that any day now a whole poop deck would be sheared off into the water. Before that ever happened, of course, a fair portion of Savannah's shipping trade would have headed for other ports. The threat to the economy of Savannah and Georgia was grave enough to send the state's congressional delegation scrambling in search of federal funds for a new bridge. After a period of tense negotiations, money was allotted and a potential calamity averted. Fears about the old bridge were replaced by curiosity about what the new one would look like.

With matters like these to talk about, there was little time for thoughts of Jim Williams. "After all," sighed Millicent Mooreland, "what more is there to say except 'Poor Jim!' "

Indeed, a more immediate concern was the sudden appearance on downtown walls, sidewalks, and dumpsters of graffiti that read A DISTURBED JENNIFER. The desperate nature of the scrawl suggested that a deranged woman was roaming the lanes, contemplating harm to herself or others. After a month of heightened anxiety and double-locking of doors, "A Disturbed Jennifer" materialized as a rock group composed of four green-haired students from the Savannah College of Art and Design. The resolution of that mystery calmed fears but did nothing to soothe Savannah's increasing impatience with the new art school.

The Savannah College of Art and Design—known familiarly as SCAD—had opened its doors in 1979 with the blessings of all Savannah. The school had taken over the boarded-up Guard Armory on Madison Square and refurbished it as classrooms and studios for seventy-one art students. Within two years, enrollment had climbed to three hundred, and the college had acquired and restored several more old and empty buildings—warehouses, public schools, even a jailhouse. SCAD's young president, Richard Rowan, let it be known that the student body would eventually grow to two thousand.

Downtown residents did not respond happily to Rowan's announcement. While the students did contribute something to the local economy, and they did bring a little life to the otherwise empty streets, they were becoming in the eyes of some people a blight on the landscape with their green hair, their odd clothes, their skateboards, and their tendency to play loud music on their stereos well into the night. In reaction, a group of downtown residents formed a Quality of Life Committee to deal with the situation. Joe Webster, who headed the committee, could be seen each day at noontime walking stiffly with the aid of a cane from his office in the C&S Bank building to the Oglethorpe Club for lunch. His route took him down Bull Street past the main entrance of SCAD, where he would invariably make his way through a small cluster of students and point silently with his cane at some offending object—a crumpled candy wrapper or a motorcycle idling noisily at the curb. On one occasion, Mr. Webster and his committee stopped in to see Richard Rowan in his office to express their concern that the fragile human ecology of downtown Savannah might not survive two thousand students. The total population of the historic district was, after all, only about ten thousand. Rowan told the committee that he would see what he could do about the loud music and that, by the by, he had recently revised his goal from two thousand students to *four* thousand.

However disruptive the college might have been to Savannah's peace and quiet, it did nothing to harm the city's physical beauty. The college restored each building it bought with taste and authenticity, and Savannah continued to receive compliments from its far-flung admirers. *Le Monde* called Savannah "la plus belle des villes d'Amerique du Nord." The National Trust for Historic Preservation focused a flattering spotlight on the city when it bestowed its highest honor—the Louise Crowninshield Award—on Lee Adler for his contribution to Savannah's restoration. Adler went to Washington to accept the award, and upon his return his fellow citizens rallied around him in customary fashion: They congratulated him for winning yet another great honor, and as soon as his back was turned, they bitterly denounced him for once again hogging sole credit for a job done by many.

While Savannah had grown accustomed to receiving compliments for its good looks, the city was thoroughly unprepared for a shockingly negative piece of news about itself that came howling out of the FBI in Washington and resounded around the world. Savannah had achieved the highest per-capita murder rate in the United States the previous year—54 murders, or 22.6 murders per 100,000 people. Savannah had become the murder capital of the United States! A stunned Mayor John Rousakis looked at the figures and complained that Savannah had been the victim of a statistical fluke. The numbers reflected murder rates in *metropolitan* areas. Unlike most cities, Savannah did not have vast outlying suburbs with thousands of untroubled suburbanites to dilute its murder rate. When the murder rate was confined to actual city limits, Savannah ranked fifteenth in the nation, which was still a troubling distinction for a city that was not even among the country's hundred largest cities.

Intending to clarify the matter, the city manager, Don Mendonsa, announced that a breakdown of police figures showed that crime in Savannah "is a black problem." Nearly half of Savannah's population was black, he said, but 91 percent of the murderers were black, and 85 percent of the victims were also black. The same was true for rape (89 percent of the offenders and 87 percent of the victims were black). Ninety-four percent of assaults and 95 percent of robberies involved black offenders. The city manager was not a racist. He expressed a compassionate concern for dealing with root causes—12.1 percent unemployment among blacks, compared with 4.7 for whites, and similar disparities in school-dropout rates, teenage pregnancies, unwed mothers, and family income.

Although racial inequalities were, if anything, greater in Savannah than in other southern cities, Savannah's blacks displayed surprisingly little hostility toward whites. On the surface, at least, a remarkable civility prevailed. A black man passing a white stranger on the street would be likely to nod and say, "Good morning," "How y'doing?" or simply "Hey." Outwardly, little seemed to have changed since William Makepeace Thackeray visited Savannah in 1848 and described it as a tranquil old city with wide, tree-planted streets and "a few happy Negroes sauntering here and there." Thackeray was not the only person to notice that slaves had smiles on their faces. W. H. Pierson wrote in *The Water Witch* in 1863: "[The slaves] are, by all odds, the happiest-looking folks in the Confederacy. They sing, while the whites curse and pray." During slavery, it was thought by some observers that the apparent good cheer of the slaves had something to do with their expectation that the roles would be reversed in the hereafter: They would be the masters, and whites would be their slaves. In the 1960s, the civil rights struggle put a temporary strain on relations, but integration was peaceful on the whole. Since then, Savannah had been governed largely by moderate whites who made it their business to stay on good terms with the black community. As a result, racial peace was maintained, and blacks remained politically conservative, which is to say, passive. There was no discernible black activism in Savannah. But it was evident that underneath their apparent complacency, Savannah's blacks were beset by an anguish and despair that ran so deep and expressed itself with such violence that it had made Savannah the murder capital of America.

If Savannah's spiritual, economic, artistic, architectural, and law-and-order concerns were not enough to keep people's minds off Jim Williams, there were plenty of distractions on the social scene. There was talk, for instance, about a standoff at the Married Woman's Card Club. Slots for membership had opened up, but competition to fill them had become so fierce that every candidate had been blackballed for two years running. No one had gotten into the club in all that time, and for the first time in memory, membership had slipped below the mandated sixteen. The stalemate was temporarily upstaged by a food-poisoning scare at one of the club's get-togethers. The ladies were just heading home at six o'clock when they discovered the hostess's cat lying dead on the front steps. Someone recalled having seen the cat nibbling a leftover portion of crab casserole only minutes before. The women thereupon trotted to their cars and drove in a swarm to Candler Hospital to have their stomachs pumped. The following morning, the next-door neighbor stopped by to say he was sorry he'd run over the cat.

Neither the Married Woman's membership crisis nor the food scare received any mention in the newspaper's society column. It was, in fact, at about this time that the newspaper announced it was discontinuing its society column altogether. The column had never been much more than a bland recitation of guest lists, but its disappearance provoked a stinging rebuke from one of Savannah's leading socialites, Mrs. Vera Dutton Strong. In her letter to the editor, which was one of the longest the newspaper had ever published, Mrs. Strong expressed "shocked disbelief" at the cancellation of the column, calling the paper's social coverage a "genuine disgrace." There was a certain irony in this, because the most compelling social gossip at the moment happened to be the test of wills currently being waged by Mrs. Strong and her rebellious daughter, Dutton.

Vera Dutton Strong was an heiress to the huge Dutton pulpwood fortune. An only child, she was a member of one of Savannah's richest society families; her mother and father had always dressed for dinner—black tie and evening gown. Throughout her childhood she had been known as "The Princess," a nickname that seemed only natural for her. She was Debutante of the Year, and at her wedding she wore an exact replica of the gown Queen Elizabeth II had worn at *her* wedding. Over the years, Mrs. Strong had shown herself to be good-humored, warm-hearted, and strong-willed. She was a founder of the Savannah Ballet Company and served as its hovering benefactress. Each year just before the Cotillion ball, society mothers would send their debutante daughters to Vera Strong so that she could teach them how to curtsy properly. A cloistered Savannahian of the purest sort, Mrs. Strong had never been to Europe, and she was past fifty when she visited Charleston for the first time.

Mrs. Strong's own daughter, Dutton, was an angel-faced beauty with long red hair and not the slightest inclination to be a princess or a ballerina, both of which Mrs. Strong had set her heart on. Dutton obediently started ballet lessons at the age of four, and soon she was dancing with her mother's ballet company. Dutton's debutante party was the only one ever held at the Telfair museum; Vera Strong hired Peter Duchin and his orchestra and commissioned a twelve-foot ice sculpture of the Eiffel Tower to highlight the "April in Paris" theme of the party. It was not until Dutton went away to school that a streak of independence began to assert itself. She skipped classes, stopped dancing, and finally dropped out of school. She came back home to Savannah, where she spent a year aimlessly hanging around the house and doing battle with her mother. "*I* never wanted to be a ballerina!" Dutton would bellow. "*You're* the one who wanted to be a ballerina!" But Mrs. Strong would have none of it. "That's nonsense! You loved dancing, or you never would have been so good at it!" After one especially energetic quarrel, Dutton stormed out of the house and moved into an apartment with an older woman who had been her mother's poodle breeder. Dutton cut her long hair short, took to wearing jeans instead of skirts, put on weight, and stopped wearing lipstick. Then one afternoon she came to see her mother to announce that she had at long last decided on a career. She would go to the police academy and become a Savannah cop.

Vera Strong took the news with uncharacteristic calm. "If that's what you really want," she said, "I pray it turns out to be everything you're hoping for." Mrs. Strong attended her daughter's graduation at the police academy with a pasted-on smile. She wore the same smile at Christmas dinner when her daughter, the former ballerina-debutante, arrived wearing a navy-blue polyester pants suit with a .38 revolver on one hip and a Mace can and handcuffs on the other.

Refusing to admit defeat, Vera Strong decided to view her daughter's choice of profession as a selfless gesture of civic-mindedness rather than a betrayal of the family heritage. In the spring, she called the Oglethorpe Club to reserve a table for Easter dinner, making a point of telling the club manager that Dutton would be going on duty immediately afterward and would therefore be in uniform. Sensing a crisis of protocol, the manager demurred and said he would have to confer with the board. Ten minutes later he called back with profound apologies: The no-trousers rule for women had never been lifted before and the board dared not do it now. Mrs. Strong forthwith denounced the manager, the board, and the Oglethorpe Club as only she could do. She then slammed down the telephone and booked a table at the more amenable but less exclusive Chatham Club.

The *Savannah Morning News* proved to be more tractable than the Oglethorpe Club. Stung by Mrs. Strong's vituperative letter, the paper reinstated its society gossip column. Understandably, the column never made reference to the red-headed ballerina and her astonishing leap from *Coppélia* to cop, or to the continuing anguish that it caused her mother.

While all this was going on, the controversy over Joe Odom and the Hamilton-Turner House continued unabated. Shortly after Joe set up the nonprofit "Hamilton-Turner Museum Foundation" to shield his illegal tour business, his neighbors countered by arguing before the Department of Inspections that, profit or nonprofit, the Hamilton-Turner House stood within one hundred yards of a school. This meant it was illegal for Joe to sell liquor at his luncheons and dinner parties. But Joe was not concerned. "The law says I can't *sell* liquor," he said. "It doesn't say I can't *serve* it." Somewhere in the gray area between selling and serving, Joe knew how to make money giving liquor to his customers, and he went right on doing it.

Liquor also played a part in a small drama involving Serena Dawes. Serena and Luther Driggers had split up, and Serena had taken to cruising the docks late at night in an effort to pick up Greek sailors. One night the police spotted her driving erratically along River Street and stopped her. Serena opted for a pose of elegant femininity, which was a feat in itself since she was wearing a shortie nightgown and fluffy white rabbit-head slippers. She batted her eyelashes and exclaimed sweetly that she had gone out to move her "cahwuh" and had gotten lost. When the policemen took her to the county jail and booked her for driving under the influence, she wanted to scream and scratch their faces, but instead she held herself in check and coyly thanked them for coming to her rescue. She mentioned that her "great-granddaddy-in-law" had been Ambassador to the Court of St. James's just to let them know they were dealing with a woman of quality. An hour later, Luther Driggers came down to bail her out, but by that time Serena had had enough of pretense. A fat black prison matron, who had taken Serena's handbag and searched it, now handed it back to her.

"You can have it back," the matron said. "It's clean."

"It is *not* clean anymore," Serena snapped, snatching the purse out of the woman's hands. "And if I *ever* catch you putting your filthy fucking hands on anything of mine again, you'll be wearing your poon-tang for a turtleneck!"

These, then, were the matters of consuming interest in Savannah, the city *Le Monde* had called "la plus belle des villes" in North America. Beautiful it was, but still very isolated and, because of that, a bit too trusting. Police had recently circulated a warning about a pair of con men who were cashing checks drawn on a nonexistent company. The con men had given their victims a sporting chance by naming their bogus company "Fly By Night, Inc.," but dozens of Savannah merchants had cashed the checks anyway. About the same time, it also came to light that the clerk in charge of handling the money in probate court did not know how to multiply and that one of the probate judges had taken advantage of the situation by dipping into the cash box. Life, in other words, went on. Savannah had community questions to resolve, such as: Should a second mall be built? Had Mr. Charles Hall ruined Whitfield Square by painting his gingerbread house a dozen shades of pink and purple? And, if so, did the city have the right to force him to repaint it in more acceptable colors?

Then one day in June, all of these questions were overshadowed by the news that the Georgia Supreme Court had once again overturned Jim Williams's conviction for murder.

The court cited two reasons for setting aside the conviction. First, it ruled that Judge Oliver should not have allowed a Savannah police detective to testify as an "expert" for the prosecution on points of evidence that the jurors were competent to evaluate on their own—the smeared blood on Danny Hansford's hand, the chair on his pants cuff, the fragments of paper on top of the gun. Second, the court faulted Spencer Lawton for waiting until his closing argument to demonstrate that the trigger on Hansford's gun was easy to pull rather than difficult, as the defense had claimed. In effect, said the court, Lawton's demonstration introduced new evidence, which should have been brought up during the trial itself, at which time the defense could have responded to it.

Williams was lucky. The reversal had been a 4-to-3 decision. The three dissenting justices argued that the errors had been harmless ones and that, in any case, they had not influenced the verdict. But none of that mattered now. Since the state supreme court had not found Williams innocent—they had merely thrown out the verdict—murder charges still stood against him. He would be tried a third time in Judge Oliver's court, and a third jury would deliver yet another verdict.

—

Williams emerged from the Chatham County Jail a little thinner than before, a little grayer at the temples, and ghostly pale from having been indoors nearly two years. He squinted in the sun. As he and Sonny Seiler walked to a car parked at the curb, a small group of reporters and cameramen followed along, shouting questions.

Did Williams think he would be acquitted at a third trial?

"Yes, of course," he said.

What would be the deciding factor?

"Money," he said. "My case has been about money from the very beginning. The D.A. spends the taxpayers' money, and I spend my own—five hundred thousand dollars of it so far. The criminal-justice system is rigged that way, in case you haven't noticed. I'd still be in jail if I hadn't been able to pay for lawyers and experts and their endless expenses. So far I've managed to stay even with the prosecution. Dollar for dollar, tit for tat."

As he approached the car, Williams looked across Montgomery Street and saw an old black woman standing at the bus stop. She was staring in his direction through purple glasses. Williams met her glance briefly and smiled. Then he turned back to the reporters.

"Well . . . maybe I shouldn't have said 'tit for tat.' As I've always said, there are forces working in my favor—forces the D.A. doesn't know anything about."

And what might they be?

"You can put them down under the heading of . . . 'miscellaneous,' " he said.

Within minutes Jim Williams was back in Mercer House, back in the news, and back on people's minds again whether they liked it or not.

Chapter 26

ANOTHER STORY

With a third trial in the offing, Jim Williams's case was approaching landmark status and attracting attention well beyond Savannah. Williams's air of cynical detachment lent spice to the expanding media coverage. *Us* magazine ("The Scandal That Shook Savannah") described Williams as having a "von Bülow-like demeanor." The editors of the photographic documentary *A Day in the Life of America* sent a photographer to Savannah with instructions to take a picture of Williams as an example of southern decadence. The photographer, Gerd Ludwig, set up his lights and cameras in Mercer House.

"He was here all day," Williams said afterward, "trying his best to capture my 'decadence' on film. I suppose I could have made it easy for him. I could have offered to pose with my most recently acquired historic relic—the dagger that Prince Yussupov used when he murdered Rasputin. That would have done nicely, don't you think? Yussupov sliced off Rasputin's cock and balls with it."

Williams took little interest in the legal side of his upcoming trial. Instead, he busied himself with the "miscellaneous" end of things, which is to say he played Psycho Dice incessantly and allowed Minerva to become a lurking presence around Mercer House. She performed the appropriate rituals for removing a curse from the house, just in case there was one, and she also cast spells on people Williams suspected of wishing him ill. By chance, I happened to see her in the midst of one of these ceremonies. It was an afternoon in March, and the annual Tour of Homes was in progress. As usual, Williams had refused to open Mercer House to the tourists, but Lee and Emma Adler had happily thrown open their doors. Williams stood at his living-room window, smoking a cigarillo and making wry comments as he watched visitors trooping up the Adlers' front steps across the street. He motioned me over to the window. Two well-dressed couples were walking single file up the Adlers' steps. Minerva was right behind them, carrying her trademark shopping bag. At the top of the steps, she paused while the others went inside; then, after looking around in all directions, she reached into the bag and flung what appeared to be a handful of dirt into the little garden below. She threw another handful down the steps. Williams laughed.

"Was that graveyard dirt?" I asked.

"What else?" he said.

"Taken from a graveyard at midnight?"

"When else?"

Minerva went inside the Adlers' house. "What on earth is she doing in there?" I asked.

"Her usual mumbo-jumbo, I suppose," said Williams. "Twigs, leaves, feathers, exotic powders, chicken bones. I told her Lee Adler controls the D.A., and that's all she had to hear. Minerva's been a very busy witch lately. She's been out at Vernonburg several times to dress down Spencer Lawton's house, and yesterday she paid a call on Judge Oliver's cottage in Tybee. She's thrown graveyard dirt at some of the best homes in Savannah, God bless her."

—

While Williams contented himself with these mystical manipulations, Sonny Seiler mounted a vigorous legal campaign to strengthen the position of the defense. He moved to suppress most of the evidence seized at Mercer House the night of the shooting on the grounds that the police did not have a search warrant; the motion was denied by the Georgia Supreme Court. His petition for a change of venue was likewise rejected. As the date for the trial drew near, Seiler found himself with essentially the same defense strategy as in the second trial. This time he would not sequester the jury, which would improve matters slightly, but he had no new evidence and no new witnesses. He had decided against using Hansford's two young hustler friends and their stories about Hansford's plan to kill or injure Williams, fearing they might backfire; besides, Hansford's penchant for violence was amply established through other witnesses. In any case, the most troublesome issue remained the total absence of gunshot residue on Danny Hansford's hand. That piece of evidence had proved decisive against Williams in both trials, despite everything the defense had done to explain it. Seiler's expert witness, Dr. Irving Stone, had testified that the downward angle of the gun, plus the blood from Hansford's hand and the delay of twelve hours before the police swabbed for residue, would have diminished the residue on Hansford's hands by 70 percent, but no more. It was unlikely that very much of the remaining 30 percent could have accidentally rubbed off on the way to the hospital, because the police had taken the routine precaution of taping paper bags over Hansford's hands before moving his body. Seiler telephoned Dr. Stone one more time to ask if there was any way he could explain a zero reading of gunshot residue. "No," Dr. Stone told him, "not with the information I have."

In addition to the gunshot-residue problem, Seiler was becoming concerned about Williams's testimony. It had been nearly four years since he had last testified, and Seiler worried that he might become confused about minor details and contradict what he had said before. Two weeks before the trial was to begin, he insisted that Williams sit down and review his prior testimony. Any deviation in his story, even the slightest detail, would give Lawton a chance to pounce on his credibility. Seiler told Williams he would bring the transcripts to Mercer House on Saturday afternoon, and they would go over them together. Saturday morning, Williams called and invited me to sit in on the review.

"Come half an hour early," Williams said. "I have something I want to tell you."

The moment he opened the door, I could tell Williams knew the odds were against him. He had shaved his mustache. Seiler had tried to make him shave it for the second trial, saying it would make him look less forbidding, but Williams had refused. Now Williams was apparently willing to do anything to ingratiate himself with the jury.

He came right to the point. "Sonny doesn't know this yet, but I'm going to change my story. I'm going to tell what really happened that night. It's my only chance to win this case."

I made no comment. Williams drew a deep breath and then began:

"The evening started out just as I've always said it did. Danny and I went to a drive-in movie. He was drinking bourbon and smoking grass. We came back to the house. He started an argument, kicked in the Atari set, grabbed me by the neck, pushed me up against the doorjamb. All that's true. Then he followed me into the study, just as I've always said. We called Joe Goodman. Right after that, Danny took the tankard in his hand and said, 'This tankard has about made up its mind to go through that painting over there.' I told him to get out. He went into the hall, I heard crashing sounds, he came back with the Luger in his hand and said, 'I'm leaving tomorrow, but you're leaving tonight.' Then he raised his arm and pulled the trigger. All that's true. It's what I've been saying all along. But here's the difference: *The gun was on safety!* When Danny pulled the trigger, nothing happened! No bullets came out. No bullets whizzed by my arm. Danny lowered the gun, took the safety off, and ejected a live round. That gave me time to reach into the drawer and get my own gun and shoot him. I fired three times. Bam, bam, bam. He fell dead. But he hadn't fired a shot. Then I thought: Goddamn, what have I done! I went around the desk, picked up his gun, fired two shots back across the desk, and dropped the gun on the floor. In the panic of the moment I didn't know what else to do."

Having said all that, Williams seemed strangely elated. "You see, it explains why there was no gunpowder on Danny's hand!" He studied me carefully, looking to see my reaction to his new story.

I wondered if my expression betrayed my astonishment.

"The police and my lawyer, Bob Duffy, arrived at the house at the same time," he went on. "I took them into the study and told them Danny had fired at me and missed, and that I'd shot him. I had a feeling I was making a bad situation worse by sticking to that story, but I didn't see that I had any choice. Well, I've been convicted twice now, so I've finally decided to tell it the way it really happened. And when I do, Spencer Lawton's case will crumble. I'll be acquitted."

"I'm not sure how you figure that," I said.

"Because it explains everything! The lack of gunpowder on Danny's hand. The live round on the floor. The pieces of paper on the gun. It all ties together!"

My guess was that Williams was using me to float a trial balloon. His new story fit the evidence well enough, and it preserved his claim of self-defense. But it was too convenient, too neat, and too late to do him much good.

"If you tell that story," I said, trying not to sound too argumentative, "you'll be admitting you've committed perjury all these years."

"Yes, of course," he said, "but so what?"

Evidently, Williams did not want to be dissuaded. So I did not tell him that I thought his new story would be music to Spencer Lawton's ears, or that if he admitted having fired all the shots, any jury—even a friendly one—would conclude that Hansford had never held a gun in his hand at all that night.

"You haven't told Sonny Seiler any of this?" I asked.

"I intend to tell him as soon as he gets here."

Good, let Sonny Seiler deal with it. It was not my business to counsel Williams anyway. I shifted the conversation to innocuous topics while we waited. I told Williams that without his mustache, he had a benign look. A jury might like that. I glanced out the window, watching for Seiler, and noticed Minerva sitting on a bench in the square.

"Is she casting a spell on somebody?"

"Probably," said Williams. "I give her twenty-five dollars a day, and I've learned not to ask questions."

Seiler arrived shortly, accompanied by his secretary and two lawyers who were assisting on the case, Don Samuel and David Botts. Seiler was out of breath. "We got a lot to cover this afternoon," he said, "so let's get going."

We assembled in the study. Williams sat at his desk, and Seiler stood in the center of the room. He was wearing a blue blazer and a red-white-and-black Georgia bulldog tie. I felt a twinge of pity for him. His case was about to fall apart. He was full of energy, impatient to begin.

"Now, Jim," he said, "we're coming into this trial with some serious problems, and I don't want to give Lawton a chance to tangle you up on cross-examination. If you get up there and say you blinked twice before you shot Hansford, he'll say, 'But, Mr. Williams, didn't you testify on an earlier occasion that you blinked *three* times?' "

"Sonny," said Williams, "before we get into all of that, there's something I want to tell you about my testimony."

"Okay," said Seiler, "but just wait a minute. I want to review where we stand. Number one: We have not been able to get a change of venue. Number two: Our motion to suppress the evidence has been denied. Number three: We've had a hell of a time trying to deal with that damned gunshot-residue test."

"I know all about that, Sonny," said Williams. "What I have to say has a direct bearing on it."

"Just hear me out. Then you can go ahead."

Exasperated, Williams sat back in his chair, arms crossed. Seiler continued.

"A couple of weeks ago, Dr. Stone told me he could not explain how Danny could have fired a gun and still had zero gunpowder on his hand. He made a suggestion, though. He said, 'Why don't you go back out to Candler Hospital and see if you can find out what they did with Hansford's body before they swabbed his hands for gunpowder. Maybe you'll come up with something.' He said the more a body is moved or touched, the more likely it is that gunpowder will be wiped off.

"I went out to the hospital yesterday and asked for the file on Hansford. They gave me the autopsy report. Nothing new about that. We've had a copy of it all along. But this copy had a top sheet I hadn't seen before. It was a green hospital admitting form filled out by the nurse in charge of the emergency room—Marilyn Case. She had written a note on it: 'Hands bagged bilaterally in Emergency Department.' This piqued my curiosity, so I called her up and asked her to explain it. She said it meant she had put bags over both of Danny's hands so the gunpowder wouldn't rub off; the coroner had called and told her to do it. I said, 'Wait a minute! The police said *they* put bags on Hansford's hands back at Mercer House! You mean to tell me that there were no bags on Hansford's hands when he arrived at the emergency room?' 'I'm sure of it,' she said. 'I bagged the hands myself.' "

Seiler was glowing. "Do you know what this means?" he said. "It means the police didn't bag the hands at all! They've been lying all along. They forgot to bag the hands! They wrapped Hansford in a blanket, lifted him onto a gurney, wheeled him into an ambulance, drove him out to the hospital, wheeled him into the emergency room, lifted him off the gurney, unwrapped him, and all that time his bare hands were flopping around and rubbing against his shirt, his jeans, the blanket—*and rubbing off all that gunshot residue!* I called Dr. Stone and told him what I'd found. 'Sonny,' he said, 'you struck gold!' "

Seiler pulled a copy of the admissions sheet out of his briefcase. "Here it is, Coach!" he said. "The death knell of

Spencer Lawton's precious gunshot-residue test. They based their whole case on it, dammit, and we're gonna kick it right between the goal posts. What's worse, Lawton was obligated to give us a copy of this sheet along with the autopsy report, and he didn't. So, we've caught him hiding the evidence again. He's gonna have fits when we hit him with it."

Seiler put the paper back in his briefcase and snapped it shut. "Okay, Jim," he said. "Your turn."

Williams sat with his chin cupped in his hand. He glanced at me, flickered his eyebrows, and then looked back at Seiler.

"Never mind, Sonny," he said. "It's not important."

—

I left Mercer House that afternoon with the uncomfortable feeling that I knew more than I wanted to know. Around midnight, I stopped in at Sweet Georgia Brown's and sat down on the piano bench next to Joe.

"I need to ask you about a point of law," I said.

"I knew you'd get into trouble writing that book of yours," Joe said. "But like I told you, that's what I'm here for."

"This is a purely hypothetical question," I said. "Suppose an unnamed person—an upstanding citizen minding his own business—happened to become privy to inside information about a criminal case. Something secret, something that contradicts sworn testimony. Would this person become an accessory after the fact if he just kept quiet about it?"

Joe looked at me and smiled broadly, while continuing to play the piano. "You wouldn't be trying to tell me Jim Williams has finally told you one of his many alternate versions of how he shot Danny Hansford, would you?"

"Who said anything about Jim Williams?"

"Oh, that's right," said Joe, "we were speaking hypothetically, weren't we? Well, according to the law, this 'unnamed person' is under no obligation to divulge his secret information, which—if it's what I *think* it is—is not all that secret anyway. Heh-heh. In fact, I was beginning to wonder how long it was going to take a certain writer from New York to find out something half of Savannah already knows."

As Joe spoke, a policeman and a policewoman approached and stood awkwardly by the side of the piano.

"Mr. Joe Odom?" the policeman said.

"That's me," said Joe.

"We have orders to place you under arrest."

"You do? What's the charge?" Joe went on playing the piano.

"Scofflaw," said the policewoman. "We're from Thunderbolt. You got six unpaid speedin' tickets and a U-turn violation."

"Any bad-check charges?" Joe asked.

"No, just the speedin' tickets and the U-turn," the woman said.

"Well, that's a relief."

"We'll have to take you to Thunderbolt in the squad car," the policeman said. "Once we book you and relieve you of two hundred dollars for bond, why, you can be on your way."

"Fair enough," said Joe, "but I'd be much obliged if you'd bear with me while I finish up a couple of things. I was just giving my friend here some legal advice. And . . ." He leaned closer to the two officers and lowered his voice. "See that old couple sitting by the ice machine? They've driven in from Swainsboro to celebrate their sixtieth wedding anniversary, and they've asked me to play a medley of their favorite songs. I'm about halfway through. I'll be done with both of these chores in about four or five minutes, if it's okay with you." The policewoman murmured it would be fine, and the two of them took seats near the door. Joe sent the waiter over with Cokes and turned back to me.

"Now, about this not-so-secret secret information," he said. "I would tell this 'unnamed person,' in case he's interested, that in all of Jim Williams's versions of how he shot Danny Hansford, there are certain consistent points. The shooting happened in the course of an argument and on the spur of the moment. It was not a premeditated killing. The victim was an out-of-control, drunk, drug-addicted kid with a history of violence, and the defendant was a frightened, angry, nonviolent older man with no criminal record. That's a scenario for manslaughter maybe, but not first-degree murder. And in Georgia, a conviction for manslaughter usually carries a sentence of five to ten years with two years to serve. Jim's already served two years."

"I suppose you could look at it that way," I said, "if you wanted to."

"Anyhow, that's my answer to your question about the 'point of law.' "

"Thanks," I said.

"And now, there is the small matter of my consultation fee—heh-heh. I'm thinking I'll waive it in exchange for a small favor. All you have to do is to follow a certain squad car out to Thunderbolt in a few minutes, then turn around and drive a certain attorney-scofflaw back to town."

"It's a deal," I said.

Joe finished his medley with a flourish. He went over to the bar and, while Mandy's head was turned, took $200 out of the cash register. On his way out the door, he stopped to pay his respects to the couple from Swainsboro. The woman wore a large pink corsage pinned above her heart.

"Oh, Joe," she said, "that was lovely. Thank you so much!"

Her husband stood and shook Joe's hand. "It ain't but midnight, Joe. Why're you leavin' so early?"

Joe smoothed the lapels of his tuxedo and straightened his plaid bow tie. "I've just been informed there's an official motorcade leaving for Thunderbolt, and I've been invited to ride in the lead car."

"My word!" said the woman. "That's a great honor."

"Yes, ma'am," said Joe. "You could look at it that way, if you wanted to."

Chapter 27

LUCKY NUMBER

Blanche Williams came into the dining room and took her seat at the dinner table for lunch.

"The cat won't eat," she said.

Jim Williams looked up from the Sotheby's auction catalog he had brought with him to the table. He looked at the cat, who was sitting motionless in the doorway. Then he returned his attention to the catalog.

Mrs. Williams unfolded her napkin and put it in her lap. "It's the same as last time," she said. "The cat wouldn't eat then either. Or the time before that. It's happened every time we've come back from the courthouse to wait for the jury to make up its mind. She's refused to eat."

Williams's sister, Dorothy Kingery, glanced at her watch. "It's one-thirty," she said. "They've been at it three hours now. I guess they're having lunch. I wonder if they'll take a break or go right on deliberating while they eat."

Williams looked up from his auction catalog. "Listen to this," he said. " 'When Catherine of Braganza, the Infanta of Portugal, arrived in England in 1662 to marry Charles II, she brought with her the largest dowry ever. Part of the dowry was the Port of Bombay in India. . . .' " He laughed. "Now, that's the kind of princess I like!"

"This makes the third time she's done it," Mrs. Williams said, "—not touched her food."

Dorothy Kingery regarded the sandwich on her plate. "Sonny says he'll call from the courthouse as soon as there's word. I hope we can hear the telephone from in here."

"I don't know how she knows," Mrs. Williams mused softly. "But she always knows."

Jim Williams suddenly closed the auction catalog and stood up. "I've got an idea!" he said. "We'll eat lunch on the dishes from the Nanking Cargo. Just for good luck."

He took several blue-and-white plates out of the breakfront cabinet and passed them around the table. His mother and his sister transferred their sandwiches from their plain white plates to the blue-and-white plates. The blue-and-white plates had been part of a huge shipment of Chinese export porcelain that had been lost in the South China Sea in 1752 and salvaged in 1983. Williams had bought several dozen plates, cups, and bowls at a highly publicized Christie's auction, and they had arrived at Mercer House within the past few weeks.

"These plates have been sitting on the bottom of the ocean for two hundred and thirty years," he said, "but they're still brand-new. When they were found they were in their original packing crates. They're in mint condition. No one has ever eaten off them before. We're the first. Funny way to preserve dishes, isn't it?"

Mrs. Williams lifted her sandwich and looked at her plate. "You can't fool a cat," she said.

—

Two weeks earlier, on the first day of Williams's third trial, the outcome had seemed a foregone conclusion—so much so that the *Savannah Morning News* had announced in a weary headline, WILLIAMS FACES YET ANOTHER CONVICTION FOR MURDER. The jury of nine women and three men seemed predisposed to hand down a third conviction; all of them, having been subjected to six years of relentless publicity, admitted that they knew about the case and were aware that two prior juries had already found Williams guilty. The tension and suspense of the first two trials had given way to a feeling of grim inevitability. Television cameras were stationed outside the courthouse once again, but this time the spectator benches in the courtroom were only half full. Prentiss Crowe declared he would not even bother to read the news reports, it was all becoming such a bore. "It's the same old story over and over," he said, "like reruns of *I Love Lucy.*"

The courthouse flack was among those who did attend. He sat slumped in his seat with one arm hooked over the back as if to keep himself from sliding off onto the floor. As usual, he was an oracle of courthouse wisdom and rumor. "Jim Williams's guilt or innocence is no longer the issue," he said. "Spencer Lawton's incompetence is the issue. The question on everybody's mind is, How long will he keep screwing up? I mean, this case is getting to be like a bad bullfight. Lawton's the matador who can't finish off the bull. Twice now, he's plunged the sword in, but the bull's still on his feet, and the fans are getting restless. Lawton looks ridiculous."

The prosecution led off with its by-now familiar repertory company of witnesses—the police photographer, the officers who came to Mercer House the night of the shooting, the lab technicians. Each responded to Spencer Lawton's questions, then submitted to cross-examination by Sonny Seiler, and left the stand. Judge Oliver nodded sleepily on the bench. The courthouse flack yawned.

"What part did you play in the removal of the body from Mercer House?" Lawton asked Detective Joseph Jordan, as he had in each of the first two trials.

"I bagged the hands," Jordan answered.

"Could you explain to the jury what you mean by bagging the hands and what the purpose for that would be?"

"Anytime there is a shooting," said Detective Jordan, "and you have reason to believe that a dead person has fired a weapon, paper bags are placed over the hands to prevent any foreign substance from getting on the hands and contaminating them, or any gunpowder residue—if there is any—from being accidentally wiped off."

A poker-faced Sonny Seiler cross-examined the unsuspecting Detective Jordan.

"What kind of bags did you use?"

"Paper bags."

"What did you bind them with?"

"I believe it was evidence tape."

"Are you absolutely sure those hands were bagged before they left the house?"

"I bagged them," said Jordan.

When the prosecution rested its case, Sonny Seiler rose to summon his first witness.

"Call Marilyn Case," he said.

A fresh face! A new witness! A change in the script! The courthouse flack leaned forward in his seat. Judge Oliver opened both eyes. Lawton and his assistant exchanged wary glances.

She was curly-headed and blond, about forty, and she wore a gray suit with a white silk blouse. She said she had worked as a nurse at Candler Hospital for fifteen years; before that, she had served as assistant coroner of Chatham County. Yes, she had been on duty in the Candler emergency room when Danny Hansford's body was brought in. Seiler handed her a copy of the hospital admissions sheet, then strode nonchalantly past Spencer Lawton and dropped another copy on the table in front of him. While Lawton and his assistant huddled over the piece of paper, Seiler placed a blowup of it on an easel in front of the jury and went on with his questioning.

"Let me ask you, Ms. Case, if you recognize this document."

"Yes, sir, I do."

"Is that your handwriting on it?"

"Yes, sir, it is."

"Tell this jury, Ms. Case, ma'am, whether or not Danny

Hansford's hands were bagged when you received him at the hospital."

"No, sir, they were not."

A murmur of surprise swept the courtroom. Judge Oliver gaveled the room to silence.

"All right, Ms. Case," Seiler went on, "so you bagged the hands yourself?"

"Yes, I did."

"How did you do it?"

"I got two plastic garbage bags, put them over both hands, and wrapped adhesive tape around the wrists."

After a brief and faltering cross-examination by a shaken Spencer Lawton, Marilyn Case stepped down from the stand. Seiler next called Dr. Stone, the forensic pathologist. Dr. Stone said that because Hansford's hands had not been bagged before he was moved to the hospital, all traces of gunshot residue could easily have been wiped off. He then added gently that by using plastic garbage bags instead of paper bags, the well-meaning Marilyn Case had actually made matters worse. "Plastic bags are an absolute no-no," he said. "They create static electricity, which can actually pull particles from the hand. Furthermore, if the body is then placed in a refrigerated morgue bin for five hours, as Hansford's body was, condensation forms inside the plastic bag, and water just kinda runs off the hands."

"In light of all that," Seiler asked, "are you surprised that there was no gunshot residue on Hansford's hand?"

"I'd be surprised if there *had* been any," said Dr. Stone.

Television stations cut into their afternoon programming with the news flash: "Shocking new evidence has come to light in the Jim Williams murder trial. . . . The district attorney has been taken by complete surprise. . . . Word around the courthouse is that Williams will walk. . . ." Later that night, Sonny Seiler arrived at the 1790 restaurant for dinner and received a standing ovation.

Lawton, having lost the use of his leading piece of evidence, shifted gears for his final argument. "We don't need the gunshot-residue test to prove that Jim Williams is guilty," he said. "It's only one piece of evidence among many." Point by point, he enumerated the surviving evidence against Jim Williams: the placement of bullet fragments, the bits of paper on the gun, the trajectory of fire, the chair leg on Hansford's pants, the blood on Hansford's hand but no blood on his gun. In particular, he focused on the thirty-six-minute gap between the time Hansford was shot and Williams's call to the police. "What did Jim Williams do in that thirty-six minutes?" Lawton asked. "I'll tell you what he did. He got another gun, went over to where Danny was lying, and shot a bullet into the desk. Then he pulled Danny's hand out from under his body and put it over the gun. What did he do for the balance of the time? I'll tell you what he did: He went around the house *selectively destroying furniture*!"

Lawton held up the police photographs of the interior of Mercer House. "This is the grandfather clock Danny Hansford allegedly knocked over. It's facedown in the hall. Notice how the base of the clock is still very close to the wall. I submit that's not where it would be if a strong twenty-one-year-old like Danny Hansford had thrown it over in a violent rage. It would have hit that tile floor and skittered down the hall. But it's barely moved out from the wall. That's because Jim Williams did it. He leaned the clock over carefully and let it drop from a few inches off the floor, high enough to crack the case and break the glass. But not high enough to damage it beyond repair. If you recall, Jim Williams told you he was able to restore it and sell it.

"Now let's see what other damage was done. A chair and a table were turned over. A silver tray was knocked off a table. An Atari set was stomped, and a half-pint of bourbon was smashed. The total damage being, what, a hundred twenty dollars and seventeen cents? I don't know. But I ask you to look at all the expensive antiques that *weren't* broken, chests, tables, paintings—worth fifty thousand dollars, a hundred thousand dollars. Ask yourself whether a young man on a murderous rampage, tearing up furniture in the home of somebody who loved antiques, would have stopped at the trifling damage he did. Of course not. That furniture was broken, if you will, by a man who loved it—by Jim Williams."

The solemn faces in the jury box gave every indication that Lawton had recouped at least some of the ground he had lost earlier. Lawton's voice was heavy with sarcasm. "What Jim Williams *didn't* do in those thirty-six minutes was call for an ambulance. He's been described as a compassionate man who makes contributions to the Humane Society. Well, he didn't even call the Humane Society to come check on Danny Hansford." A young female juror wiped her eyes with a handkerchief. "We can spot them the gunshot-residue test," Lawton said. "We don't need it to convict Jim Williams."

By the end of the day, the palpable shift in the jury's mood had alarmed Sonny Seiler. Lawton had effectively rebuilt his case around the surviving pieces of physical evidence, diverting attention from the embarrassment of the bagged hands. There was nothing Seiler could do about it now; he had already rested his case and delivered his closing argument. The judge sent the jury home for the night. The next morning he read his instructions, and the jury retired to consider its verdict.

—

Back at Mercer House, the Williamses finished their sandwiches in silence. Mrs. Williams folded her napkin and gazed out the window. Dorothy fidgeted with a spoon. Williams flipped through the Sotheby's catalog, not really reading.

The telephone rang. It was Sonny Seiler reporting that the jury was having hamburgers for lunch. At four-thirty, Seiler called again to say that the jury had asked to have a dictionary sent in. One of the jurors did not know the meaning of the word "malice."

At five-thirty, Judge Oliver sent the jury home for the weekend, still deadlocked. Seiler had learned from the bailiffs, who were notorious for prying and telling tales, that the jurors were evenly split. Deliberations resumed at ten o'clock Monday morning. Around noon Seiler noticed that the bailiffs had suddenly stopped talking to him. They averted their eyes when he passed in the corridor. It was an ominous sign. "That means a decision is coming down in favor of the prosecution," he said.

By three o'clock, the split had widened to 11-to-1 in favor of conviction. The forewoman of the jury sent a note to the judge. "There is one person who refuses to change her mind no matter what we say or do." Within minutes, the bailiffs let it be known that the lone holdout was a woman named Cecilia Tyo, a feisty divorcée in her late fifties. Mrs. Tyo had told the other jurors that years ago she had found herself in a life-and-death situation not unlike the one Jim Williams described. Her live-in boyfriend had come into the kitchen in a drunken rage and tried to strangle her while she was cooking dinner. Just as she was about to black out, she grabbed a fillet knife and stabbed him in the ribs, wounding but not killing him. Mrs. Tyo said she understood the meaning of "self-defense" better than anyone else on the jury, and she would not change her vote. "My three children are all grown up," she said. "I don't have to go home and cook. I don't have any responsibilities. I can stay here as long as any of you can."

At five o'clock, the judge summoned all parties into the courtroom. Williams came from Mercer House, Seiler from his office. The jury took its place in the jury box. Mrs. Tyo, her white hair wound in a bun, sat with her jaw set, staring sullenly at the floor. She neither looked at nor spoke to the other jurors.

"Madam Foreman, have you arrived at a verdict?"

"I'm sorry, Your Honor," the forewoman said, "we have not."

"Do you believe that if you deliberate further you will get a verdict?"

"I'm beginning to believe, Your Honor, that we could deliberate until hell freezes over and not get a verdict."

Sonny Seiler moved for a mistrial, but Judge Oliver

brusquely denied it. Instead, over Seiler's objections, he read a "Dynamite Charge" to the jury, which essentially told them in blunt terms to stop dawdling and come to a unanimous decision. He then adjourned the proceedings until ten o'clock the next morning, admonishing the jurors, as he had done many times before, not to read, listen to, or watch news reports of the trial, and not to discuss the case with anyone.

—

Jim Williams drove home from the courthouse, but instead of going inside, he walked across the street into Monterey Square and sat down on a bench next to Minerva.

"My lawyers have fucked up again," he said. "There's only one juror who's still on my side. It's a woman."

"How strong is she?" Minerva asked.

"I don't know. She's pretty ornery, I think, but she'll be under a lot of pressure tonight. The D.A. knows who she is, and he's desperate to break her. We've got to stop him."

"Do you know where she live at?"

"I can find out. Can you protect her?"

Minerva gazed into space. "There's things I can do."

"Well, this time I want you to use your most potent weapons."

Minerva nodded. "When I git through layin' down my shit, she'll be safe all right."

"Do me a favor," said Williams. "When you do whatever you're going to do, use something that belonged to Dr. Buzzard. Like one of his old socks, or a shirt, or a comb. Anything."

Minerva gave Williams a look of irritation. "I didn't keep none a his socks. And if I did, I wouldn't know where in hell to start lookin' for 'em in that mess I got in my house."

"Well, but you have other things of his."

"I don't know. I didn't keep nothin'. I didn't really know the man that good."

"Now, Minerva, we've known each other too long for that." Williams spoke as if he were addressing a recalcitrant child. "Those are his purple spectacles you're wearing, aren't they?"

Minerva heaved a sigh. "Let's see. I think I ran across a pair a his shoes the other day. Oh Lord, I don't know what I done with them shoes."

"It doesn't have to be a shoe. What else have you got?"

Minerva gazed up into the tree. "Well, somewhere, if I have the strength to look I might find something. Yeah . . . something." She smiled. "I think I even got his false teeth somewhere."

"Well, now's the time to use them," said Williams, a note of urgency entering his voice. "I don't want anybody messing around with that woman tonight."

"They may try messin'," said Minerva, "but if they do they gonna fall sick real quick. May even die."

"That won't do me any good," Williams said. "I don't want anybody getting to her *at all*. Period. What can you do about that?"

"I will go to the flower garden later tonight," she said. "At dead time. I'll talk to the old man."

"Good."

A smile spread itself across the moonscape of Minerva's round face. "And then when I git through dealing with your business, I'll make him give me a number."

"Oh, don't do that, Minerva! You know he won't give you one. You'll just make him angry. No, no. Tonight's not a good night for that."

Minerva's smile withered to a pout. "But I need a number to play so I can git me some money," she said.

"All right, goddammit, I'll give you the number myself right now!"

Minerva looked sharply at Williams.

"You've always said I was 'wise,' " he said.

"Yes, I know. You was born with a veil over your face, baby. You do have the gift."

"Tell me how many numbers you need."

"I need a triple number—like one, two, three. It can be the same number three times or three different numbers."

"All right," said Williams. "Let me concentrate for a second. Then I'll give you a number that will win you a handful of money." Williams closed his eyes. "The numbers are . . . six . . . eight . . . and one."

"Six-eight-one," Minerva repeated.

"That's right. Now, how much money does it take to play it? A dollar, five dollars, ten dollars?"

A flicker of doubt crossed Minerva's face. "You might be teasin' me."

"I don't tease," said Williams. "But you haven't answered my question. What does it take to cover the bet?"

"Six dollars."

"How much would you win if you won?"

"Three hundred. But hey, this thing play two tracks," she said. "Which track to play? New York or Brooklyn? Me, I play New York track. I don't want to play six-eight-one on New York and have it come Brooklyn. Which one to play?"

"Can't you play both?"

"Hell, no. That would take another six dollars. And listen, the man that writes the numbers for the other track, for Brooklyn, he live seventy miles from me. So I got to have a number for the New York track."

Williams closed his eyes again. "Okay. I see it now. It's the New York track. Play six-eight-one on the New York track. You'll win three hundred dollars for sure. I'll give you the six dollars to cover the bet."

Minerva took the money.

"But remember one thing," said Williams. "Six-eight-one will work only if you leave Dr. Buzzard alone tonight and don't hound him for a number. If you bug him, six-eight-one will automatically become worthless."

"I'll leave him be, baby."

"Good," said Williams. "I want the two of you to concentrate on only one thing tonight. Keeping Mrs. Tyo on my side. I don't want you or the old man wasting energy on numbers again until this thing is over."

Minerva nodded solemnly.

"And don't you worry about the three hundred dollars. It's as good as in your pocket. Do you follow me?"

Minerva stuffed the six dollars into her bag. "Yeah, baby, I follow you."

—

The third floor of the Chatham County Courthouse was a scene of turmoil and confusion at ten o'clock the next morning. The doors of Judge Oliver's courtroom remained chained and padlocked. The crowd of spectators milling around in the corridor was augmented by the presence of Sheriff Mitchell and a half dozen of his deputies. The sheriff and his men had come to the courthouse in anticipation of a guilty verdict; afterward they would escort Williams through the underground passage to jail. But the padlock on the courtroom door was unusual. It meant that the session would be delayed in starting. Something unexpected had happened. This is what it was:

At seven that morning, Spencer Lawton had received a telephone call from a paramedic who worked for LifeStar, an emergency medical service. The paramedic said that at two-thirty an anonymous woman had called the service and asked medical questions pertaining to "a shooting between an older man and a younger man." How long would it take blood to congeal on a person's hand? How quickly would a person die if he had been shot in the aorta? Though she refused to identify herself, the woman eventually admitted she was a juror in the Jim Williams case and that she was the only one who believed Williams was innocent. She added that the other jurors had commented that the case was about a couple of faggots and that they should just convict Williams and go home.

Lawton immediately called Judge Oliver and demanded that Mrs. Tyo be expelled from the jury for discussing the case outside the jury room and be replaced by one of the alternate jurors. This would all but guarantee a guilty verdict. Seiler, when he heard about it, insisted the judge declare a mistrial.

At ten o'clock, while the crowd buzzed in the corridor outside the locked courtroom, Judge Oliver convened a star-chamber session in his office in an effort to deal with the situation. In the presence of Lawton, Seiler, a court stenographer, and the paramedic, the judge summoned each of the jurors individually and asked them under oath if they had called a paramedic in the middle of the night to discuss the case. Each said no, including Mrs. Tyo, although when Mrs. Tyo left the room the paramedic told the judge, "That voice is familiar to me."

Out in the corridor, speculation centered on three possibilities: that Mrs. Tyo had made the call, that the paramedic had been duped by someone acting in league with the prosecution, and that the paramedic was in active collusion with the prosecution. Having failed to get a confession out of anybody, Judge Oliver reopened the courtroom and called the court back into session. Once again, he asked the jurors if any of them had discussed the case with a paramedic. None spoke up. Mrs. Tyo, looking distressed, held a handkerchief to her mouth. She had confided to the forewoman that she had recently suffered a heart attack and was afraid she might be on the verge of having another. Seiler moved for a mistrial. The judge rebuffed him and sent the jury, including Mrs. Tyo, back into deliberations.

In the expectation that something might happen soon, Williams went out into the corridor to wait. Minerva was sitting alone at the far end. He walked over and stood in front of her. She spoke to him as if in a trance.

"Last night I done took the old man's teeth and buried them in that lady's yard. Just like you said."

"They've been up to mischief anyhow," said Williams. "They've concocted a story, and they're trying to throw her off the jury."

"That would be they only hope," said Minerva. " 'Cause she ain't switchin' sides. That's for sure, and I ain't lyin'. The old man done took the case his self this time. Uh-huh. And after midnight, me and Delia worked the D.A. and the judge up one side and down the other."

Williams smiled. "Did you play that number I gave you?"

"Didn't have no time to play it. I been too busy."

—

About noon, the judge called the jury back into the courtroom and asked if there had been any movement toward a decision. There had not. Reluctantly, he declared a mistrial and gaveled the proceedings to a close. Amid the ensuing commotion, Spencer Lawton's voice could be heard calling out to the judge. "For the record, Your Honor, I will ask the court administrator to set this case down for a retrial as soon as possible!"

A fourth trial would set a record. Jim Williams would become the first person ever to be tried four times for murder in the state of Georgia. The courthouse flack laughed and slapped his thighs and hooted that the matador was now bloodier than the bull. Downstairs, the television crews converged on Lawton, who, though bloody, was still unbowed. "After three trials," he said, "the score is thirty-five to one for conviction. I'm confident that if we get a jury that is willing and able to decide, we'll get the right verdict." As he spoke, a small crowd gathered around him. Minerva stood on the periphery, a broad smile on her face and three crisp one-hundred-dollar bills crumpled in her hand.

—

Later that evening, Williams sipped Madeira and played round after round of Psycho Dice. His gray tiger cat, having just eaten her first bite of food in two days, lay sleeping in his lap. Williams calculated that his third trial had cost him roughly a quarter of a million dollars.

"As far as I'm concerned," he said, "only three hundred dollars of it was worth a damn."

Chapter 28

GLORY

Lillian McLeroy came out on her front steps to water her plants and get a closer look at the commotion in Monterey Square. Ladies in hoopskirts and men in frock coats were milling around in the bright morning sun, along with blue-uniformed soldiers with muskets slung over their shoulders. Clouds of dust rose up from the street in front of Jim Williams's house as workmen raked truckloads of dirt over Bull Street to make it look like an unpaved nineteenth-century road. The panorama was startling, but the eerie sense of having seen it all before sent a shiver through Mrs. McLeroy. Monterey Square this morning looked just the way it had looked ten years before when the movie about the assassination of Abraham Lincoln was being filmed. The movie crews were back again, with their lights and cameras and the big vans parked across the square. This time they were filming *Glory*, a movie about the first black regiment in the Union Army during the Civil War. Mrs. McLeroy looked toward Mercer House, half-expecting to see Jim Williams drape another Nazi flag over his balcony.

But Jim Williams was not inclined to do that this time. In fact, instead of opposing the filming, he had let the filmmakers use his house. He had let them bring their equipment in and hang lace curtains in the living room to give Mercer House the look of a mansion in Boston in the mid-1860s. Earlier, Williams and the producer had sat down in his study and, over cigars and Madeira, negotiated a fee. The producer offered $10,000. Williams leaned back in his chair and smiled. "Eight years ago I shot a man who was standing right about where you are now. In a few weeks I'll be going on trial for murder, for the fourth time, and my lawyer is a man of expensive tastes. Make it twenty-five thousand and you have a deal."

—

The legal wrangling over a fourth murder trial had dragged on for nearly two years. Sonny Seiler first asked the court to bar another trial on the grounds that it would put Williams in double jeopardy. The motion was denied, and so was Seiler's appeal. Both Seiler and Lawton then demanded in separate motions that the court disqualify the other from further involvement in the case. Seiler, citing Lawton's concealment of evidence, said Lawton had been guilty of "prosecutorial misconduct of the highest order." Lawton countered that Seiler had defended Williams "in a negligent, incompetent and unethical manner." (This accusation was based largely on Lawton's contention that the young hustler friends of Hansford had been bribed by Williams and Seiler for their affidavits. There was no proof of that allegation, however, and neither of the two witnesses had ever been used in court.) Both motions were denied. The fourth trial would go forward.

On one issue all parties were agreed: that it would be impossible to find a single juror in Savannah who did not already have strong opinions about the case and about the taxpayers' money being spent on it. So, on the morning the filming of *Glory* began at Mercer House, Sonny Seiler went into superior court and asked for a change of venue. He knew it would be granted this time and prayed only that the trial would not fall into the fire of some redneck outpost after the frying pan of Savannah.

In the end, the honors went to the city of Augusta. Spencer Lawton considered it a victory, cheerfully telling friends that Augusta was a "cow town" and that Williams would be convicted for certain. Sonny Seiler was not so sure about that.

The second oldest city in Georgia, Augusta lay 130 miles upriver from Savannah on the fall line of the Appalachian piedmont. The city's population of fifty thousand was scattered about its sloping terrain in a descending hierarchy that closely followed the lay of the land. On the Hill and the high ground to the north, rich families lived in fine houses and played golf at the Augusta National Golf Club, home of the annual Masters Tournament. At the foot of the Hill, the city's old tree-shaded boulevards served as a commercial core and a middle-level residential zone. Farther south, the town descended into a vast, low-lying marshland of working-class houses, mobile homes, shanties, Fort Gordon army base, and a backwoods thoroughfare made famous by Erskine Caldwell as a symbol of rural squalor—Tobacco Road.

So Augusta had its sophisticates and its cruder elements. But when the selection of jurors began, it became clear that whether they lived on the Hill or in the swamp, Augustans all had one thing in common: They had never heard of Jim Williams.

Reporters and television crews came up from Savannah to cover the trial, but the local media virtually ignored it. There were no big headlines in the Augusta newspapers, no news flashes interrupting television programs, no crowds overflowing the gallery. Every weekday for two weeks, a jury of six men and six women calmly assembled in the Richmond County Courthouse to listen and watch as the trial unfolded. They were fascinated, even titillated, and yet they remained detached. They had not lived with the Jim Williams case as people in Savannah had lived with it. Mercer House, with all its grandeur and significance, was merely a house in a photograph to them; it had not figured in the landscape of their daily lives. Jim Williams had not climbed the social ladder in their very midst, arousing feelings of admiration, envy, and outrage as he had done in Savannah over the last thirty years. One prospective juror gave Sonny Seiler a reason to hope that the issue of homosexuality would not be as much a negative in Augusta as it had been in Savannah. "I have no use for gays," the man admitted during jury selection, "but I don't mind it so much if they live somewhere else."

—

By the time the fourth trial began, Sonny Seiler had worked his presentation into an act of highly polished showmanship, focusing his energies on his strongest line of attack—the incompetence of the police. When Detective Jordan took the stand and claimed that he had put bags on Danny Hansford's hands, Seiler gave him a brown paper bag and a roll of evidence tape, held out his right hand, and asked him to tape the bag over it. Seiler then paced up and down in front of the jury, waving his bagged hand in the air, leaving no doubt that if Jordan *had* bagged Hansford's hands, no one at the hospital could possibly have failed to notice it. Seiler ridiculed the prosecution for inconsistencies in the statements of its expert witnesses—most notably Dr. Larry Howard, director of the State Crime Lab. Dr. Howard had claimed at one trial that Williams could not have fired all his shots at Hansford from behind the desk; at another, he said Williams *could* have done it. At different times, Howard had said that Danny Hansford's chair had fallen backward, sideways, and forward. Seiler gleefully brandished a memo that showed how officials at the state crime lab had originally planned to conceal the results of the gunshot-residue tests if they did not help the prosecution. "If you do want to report the test results," one official wrote to another, "just let us know. The grand jury hearing is June 12."

"They all play footsie together," Seiler piped, "and it's just disgusting. They were *thirsting* for a conviction. They were saying to each other, 'Let's see if the residue tests cut our way. If they do, we'll use them. If they don't, we'll forget it.' "

Seiler kept the jury well entertained, and by the middle of

the first week they had nicknamed him "Matlock," after the lawyer played by Andy Griffith in the popular television series. That was a good sign, and Seiler knew it. Several times in his closing remarks, he moved the jurors to laughter. That was another good sign. "Jurors never laugh if they're about to send a man to prison," he said.

Minerva made only one appearance at the trial, and when she did she told Williams she felt movement in his favor. "But listen," she said, "just in case something go wrong, be sure you put your drawers on backwards. That way you'll get a shorter sentence."

The jurors reached a verdict fifteen minutes after they sat down to deliberate, but they stayed in the jury room another forty-five minutes, afraid they might seem too hasty if they sent word to the judge right away. They had found Williams not guilty.

—

Having been acquitted at last, Jim Williams could never again be tried for murder in the shooting of Danny Hansford. It was over—the worry, the dread, the expense. Because he had been found innocent of any crime in Danny Hansford's death, his insurance company would step in and settle with Hansford's mother. So that burden was lifted as well.

Back at Mercer House, Williams poured himself a drink and considered his options. For the first time in eight years, he was a free man. Mercer House was his again, no longer held as collateral for his jail bond. He could sell the house if he wanted to. It was worth over a million dollars, more than ten times what he had paid for it. He could rid himself of the unhappy memories and buy a penthouse in New York, a townhouse in London, or a villa on the Riviera. He could live among people who did not automatically think of guns and killing and sensational murder trials every time they looked at him. Williams's dark eyes sparkled as he thought about the possibilities. Then a smile crossed his face.

"No, I think I'll stay right here," he said. "My living in Mercer House pisses off all the right people."

Chapter 29

AND THE ANGELS SING

Six months after his acquittal, Jim Williams sat down at his desk to make plans for his first Christmas party in eight years. He called Lucille Wright and asked her to prepare a low-country banquet for two hundred people. He hired a bartender, four waiters, and two musicians. Then he took out his stack of index cards and embarked on the most delicate and satisfying task of all: compiling his guest list.

Williams considered each card carefully before consigning it to the In stack or the Out stack. He put most of the regulars promptly on the In stack—the Yearleys, the Richardsons, the Bluns, the Strongs, the Crams, the Macleans, the Minises, the Hartridges, the Haineses. But he hesitated when he came to the card of his old friend Millicent Mooreland. Though she had been steadfast in her belief that Williams was innocent, she had made the grievous mistake of not attending his last party on the grounds that it had come too soon after Danny Hansford's death. For this transgression, Williams now put her on the Out stack. She would do penance this year. She would be chastened, and then she would be restored to grace next Christmas, assuming she did nothing to displease Williams before then.

As for Lee and Emma Adler, Williams simply dropped their card into the wastebasket. Williams had no need to curry favor with the Adlers anymore. Lee Adler had been up to his old tricks, anyway. He had just returned from the White House, where he had received a National Medal of Arts award and posed for photographs with President and Mrs. Bush. This only made him more hateful to Williams and to most of the people who would be attending his party. On top of that, Adler had become embroiled in a bitter fight locally over his plan to build new Victorian-style housing for blacks in downtown Savannah. Adler's scheme called for row upon row of identical houses covered with vinyl siding and jammed together with no lawns or green spaces in between. The Historic Savannah Foundation had risen up in angry opposition, decrying the substandard quality of Adler's proposed dwellings. Adler had been forced to redesign the project, putting in green spaces and replacing vinyl siding with wood. Jim Williams knew that the guests at his Christmas party would be eager to exchange views about Lee Adler's latest activities without fear of being overheard by either him or Emma. No problem; they would not be there.

Williams also dropped Serena Dawes's card into the wastebasket—but sadly, and for a different reason. Some months earlier, Serena had decided that the 1930s and 1940s—the days of her glamorous full-page ads in *Life* magazine—had been the high point of her life and that it would be downhill from here on. She announced that she would die on her birthday, and she thereupon refused to leave the house or receive visitors or eat. After several weeks, she was taken to the hospital, where one night she summoned her doctor and nurses and thanked them graciously for looking after her. By morning she was dead. She had not died of starvation or committed suicide by any conventional means. She had simply willed herself to die, and being a strong-willed woman, she had succeeded. She had missed dying on her birthday by two days.

Serena's death was not related in any way to the end of her affair with Luther Driggers, but Williams paused when he came to Driggers's card anyway. Luther Driggers had been the focus of much attention in recent months. He had been struck by lightning. It had happened at the height of one of Savannah's typical summer-afternoon thunderstorms. Driggers had been lying in bed with his new girlfriend, Barbara, when a wiry tongue of fire licked out from the charcoal-gray sky and enveloped his house.

Barbara's hair suddenly stood on end. The first thought that ran through Driggers's head was that he had never had that kind of effect on a woman before. But then he smelled ozone in the air and knew it meant they were surrounded by a huge electrical charge. "Get down!" he yelled. Then it struck. Luther was thrown to the floor, and Barbara was knocked unconscious for several minutes. Later, when the power was restored, they discovered that the lightning had melted the innards of the television set.

At first, Driggers did not connect the lightning with his subsequent episodes of dizziness and an increasing tendency to fall downstairs and lose his balance in the shower. He had been drunk most of his life, and those things seemed attributable to liquor. But when he stopped drinking, the dizziness continued. Doctors found and removed from his brain a semifluid mass the size of a golf ball and the consistency of motor oil.

In the months that followed, Barbara's stomach began to swell, and that did seem to be a direct consequence of the events of that tempestuous afternoon. They decided that if the baby was a boy they would name it Thor (after the Norse god of thunder). If it was a girl they would name it Athena (after the Greek goddess who carried Zeus' thunderbolt). But Barbara was not pregnant after all. The lightning had damaged her internal organs, much as it had done to the television set, and within months she became sick and died. Driggers, though otherwise healthy, once again took to walking out of Clary's drugstore without eating his breakfast. The old fears about his demons resurfaced, and once again people spoke darkly about the possibility that he might dump his bottle of poison into Savannah's water supply.

"Anyone who believes that is a fool," Driggers told me one morning in Clary's.

"Because you wouldn't dream of doing it, would you," I said.

"Oh, I might very well do it," he said, "if I *could*. Unfortunately, it's not possible. Do you remember what I told you the day I first met you? That Savannah's water came out of a limestone aquifer? And that *that* was the reason why your toilet bowl was encrusted with crystallized scum? Well, for the same reason—that Savannah's water comes from an aquifer deep in the earth—I couldn't poison it if I wanted to. I couldn't get to it. Now, if there were an aboveground reservoir, I could dump poison in it very easily. But there isn't."

"I'm relieved to hear that," I said.

"Don't be too relieved," Driggers replied. "With all the industrial pumping going on, salt water has already begun to seep into the aquifer, and it will soon be unusable. Then we'll have to drink the filthy water from the Savannah River. And my poison couldn't make that water any worse than it already is."

Jim Williams held Driggers's card between his thumb and forefinger, imperiously weighing the pros and cons. Luther Driggers was a friend of long standing, but Williams recalled how Driggers had ridiculed him for not being clever enough to dispose of Danny Hansford's body before the police had come, implying that Williams had been guilty of murder and therefore should have removed the evidence. Driggers's card went onto the Out stack.

Williams hesitated again when he came to the card of Joe Odom. Joe had first made it onto Williams's guest list upon his marriage to his third wife, Mary Adams, whose father happened to be chairman of the board of the C&S Bank. That marriage had catapulted Joe into Savannah's highest social circles. By the time of his divorce, he had become such a popular figure in his own right that Williams continued to invite him to his parties despite his increasing financial embarrassments. Lately, however, Joe Odom's fortunes had taken a precipitous plunge.

In July, the landlord of Sweet Georgia Brown's had padlocked the bar, evicted Joe for nonpayment of rent, and sued for arrears. Joe filed for bankruptcy. Mandy, who had lost more than $5,000 in the collapse of the bar, took her losses in stride until she happened to overhear Joe referring to another woman as "my fourth wife-in-waiting." With that, she stomped out of the Hamilton-Turner House, swearing vengeance. Her revenge took a particularly devastating form, as Joe learned when he looked at his newspaper one November morning and saw the headline ATTORNEY JOE ODOM INDICTED FOR FORGERY.

According to the article, Joe had been charged with seven counts of faking the signature of Mandy Nichols, his partner in the "now-defunct jazz bar" Sweet Georgia Brown's. The seven checks totaled $1,193.42. Forgery was a felony offense punishable by up to ten years in jail.

Joe knew at once what Mandy had done. She had sifted through the canceled checks from the Sweet Georgia Brown's checking account—the account they had put in Mandy's name because Joe's name had been anathema to every bank in Savannah—and she had picked out seven checks that Joe had signed in her absence.

Joe stood in his front hall, newspaper in hand, absorbing the enormity of the crisis before him. It dawned on him that the sheriff would soon be arriving with a warrant for his arrest, so he pulled on a shirt and a pair of pants, climbed out a rear window, jumped into his van, and headed south on I-95. He had no intention of spending the weekend with sheriffs, bail bondsmen, and lawyers. Not this weekend anyway. The Georgia-Florida football game was on Saturday, and Joe would definitely be there. Nothing took precedence over the Georgia-Florida game. Ever. Not even a felony indictment.

"The sheriff can wait," Joe said when he called friends from Jacksonville to inform them of his whereabouts. "I'll be back on Monday."

Upon his return, Joe appeared in federal court and told the judge that the seven checks were not really forgeries but rather an unorthodox way of doing business. He pointed out that one check had been made out to the linen service, another to the phone company, and another to the plumber—all to pay legitimate expenses for his and Mandy's business. He produced deposit slips showing that he had put more money into the account than he had taken out with the seven checks. He concluded by saying that if he had really intended to commit forgery, he would have taken more than $1,193.42.

But forgery was forgery regardless of the amount. Furthermore, Joe could not quite explain why the two largest checks had been made out to cash. In the end, he had no choice but to plead guilty. The judge sentenced him to two years' probation, stipulating that as a first offender he could wipe his record clean if he made restitution within a year. If he did not, he would go to prison for the remainder of his term.

Jim Williams put Joe's card squarely on the In stack. Yes indeed. Joe Odom would be the man on the spot for a change, the man on the receiving end of the opprobrious glances. Joe would take it all very much in stride. Williams admired that about him, his resilience. Despite his mounting problems, Joe was still the gregarious, table-hopping, good-natured man-about-town. In fact, it was Joe Odom's smiling face that first caught my eye when I arrived at the party.

"Well, it looks like you'll have a happy ending for your book," he said. "I mean, just look around you. Jim Williams isn't a convicted murderer anymore, and I won't be a convicted forger just as soon as I pay Mandy the one thousand, one hundred and ninety-three dollars and forty-two cents I don't really owe her. We're all out of jail, and it's party time again. If that isn't happiness, what is?"

I was mulling over Joe Odom's formulation for happiness when Minerva appeared before me in a black-and-white maid's uniform. She was carrying a tray of champagne glasses. Guests gathered around and helped themselves, and when the tray was empty Minerva moved closer to me.

"I need to git me some devil's shoestring," she said under her breath.

"What's that?" I asked.

"It's a root. Some people calls it 'the devil root.' I calls it my baby, 'cause it works good for me. I didn't bring none with me, though, and I need some before midnight. Trouble's brewing. It's that boy again."

"Danny Hansford?"

"Uh-huh. He's still workin' against Mr. Jim."

"But what can he do now?" I asked. "Jim Williams has been acquitted. He can't ever be tried again for killing Danny."

"There's plenty that boy can do!" Minerva said. "He don't need no murder trial to cause hell. The boy died hatin' Mr. Jim, and that's the meanest kind of curse you can have against you. It's the hardest one to git undone."

Minerva's eyes narrowed. "Now listen," she said, "I need to git me some a that root, and I know where there's some growin'. It ain't but two-three miles from here. Mr. Jim can't take me there on account of this party goin' on, so what I need to know is, will you drive me?" I nodded that I would, and Minerva told me to meet her in the square by the monument at eleven.

If the angry ghost of Danny Hansford was hanging heavy over Jim Williams's party, it did not dampen the mood even slightly. Sonny Seiler was present, rosy-cheeked and smiling, accepting congratulations for his acquittal of Williams and condolences for the recent death of Uga IV, who had been felled by kidney failure at home while watching a Georgia basketball game on television. The bulldog mascot was buried in a private funeral service near Gate 10 of Sanford Stadium, alongside the graves of Uga I, Uga II, and Uga III. Seiler chose a successor, and within two weeks the state of Georgia sent him a new license plate for his red station wagon: UGA V.

Blanche Williams, who had been the soul of stoicism throughout her son's ordeal, wore an evening gown and a pink corsage. She pronounced herself as pleased as she could be. She was eighty-three, she said, and now that her son was safe the good Lord could take her anytime He pleased.

Jim Williams was decked out in black tie and Fabergé cuff links. He circulated among his guests, laughing heartily and displaying an ease and contentedness he had not shown in many years. He raised his eyebrows slightly when I told him I had agreed to take Minerva on an errand later on.

"I think she's going a little overboard this time," he said, "and I told her so. I'm afraid she may be getting too fond of the twenty-five dollars I pay her each time she does a little rootworking for me. But it doesn't matter. She'll never cost me a fraction of what I've had to pay my lawyers."

At eleven o'clock Minerva and I got into my car, and in a few minutes we were heading west on the road toward the airport.

"It's growin' wild just this side of an overpass," she said, "but I don't remember which overpass."

We pulled off the road at the Lynes Parkway overpass. Minerva took a flashlight out of her satchel and thrashed around in the brush. She came back empty-handed. She had no luck at the second overpass either. At the third, she foraged farther afield and returned carrying a handful of weeds and roots.

"We got the roots," she said, "but we ain't through yet. Now we got to go see the head man."

"Dr. Buzzard?" I asked. I was beginning to suspect I had been duped into taking part in a long and involved expedition. Dr. Buzzard's grave was in Beaufort, an hour's drive each way.

"No, not him," she said. "He done all he's gonna do. We're gonna see the *real* head man now, the only one who can put a stop to this thing." She did not elaborate, and in moments we were riding east toward the beach, open fields and marsh grass spreading out into the darkness on all sides.

"Jim Williams doesn't seem as worried as you do about Danny Hansford," I said.

The oncoming headlights glinted off Minerva's purple lenses. "He is worried," she said softly, "and he should be. 'Cause *I* know . . . and *he* know . . . and *the boy* know . . . that justice ain't been done yet."

She stared ahead, unblinking, and spoke as if in a trance. "Mr. Jim haven't told me nothin'," she said. "He didn't need to. I seen it in his face. I heard it in his voice. When people talks to me, I don't hear the voice, I see a picture. And when Mr. Jim spoke, I saw it all: The boy fussed at him that night. Mr. Jim got angry and shot him. He lied to me, and he lied to the court. But I helped him anyway, 'cause he didn't mean to kill the boy. I do feel sorry for the boy, but I always takes the side of the living, no matter what they done."

We crossed a low bridge over the inland waterway onto Oatland Island. After taking several turns, we came to a boat ramp that led down to the edge of a wide creek.

"Do you want me to wait here?" I asked.

"No, you can come too," she said, "but only if you keep real quiet."

We left the car and walked down the ramp. The air was still, except for the sound of a small motorboat somewhere out in the middle of the creek. Minerva looked into the darkness and waited. It was the night of the new moon, she said, which was why it was so dark. She said new-moon nights were the best nights to do her kind of work. "Before I left my house tonight," she said, "I fed the witches. That's what you got to do when you havin' trouble with evil spirits. You got to feed the witches before you do anything else."

"How do you do that?" I asked. "What do witches eat?"

"Witches loves pork meat," she said. "They loves rice and potatoes. They loves black-eyed peas and cornbread. Lima beans, too, and collard greens and cabbage, all cooked in pork fat. Witches is old folks, most of them. They don't care none for low-cal. You pile that food on a paper plate, stick a plastic fork in it, and set it down by the side of a tree. And that feeds the witches."

The motorboat's engine clicked off. An oar splashed in the water.

"That you, Jasper?" Minerva called.

"Uh-hunh," a low voice answered. A shadowy form was taking shape twenty yards offshore. It was an old black man in a slouch hat. He was paddling a small wooden boat. Minerva nudged me. "He ain't the head man," she whispered. "He's just takin' us to him." Jasper touched his hat as we got in, then pushed off with the paddle and started up the motor again. As we moved into the blackness, Minerva dipped her handful of roots into the water to clean off the dirt. She broke off a piece and put it in her mouth. The boat rode low in the water. I sat perfectly still, afraid that if I made the slightest movement we might capsize.

A solid wall of trees rose before us on the opposite shore. It was a forbidding black mass without a single light visible. Jasper turned off the engine and paddled until the boat scraped the sand. We all got out. Jasper pulled the boat onto the shore and sat down to wait.

Minerva and I climbed to the top of a low rise. Slowly, as my eyes adjusted to the darkness, I became aware of dense shrubbery around us and of the ghostly drapery of Spanish moss. We moved deeper into the trees, and I began to make out solid shapes rising from the ground—obelisks, columns, arches. We were in Bonaventure Cemetery. I had come to this place many times since Mary Harty had brought me here on my first day in Savannah, but never after dark. I recalled now what Miss Harty had told me—that late at night if you listened closely you could hear echoes of that long-ago dinner party with the burning house and the guests proposing toasts and throwing their wineglasses against a tree trunk. All I heard tonight was the wind sighing through the trees. Then it occurred to me why I had never come here this late: The cemetery shut its gates at dusk. We were trespassing.

"I don't think we're supposed to be here now, Minerva," I said. "The cemetery's closed."

"Can't do nothin' about that," she said. "Dead time don't change for nobody."

"But what if they have a night watchman?" I asked.

"I has worked this flower garden many times and never had no trouble," Minerva said firmly. "The spirits is on our side. They will watch over us." She shined her flashlight on a piece of paper with a hand-drawn map on it.

"What if they have guard dogs?" I asked.

Minerva looked up from her map. "Now listen," she said, "if you're afraid to come with me, you can go back and wait with Jasper. But make up your mind, 'cause it's already twenty till midnight."

In truth, I was beginning to feel the protective force of Minerva and her spirits. So I followed as she set off, map and flashlight in hand, mumbling to herself. Bonaventure at night was a vast and somber place, nothing like the friendly little graveyard in Beaufort where Dr. Buzzard was buried and where boys played basketball on a floodlit court a hundred yards away. Before long, we came upon a somewhat more open terrain with a few scattered trees and modest tombstones in orderly rows. Minerva paced off several rows and turned right. Halfway down the row, she stopped and looked again at her map. Then she turned and shined the light on the ground behind her. "There it is," she said.

At first I saw nothing. No headstone, no tomb. But when I stepped closer I noticed a small granite tile set into the ground, flush with the sandy soil. The beam of Minerva's flashlight illuminated the inscription: DANNY LEWIS HANSFORD MARCH 1, 1960, MAY 2, 1981.

"That's him," she said. "That's the head man in this thing. He's the one that's causin' all the trouble."

Deep double tire tracks bracketed Danny Hansford's marker. Utility trucks had apparently driven back and forth over his grave. There was even a spot of crankcase oil on the gravestone. It made a silent mockery of Danny's boast that he would get a big tombstone if he died in Mercer House. Minerva knelt in front of the marker and gently wiped away the loose sand.

"Pitiful, ain't it?" she said. "Now I know why he haven't let go. He ain't happy here. He got a nice oak tree and a dogwood overhead, but he ain't happy." She dug a small hole next to the grave and slipped a piece of root into it. Then she reached into her shopping bag and took out a half-pint bottle of Wild Turkey. She poured a few drops into the hole, then put the bottle to her lips and drank the rest.

"You can drink all you want to when you're at the grave of a person who loved to drink," she said. "You'll never get drunk, 'cause the dead will take the fumes away from you. By the time you pull the top off the bottle, they done beat you to it. You can drink for hours. Mr. Jim told me the boy loved Wild Turkey, so I give him a little drink to get him in a better mood. Me, I like to dip snuff. When I die, you can carry me my favorite snuff. Peach or Honeybee. Put it under your lower lip when you sit by my grave."

Minerva seemed in a better mood herself. She dumped the contents of her shopping bag on the ground and motioned for me to step back and give her room. Then she began to speak in that faraway voice.

"Where they got you now, boy? Has they got you in heaven? If you ain't in heaven yet, you wanna git there, don't you? 'Cause, face it, boy, you gonna be dead a *lonnnng* time. So, now listen. The only way you gonna move up is if you *quit playin' with Mr. Jim!*"

Minerva leaned to within a few inches of the gravestone, as if whispering into Danny's ear. "I can help you, boy. I got connections! *I has influence!* I knows the dead. I will call on them and tell them to lift you up. Who else gonna do that for you? Nobody! Do you hear me, boy?"

She cocked an ear to the grave. "I think I'm hearin' somethin'," she said, "but I ain't sure what it is." Minerva's hopeful expression slowly turned into a scowl. "Sounds like laughin'. Dammit, it *is* laughin'. He's just laughin' up a storm at me, that's what he's doin'."

Minerva gathered her paraphernalia and stuffed it angrily back into her bag. "Dammit, boy, you ain't no better than my old man. I swear you won't git no help from me."

She rose to her feet and headed down the row of tombstones, lurching and muttering. "You think you had a hard life, boy. Hell, you ain't got no idea. You never had no bills to pay, no kids to feed, no house to clean. You done had it easy. Well, you can just lay there now. That'll teach you."

Minerva charged through the darkness, the beam of her flashlight bouncing ahead of her. We passed the graves of

Bonaventure's two most famous residents, Johnny Mercer and Conrad Aiken—Mercer's epitaph affirming a hereafter in which angels sing, Aiken's raising the specter of doubt and of destinations unknown. Danny Hansford would have to chart his own course now. Minerva had washed her hands of him. At least for the time being.

Once we were back in the boat, she lightened up. "I'll leave him lay there for a while," she said. "Let him worry he missed his chance to git raised up into heaven. Next time I come he'll be glad to see me. I'll carry him some Wild Turkey and some devil's shoestring, and I'll give him another chance. Oh, he'll back off Mr. Jim by and by. Uh-huh. Then I'll raise him up, and he won't laugh at me no more. You wait and see. Him and me is gonna be such good friends, he'll be givin' me numbers before long so I can play 'em and git me some money!"

—

Less than a month later, on the morning of January 14, 1990, Jim Williams came downstairs to feed the cat and make himself a cup of tea. After doing that, but before picking up the newspaper from the front stoop, he collapsed and died.

News of Williams's sudden death at the age of fifty-nine immediately gave rise to speculation that he had been murdered or that he had taken an overdose of drugs. But the coroner announced that there had been no indication of foul play or drug abuse and that Williams appeared to have died of natural causes, most likely a heart attack. After an autopsy, the coroner was more specific: Williams had died of pneumonia. This started another rumor—that he might have died of AIDS. But Williams had shown no signs of being ill; in fact, only a few hours before dying he had attended a party where he had been in good spirits and in apparent good health.

Minerva, of course, had her own idea about what had happened. "It was the boy that done it," she said. A little-noticed detail of Williams's death lent an eerie ring of truth to her pronouncement. Williams had died in his study, in the same room where he had shot Danny Hansford. He had been found lying on the carpet behind the desk in the very spot where he would have fallen eight years earlier, if Danny Hansford had actually fired a gun and the shots had found their mark.

Chapter 30

AFTERWARD

Two days after Williams's funeral, I paid my respects to his mother and sister at Mercer House. As I was leaving, a horse and carriage came clopping around the square and slowed to a stop in front of the house. From the sidewalk, I could hear the tour guide telling her three passengers that General Hugh Mercer had built the house during the Civil War, that the songwriter Johnny Mercer had grown up in it, and that Jacqueline Onassis had once offered to buy it for $2 million. To this by-now familiar routine, the tour guide added that filmmakers had used the house the previous spring to shoot scenes for the movie *Glory*. But she said nothing about Jim Williams or Danny Hansford or the sensational murder case that had captivated the city for so long. The tourists would leave Savannah in a few hours, enchanted by the elegance of this romantic garden city but none the wiser about the secrets that lay within the innermost glades of its secluded bower.

I, too, had become enchanted by Savannah. But after having lived there for eight years, off and on, I had come to understand something of its self-imposed estrangement from the outside world. Pride was part of it. Indifference was too, and so was arrogance. But underneath all that, Savannah had only one motive: to preserve a way of life it believed to be under siege from all sides. It was for this reason that Savannah had discouraged Prudential from establishing its regional headquarters in the city in the 1950s (and why Prudential ended up in Jacksonville instead). It was why Savannah had given Gian Carlo Menotti's Spoleto U.S.A. Festival the cold shoulder in the 1970s (and why the festival finally settled in Charleston). Savannah was not much interested in what went on outside Savannah. It had little enthusiasm for the popular culture, as headline entertainers like Eric Clapton, Sting, George Carlin, and Gladys Knight and the Pips discovered when they brought their acts to Savannah and found themselves playing to half-empty auditoriums.

Savannah spurned all suitors—urban developers with grandiose plans and individuals (the "Gucci carpetbaggers," as Mary Harty called them) who moved to Savannah and immediately began suggesting ways of improving the place. Savannah resisted every one of them as if they had been General William Tecumseh Sherman all over again. Sometimes that meant throwing up bureaucratic roadblocks; at other times it meant telling tourists only what was good for them to know. Savannah was invariably gracious to strangers, but it was immune to their charms. It wanted nothing so much as to be left alone.

Time and again, I was reminded of what Mary Harty had told me on my first day in town: "We happen to like things just the way they are!" I had no idea how deeply that sentiment ran until a revealing incident occurred late in my stay. The Chamber of Commerce hired an outside team of urban consultants to study Savannah's economic and social problems. When the consultants submitted their final report, they appended a note saying that in the course of their research they had asked twenty prominent Savannahians where they thought the city should be in the next five, ten, and fifteen years. None of them had ever given the matter any thought.

For me, Savannah's resistance to change was its saving grace. The city looked inward, sealed off from the noises and distractions of the world at large. It *grew* inward, too, and in such a way that its people flourished like hothouse plants tended by an indulgent gardener. The ordinary became extraordinary. Eccentrics thrived. Every nuance and quirk of personality achieved greater brilliance in that lush enclosure than would have been possible anywhere else in the world.

ACKNOWLEDGMENTS

I owe a great debt of thanks to several dozen Savannahians who appear as characters in this book, some under their own names, some under pseudonyms.

In addition, a number of people in Savannah, who are not necessarily portrayed in these pages, were helpful to me in various ways: Mary B. Blun, John Aubrey Brown, Peter and Gail Crawford, Mrs. Garrard Haines, Walter and Connie Hartridge, Jack Kieffer, Mary Jane Pedrick, and Ronald J. Strahan.

Two people have won my everlasting affection and gratitude for their energy and enthusiasm in guiding this book into finished form: my agent, Suzanne Gluck, and my editor, Ann Godoff.

For critical readings of the manuscript and other forms of advice and counsel, I am also grateful to Stephen Brewer, Rachel Gallagher, Linda Hyman, Joan Kramer, Russell and Mildred Lynes, Carolyn Marsh, Alice K. Turner, and Hiram Williams.

Of all those who helped me, however, no one took a greater interest, nor followed the progress of this book more closely, than Bruce Kelly. A Georgian, a landscape architect of extraordinary genius, and a true friend, it was he who suggested I write this book in the first place and who, more than anyone else, remained supportive and encouraging throughout the long years I took to do it.